John A. Haddock

A Souvenir of the Thousand Islands of the St. Lawrence River

John A. Haddock

A Souvenir of the Thousand Islands of the St. Lawrence River

ISBN/EAN: 9783337240684

Printed in Europe, USA, Canada, Australia, Japan

Cover: Foto ©ninafisch / pixelio.de

More available books at **www.hansebooks.com**

SECOND EDITION — REVISED AND CORRECTED

A SOUVENIR

OF THE

Thousand ✠ Islands

OF THE

ST. LAWRENCE RIVER

FROM

KINGSTON AND CAPE VINCENT TO
MORRISTOWN AND BROCKVILLE

WITH

Their Recorded History from the Earliest Times, their Legends, their Romances,
their Fortifications and their Contests

INCLUDING BOTH THE

American and Canadian Channels

PROFUSELY ILLUSTRATED

With Views of Natural Scenery, as well as Pictures of Many Summer Villas, Steamers, Fishing Scenes, etc.

EDITED AND PUBLISHED BY

JNO. A. HADDOCK, of Watertown, N. Y.

A Native of Jefferson County, N. Y.

Under the Patronage of the Thousand Island Club of Alexandria Bay

PRINTED AND BOUND BY THE
WEED-PARSONS PRINTING COMPANY

ALEXANDRIA BAY, N. Y.
1896

COMMENDATORY.

OFFICE OF CORNWALL BROS.

ALEXANDRIA BAY, N. Y., *October 31, 1894.*

Mr. JOHN A. HADDOCK:

Dear Sir — I have heard that you are about preparing an elaborate and highly illustrated history of our river, to be sold as a more worthy Souvenir of our river and islands than has yet appeared. I have for some years felt the want of such a book, many copies of which my sons could sell over their counter here if it could have been procured. Having known you personally many years, I have full faith in your ability and zeal for the preparation of such a work, and I wish you much success and encouragement in your labor, which will, I hope, be remunerative.

Your friend,

ANDREW CORNWALL,

One of the original owners of all the American Islands from Round Island to Morristown.

LAW OFFICES OF JAMES C. SPENCER, 280 BROADWAY, NEW YORK.

Mr. JOHN A. HADDOCK, WATERTOWN, N. Y.:

My Dear Sir — Having heard you express your ideas as to a needed book which should suitably illustrate the natural beauties of the Thousand Island Archipelago of the St. Lawrence, with views of leading cottages and sketches of the individuals occupying them, I take pleasure in approving your plan, and do not hesitate, from my knowledge of you personally, to fully believe you will carry out all you undertake in making a book which will be a Souvenir to be treasured by all who can appreciate the grandest river and the most beautiful islands upon the globe. Wishing you great success, I remain,

Very truly yours,

Summer residence,
   MANHATTAN ISLAND,
      ALEXANDRIA BAY, N. Y.

JAMES C. SPENCER,
   Vice-President Thousand Island Club.

COPYRIGHTED, 1895.
ALL RIGHTS RESERVED.

INTRODUCTORY.

There have been many attempts to depict the Thousand Islands, with their ever-varying, changeful scenery, and the opulence of their later adornment. Some of these efforts have been honest but inefficient, some sporadic and fitful, others resulting only in a poor attempt to make money out of a subject too grand for such a purpose. And so, year after year, these Islands have lacked a chronicler and a delineator who should present important improvements as well as natural scenes upon the printed pictorial page. The inquiry for a book that should meet this constant and earnest demand for truthful delineation of the fairest spot on earth, has induced a few gentlemen, some of them connected with the Thousand Island Club, to prompt the undersigned to present to the public something that should measure up to the occasion. Accordingly the subscriber, who is the latest Jefferson County historian, has given his attention to the subject, and he now presents to the property-owners upon the river and to the vast number who yearly visit this region, the result of his labors, and he believes that it faithfully portrays the river and its islands as they exist to-day, as well as the grand improvements made and being made there.

It is in no sense a money-making scheme, the promoters being only desirous that the book shall pay its own way, as it should, and be a fair representation, up to date, of the Islands of the St. Lawrence and their present environment, and be at the same time, also, a fair illustration of the progress made up to 1896 in the art of typography and artistic decoration.

In this spirit, then, this Book is issued, in the full belief that it will fill a want which has been felt for the past seven years among the intelligent and appreciative class who come annually to this section, the importance of which appears now to be permanently established.

JNO. A. HADDOCK,
WATERTOWN, N. Y.

Address on the River,
CLAYTON, N. Y.

SONG OF THE ST. LAWRENCE.

By WILL CARLETON.

I.

I am marching to the sea —
To my king, the mighty sea;
In his tent he waits for me —
 In his tent, with walls of blue,
 Decked with flags of brightest hue,
In his starlit, sunlit tent,
O'er the head in splendor bent.

II.

I have messages in store,
 For my king, the mighty sea;
Great Superior's solemn word,
Huron's answering voice is heard;
Erie's shelving walls of land,
Clad with wealth and comfort o'er;
Stern Niagara's thunder-pour,
Great Ontario's prosperous strand,
Decked with city-pictures grand —
 All send messages by me,
 To their king, the mighty sea.

III.

All my treasures I must leave —
 All my thousand tree-fringed isles,
 All my shore-hills clad in smiles —
All the shadows that they weave,
All my woods, with eyes of blue,
All the cottages of white,
Bathed in dim reflected light;
Would that I might take them too,
Floating eastward down with me,
For an offering to the sea!

IV.

Stately ships with plumes of black,
Follow on my gleaming track;
Villages with sails of white,
Decked with banners brave and bright;
Funeral trains of forest trees,
Journey with me to the seas —
Travel with me toward the main —
March amid my glittering train.

V.

Down the rapid's giddy stair
 Rush I headlong as in fear;
Past the crags that linger there —
 Past th' old gray rock's constant sneer,
To my death-like, deathless fate,
Where my lord and king doth wait.
Panic-struck, I rush and rave,
As some mortals toward the grave,
Rush and rave and hurry on,
With my task no nearer won.
But or tranquil or in haste,
Frowning wild or placid-faced,
Eastward still my soul is set:
I am loyal, even yet !

VI.

Times, in broad blue lakes I tarry,
 Kept in couches soft and low;
Lulled to sleep as if by fairy,
 Breeze-caresses sweep my brow.
Sun-caresses thrill my soul,
Shadow-hands my ways control;
In the night's unlaughing glee,
Stars come out and smile at me;
Zephyrs from the wooded west,
Pause awhile, with me to rest.
"Here," I plead, "that I might stay
Many a night and many a day !"
But the cry is "Onward ! On !"
Never, till my journey's done,
Can I tarry well or long,
Can I hush my marching-song.
I am marching to the sea —
To my king, the mighty sea;
In his tent he waits for me,
In his tent, with walls of blue,
Decked with flags of brightest hue
In his starlit, sunlit tent,
O'er the head in splendor bent;
On his calm, majestic breast,
I will lie, in changeful rest.

THE HAPPY ISLANDS.

By GEORGE C. BRAGDON.

There, where a Thousand Islands sleep,
Come pulsing from Niagara's leap
The blended lakes with tireless sweep —
Vast lakes, which float the grain and ore
Of mighty States from shore to shore,
A thousand billowy miles and more.

'Tis there the centering waters meet
In rush sublime and beauty sweet,
Which we with happy thrills shall greet —
We who in fevered towns have sighed
For green and watery spaces wide,
And Nature's murmuring love beside.

Ah, here they are! The river here,
Swift, slow, tumultuous, crystal-clear,
Lapping the islands which uprear
Their rocky heads with crests of trees,
Has sure enchantments to release
The heart, and change its pain to peace.

Hail! River of the Thousand Isles!
Which so enchants and so beguiles
With countless charms and countless wiles;
Flow on unpent, forever free
And pauseless to the ocean-sea
Which belts the globe's immensity.

Not there our goal. Here, here we stay
Amid the islands green and gray,
Nor strive, but idly float and play
Along the river's glints and gleams,
And yield to reveries and dreams
With which the quickened fancy teems.

Here where the airs are always pure,
And wave and earth and sky allure,
And whisper, "Let the best endure,"
The wiser thoughts and instincts grow,
Hearts truer feel and surer know,
And kindle to a tenderer glow.

St. Lawrence River, here we rest,
And here we end our wandering quest
To reach the Islands of the Blest.
Where Nature's sweetest sweets abound
And sacred waters, sacred ground —
The Earthly Paradise is found!

LEADING ARTICLES

IN

HADDOCK'S SOUVENIR OF THE ST. LAWRENCE.

[SEE INDEX ALSO.]

Many full-page illustrations.
A grandly written introduction.
Two beautiful poems, by George C. Bragdon and Will Carleton.
The Chain of Title.
Biographies of E. G. Merrick, Judge Spencer, Governor Flower, Gen. W. H. Angell, and others.
Canada's West Point.
General description — legends, romances, Indian histories and warlike expeditions.
Carlton Island.
Gen. Alvord's two superior articles, "Men I have met upon the Great River."
Thousand Island Park, Chas. Crossmon, Crossmon House, a Bonaparte in Northern New York.
The Mystery of Maple Island, connecting the assassination of President Lincoln with a death on this great river.
Old Fort Frontenac and Modern Kingston.
H. Walter Webb, Third Vice-President N. Y. C. R. R.
Theo. Butterfield, Gen. Passenger Agt. R. W. & O. R. R.
Col. Z. H. Benton.
Pictures of many steamboat men, with biographical sketches of their lives.
The Red Cross.
The Whittlesey Affair.
The great Balloon Voyage of LaMountain and Haddock.
The Awakening of Henry Backus.
The Waterway from Chicago to the Ocean.
The Patriot War in Canada.
The War of 1755.
Travellers' description of the Thousand Islands; some favorable, some critical.
Poetry of the Thousand Islands.
Geology of the Thousand Islands.
Why the River runs where it does? — an able article by Prof. Hines, of Watertown.
Light-houses of the Islands.
Early recollections of Alexandria Bay.
The St. Lawrence in War Days.
Round Island and the Frontenac.
Frank Taylor, the artist.
Carlton Island in the Revolution.
Gananoque, past and present, illustrated.
Brockville, illustrated.
How the Indians learned to run the Rapids.
First printing on the St. Lawrence, by General Neilson.
The Fowlers, the Spicers and the Esselstyns.
La Salle and Frontenac, and many other articles, references and incidents.

A STURGEON CAUGHT IN THE ST. LAWRENCE.

It is a curious fact that great changes take place in the habitat of the finny tribe. Perhaps the most lasting fishing grounds are those off Newfoundland, the straits of Belle Isle and Southern Labrador, where the smaller sized codfish have swarmed in vast quantities for over 200 years. Forty-five years ago the cisco was the most prolific fish in our own Lake Ontario. The numbers caught were well-nigh marvelous. Now, they are far less numerous. In 1850 there were comparatively few black bass in the St. Lawrence or the lake. Now, they are the gamiest fish to be found, and vast numbers are caught by expert anglers. We might enumerate other varieties that were once plentiful but are now scarce. We show above a large sturgeon, a fish once often caught in the St. Lawrence, but not now so plentiful.

THE THOUSAND ISLANDS.

INTRODUCTORY AND DESCRIPTIVE.

THERE is in North America a mighty river, having its head in remote lakes, which though many in number, are yet so great that one of them is known as the largest body of fresh water on the globe — with a flow as placid and pulseless as the great Pacific itself, yet as swift in places as the average speed of a railway train. Its waters are pure and azure-hued, no matter how many turbid streams attempt to defile them. It is a river that has no freshets nor scarcely any drying up, no matter how great the rain or snow-fall or how severe the drouth on all its thousand miles of drainage or of flow — so grand and yet so lovingly beautiful as to enthrall every appreciative soul.

It rises in the great fresh-water sea, and ends in the great Atlantic — some places ten miles wide, at others less than a mile. This great river has never as yet had a respectable history, nor more than an occasional artist to delineate its beauties. It runs for very many miles between two great nations, yet neglected by both, though neither could be as great without it — a river as grand as the La Plata, as picturesque as the Rhine, as pure as the Lakes of Switzerland. Need we say that this wonderful stream is the ST. LAWRENCE, the noblest, purest, most enchanting river of all God's beautiful earth?

This noble stream drains nearly the whole of that vast region lying between the 41st and 49th degrees of north latitude, and the 60th and 93d parallels of longitude — a region perhaps not as extensive nor as productive as that drained by the mighty Mississippi, yet the flow of water in the St. Lawrence must exceed that in the Mississippi, for the current in the former is rapid, while the latter, except in great freshets, is contented with a medium flow. Rising in 49° north latitude, the waters of the St. Lawrence flow down through their many lakes to near the 41st parallel, whence they are impinged towards the north, and at Cape Vincent take an almost northeast course, following that general direction until they reach the great sea — entering it on almost the same meridian of longitude that crosses its remote source in British North America. Why its history has so long remained unwritten, and why this noble river is not more generally known, is perhaps accounted for in part by the fact that the St. Lawrence traverses a region of country remote from the great thoroughfares of the world's commerce or trade. It lies along the boundary line of business. Its banks, to be sure, are dotted here and there with thriving towns and cities, several of considerable importance in the world's traffic, but its grand use is in connecting the great lakes with the ocean. The region through which it passes is one of great interest. The geological formation attracts the attention of the student and the artist. It bears on its face the unmistakable traces of a primeval condition, found nowhere else on our continent, and probably not in more striking beauty anywhere on the face of the globe. Its picturesque windings, pure water, wonderful atmosphere, and great and varied beauty of scenery, are witnessed in such wonderful and lavish profusion nowhere else.

The air is an element of more worth than weight, and exceeds all others in its ability to impart pleasure and comfort, as well as to pain and annoy. Every pleasure or pain is affected by the quality of the air we breathe. The atmosphere has not only to do with our temporal happiness and comfort, but it has very much to do with making character. It has been observed that the inhabitants of high, rugged countries, who breathe the clear, pure air of heaven, are those who come nearest to living the lives of noble freemen. The spirit of liberty and honor is said to inhabit the mountains, while the spirit of dependence, sloth and venality is found in the humid, luxurious low countries; and as man, so nature partakes of that spirit and element which build up and beautify. The air of the St. Lawrence region is one of its greatest attractions. It is pure, clear and invigorating. The early dawn and the evening twilight there are among the loveliest on the globe.

Next to air in importance comes water, the eldest daughter of creation. It was upon the water that the spirit of creation first moved. It is coupled with water that the greatest beauty in nature is found. It is the element that God commanded to bring forth living creatures abundantly; the element without which all creatures on land, as well as those within its folds, must perish. Moses gives it the first place, and justly so, because out of it all things came. Nowhere is there a stream which resembles the St. Lawrence in the particular feature of its purity and the rarefying influences of the atmosphere. Throughout its entire length this great stream has the clearness and purity of a mountain spring, and the water and air combine to make more beautiful and enjoyable those natural attractions in scenery for which it is fast becoming known to the traveler and the world in general. Yet its wonderful breadth of attractiveness, in all its wide range, is even now imperfectly understood.

If the waters of the St. Lawrence are attractive and full of enjoyment and recreation for the pleasure-seeker, its thousands of beautiful islands present pictures grand and sublime — pictures of which the poet painters have only dreamed. Its romantic and unwritten history is only an attractive field in which facts assume the air of fiction. The romance of American history is an interesting and important harvest, which is fast passing away, and soon will be lost forever, unless garnered into the great treasure-house of the printed page, where it can be preserved for the coming ages. No section of the continent is the scene of events more important and numerous, in our unwritten history, than that through which this great river flows. For it has been the principal artery along which the pulse of civilization throbbed for ages in its struggles to penetrate the unknown region of the inland seas of the far West.

Its civilization is older than that of any other section of the continent. The scenes and struggles on its banks have been nobler, grander and more persistent than those of any other section. Nowhere else can be found such determined and Herculean efforts. Coupled with this, in turn, have come some of the sublimest and grandest examples of Christian faith and forbearance to be found anywhere, for the civilization and conversion of the native North American and the possession of this continent. Almost every village and hamlet — especially of the lower portion of the river — has a history full of stirring records, important in the first settlement of this continent, while the upper St. Lawrence is closely identified with all the leading events of the early history of our own country; and, in addition to this, has an interesting local history, illustrative of the events and trials undergone by a struggling pioneer people for the enjoyment of the priceless boon of Liberty.

To reach back down the line of years past, and gather up the forgotten and almost lost scenes and incidents, and weave about these newly-discovered sources of beauty and popular resources of pleasure the history of early days and discoveries, and preserve it all, embellished by the hand of the artist, for future ages, is not a work of ease, though we have found it a work of pleasure. History will take us back more than fifteen hundred years, and we find that there are few martyrs in the Church of Rome whose name or fame rests upon a more lasting or better foundation than that of St. Lawrence. And yet in the New World it has found a fame and foundation that shall be admired long ages after the story of his deeds and even the holy church which canonized his bones may have been forgotten. It is gratifying to know that the object of our adoration is so honorably and worthily christened, although in learning this we are reminded of the ceaseless spirit of change written upon all things. St. Lawrence the martyr has become St. Lawrence the river.

The stereotyped falsities of history are very many in America, and they creep upon us with our eyes wide open. They come because legend has taken the place of fact. The writer who would dare seriously to dispute the claim of Columbus to the honor accorded him for nearly three hundred years, would be bold indeed; and yet the position that he was not the discoverer of America has been attempted to be maintained. The Pilgrims landed at Plymouth Rock, and came to found a government where they could enjoy religious freedom and liberty, and open an asylum for the oppressed of all other countries. But long before them there came a colony whose sole purpose was TO FISH; and the nation they founded has vied with the others, and grown mighty and formidable in wealth and greatness. It seems not altogether unlikely that the American nation may develop characteristics which will be better evidence of its origin and the original purpose of its founders than can be found in the piety or exalted purpose of the Pilgrims. So, everywhere, the great incentive to explore and extend government bounds and influence has been that gain might follow religion.

As early as 1500, great fleets of British and Norman sailors visited Newfoundland, whose cod-fisheries were even then known throughout the Old World. The coasts of Newfoundland and Labrador were visited many times by these great fleets before any attempt was made at exploring the Gulf of St. Lawrence or the river, even at its mouth. The Spaniards had then begun to seek for treasure on the southwest coast of America. Faint glimpses of the great father of waters had gone out to the world, and strange stories came from the Indians of its source and the great lakes beyond. Jesuit missionaries, little by little, dared to penetrate the great unknown, and suffer the cruelties and hardships of life in a wilderness dominated with savage men and beasts. Spain was pushing her researches, and the Old World was filled with reports of strange people and of a strange land. Of course, fiction and romance are never idle, and they clothed the whole in wonderful beauty and decked the New World with gold, precious stones and gems of rarest worth and excellence.

It was under these circumstances that Jacques Cartier, a French sea captain, in 1534, came with two vessels to explore the great river that empties through the Gulf into the Atlantic, which had been known by the Labrador and Newfoundland fishermen for nearly a hundred years. He landed at the mouth of the river in the Spring, and had not proceeded far — in fact, had not entered the river at all — before he became satisfied that the Spaniards had been there before him; and as he progressed further, he found unmistakable evidence that these restless, undaunted explorers had several times visited those shores in search of mines. They had ascended the river some distance, but abandoned the search after amusing themselves by cruel treatment of the innocent natives. It is claimed by some that the name of Canada comes from a corruption of their expression of disgust and disappointment —"Aca-Nada" (here is nothing), which the natives picked up and held on to, without knowing its meaning, for the purpose of designating the place and associating with it the strangers who came. Whatever may be the merit or truth of this story, it has the authority of the oldest and best historian of Canada (Heriot).

Cartier returned to France during the Summer, having accomplished little or nothing by his journeying. The next year he made another voyage to the Gulf, which was almost as barren of results as his first one. He effected a landing on the north entrance of the great river, and called the place St. Nicholas, which name it still bears. He also named a bay on the same coast St. Laurence, for the reason that he entered the bay on the 10th of August — St. Laurence's fast-day. Thence the name has spread the entire length of the river. The Spaniards were the first to explore the river, but by a strange coincidence, a Frenchman names it after a saint of Spanish birth and education.

Cartier passed up the river on this voyage as far as where Montreal is now situated, and there he remained during the Winter, becoming acquainted with the natives, trading with them and studying their habits, customs and language. This point was at that time something of an Indian village, under the name of "Hochelaga." In the Spring he returned to France, and for four years the wars and internal troubles of his own country prevented any further visits or explorations.

About 1542 King Francis First issued letters to Francis de la Roque, Seigneur de Robervale, giving him power of the King over "Canada, Hochelaga, Saguenay, Terre Neuva, Labrador," and other countries or "cities" of the New World. The commission was almost equal to the command to go forth and possess the earth. Six ships embarked in this expedition, Cartier accompanying it as chief captain. A portion of the party settled at Quebec, but the most of those who remained settled at Montreal — Cartier among the number. The vessels returned to France laden with furs which were gathered during the Winter. The next year they came again, and found the little colony in good condition. Cartier then explored the river to the mouth of the Saguenay, and the new scenes could hardly be believed even by those who were in the midst, much less by those who listened to the report of them. This feeling is still shared in a pleasurable degree by those who behold for the first time the scenery of the lower St. Lawrence and its tributaries. A third expedition to Canada was undertaken two years after, under Roberval, but it proved a failure — all the ships being lost, and no survivor was left to tell the story.

The growth of the French colony was very slow, and its history is one of great hardships and privations. The rigorous climate, the bloodthirsty and hostile natives, the great number of wild beasts, all combined to neutralize and circumscribe every effort at happiness, and even a tolerable existence was hardly attainable. Then follow the expeditions of Champlain, who traversed the discoveries of Cartier, and penetrated still farther west, and reached out to the north and south through the tributaries of the great river; and for the first time the exploration of the country was begun in earnest. Companies were formed, and aid and assistance obtained from the French government, and large investments were made by capitalists and speculators. The Indian wars and massacres which followed have scarcely parallels in American history. The great tribes of Algonquins, Hurons and Iroquois roamed at will from the upper Mississippi to the Gulf of St. Lawrence, and began to look with jealous eyes upon the incursions of the white man. The fur-trade began to be the great business of the colonists, and the St. Lawrence river was the thoroughfare by which the tribes from the lake country were enabled to reach Montreal, where they disposed of their stock of skins. It was by this trade that the river was really opened up to the adventurous white man.

The events of these years, and the progress of civilization are interesting; they are the very romance of American history, and pertain to that which is fast becoming the most enjoyable and pleasing portion of our continent in Summer. From the foot of Lake Ontario to Prescott is a continued stream of romance and beauty, which our artist will portray by his camera. Surely the region in Summer is one calculated to make us ask, as we move amid the delights,

"Was it not dropt from heaven?"

Not a breath but bears enchantment; not a cliff but flings on the clear wave some image of delight. Every turn and motion of the boat brings new views, new scenes, new life: scenes that fascinate the eye, and pictures that draw the soul in wondering admiration to the great Artist Divine. Be it ours to muse on such scenes ; ours to glide through them from daybreak till the beautiful night creeps on and broods in solemn stillness over all. Through all the years of life the memory of such scenes last ; they come in dreams, and we revisit them in memory's treasure-house. They draw us nearer the really good and beautiful which we all some day hope to enjoy.

The work in hand is one of importance to Canada and the United States, and is of especial interest to persons who live within the section of country covered by it, as well as to all admirers of American scenery. The scope and design is sufficiently broad to comprehend everything of interest. The picturesque portions are within the limits named, and they are artistic. Views of scenery and of villas alone will make the work of great value. The scenes will not only be new, never before having been presented to the public in this complete form — but the enjoyment and improvement of them by the pleasure-seekers who make the islands their permanent Summer homes, is also a new feature in American Summer-life, and adds very much to the natural beauty. These islands are petty kingdoms, lying in close and friendly proximity to each other — ruled by no power except the wishes, comfort and happiness of those who call them " Home." In the upper St. Lawrence there are over fifteen hundred of these islands. A large portion of them are owned by wealthy persons, many of whom have built upon them fine residences, and laid out tasteful grounds. Within the past few years the improvements in this direction have been very great. One immense camp-meeting enterprise has called into existence hundreds of fine cottages on the largest island, and many desirable residences on the lower end of the same, while every island, during the summer months, seems to bear its portion, if not of permanent Summer-homes, of transient tenting or camping parties. Skiffs and steam yachts being the only means of getting from island to island, or from an island to the main shore, they are of necessity numerous, and handsome and expensive ones are plenty. They move silently about, with fishing or visiting parties, in the day-time; and when the soft evening air, so peculiar to this region, has settled down, and the beautiful sunset faded out, the different islands will become illuminated ; boats loaded with happy pleasure-seekers glide about among them ; then it is that the search-light expedition gets in its weird work ; the music of bands and of voices floats out upon the pure, clear air, over the placid waters — and the heart cannot but respond in its fullest gladness. Nowhere on earth, away from the silent Adriatic, has the poet's dream of Venice been so fully, rapturously realized. For fully forty miles in the upper St. Lawrence (between Kingston, Cape Vincent and Brockville), where these islands are thickest, the scenery by day is grand and inspiring, while the illuminations, the music, the flashing boats and the festivities make the evenings enchanting.

THE CHAIN OF TITLE.

THE importance of these islands, which form the northwestern boundary of Jefferson county, demands historical consideration distinct and separate from the towns in which they are situated. Cape Vincent, Clayton, Orleans and Alexandria each claim a part of the islands, since they are mapped and described as belonging to the towns which front upon the river opposite. The islands proper really begin at Cape Vincent and Kingston, and extend to Morristown and Brockville, about thirty-eight miles below, and are about 1,500 in number.

The author has been sometimes puzzled what to believe as he listens to diverse statements of the same general facts as related by different individuals. To understand the errors of many such statements, at once demonstrates the unreliability of oral testimony, and shows the importance of serious investigation before making a record for the printed page. It was once believed by many that Wellsley Island was for a time held half-and-half by both Canada and the United States. The inconsistency of such a location of the dividing line between two governments will be apparent to the most casual observer. But under such misinformation there were numerous settlements by Canadians upon that important island, claiming that they were within the limits of their own country. The truth is that in the treaty division of these islands there was no attempt to divide any island. The treaty called for a line running up the "main channel of the St. Lawrence," but when the commissioners came on to locate the line, they found two main channels, both navigable, though the southeast (the American) channel was by far the straightest, and is undoubtedly the main channel of the river at that point; and so the commissioners "gave and took" islands under the treaty, Wellsley Island falling to the United States because so near its main shore, and Wolfe Island going to the Canadians for a similar reason.

The place which this beautiful region holds in American history is second only to that occupied by New England and Plymouth Rock, while the memories and traditions which cluster around it are as thrilling and romantic as are to be found in the new world. Wars, piracy, tragedy and mystery have contributed to its lore. The people of the United States should ever bear in mind that this river was discovered by the Spanish, conquered by the French, again conquered by the English, whose footprints have become indelible. That nation yet controls the whole river for long distances, and is half owner for yet other long distances. It is the grand highway for both Canada, England and America. May it ever remain such.

The St. Lawrence was discovered by Jacques Cartier, the French explorer, in 1535, but he did not proceed farther up the stream than to explore the St. Louis rapids above Montreal. There is much uncertainty as to the identity of the white man who first gazed upon the beautiful scene presented by the Thousand Islands. The early discoverers were less interested in scenery than in the practical things which pertained to navigation, trade and travel, and the spreading of Christianity. Champlain, in 1615, beginning at the western end of Lake Ontario, explored that lake and the St. Lawrence to Sorel river, thus passing through the Thousand Island region on to Lake Ontario and the Bay of Quinte.

How or when or by whom the world's attention was first called to this archipelago is certainly a matter of doubt, but certainly at an early date it had impressed itself upon the lover of the grand and beautiful, for at least two centuries ago the French christened it "Les Mille Isles"—The Thousand Isles. The later and more completely descriptive English name for it is "The Lake of a Thousand Islands." The St. Lawrence has marked the line of separation, and the Thousand Islands have been the scene of some of the important campaigns in four great conflicts between nations. The first was the Indian war between the Algonquins and the Iroquois, which continued many years, with occasional intermissions. The second struggle was between the French and English, and some of its hostile meetings and victories and defeats took place among the islands and on the neighboring shores. In the American Revolutionary war with England, and that between the same forces in 1812, the defense of this locality was of decided importance, but its joint occupancy was settled by the wise men of both countries.

Some of the most exciting incidents of that disgraceful military adventure known as the Patriot War, with its intermittent outbreaks from 1837 to 1839, took place on this part of the river, notably the burning of the Canadian steamer Sir Robert Peel, on Wellsley Island, on the night of May, 29, 1838, and the battle of the Windmill, near Prescott, Ont., November 13, of the same year.

The development and wonderful increase in the value of these islands have been more especially due to influences which have originated at Alexandria Bay. The islands were transferred to the State of New York through the several treaties with the aboriginies, following the same chain of title by which the main shore, from the Hudson to the St. Lawrence, came under the proprietary and governing control of the State. The dividing line between the United States and Canada passes somewhat arbitrarily among the islands, varying in size from a small pile of rocks covered by a few stunted trees, to others quite large—one of them (Wellsley Island) containing nearly 10,000 acres of arable land. This valuable island was conceded to the United States under the treaty with England, negotiated at the close of the war for independence. The State of New York, by patent under its great seal, conveyed the islands to Colonel Elisha Camp, a distinguished citizen of Sackets Harbor, N. Y. In 1845 Azariah Walton and Chesterfield Parsons purchased (not from Col. Camp, but from Yates & McIntyre, of lottery fame, whose title came from Camp), the northwest half of Wellsley Island and "all the islands in the American waters of the river St. Lawrence from the foot of Round Island (near Clayton) to Morristown," a distance of some thirty-five miles. The consideration was $3,000. Eventually the Parsons interest was purchased by Walton, who became sole owner, and continued as such until the firm of Cornwall & Walton was established in 1853, when they purchased nearly the whole of the remaining half of Wellsley Island, and then that firm became sole owner of all these islands, having vested in them all the rights and title originally granted Colonel Camp by the State of New York. To Hon. Andrew Cornwall, for nearly fifty years at Alexandria Bay, and always its devoted friend and advocate, is due the greatest credit for the movement which has developed the Thousand Islands, and he is yet spared to greet each season the great company who come year by year to enjoy the grand river. A brief sketch of his life should be published and appreciated. He is the patriarch of the American side of the upper St. Lawrence.

The value of the islands was quite nominal until they fell under the new firm's control, and even for several years afterward. Eventually there grew up a demand for them, and they were sold low, but with a clause in the conveyance requiring a cottage to be erected within three years. Col. Staples obtained as a free gift the grounds upon which he erected the Thousand Island House. As an indication of the present value of at least one of these islands, it is now made public that $10,000 was offered and refused for an island sold by Cornwall & Walton for $100. The Canadian islands were not, of course, included in the grant to Camp, Yates & McIntyre, or to Cornwall & Walton. A considerable number of these Canadian islands were lately sold by that Government.

A RAINY DAY AT THE ISLANDS.

SUNSHINE and daylight are at their best among these islands. But even a rainy day has its compensations. Then the men stay around the hotels, and devote themselves to the ladies, who are not so much given to fishing as are their escorts. The book that was but lately cast aside for something promising greater zest, is now resumed at the turned-down page, and the promised letter is thought of and leisurely written. The ladies gather upon the verandas of the hotels, and with crocheting and talk and exchange of experiences, pass away the time. Many predictions are made as to the duration of the rain, and with friendly chat, not disguising an occasional yawn, the hour for an early dinner soon arrives, and after that comes the afternoon nap, the early tea and then the pleasures of the evening. Some dance, the young brides and the other bright ones who are very willing to become brides and share in the happiness they watch so intently, these steal away to the darker corners of the verandas, where confidences and an occasional pressure of the hand (possibly a kiss) may be indulged in without too much publicity. So, almost unflaggingly, the day passes away, and John, the oarsman, promising fair weather to-morrow, stillness and sleep creep over the happy company, who are willing to declare that even a rainy day is enjoyable among the Thousand Islands, where the soft outlines of the ever-varying shore are half hidden, half revealed through the rainy mist, as if waiting for the sun's enchanting power to develop their hidden mysteries and reveal their entrancing, restful beauties. This is indeed that "Port of Peace," into which, when once you have sailed your boat, you are glad to stay, and you leave the spot with sad regrets, to be remembered always as the place where the soul is lifted up to God in glad thankfulness that He ever made such a resting spot for His weary children, who, through many pilgrimages in many lands, at last find here a spot that fills the hungry soul with satisfaction.

Now, as to Health.

All who have ever remained here for a week are conscious that after the third or fourth day there is a peculiar change in the system. If you have been troubled with insomnia, it begins to leave you, and natural, restful sleep asserts its sway. You like to sit and rest, your legs become lazy, and you are not at all anxious for long walks. The hotel's shady settees have become matters for consideration; you conclude, after much argument, which is the easiest one, and best protected from the sun. You yawn often, and wonder what has come over you. You can lay down and take a nap at almost any hour after 10 A. M. You languidly push aside the newspaper whose leaders only last week were read with the most intense interest. The spirit of Rest creeps upon you almost unawares, for your system is being fed upon the ozone of this health-giving spot. The very air becomes an active ally in behalf of your overworked nerves, and before you are aware of it, you begin to fill up with reserve force, that shall stand you in good stead in the city's heat and push.

These beneficial influences are within the reach of all. There are now hotels and boarding-houses at Alexandria Bay, Thousand Island Park, Clayton, Cape Vincent, Westminster Park, Round Island, and at many other resorts, where the poor man can find entertainment within his means, and the rich man, too (much as he is criticised), may also find comforts adapted to his desires. In former times there were only the more expensive resorts, and that kept away the middle-class of summer tourists. That is all changed now, and every condition except the chronically poor can find boarding houses within their means. It will not be long before this great national Vacation Park, 38 miles long, will be eagerly sought by all conditions of society, from the skilled mechanic to the millionaire.

The Value of Rest.

Many people make the mistake of supposing that a summer vacation is not complete unless devoted to various sorts of physical exercise. It seems to be taken for granted that the energies of body and mind cannot be recuperated except by trips and diversions that call for muscular effort. Summer resorts that do not offer such opportunities are often thought to be wanting in proper attractions. There is another class of people, such as artists, teachers and clergymen, who seek places where they may pursue their usual work amid new surroundings. Under suitable restrictions perhaps no harm comes from this. Change of air and of diet are beneficial, and new faces and new scenery tend to break up the monotony of all toil and care. There are not enough people, however, who appreciate the value of a period of absolute rest, an entire cessation from activity. Just as land is better for being allowed to lie fallow, the physical and mental energies of man are better for being allowed to repose for a time. Nothing is lost by permitting mind and body each year to indulge thus in a few days' slumber. A short season spent in lounging about the Thousand Islands, watching the shifting water, or in idling in the woods and fields, with their fresh odors and changing views of hill and dale, light and shade, island and shore, as they intermingle and then separate, will often fill the frame with new vigor and the ind with new impressions. Particularly is uch a change beneficial when the thermometer is up among the nineties. Then, if ever, the energies should be carefully husbanded. The English philosopher who asserted that Americans work too hard and take too little leisure, stated a truth which intelligent foreign visitors have frequently noted. This warning has a special timeliness just at present, and the seeker after a spot where the very soul may rest will find his El Dorado among the Thousand Islands.

HON. ELDRIDGE G. MERICK.

It is fortunate for our history that we are able to present to our readers, from an entirely reliable source, a very circumstantial and accurate record of the life of one of the great river's most widely known, distinguished and able denizens, who rose from small beginnings to the very first rank in business and in citizenship. Indeed, the writer remembers no man in Jefferson county who was superior to Mr. Merick. There were two or three, Hon. Orville Hungerford, Hon. C. B. Foard, and perhaps Gen. Wm. H. Angel, who stood as high in probity and faithfulness to friends and to society, and were as patriotic and high minded as Mr. Merick, but he had no "superior" in his adopted county, nor in Northern New York, nor on the river.

He was the fifth child in a family of nine children, six boys and three girls, and was born March 6, 1802, in Colchester, Delaware county, N. Y., from which place he moved with the family to Sherburne, Chenango county, at the age of about four years. The section to which the family removed was almost an unbroken wilderness, with few inhabitants and no schools or opportunity for obtaining an education. The principal amusement for a boy of his age was picking up the brush and burning it, preparing the land for crops. The first school he attended was at the age of nine. The school held for only four months. At the end of the four months he was able to read a newspaper fairly well. He continued at home, himself and brother carrying on the farm, until eleven, at which time he went to live with a man named Clark. That family had no children, and Eldridge was treated as their own child. Mr. Clark had a small farm on the Chenango river, which this boy carried on principally, with occasionally a little help from the owner. His business, after getting through with the work of the farm in the fall, was to chop and put up ten cords of wood before going to school the first year, increasing it five cords each year until he got twenty-five cords, which was all that was needed for the family. Eldridge attended the country school from three to four months each winter, until seventeen years of age, and then he commenced teaching. When Mr. Clark went to St. Lawrence county in 1820, young Merick went with him, remaining there until twenty-one years of age.

Arriving at majority, the people with whom he lived not being in a situation to do anything for him, he found it necessary to shift for himself. His first effort was a contract for building a stone wall at Russell, St. Lawrence county, after which he went to Watertown, Jefferson county, working there for several months, and delivered the material for the old stone Presbyterian church; thence to Sackets Harbor, to work for Festus Clark, a brother of his former employer, as clerk in a small store. Remaining there for a short time, he went to Depauville, in the same capacity, with Stephen Johnson, who had a country store, and was also engaged in the lumber business for the Quebec market.

He remained with Mr. Johnson two years, superintending his lumber business largely, and while there became acquainted with Mr. Jesse Smith, who had been furnishing Mr. Johnson with means to carry on his lumber business. Mr. Johnson was unfortunate in business and failed at the end of two years, and was sold out by the sheriff, which sale was attended by Mr. Smith as a creditor, and knowing it threw young Merick out of employment, he offered him a situation, which was gladly accepted. This was about 1826. Mr. Smith was doing a very large mercantile and manufacturing business for those times. After being with him for a little over a year, he sent Mr. Merick with a store of goods to Perch River, and the following Summer sent him to Quebec to look after his lumbering interests, and in the Fall of the same year offered him a partnership and an interest in the business, which was accepted, and so young Merick became the manager. The business developed into a pretty large one, devoted principally to lumber designed for the Quebec market, and also the building and running of vessels. The timber and staves, which were the principal business, were obtained about the head of Lake Ontario and Lake Erie, extending into Lake Huron, and were transported by vessels across the lakes to Clayton, on the St. Lawrence, and there made into rafts for transportation to Quebec. Of these rafts there were several made up every year, amounting (according to their size) to $40,000 or $50,000 each. These rafts had to be made very strong to run the rapids of the river, seven or eight in number. Each stick of oak timber was tied up with large oak wisps, forming what was called a dram, and from ten to twenty or thirty drams in a raft. The rafts were propelled by a number of small sails, but usually went but little faster than the current. At the rapids a pilot and extra men were taken to conduct the raft through the rapids; a pilot for each dram or section, the raft being divided into several sections for running the rapids. Sometimes a large raft required from 200 to 300 men. Frequently they would get broken up in the rapids and run ashore, attended with considerable loss and expense in saving the pieces. Arriving at Quebec, they were usually sold on from two to six months' time, but the percentage of loss by bad debts was very small. Better facilities were needed for transporting this square oak timber, and a ship-yard was established at Clayton. After Mr. Smith removed to Ohio, Mr. Merick continued the timber trade, adding forwarding and grain business, associating with Messrs. Fowler and Esselstyn.

The business in the winter was arranging and superintending the shipments, selecting the timber in the country, and getting it forwarded for shipping, and in building vessels, of which the firm generally had one or more on the stocks. They built, with one or two exceptions, all the steamboats forming the justly celebrated line on Lake Ontario and the River St. Lawrence, on the American side.

The "Reindeer" fleet, which at one time numbered fourteen vessels, were built at his Clayton yard; also three steamers of the Ontario Navigation Company, all of them having his careful supervision.

With D. N. Barney & Co., he built, about 1844, the steamer Empire, to run between Buffalo and Chicago. Her increased tonnage and decks attracted much attention, with many prophecies of failure, but she proved a success and was the vanguard of the fine fleet of lake transports.

When the Grand Trunk Railroad was built, however, following up the St. Lawrence and Lake Ontario, the competition ruined the business of these passenger steamers. The line ceased to be remunerative, and the boats were sold, some to go to Montreal; one went to Charlestown, S. C., and afterwards was engaged in the rebel service in the war of the rebellion.

He had previously established a house in Cleveland, one in Oswego and one in Buffalo, the object being to furnish business for the vessels on the lakes. Each additional facility only showed the necessity of still further facilities. The firm decided to build a large flouring mill in Oswego, which had the largest capacity of any mill in the country at that time, turning out from 1,000 to 1,200 barrels a day, and having thirteen runs of stone.

He was interested in railroad building in Ohio, but it was before the days of floating bonds and watering stocks, but not of incompetent, reckless superintendents. The enterprise was a failure. But through their railroad enterprise the firm was enabled not only to con-

ELDRIDGE G. MERICK.

trol the wheat over the road and to market by vessels, but for the mill at Oswego. During the war, or at the close, the mill was making very large profits, from $1 to $2 a barrel, but unfortunately it took fire and burned down, with a large stock of grain and flour on hand. The loss was pretty well protected by insurance, but the profit which they would have made if the mill had not burned down, could not have been provided for. The actual loss was nearly $150,000.

Perhaps his first and greatest financial loss was through the failure of a large commission house (Suydam, Sage & Co.) in New York, in 1850. But that loss brought generous and prompt proffers of aid from business men in Watertown, Kingston and Quebec, which were long after most gratefully remembered. The great financial disasters of 1857 and 1873 also brought misfortune to him, as well as to many others. He was greatly helped in all these reverses by the confidence that his creditors had in his ability and strict integrity, steadily refusing compromises when offered. He paid dollar for dollar, though often at great sacrifice of property. For many years Mr. Merick was president of the Sackets Harbor Bank, relinquishing the position on leaving Jefferson county.

For many years he found Clayton was too much at one side for the prompt and successful management and oversight of his varied interests. He was strongly attached to the people of Jefferson county and the beautiful St. Lawrence, and it was with many regrets that he left his old friends and pleasant home, with all the associations of youth and manhood, to make a home, in 1859, at the more central point, Detroit. Here he took an honored position among the business men of the city, many of whom sought business advice from him, glad to profit by his large experience. In addition to other business, he bought an interest in the Detroit Dry Dock Company for the firm of Merick, Esselstyn & Co. John Owen, Gordon Campbell and Merick, Fowler & Esselstyn each owned one-third of the Dry Dock stock—the total stock being $300,000.

Mr. John Fowler, a partner of the firm of Merick, Fowler & Esselstyn, died in May, 1879. The surviving partners purchased his interest in the business, and continued under the name of Merick, Esselstyn & Co.

After the failure of 1873, Mr. Merick was too old a man to again do business with his former confidence and success.

In 1829 Mr. Merick married Miss Jane C. Fowler. She died in 1881, leaving four surviving children — all of whom have proven useful and honored members of society.

Mrs. Cyrus McCormick, who was Mr. Merick's niece, was the daughter of Melzar Fowler, born at Brownville, N. Y., and survives her distinguished husband, who was that C. H. McCormick, so long the leader in manufacturing reapers for the harvest field, whose machines have gone into all lands. He was the one to introduce that inestimably valuable machine into England, as is so well spoken of in Haddock's History.

Mr. Merick was very early interested in the temperance movement. It had been the custom to put whisky among the necessary stores for every raft and vessel. He very soon realized the injury it was doing, made liquor a contraband article, supplied tea and coffee instead, and made it his personal duty to visit cabin and forecastle, to confiscate and throw overboard any spirits smuggled on board.

The sailors who manned his vessels came from the adjacent farms and villages. Young men, beginning as cabin boys, or before the mast, were frequently advanced as they proved worthy and capable to be mates, captains and shareholders, and all looked up to him as to a personal friend and father.

One who had sailed for him thirty-five years wrote: "The accounts for these years aggregated more than half a million of dollars, but never an error to the value of a cent in his books, never a sour look or unkind word. I was always treated more as an equal than as a servant." Another who served him forty years said: "I have received from him nothing but kindness. When in need of aid or counsel his generous heart always responded to my wants. In prosperity and adversity, sunshine and storm, he was always true to principle, and true to himself as a man, ever following the Golden Rule."

Mr. Merick had no political aspirations, beyond wishing to do the best possible for his own township, of which he was several times supervisor. He was a strong Whig, and gave money, time and influence to promote the interests of that party. Twice he was nominated for Congress, and ran ahead of his ticket; once both parties wished to unite upon him as their candidate, but his business interests would not permit him to accept the nomination. He was also one of the Electoral College, voting for President William H. Harrison.

The title of judge was given him when he was appointed associate judge of Jefferson county, but he felt that it rightfully belonged only to a man of legal training and ability.

The Patriot War of 1837-38 caused much trouble and anxiety all along the border, and brought together many of the best men of Northern New York and Canada to council together and take such measures as would insure peace.

One of the Canadian members of that committee of arbitration wrote: "How much the high character and the confidence inspired by your father in Canada, assisted in allaying the irritation which existed on both sides of the line. To him many misguided men owe their deliverance from extreme peril. I well remember the effect upon my own mind, not a little exasperated at the time, by his explanations as to the sincere, but mistaken views which induced many good and worthy people to engage in or extend aid to what they suppose to be a movement in assisting the oppressed."

Mr. Merick, deploring his own inability to obtain a collegiate education, was ready to aid young men with such aspirations. The success of many business men was owing to the counsel and substantial aid he gave. Academies, colleges, churches, public and private charities were cheerfully aided by him as "the Lord prospered him."

His noble, courtly bearing, his unassuming manner, his thoughtfulness, tenderness and benevolence, his faithfulness and integrity make a rich legacy to children and children's children.

It had always been his thought that a business man should keep at work till the end of life. In the winter of 1887-88, realizing from his advanced years that his strength was fast failing, he decided to sell the remaining vessels of the fleet. Friday, February 10, 1888, the contract was made for selling the last one. Saturday, February 11, the papers were to be signed. He tarried a little in the morning, perhaps not quite as well as usual, after a somewhat restless night — his mind no doubt busy with reminiscences of the past, and saddened by the change of affairs. The mail brought news from absent loved ones. While talking with his daughter, sitting beside him, of the good tidings received, his head dropped, one sigh was given, "the silver cord was loosed," "the golden bowl was broken,"— he had gone from his work to his rest and his reward.

Thus passed away, after an honorable and a useful life, one of the most widely-known and justly-honored of the river men, who came to man's estate in Jefferson county, and spent the flower of his life there. His death occurred at Detroit, February 11, 1888, in his 86th year.

Mr. Merick and wife reared a family of four children. They were:

MARIA D., wife of Isaac L. Lyon, a native of Ogdensburg, N. Y. They reside at Redlands, Cal.

ERMINA G. MERICK, wife of E. J. Carrington, of Fulton, N. Y. They reside at Detroit, Mich.

MELZAR F. MERICK, died March 28, 1893. His wife was Mary Whittlesey, of Danbury, Conn.

JEANNIE C., wife of G. N. Chaffee, of Detroit, Mich., which is their home.

Mr. Merick was in many respects a peculiarly able man, and should be spoken of apart from his many business enterprises. Judgment was the leading quality of his mind. To strangers he appeared reserved, the result of his native modesty, and not the outgrowth of any feeling of superiority or of self-elation.

ROSWELL PETTIBONE FLOWER.

His soul was too great and his judgment too solid for any such folly as that. He was eminently democratic, simple in his manners and his tastes, as have been all the really great men the writer has encountered. Mr. Merick was not a sharer in the command of armies, nor is it probable that he ever knew what it was to be thrilled by a bugle call or beat of drum; yet he intensely appreciated the struggle endured by the Union armies, whose perils he would surely have shared had he been of suitable age. He was a patriot in the highest sense of that term. Amidst all the duties of his exacting business, he was a consistent Christian; the traveling Methodist minister always found a welcome at his fireside, both from him and his amiable wife, a fact the writer has heard the late Rev. Gardner Baker speak of with grateful tears. Mr. Merick's unostentatious and democratic ways made him life-long friends, for his manner invited confidence, and confidence in him meant safety. Children and animals never shunned his society, for they intuitively perceived his gentleness under his greatness. Viewed in any light, as a man of affairs, the possessor and dispenser of large wealth, as the unostentatious but ever vigilant citizen of a free country, or as the sincere Christian, he possessed so many excellencies that he fell but little short of earthly perfection. He left a memory in Jefferson county that remains peculiarly sweet, and entirely untarnished. And it is fitting to hold up such a character to the admiration of the youth who come after him, as an evidence that the age in which he lived was not altogether one of greed and money-getting, but was adorned now and then by souls as grand as can be found in the records of any people. And so Eldridge G. Merick passes into history as one of the very ablest and best of his time.

GOVERNOR ROSWELL PETTIBONE FLOWER.

[See Portrait.]

WE scarcely need apologize for introducing into this River book the portrait and biographical sketch of Governor Flower. His childhood was spent only twelve miles from Alexandria Bay, a spot he often visited in his youth, and he has grown to be one of whom his fellow citizens, and more especially those who knew him in early life, are very proud. His career is an incentive to every boy and young man in the State.

He was born August 7, 1835, at Theresa, Jefferson county, N. Y. His father, Nathan Monroe Flower, whose ancestors came to Connecticut in 1696 and settled in New Hartford, was born at Oak Hill, Greene county, in this State. Nathan Flower learned the wool-carding and cloth-dressing trade in his father's mill at Oak Hill, and when he became of age established business for himself in Cooperstown, Otsego county. At Cherry Valley, in the same county, he married Mary Ann Boyle, and soon after moved to the northern wilderness and established a wool-carding and cloth-making business at Theresa. Nine children were born to them, seven sons and two daughters, of whom Roswell Pettibone Flower was the fourth son and the sixth child. Their father died when Roswell was only eight years old. Their mother conducted the business for a couple of years, and young Roswell was put to work at picking wool eight hours off and eight hours on daily, during the summer season, for a couple of months, and the rest of the time he was sent to school. The family had a farm of 30 acres near the village, and another one of some 200 acres eight miles out. The children worked on these farms, chopping wood for the house in the village, and raising hay and oats, wheat and potatoes. There was nothing on the farm that young Roswell could not do. Until he was fourteen years of age he was occupied at school, and night and morning did what work he could to help support the family. His brothers being older than he, it was not Roswell's luck to have a new suit of clothes until he was able to earn the money himself. His mother would cut down the clothes of the older boys to fit him, and stories are told, even in these days, at Theresa, of the anguish of mind which young Flower suffered over this matter of hand-me-downs. His sister Caroline married Silas L. George, a merchant of Theresa, and Roswell was employed by him for $5 a month and board. In the winter he attended the Theresa High School, conducted by Mr.

Goodenough, and worked for his board until he was sixteen years of age, when he graduated. To get his spending money Roswell did odd jobs of sawing wood and carrying it upstairs for the lawyers of the village. Twenty-five cents was a good deal of money in those days, and rather than ask his mother for the money, he preferred to saw half a cord of wood and carry it upstairs. Farm hands were scarce in haying time, and being a strong and active young man, he could command good wages, and frequently left the little country store for two or three weeks to help out some farmer who was anxious to get his crops in. He also worked in a brick yard, driving a yoke of stags around the vat to tread out the clay, for which he received the munificent sum of $1.50 a week, not counting Sundays.

AS A VILLAGE SCHOOLMASTER.

After he graduated from the High School he found an opportunity to teach in a little school a mile from town. The scholars in those days often desired to have a bout with their master before they would become tractable. Mr. Flower taught out the balance of the term in the red school house below the village and "boarded around" among the parents of his scholars a week or less in a place, in the regular old New England fashion, which still obtains in the way-back districts of Northern New York.

His first day in school, during the noon intermission, the biggest boy came to him for a "square-hold" wrestle. Mr. Flower accepted the challenge and easily threw the lad. After he had thrown the larger boys he found them all, with one exception, ready to recognize his authority. One day in the spelling class this boy, who was about twenty-one years old, declined to pronounce his syllables, but after a tussle Roswell succeeded in making him pronounce them correctly. He then gave notice that he would hold a spelling school that evening, and stated that he desired only those of the scholars to come who would be willing to do their best. During the intermission this young man said he was coming to school that evening, but that he would not spell. Roswell was boarding at the time with the family of Edward Cooper, with whom lived a young man of twenty-two named James Casey, now a merchant at Theresa. The young teacher talked over the expected trouble and arranged that Casey should choose for one side of the school, and if this obstreperous young fellow should make his appearance Casey should elect him to his side, and if he made any fuss in spelling, the two should join forces and put him out. The evening school had not been opened more than ten minutes before this young man came in and sat down behind one of the old-fashioned desks. He was immediately chosen, but said he would not spell. Then young Flower told him that he must spell or leave the school. He replied that he would be —— if he would spell, and that he would be —— if he would leave the school. Mr. Flower insisted, which only called forth a repetition of the offensive remark. The schoolmaster then called upon anybody present who desired to resent the insult to the school and the teacher to assist him in putting the offender out of doors; whereupon young Casey rose up, and Roswell, grabbing the young man by his shoulder and his assistant by his feet, he was speedily ejected. But he was not conquered. He went over to the hotel a few rods distant and persuaded one of the trustees and a big chap by the name of William Wafful to come over and whip the teacher. Nothing daunted, Roswell stated the case to his belligerent visitors and then said to the young man: "Now, sir, you must either spell or leave this school again." This conquered the youthful Samson, and he spelled without further trouble. After school was out the colossal Mr. Wafful remarked that if this young man had not spelled then he would have whipped him himself.

When he was in his eighteenth year Mr. Flower had an offer to go to Philadelphia (Jefferson county) as a clerk in a general merchandise store. His employer was a Mr. Woodward, who failed two months afterward, and the young man, thrown out of employment, was forced to return to Theresa. That spring and summer he did work on his mother's farm, and earned a ton of hay by working nine days and a half in the field, mowing grass and "keeping up his end" with eleven men in mowing.

During his boyhood he always went barefoot in the summer months, and he once remarked in a speech, while running against William Waldorf Astor for Congress, that until he was fifteen years old he did not feel at home in the summer time unless he had a stone bruise or two on his feet, and that he had warmed his feet many a morning when driving up the cows in the crisp autumn weather on a spot where a cow had lain the night before.

SIX YEARS OF EARLY MANHOOD.

In August, 1853, Mr. Flower had an offer to go into the hardware store of Howell Cooper

& Co., at Watertown. After remaining there a month he had another offer which was more to his liking and which he accepted. It was to become deputy postmaster at Watertown at $50 a month and board. He occupied this position under Postmaster William H. Sigourney for six years. The first $50 he saved he invested in a gold watch, which he sold a few months later to a young physician for $53, and took his note for it. Mr. Flower still has that note. Mr. Flower managed to save some money out of his wages, and at the end of his term in office had accumulated about $1,000, with which he purchased the interest of Mr. Sigourney in a jewelry business, the firm name being Hitchcock & Flower, at 1 Court street, Watertown. His aptitude for business enabled him to advance the interests of the firm, and in a couple of years he bought out his partner and continued alone in the business until 1869.

Mr. Flower was married on December 26, 1859, to Sarah M. Woodruff, a daughter of Norris M. Woodruff, of Watertown. Three children were born to them, of whom only one is living, Emma Gertrude. She was married to John B. Taylor, of Watertown, January 2, 1890. While in the Watertown post office Mr. Flower's spare time was taken up, not in social entertainments, because he had no money to enter such society, but in reading whatever he thought might be useful to him in the future. He made himself thoroughly familiar with the "Federalist" and kindred works, and having an idea of some day becoming a lawyer, he got a little knowledge of Blackstone and Kent; but his natural bent was for business, and he never attempted the law.

Business in New York.

In 1869 Henry Keep, the well-known capitalist, who had married Miss Emma Woodruff, a sister of Mrs. Flower, was on his deathbed. Two or three weeks before he died he sent for Mr. Flower to come to New York, and during his sickness gave him a pretty good idea of the character of the men with whom he had been surrounded in the business world. Mr. Keep had been president of the New York Central and treasurer of the Michigan Central and Lake Shore, and was president at the time of the Chicago and Northwestern railroad. He knew it would take a man of good common sense and quick perception to aid his wife in the management of his large property after his death, and in Mr. Flower he thought he recognized those qualities. In answer to a question by Mr. Flower, in order to get his opinion of Daniel Drew, as to whether Drew was an honest man, Mr. Keep, who was very reticent, did not reply for some ten minutes, and then said: "He is as honest a man as there is in the State of New York, but for fear that somebody else will cheat, he will always begin first." Immediately after Mr. Keep's death Mr. Flower removed to New York and took charge of his late brother-in-law's estate, the value of which has more than doubled under his management. It was then worth $1,000,000, and now under Mr. Flower's management it has expanded to $4,000,000. The properties in which the estate was invested caused Mr. Flower to be a frequent visitor to the West, and since 1870 he has made extended trips all over the United States, and has a personal knowledge of the possibilities and natural resources of almost every section of the country. Governor Flower's fortune, which is estimated in the millions, has not been made by speculation in Wall street, but by the shrewd purchasing of properties, which, by careful and prudent management, have developed and proved valuable investments.

His Career in Wall Street.

In 1872 Mr. Flower was at death's door for several weeks, but after four or five months' sickness he finally recovered. His physicians then advised him to take all the outdoor exercise possible. At this time the brokerage and banking firm of Benedict, Flower & Co., was dissolved, and Mr. Flower gave his entire attention to the management of his sister-in-law's estate and other estates which had been placed in his care. He found a New York office necessary, and so established himself at 52 Broadway. His younger brother, Anson R. Flower, was brought to New York from Watertown in order to become acquainted with the business, that he might take charge of it in Mr. Flower's absence; but, strange to say, the more the latter tried to get out of business the more he got into it, and the firm of R. P. Flower & Co. found itself doing a large commission trade without any attempt having been made to push it — so large, in fact, that another brother, John D. Flower, and a nephew, Frederick S. Flower, were taken into the firm, and not until 1890 did Mr. Flower relinquish his interest in the concern and become a special partner. But in the meantime he had managed to get the "out-of-door" exercise which the doctors had suggested through the State sportsman's clubs. In 1877 Mr. Flower attended the convention of these clubs at Syracuse and won a prize, consisting of a corduroy hunting suit, over a field of 113 entries. Thirty-two of them had tied at twenty-one yards' rise, and they had to go back to the twenty-five yard score. Then all that were left had to go back to thirty-one yards and shoot until somebody dropped out. Mr. Flower and ex-Attorney-General Tabor were the last competitors in the contest, and Mr. Flower finally won the clothes and still wears them on the hunting expeditions which he frequently takes after woodcock, duck and partridge.

ALWAYS ACTIVE IN POLITICS.

In politics Mr. Flower has always been a Democrat. He cast his first vote for Buchanan, and has been a constant and active worker for his party. He was chairman of the county committee for several years and helped to start the nucleus of an organization which has been known throughout the State as one of the best equipped political organizations within its borders. Mr. Flower was an active Mason in his younger days, being at one time high priest of the Watertown chapter. One day, going down to the grand chapter, at Albany, he met on the cars Samuel J. Tilden and his secretary, John D. Van Buren. Mr. Tilden asked him what he thought about the State, and Flower replied that he did not believe Mr. Tilden would the next year be chairman of the State Committee for the reason that he did not seem to recognize the fact that a man under fifty years of age has any influence in politics. He told Mr. Tilden that it was the young men who would control the party, and that he must extend his acquaintance among them or be prepared to step out. Mr. Tilden replied that he would like to have the young men with him, but that he had no opportunity of coming in touch with them; that his friends didn't seem to think it was worth while. Mr. Flower then told Tilden that Jefferson county had sent to Colonel Van Buren the year before the best scheme for organization of a party that had up to that time made its appearance, and that if he would organize the party throughout the State on the basis of recognizing the merit of young and active workers, instead of the "has beens," he would be sure to carry the State at all times, and might continue at the head of the organization as long as he saw fit. Van Buren confirmed this opinion. About a month later Hon. Allen C. Beach, of Watertown, received a telegram from Mr. Tilden, asking him to come to his house and spend two or three weeks, as he wanted to extend the suggested organization throughout the State. It was thus that the famous "Tilden machine" was started. It was Flower's suggestion to organize it and Tilden's perseverance which extended it. In 1877 Flower was Chairman of the Democratic Executive Committee when the party won the campaign, though there was a bolt against the ticket.

A TERM IN CONGRESS.

After his son's death, in 1881, Mr. Flower was induced to run for Congress in the Eleventh Congressional District against William Waldorf Astor. The representative of this district had been Levi P. Morton, until he resigned to take the position of Minister to France. Mr. Morton had been elected by over 4,000 majority. In that campaign, after Orlando B. Potter had declined the Democratic nomination, Mr. Flower accepted it on the platform that he would not purchase a vote to secure the election, and on that he made the issue and was elected by 3,100 majority. In the Forty-seventh Congress he was appointed a member of the Committee on Banking, and almost immediately took a prominent part in the discussion of financial questions. Mr. Flower recently said to the writer: "When I was elected to Congress, although I was pretty thoroughly conversant with practical banking methods, I knew nothing of the theories of finance, but I soon learned that if I was to be of any use in Congress I must do a little reading, and with the aid of books from the Congressional Library, I soon pretty thoroughly mastered the subject. I found it much the most interesting subject I had ever studied. It is better reading than the best novel that ever was written." During his first term in Congress he also made speeches on the Chinese question, on the River and Harbor bill, and a notable one on the reduction of taxes.

A UNIQUE POCKET COMPANION.

Mr. Flower would hardly be called a good speaker, but he was called on frequently in his county to talk from the platform, particularly during the Seymour and Blair campaign of 1868. Endeavoring to fill that want of many public speakers — the possession of a copy of the Constitution of the United States in convenient size to carry in his pocket — he searched the book stores of Watertown, but was unable to find one. Happening into a little corner shoe-store he saw tacked to the bench of a grizzled old cobbler a little primer containing inside the Constitution and outside the advertisement of a fire insurance company. James Muldoon, the shoemaker, gave Mr.

Flower the book, and he has it yet, always carrying it in his pocket for easy reference. In 1876, when visiting Chicago, Mr. Flower had his memorandum book stolen, which contained the present of the cobbler. While in Europe some months later he received a note from the proprietor of the Grand Pacific Hotel, saying that his book had been found in a lumber yard, and would be returned to him. The Constitution turned up inside in perfect order, and in 1883, when making a speech in Congress on giving power to the President to veto separate items in the Appropriation bill, Mr. Flower produced the cobbler's copy of the Constitution, and, considering its adventures and the value a pamphlet copy would be to many persons, as it had been to him, he asked that it, together with the substantial amendments, be printed in the Record to accompany his remarks, that with them, it might be distributed to the people. Over 500,000 copies of this somewhat unique document were circulated by himself and other members of Congress.

A GUBERNATORIAL POSSIBILITY AND ALREADY A NATIONAL LEADER.

In 1882 there was a general demand throughout the State for his nomination to the office of Governor. In the Democratic convention Mr. Flower received 134 votes against the same number for General Slocum, and sixty-one for Grover Cleveland, of Buffalo. The strife between Tammany and the County Democracy was so great at that time that it was thought better politics to nominate a man outside of the city of New York. Consequently Mr. Flower made way for Cleveland, who was declared the choice of the convention. In this same year, 1882, Mr. Flower refused a renomination for Congress, having stated in his first canvass that he would not accept a second nomination and that he would leave the district in such a condition after one term that any good Democrat, no matter how shallow his pocket, might be nominated and elected in it. He was at this time offered the unanimous nomination of both factions of his party, and was assured that the Republicans would make no nomination if he would consent to run, but he preferred to carry out his pledge to the people when he ran against Mr. Astor. Orlando B. Potter was nominated and elected in his place, Mr. Flower taking the stump for him. Mr. Flower has been a member of the State Executive Committee every year since that time, and has given valuable aid to the Democratic party managers. In 1885 he attended the Democratic State Convention as a looker-on; not as a candidate for office. The convention nominated David B. Hill for Governor. Several delegates had asked Mr. Flower to accept the nomination for Lieutenant-Governor, but he refused. He left Saratoga the morning before the convention adjourned, but when he arrived at his country home in Watertown, he found that he had been unanimously nominated for Lieutenant-Governor. He immediately declined the honor, stating his reasons for doing so. The State Committee was called together and nominated in his place Colonel Jones, of Binghamton, he "who pays the freight."

Mr. Flower, in 1882, was made chairman of the Democratic Congressional Committee, and ran the campaign that year which resulted in a majority in the House of fifty for his party. In the Presidential campaign of 1888 Mr. Flower was selected as one of the four delegates-at-large to the National Democratic Convention at St. Louis, which nominated Mr. Cleveland for President, and was chosen chairman of the delegation. In the same year, when it seemed probable that the two Democratic factions in the Twelfth district might each run a candidate for Congress, they united on Mr. Flower, and asked him to accept the nomination. This he did, with some hesitation, and only in order to help the election of the Presidential and Gubernatorial nominees.

AGAIN IN CONGRESS.

In the Fifty-first Congress Flower was appointed a member of the House Committee on Ways and Means, and also a member of the Committee on the World's Fair. His efforts toward securing the location of the fair in New York have been recognized by the city and State, and his speech on that subject contained about all the points in favor of New York that could be put into thirty minutes.

Mr. Flower once remarked to the writer that his success in Congress was chiefly due to the fact that on whatever committee he was placed he tried to learn as much about his work if not more than any other member of the committee. On the Ways and Means Committee in the Fifty-first Congress, by the questions he asked at the hearing held before that committee, he showed his familiarity with many subjects, and with distant sections of the country and their industries. There was no just claim before Congress for the pension of a Union soldier that he did not champion, believing that if a soldier received a pension to which he was not entitled the government was to blame and not the soldier, for there are in each Congressional district three surgeons by whom the soldier is examined before he is allowed a pension. Mr. Flower also made a strong speech in the Fifty-first Congress in favor of the election of postmasters by the people, and offered an amendment to the Constitution to that effect. Because of his thorough knowledge of the West and its needs he was enabled to make in Congress a speech on the irrigation question, which attracted a great deal of attention, and which was made the basis of the Senate Committee's report on that subject.

THE CANVASS OF 1890.

Mr. Flower was chairman of the Democratic Congressional Campaign Committee in 1890. The committee had very small means, but his organizing powers were brought into play with great success. The campaign was quietly but systematically conducted. Campaign documents were circulated in large numbers, and the result was the largest Democratic Congressional majority ever obtained in an election in the United States. Mr. Flower created the impression that he was doing nothing, even counseling some of the leading newspapers of his party to pitch into him and accuse him of inaction, in order to arouse the Democratic rank and file to the necessity for active effort on their part. He believed that a full vote of his party meant a great Democratic triumph, and the outcome justified his belief.

Mr. Flower was nominated for Governor at the Democratic State Convention of 1891, and was elected by a plurality of 47,937 over Jacob Sloat Fassett.

HOW HE SPENDS HIS MONEY.

Mr. Flower has never turned his back on any charitable institution that he could consistently befriend, as the people of the State can testify. He has always made it a rule to give away in charity a certain portion of his income — for many years all that he did not need for his own living expenses — believing that when a man had wealth he should distribute it while he is alive in order that there be no contest over it when he dies.

Mr. Flower's parents were Presbyterians, and on a visit to Theresa a number of years ago he found that the church which he had attended as a small boy had run down and that the building itself was in a dilapidated condition. At considerable expense he had the church rebuilt, and it is now a beautiful little structure — a fitting memorial to Mr. Flower's parents. On the death of his son. Henry Keep Flower, in 1881, Mr. and Mrs. Flower gave St. Thomas church, in New York city, of which Mr. Flower is a vestryman, $50,000 to erect on Fifty-ninth and Sixtieth streets and Second avenue a four-story building to be known as St. Thomas' house, to be used for parish work. The structure has rooms occupied by an American Sunday school of 500 children, a German Sunday school, and a Chinese Sunday school. On the lower floor is a diet kitchen and on the second floor an institution to teach young girls how to sew and mend. The next floor is a club room where the boys play checkers and backgammon, and on the upper floor is found a library for a club of young men. All these institutions are carried on by the charitably disposed of St. Thomas' church. On the inside of the building on the wall is a marble slab, upon which is incribed: "Erected to God by Roswell P. Flower and Sarah M. Flower, in memory of their son, Henry Keep Flower."

Mr. Flower's brother, Anson, is a vestryman in Trinity church in Watertown, and Mr. Flower joined him in building a $100,000 home for that parish. The homœopathic school of physicians in New York city were erecting, a few years ago, a college, but had no hospital in which to teach young students anatomy and the use of the knife in practical surgery. Mr. Flower erected for them, at the corner of Avenue A and Sixty-third street, the Flower Hospital, which supplies this need. But this by no means completes the list of beneficiaries of the family. Henry Keep's widow has erected at a cost of $100,000, in the suburbs of Watertown, a home for old men and women called "the Henry Keep Home." As Mr. Flower truly says: "What better use could be made of the money of Henry Keep, whose father died in the poor house, than to erect, with some of it, a home for aged men and women?" Henry Keep's widow has also given $100,000 for the Ophthalmic Hospital at Twenty-third street and Fourth avenue, New York.

The writer has known Governor Flower from his earliest infancy, having at one time been a law student in the office of the Governor's father, and upon terms of daily intimacy with that estimable family of children, all of whom have grown up into useful and honored members of society. The Governor's most pronounced trait of character is his ability to level up to the demands of every situation in which he has been placed. When a boy, he could do more work than any other boy of his age in his native town, and Theresa was full of smart, athletic young fellows. Roswell was in "dead earnest" all the time, thorough in whatever he undertook, of a pushing, vigorous manner, ever on the alert, and putting the best foot forward every time. He was always hard at work, but when he had made half-a-dollar by industry he was liberal with it — ready to divide with his brothers or with the neighbors' boys. He was always a "trusty" boy — his word would go as far when fifteen years of age as any full-grown man in Theresa. He had a self-possessed and honest way that gave him standing. It is not remarkable that a boy with such traits has made a successful, trusty, honest man. I have read his speeches in Congress and his State papers since he became Governor. Their erudition and ability, and their matter-of-fact way of dealing with public affairs have not surprised me, for I knew the boy and the quality of the stock from which he sprang. His father was a nobleman if ever there was one in Northern New York, and his mother was one of the most faithful, industrious and home-making women of her day.

It is easy to say, and easier yet, perhaps, to suspect that what we print here may be largely due to the desire men usually feel to compliment and perhaps flatter men who have reached high positions or acquired great wealth. Governor Flower is too well known in his native county to need aught but honest praise from any source. Though a tireless partisan and an uncompromising Democrat, he has never lost a friend through any political divergence of view. Honest in his own opinions he does not hesitate to accord those who differ with him the same honesty of purpose. Springing from the middle walks of life, neither poor nor rich, nor yet a college graduate, but graduated from that wonderful developer of practical common sense, every-day human experience, he possesses the robustness and mental health which such an origin might be expected to transmit. His face is all expression, showing an exquisitely penetrating and mobile intellect, easily stirred to noble emotions and brimming over with goodness. He is a delightful companion, welcome in every circle, but shines brightest and most hopefully to those who share his daily life and "know him best of all." His life has been a blessing to so many, here and elsewhere, that his personal popularity is not so remarkable when we consider the foundation upon which it is mainly built — an unselfish desire to do good.

THE WATERTOWN RESIDENCE.

Although Mr. Flower has for some 20 years had a winter home in Fifth avenue, New York, he still spends his summers in Watertown, where, upon Arsenal street, he occupies a cozy, pretty house. There are 50 dwellings in Watertown surpassing it in splendor of appearance, more modern, with a greater evidence of the luxuries of life, but none having more the look of a real home. The house was built over fifty years ago, by Norris M. Woodruff, Mrs. Flower's father, and has the rambling, comfortable look of that period in architecture. It is a wooden building painted white — a cleanly, dazzling white, which seems to have been so attractive in the eyes of the last generation — and it has the usual accompaniment of bright green blinds. The house stands a little back from the street, having sufficient space for some handsome beds of flowers and a perfectly trimmed green lawn, while back of the house one sees a fine garden and clumps of handsome trees. Mr. Flower transacts his business in a comfortably-arranged office in the Flower Block.

HON. JAMES C. SPENCER,

Ex-Judge New York City Superior Court, is another of the men who have done much to embellish nature. An extended account of his lovely property, "Manhattan," may be found elsewhere. He is a native of Fort Covington, Franklin county, N. Y. His father, the late Judge James B. Spencer, was one of the early settlers of Franklin county, and was a prominent and respected citizen and recognized political leader in the northern part of the State, having held many important positions, including that of Judge and Representative in the State and National Legislatures. He also distinguished himself in the War of 1812, participating actively in the important engagements of that contest, including the battle of Plattsburg. In politics he was a Democrat of the Jefferson, Madison, and Jackson school. He was the personal friend and colleague of Silas Wright, and was recognized and appreciated by that great man and other prominent Democrats of the State of New York, as an intelligent and reliable political coadjutor, in the struggles of more than a quarter of a century to secure and perpetuate Democratic ascendancy in the State. He also enjoyed the confidence and esteem of all his fellow-citizens who knew him, without regard to political differences. He died in the year 1848, at the age of sixty-eight.

This branch of the Spencer family and that represented by the late Chief Justice Ambrose Spencer, and his son, Honorable John C. Spencer, were kindred, and claim a common ancestry. The family emigrated to New York from Connecticut, their original place of settlement in the New World, springing from an English ancestor, William Spencer, who came to Cambridge, Mass., before or early in the year 1631.

It appears that he returned to or visited England afterwards, for he married his wife, Alice, in that country about the year 1633. He was again a resident and a prominent man in Cambridge in 1634-5, and was afterwards one of the first settlers in Hartford, Conn. He was the eldest of three brothers, all of whom were among the early settlers of Hartford.

The family of the present Judge Spencer, on the maternal side, were purely Irish. His grandfather emigrated to this country from Ireland prior to the American Revolution, and served his adopted country as a soldier during the War of Independence.

Judge Spencer, before he had fully attained manhood, was thrown upon his own resources, and acquired his education and profession mainly by his own exertions. He commenced the practice of law in 1850, in his native county, and soon became popular and respected in his profession.

In 1854, he removed to Ogdensburg, St. Lawrence county, and, with judge William C. Brown, formed the legal firm of Brown & Spencer, which for many years enjoyed a successful and profitable practice in the courts of Northern New York. In 1857 he was appointed United States District Attorney for the Northern District of New York.

The performance of the duties of that office extended his professional acquaintance into nearly every county of the State. After the expiration of his term of office, he removed to the city of New York and entered upon the practice of his profession in that city. His energy and industry, added to his former professional reputation in the State, soon brought him clients and a very successful business.

In 1867, he entered into partnership with Hon. Charles A. Rapallo and other legal gentlemen, under the firm name of Rapallo & Spencer, which became familiar to the public and in the courts as associated with some of the most important causes of the day, including the famous Erie controversy and equally important litigations connected with railroad and steamship companies. The existence of that firm terminated with the election of its senior members to the bench — Mr. Rapallo to the Court of Appeals, and Mr. Spencer to the Superior Court of New York He was a candidate at a later day for reëlection as judge, but was defeated by a small majority.

On his retirement from the bench and return to the active practice of his profession in New York city, the Judge was heartily welcomed, and his old clients renewed their allegiance. As years have worn away he has become more attached to his Manhattan Island (see description elsewhere), and there he spends much of each summer, a practice dating back for twenty years. He has improved and beautified every thing he has touched, and is known as a liberal, progressive gentleman, taking a deep and healthy interest in all that relates to the St. Lawrence and the improvement of its Islands. Such men become, in a sense, public benefactors, and their memory should not die for want of proper recognition, nor their example be lost upon posterity.

CANADA'S WEST POINT.

THE ROYAL MILITARY COLLEGE AT KINGSTON.

BY J. JONES BELL, M. A.

WITH a frontier extending across a continent, bordering on a nation from which several hostile raids on behalf of "Irish independence" have taken place, and with a half-breed and Indian population in her own northwest, which has on two occasions broken out into open rebellion, Canada finds it necessary to maintain the nucleus of a military force, which shall be available on short notice to defend her frontier or to put down rebellion. She cannot afford to maintain a standing army, but she has three batteries of artillery on permanent service and a cavalry school, four infantry schools and one mounted-infantry school, at which the officers and non-commissioned officers of the Volunteer Militia may receive such a training as will fit them to take command and give instruction to the volunteers, who, taken from the field or workshop, would otherwise be wholly untrained and undisciplined.

But while her volunteers have given a good account of themselves when occasion called them into active service, and while her schools of military instruction have been the means of placing good officers at their head, it was felt that something more was needed to complete the system, and accordingly the Parliament of Canada, in 1874, passed an act authorizing the establishment of a Royal Military College "for the purpose," as the act states, "of imparting a complete education in all branches of military tactics, fortification, engineering and general scientific knowledge in subjects connected with and necessary to a thorough knowledge of the military profession, and for qualifying officers for command and for staff appointments."

In selecting a site for the college the government naturally turned its eyes to three places which were specially adapted for the purpose by virtue of their historical associations and the possession of extensive fortifications which might be utilized for technical training. These were Halifax, Quebec and Kingston. The latter was ultimately chosen, for, in addition to being the most central, it possessed certain buildings which could be utilized.

After the conquest of Canada, Kingston, the site of Fort Frontenac, built in 1673 by the French commander after whom it was named, became a military post of great importance. During the war of 1812 it was the British naval station for the lakes. A dockyard was established on a low promontory which juts out between the Cataraqui river and a small inlet of the St. Lawrence called Navy Bay. At this dockyard Sir James Yeo built his fleet for Lake Ontario. After the war the dockyard was dismantled, but a large three-story stone building remained, known as the Stone Frigate, which had been occupied by the marines. This, with a large blacksmith shop close by, was utilized for the college. [See building at left center of picture.]

In 1876 the first classes were opened, eighteen cadets being admitted. The staff consisted of a commandant, a captain and three professors. As the classes grew, more accommodation was required, and a large building, of the grey limestone for which Kingston is famous, was added. It contains offices, reading and mess rooms, library, class rooms, laboratory, hospital and kitchen. The Stone Frigate became a dormitory, and the blacksmith shop was converted into a well-equipped gymnasium.

The main building faces a spacious parade ground, with tennis lawn and cricket ground, and opposite, on the point, is Fort Frederick, a battery which guards the entrance to the harbor, with a martello tower at its apex.

Though modeled after Woolwich, the college is intended to give the cadets a training which will fit them for civil as well as military life. The course, which is four years, though provision is made for a two years' course in certain subjects, embraces English, French, drawing, mathematics and mechanics, engineering, surveying, fortification, architecture, astronomy, chemistry, geology, mineralogy, physics, electricity, tactics and strategy, signaling, military law and administration, military drill, gymnastics, fencing, swimming and riding. A few of these subjects are voluntary, but most of them are obligatory. A rigorous examination has to be passed by candidates for entrance, and if more reach the minimum than can be admitted — two from each of the twelve military districts into which Canada is divided — those who make the highest number of marks are given the preference. The age of admission is from fifteen to nineteen.

The military staff consists of a commandant, staff adjutant and seven professors and instructors, four of whom are graduates of the college, and two of the latter hold commissions in the regular army. Five of the staff are officers of the active list of the imperial army, lent to the college for a five years' term, at the close of which they are required to rejoin their command. Two are officers of the retired list. There is a civil staff of five, holding permanent appointments from the government. The presence of imperial officers gives a standing to the institution which it would not otherwise possess, and helps the proper training of those of the cadets who are destined for commissions in the regular army. The government was fortunate in the choice of the first commandant, COL. HEWITT of the Royal Engineers, who, in addition to being an accomplished scholar and a good soldier, was possessed of great tact and energy, and knew Canada from former service. To his skill is due in large measure the success which attended the college from its very outset, and his guiding hand directed it through the difficulties which invariably attend the early career of a new institution, which, in this case, was to a large extent an experiment. Having completed his term he returned in 1886 to Plymouth, and was succeeded by COL. OLIVER of the Royal Artillery, who had been professor of surveying and astronomy from the beginning, and who proved himself to be a worthy successor. The present head of the institution is MAJ.-GEN. CAMERON, late of the Royal Artillery.

SIR FREDERICK MIDDLETON, now retired from the command of the Canadian forces, took a deep interest, officially and personally, in the college, and during its early days helped it with counsel and advice, which his experience at Sandhurst well qualified him to give. The general officer commanding the militia is ex-officio president of the college.

The entrance examinations are held in June at the headquarters of each military district, and the twenty-four successful candidates report themselves at the opening of the term the following September. The first week is spent in being uniformed and drilled into some kind of form. The second week the old cadets return, and the garrison settles down to hard work. The daily routine embraces drill and class parades, study and other duties. From reveille to tattoo, with the exception of two hours — from four to six, during which he is free — the cadet is under the eye of authority in the class or lecture room or on parade. There is none of that loitering which so often takes place at civil colleges, none of that individual liberty which often means license. The cadet has, however, two half holidays, on Wednesday and Saturday, when he may go out on pass till eleven o'clock, or with extra leave till one. Balls and parties in Kingston are timed for these days, for the cadet, with his gay scarlet uniform, is an important factor in the social world. While attending the college the cadets are of course subject to the Queen's Regulations, the Army Act, the Militia Act, and such other rules and regulations as Her Majesty's troops are subject to.

The physical training is excellent. SERGT.-MAJOR MORGAN, of the Scots Guards, presides over this department, and well qualified he is to fill the position. Cadets who pass four years under his instruction come out with deep chests and erect figures, and show what a thorough physical training can accomplish.

One of the rewards of good conduct is promotion to the rank of non-commissioned officer, the commandant having authority to appoint such from among those best qualified. Proud is he who is invested with the chevrons, or given the right to wear the sergeant's sash.

But while subject to strict discipline the cadets have opportunities to cultivate their social qualities. One of the events of the season is the annual sports, which take place in September. The campus is alive with carriages and pedestrians, while pretty girls, with their chaperons, form the center of groups engaged in animated conversation, or watching with interest the various competitions of speed and skill. Races, jumping competitions and steeplechases follow each other in quick succession, while the tug of war between the right and left wings creates almost as much interest as the struggle on the Isis between the college eights. The games over, all adjourn to the gymnasium, where the prizes, more substantial than the crown of ivy at the Olympic games, are distributed to the victors. Tea and an impromptu dance follow in the college halls.

A ball is given at Christmas by the staff and cadets, and a yet more elaborate entertainment of similar character at the close of the college year in June. On closing day a series of field manœuvers takes place, with blowing up of imaginary fortifications and fleets, and an exhibition of drill and bayonet exercise, after which the results of the examinations are announced, the prizes distributed, and the session brought to a termination. The governor-general, the minister of militia, or someone else high in authority, is secured, if possible, to distribute the prizes and make a speech. Four commissions, one each in the engineers, artillery, cavalry and infantry branches of the imperial service, are available, the cadets who stand highest on the honor roll, if otherwise eligible, being entitled to them in the order named. The first two are eagerly sought, the third generally goes a-begging, as there are few Canadian youths with sufficient means to keep up a position in such an expensive branch of the service, in which case an additional commission in the infantry is generally substituted. All who have taken the full four years' course, and qualified in all the obligatory subjects, are entitled to receive a diploma of graduation, those who have specially distinguished themselves also receiving honors. Those who leave at the end of two years, and pass the subjects required, receive a certificate of military qualification only.

After the official proceedings are over on the closing day the cadets have a parade of their own, when the members of the graduating class have to undergo an ordeal of hand-shaking and leave-taking in true college form. A valedictory dinner in the evening follows, and then steamer and car bear the cadets off, and the halls are deserted for three months.

Some of the passed cadets of the college have already won fame for themselves. The name of STAIRS, who accompanied STANLEY in his march through darkest Africa, is well known the world over. LIEUT. HEWITT served in the Soudan and bears a medal won on the banks of the Nile, and LIEUT. DOBELL has distinguished himself for bravery in Burmah.

Occasion has not yet arisen to call into full play the energies of the rapidly-growing members of the graduates of the Royal Military College, and it is therefore too early to judge of its full benefit to Canada. But the opinion of LORD LANSDOWNE, expressed when governor-general, is worth quoting. These are his words:

"There is no Canadian institution of which Canada should be prouder or which will do better service to the country and to the empire. It forms an interesting and distinctive feature in the military system of the Dominion. That system, as I understand it, is based upon the recognition of the fact that Canada cannot afford in her own interests, or in those of the empire, to disregard those precautions which every civilized community takes in order to ensure its own safety from internal commotion or external attack. Upon the other hand it is a system entirely opposed to the establishment of a numerous standing army or to the withdrawal of a large body of citizens from the peaceful pursuits which are essential to the progress and development of the country.

"That being so, it is clear that in case of a national emergency the Dominion would have to trust largely to the spontaneous efforts of its own people, to the expansion of its existing organization, and the rapid development of the resources already at our command.

"But, gentlemen, it is needless for me to point out to you that there is one thing which it is impossible to produce on the spur of the moment, and it is a body of trained officers, competent to take charge of new levies or to supervise operations necessary for the defense of the national territory, and therefore it appears to me that we cannot overrate the value of an institution which year by year is turning out men who have received within its wall a soldier's education in the best sense of the word and who, whatever their primary destination, will, I do not doubt, be found available whenever their services are required by the country."

The cost of education at the Military College is not unreasonable. Each cadet is required to deposit annually $200 to cover the cost of messing and quarters, and in addition $200 the first year and $150 each year afterwards for uniform, books and instruments. The messman receives forty-six cents per day for each cadet present. Extras are obtainable at fixed prices. No cadet is allowed to spend more than $2 per month, non-commissioned officers more than $4, for extras, which they pay out of their pocket money.

In addition to the full course of four years and the military course of two years, provision has been made at the college for officers of the militia, who require higher instruction than the military schools afford, to take a three months' course, one class being instructed each year. By this means a number of officers have been enabled to qualify for important positions in the service.

Taken all in all, Canada's West Point has been an unqualified success.

AN INTERNATIONAL BOOK.

IT has been the constant endeavor of the editor of this book to preserve its international character, not forgetting for a moment that Canada has a much more extended proprietorship over the St. Lawrence river than has the United States. For many miles below Montreal the river runs through territory exclusively Canadian. No sincere patriot would desire to disturb, by word or deed, the friendly relations existing between the two great English-speaking peoples, whose united voice could control any matter of public policy, either in America or in the east. Canada is a vast country, larger than the whole United States in extent, for her territory extends very far north and joins our own country upon the north Pacific ocean. There have been efforts in the past, participated in by hair-brained plotters, to disturb the fraternal feeling between the two countries, but such efforts now find but slight recognition upon either side of the line. The press of both countries is friendly to fraternal feelings, and the public official business upon the whole frontier, from the farthest west to the dividing line upon the east, is conducted without serious disturbance.

GENERAL DESCRIPTION,

Historical and Otherwise, with some Opinions of Travellers.

THE route of the St. Lawrence has long been noted for the variety and beauty of its scenery. The traveller coming up from the sea, should he turn aside to explore the chasm of the Saguenay, would witness a scene of grandeur scarcely equaled by any other of its kind in any part of the world. Further up, the Rapids of the St. Lawrence present in succession displays of majestic power and volume that command admiration, and on finally reaching the level or navigable waters above, the approach to the first of the Great Lakes leads throught a labyrinth of islands, which, for variety of scenery and quiet beauty, have seldom failed to awaken the enthusiasm of the traveller.

To this group of islands, with their historical associations, and the impressions which their scenery has inspired, the greater part of this volume is devoted.

In arranging the materials of this work, the editor has been engaged in no small degree in presenting the thoughts of others; but, believing that the enjoyment of this scenery would be enhanced by learning the manner in which it has impressed those who have witnessed it in the years that are past, he has sought to present as wide a range of these impressions as opportunities allowed, yet not failing to present much that is original and never before published.

No one will doubt that places acquire extraordinary interest when associated with great events, or even when linked with the ideal incidents of poetry and romance. In allusion to the interest which these associations impart to so many places in the Old World, while there are comparatively few in the New, the naturalist Wilson, in whom were united a keen perception of the beauties of nature and a highly poetic temperament, in the opening part of his Foresters, says:

" Yet Nature's charms, that bloom so lovely here,
Unhailed arrive, unheeded disappear;
While bare, bleak heaths, and brooks of half a mile
Can rouse the thousand bards of Britain's Isle.
There, scarce a stream creeps down its narrow bed,
There, scarce a hillock lifts its little head,
Or humble hamlet peeps their glades among,
But lives and murmurs in immortal song.
Our western world, with all its matchless floods,
Our vast transparent lakes and boundless woods,
Stamped with the traits of majesty sublime,
Unhonored weep the silent lapse of time;
Spread their wild grandeur to the unconscious sky,
In sweetest seasons pass unheeded by;
While scarce one Muse returns the song they gave,
Or seeks to snatch their glories from the grave."

In some of the prose descriptions that follow, the reader will find a poetry of sentiment and imagery of thought that cannot fail to engage the attention. In others, there are incidents and events described that may add new interest to this region, especially those relating to the accounts of travel in the olden time, with the humble accomodations and the discomforts of the period, that afford a striking contrast with the exact appointments and the ample luxuries of the present day.

EARLY INDIAN HISTORY.

"In the beginning," so far as history or tradition extends back into the past, this region was the border-land of the Algonquin and the Iroquois,— the former dwelling for the most part to the northward and eastward, while the latter, at least in the later period, had their principal homes along the lakes and rivers of Central and Western New York.

The early historians of Canada record the fact that a bloody war was going on between the Adirondacks or Algonquins on the St. Lawrence, and the Iroquois or Five Nations of the region now included in Central and Western New York, when the country was first visited by the French. Champlain took part in this war on the part of the former, and by the use of fire-arms, hitherto unknown in Indian warfare, turned the tide of success for a time in favor of his allies — but gained thereby the lasting hatred of their enemies towards the French. The origin of this warfare is traced by tradition to a long time before the first appearance of the white man, and although not measured by moons or seasons, it still appeared to be consistent, and probable,— and according to the little that could be gathered, was as follows :

The Algonquins and the Iroquois had lived for a long time in harmony, the former being the stronger, and chiefly subsisting by the chase, while the latter were more inclined to fishing and agriculture. Now and then the young men of the two races would go out on their hunting expeditions together, but in these the superiority of the man who killed the game, over him who skinned and dressed it, was always insisted upon, and when the party saw an opportunity, it was the business of the one to pursue and slay, and of the other to stand by and see it done.

At one time, half a dozen of each class were out in the winter on a hunting excursion together. They saw some elk and immediately pursued them, but the Algonquins, presuming on their superiority, would not suffer the young Iroquois to take part, at the same time giving them to understand that they would soon have business enough on hand in taking care of the game they were about to kill. Three days were spent in vain pursuit, for although they saw there was an abundance of game, ill-luck followed them at every step.

At length the Iroquois offered to go out themselves, and the former, not doubting but that a like failure would soon put an end to their unwelcome comments upon their own efforts, consented. The tide of success turned in their favor, and the Iroquois soon returned with an abundance of game. Mortified at this result, the jealous Algonquins the next night killed all of their successful rivals as they lay sleeping. The crime, although concealed and denied, was soon discovered, and the Iroquois at first made their complaints with moderation — simply asking that justice should be done to the murderers.

No attention was paid to these complaints, and the injured party took justice into their own hands, solemnly vowing to exterminate the haughty race or perish in the attempt. Long series of retaliatory inroads were from this time made by each into the territories of the other, which finally ended greatly to the advantage of the Iroquois, and in the almost total annihilation of their enemies. The St. Francis Indians are a remnant of this once powerful tribe.

HIAWATHA.

The legend of Hiawatha has been rendered familiar to most readers of American poetry by the metrical version of Longfellow, and the prose of Clark, Schoolcraft and others, and much controversy has been had with respect to the author of the legend as it first appeared in English. We accept, as fully reliable, the statement made by the late Hon. J. V. H. Clark, of Manlius, author of the History of Onondaga County, in a letter to the New York Tribune, in January, 1856, in which the claims of various writers and the dates of their publications are precisely stated.

The legend relates to the origin of the League of the Iroquois, at a time which no record fixes by date, and no circumstance acceptable to the historian would lead him to locate otherwise than somewhere in that period clouded in the uncertainties of the forgotten past. We cannot present its beginning, which was in this region, more appropriately than in the original language of Mr. Clark:

"Hundreds of years ago, Ta-oun-ya-wat-ha, the Deity who presides over fisheries and streams, came down from his dwelling place in the clouds to visit the inhabitants of the earth. He had been deputed by the Great and Good Spirit, Ha-wa-ne-u, to visit streams and clear the channels from all obstructions, to seek out the good things of the country through which he intended to pass, that they might be more generally disseminated among all the good people of the earth — especially to point out to them the most excellent fishing grounds, and to bestow upon them other acceptable gifts. About this time, two young men of the Onondaga Nation were listlessly gazing over the calm blue waters of the Lake of a Thousand Isles. During their reverie they espied, as they thought, far in the distance, a single white speck, beautifully dancing over the bright blue waters, and while they watched the object with the most intense anxiety, it seemed to increase in magnitude, and moved as if approaching the place where they were concealed, most anxiously awaiting the event of the visitation of so singular an object — for at this time no canoes had ever made their appearance in the direction whence this was approaching. As the object neared the shore, it proved in semblance to be a venerable looking man, calmly seated in a canoe of pure white, very curiously constructed and much more ingeniously wrought than those in use among the tribes of the country. Like a cygnet upon the wide blue sea, so sat the canoe of To-oun-ya-wat-ha upon the Lake of a Thousand Isles.

"As a frail branch drifts towards the rushing cataract, so coursed the white canoe over the rippling waters, propelled by the strong arm of the god of the river. Deep thought sat on the brow of the gray-headed mariner; penetration marked his eye, and deep, dark mystery pervaded his countenance With a single oar he silently paddled his light-trimmed bark along the shore, as if seeking a commodious haven of rest. He soon turned the prow of his fragile vessel into the estuary of the 'double river,' and made fast to the western shore. He majestically ascended the steep bank, nor stopped till he had gained the loftiest summit of the western hill. Then silently gazing around as if to examine the country, he became enchanted with the view, and drawing his stately form to its utmost height, he exclaimed in accents of the wildest enthusiasm, Osh-wah-kee, Osh-wah-kee."

He approached the two young hunters, gained their confidence, and having drawn from them a knowledge of the difficulties under which they labored, disclosed to them the spirituality of his character, and the object of his mission. He invited them to attend him in his passage up the river, and they witnessed many things which could only be accounted for as miracles, or be described but in the wonders of Indian mythology. He ascended to the lesser lakes, placed all things in proper order for the comfort and sustenance of man, taught them how to cultivate corn and beans, which had not before been grown by them, made the fishing ground free, and opened to all the uninterrupted pursuit of game. He distributed among mankind the fruits of the earth, and removed all obstructions from the navigable streams. Being pleased with his success, he assumed the character and habits of a man, and received the name Hi-a-wat-ha, (signifying "very wise man,") and fixed his residence on the beautiful shores of Cross Lake. After a time, the country became alarmed by a hostile invasion, when he called a council of all the tribes from the east and the west, and in a long harangue urged upon them the importance of uniting themselves in a league for their common defense and mutual happiness. They deliberated upon his advice, and the next day adopted and ratified the League of Union which he recommended. As Lycurgus gave law to the Spartans, and swore them to faithfully observe its precepts until his return from a journey, and then departed to return no more, so Hi-a-wat-ha, having brought the council to a close, and as the assembled tribes were about to separate on their return home, arose in a dignified manner, and thus addressed them;

"Friends and Brothers: — I have now fulfilled my mission upon earth; I have done everything which can be done at present for the good of this great people. Age, infirmity and distress sit heavily upon me. During my sojourn among you I have removed all obstructions from your streams. Canoes can now pass everywhere. I have given you good fishing waters and good hunting grounds; I have taught you how to cultivate corn and beans, and have learned you the art of making cabins. Many other blessings I have liberally bestowed upon you.

"Lastly, I have now assisted you to form an everlasting league and covenant of strength and friendship, for your future safety and protection. If you preserve it without the admission of other people you will always be free, numerous and mighty. If other nations are admitted to your councils, they will sow jealousies among you, and you will become enslaved, few and feeble. Remember these words: they are the last you will hear from the lips of Hi-a-wat-ha. Listen, my friends; the Great-Master-of-Breath calls me to go. I have patiently waited his summons. I am ready: Farewell."

As the wise man closed his speech, there burst upon the ears of the assembled multitude the cheerful sounds of the most delightful singing voices. The whole sky seemed filled with the sweetest melody of celestial music; and heaven's high arch echoed and re-echoed the touching strains till the whole vast assembly was completely absorbed in rapturous ecstacy. Amidst the general confusion which now prevailed, and while all eyes were turned towards the etherial regions, Hi-a-wat-ha was seen majestically seated in his canoe, gracefully rising higher and higher above their heads through the air until he became entirely lost from the view of the assembled throng, who witnessed his wonderful ascent in mute and admiring astonishment — while the fascinating music gradually became more plaintive and low, and finally sweetly expired in the softest tones upon their ears, as the wise man Hi-a-wat-ha, the godlike Ta-oun-ya-wat-ha, retired from their sight, as mysteriously as he first appeared from The Lake of a Thousand Isles, and quietly entered the regions inhabited only by the favorites of the great and good spirit Ha-wah-ne-u.

In the legend, as rendered by Longfellow, no allusion to this region is specifically made, and the scene of events is located in the west, on the south shore of Lake Superior, in the region beyond the Pictured Rocks and the Grand Sable.

CREATION OF THE INDIAN RACE.

Among the traditions of various Indian tribes we find a legend of their creation, which, although differing more or less in details, agrees in ascribing their origin to a people who came out of the ground. Of this mythological belief we have an interesting example in this part of the world, as given by M. Pouchet, a French writer of acknowledged merit, who recorded what he saw and heard. This writer was an officer in the French service, and commanded Fort Levis, on the Oraconenton Isle, a short distance below Ogdensburg, when this last stronghold of the French was captured by Lord Amhurst in 1760.

He subsequently prepared a history of the events in which he had himself borne an important part, which was published some years after his death, and in this he gives much information concerning the Indians who then inhabited this region. In describing the shores of Lake Ontario, he speaks of a great arc of sand hills along the eastern end of the lake, behind which are marshy meadows, through which the rivers wind. This description clearly identifies these streams with those now known as the North and South Branches of Sandy Creek, in the town of Ellisburgh, Jefferson county, which unite just above the point where they enter the lake. They are remarkable in this, that at the head of the South Branch is the place where the traditions of the Iroquois fix the spot "where they issued from the ground, or rather, according to their traditions, where they were born."

TRACES OF INDIAN RECORDS ON THE ST. LAWRENCE.

Opposite the village of Oak Point, in Elizabeth Township, Canada, there existed in 1850, and perhaps does still, a rude representation of a canoe with thirty-five men, and near it a cross. On the rocks below Rockville there were two similar paintings, each being a canoe with six men. A deer rudely painted on the rocks was found on the shore of Black Lake, a few miles inland from Morristown, and doubtless other rude sketches of the kind may be found. These are probably of comparatively modern origin, or at most not earlier than the time of European settlement. They may have been significant of some event at the time when made, but whatever the objects may have been, they have passed into oblivion with the memory of those who made them.

GENERAL DESCRIPTION.

EXPEDITIONS OF DE COURCELLE AND DE TRACY.

In the papers relating to De Courcelle's and De Tracy's expeditions against the Mohawk Indians (1665-6), in describing the routes leading into the Iroquois country, the navigation of the St. Lawrence is mentioned as exceedingly difficult until the rapids are passed.

"But when the mouth of the Great Lake is reached, the navigation is easy, when the waters are tranquil, becoming insensibly wider at first, then about two-thirds, next one-half, and finally out of sight of land; especially after one has passed an infinity of little islands which are at the entrance of the lake in such great numbers, and in such a variety, that the most experienced Iroquois pilots sometimes lose themselves there, and have considerable difficulty in distinguishing the course to be steered in the confusion, and, as it were, in the labyrinth formed by the islands. Some of these are only huge rocks rising out of the water, covered merely by moss or a few spruce or other stunted wood, whose roots spring from the clefts of the rocks which can supply no other aliment or moisture to these barren trees than what the rains furnish them. After leaving this abode the lake is discovered, appearing like unto a sea without islands or bounds, where barks and ships can sail in all safety so that the communications would be easy between all the French colonies that could be established on the borders of this great lake which is more than a hundred leagues long, by thirty or forty wide."

FRENCH MISSIONARIES.

Among the pioneers of discovery were the missionaries who were sent out to gain the friendship and secure the conversion of the Indian tribes of the interior. These zealous men allowed no obstacles or dangers to interrupt their efforts or dampen their ardor, but with an energy and perseverance that cannot fail to excite our admiration, they pursued their way to the remotest parts of the interior, where some lived many years among the savages amid all the privations of a wilderness, and others were murdered, or miserably perished in the solitudes of the forest. We can here mention but a few of these pioneers and discoverers:

François de Salignac de Fenelon, half brother of the illustrious French writer, the Archbishop of Cambray, came to Canada in 1667, and was for some time engaged in the Indian missions at Toronto and elsewhere.

The Abbe Fenelon accompanied the Count de Frontenac to Lake Ontario in 1673.

Louis Hennepin, a Franciscan, came to Canada in 1675, and was stationed the next year at Frontenac, Kingston. He was afterwards sent by La Salle to explore the country, and was the first European who saw the Mississippi river. In 1697 he published an account of remote regions that he pretended to have visited, but which is now regarded in part at least as a fiction. Father Marquette also made extensive journeys in the west, and died at Mackinaw, May 14, 1675. Ménard, Allouez and many others passed this way on their journeys to distant points, but these men were, as a rule, little given to romantic descriptions, and their "relations" pertain more to the proper object of their missions, than to the scenery that they passed.

Father Emmanuel Crespel, in a little work published in 1742, describes some incidents of a journey into the Indian country on the Upper Lakes. He was fifteen days going from Montreal to Frontenac, and was there detained some time in waiting for a vessel to Niagara. This was of about eighty tons burthen, and apparently the only one then on the lake. The passage was made in less than thirty-six hours. The lake was very calm and he sounded with a line of a hundred fathoms without finding bottom.

On his return he remained two years at Frontenac, when he was recalled to Montreal, and soon afterwards was sent to La Pointe de la Chevelure on the east side of Lake Champlain, in the present State of Vermont, and opposite the French post at Crown Point.

FIRST MILITARY ESTABLISHMENT UPON LAKE ONTARIO—FORT FRONTENAC.—(1673.)

In order to protect the French interests, the Count de Frontenac resolved to establish a military post at the outlet of the Lake, and with the view of impressing the natives with the power of the French, he resolved to take two flat bottomed canoes up the rapids, and even to mount them with cannon, to inspire them with awe. The boats were built after a particular model, painted unlike anything ever seen before, and were each manned by sixteen men. With these and about one hundred and twenty bark canoes he left Montreal on the 16th of June, and in about three weeks reached the beginning of smooth-water navigation. Hearing that the Indians had assembled in great numbers, and were uneasy about the object of his expedition, he resolved to proceed with caution, in one body, and in closer column than before. The weather was so serene, and the navigation so smooth, that they made more than ten leagues the first day, and went into camp at a cove about a league and a half from Grenadier Island, where the eel-fishing begins. In his Journal he says:

"We had the pleasure on the way to catch a small loon, a bird about as large as a European Outarde, of the most beautiful plumage, but very difficult to be caught alive, as it dives constantly under, so that it is no small rarity to be able to take one. A cage was made for it, and orders were given to endeavor to raise it, in order to send it to the King. On the 11th [of July], the weather continuing fine, a good day's journey was made, having passed all that vast group of islands with which the river is spangled, and camped at a point above the river called Gananoque, up which many of them go hunting. It has a very considerable channel. Two more loons were caught alive, and a kind of deer, but the head and antlers are handsomer than the deer of France."

The narrative continues with an account of the regal manner with which the Count de Frontenac entered the lake, and the interviews he had with the Indians. In short, nothing which pomp and ceremony—the waving of banners, martial music, and the discharge of cannon could do, was omitted, to impress the wondering natives with an overwhelming idea of the omnipotence of the French. The speeches and proceedings of the occasion are all found fully recorded. The outline of a fort was at once traced out, and its construction commenced. Beginning work by daylight on the 14th, the ground was cleared before night. The Indians were astonished to see the large clearance made in a day—some squaring timber in one place; others fetching pickets; and others cutting trenches, all at the same time, and with the greatest dispatch and order.

EXPEDITION OF DE LA BARRE.—(1684.)

De La Barre, Governor of Canada from 1682 to 1685, had distinguished himself in the West Indies, where he had taken Antigua and Montserat from the English. In 1684, he repaired to Fort Frontenac, and ordered three vessels which the French had built upon the lake to be repaired, with the design of crossing to the country of the Iroquois, and frightening the people into his own terms of peace. His army consisted of 600 soldiers, 400 Indians, and 400 men for carrying provisions, besides 300 men left in the fort.

The Governor tarried six weeks at Frontenac, his encampment being near a pestilential marsh, causing so great sickness and mortality that he found himself unable to accomplish his object by force of arms. He accordingly resolved to effect what he could by treaty, and having vainly hoped to obtain the co-operation of Gov. Dongan, he sent agents to invite the Five Nations to a council. The Governor of New York, although in sympathy with the religious influences so actively employed by the French, did not consent to any concurrence, but secretly put every obstacle in the way; and in this he so far succeeded, that the Mohawks and Senecas remained at home. The other tribes, who were more under the influence of the French missionaries, sent representatives to meet him, consisting of Garangula and thirty warriors. The place of meeting was at the mouth of Salmon river, at the eastern end of Lake Ontario, about forty miles from Onondaga castle.

After remaining two days in the French camp, the Governor proceeded to address the Indians, a circle being formed by the French officers on one side, and Garangula and his warriors on the other.

We have not space to print the speeches made upon each side by the "high contracting parties," but De la Barre entirely failed in placating or overawing the Indians, who became insolent, and at last openly defied that officer, who was soon compelled to retreat, and his command reached Frontenac (Kingston) at last much demoralized. The expedition was so much of a failure as to be almost stigmatized as puerile.

EXPEDITION OF DE NONVILLE.—(1685.)

In 1685, the Marquis De Nonville made an expedition into the Genesee country, but left no record of local interest concerning the islands.

THE AVENGING INROAD OF THE IROQUOIS UPON THE FRENCH—(1688.)

Early in July, 1688, an act of perfidy on the part of the French brought down upon their settlements the terrible vengeance of the Iroquois. Passing down the St. Lawrence, they landed at Lachine on the 26th of July, and fell upon the unsuspecting inhabitants, burning, plundering and massacreing in all directions, and almost up to the defenses of Montreal. They lingered weeks in the country, laid waste the settlements far and wide, and returned with the loss of only three men. The French lost about a thousand persons by this inroad, and many prisoners were carried off for a fate worse than sudden death.

The French at Fort Frontenac were obliged to burn the two vessels they had on the lake, and abandon the fort, first setting a slow match to the powder magazine. The fire happened to go out before the powder was reached, and the place was soon plundered by the Indians. The garrison set out in seven bark canoes, travelling only by night, and hiding by day, and after much difficulty reached Montreal with the loss of one canoe and all on board.

De Nonville witnessed the devastation of his colony without daring to resist the enemy while engaged in their work of ruin, nor on their return. He was succeeded the next year by Frontenac.

ONONDAGA EXPEDITION OF THE COUNT DE FRONTENAC.

In 1696 the Count de Frontenac made an incursion into the country of the Onondagas, but the only mention that he makes of this region is his encampment for a night upon what is now known as Grenadier island.

SUBSEQUENT OPERATIONS OF THE FRENCH ON LAKE ONTARIO.

During the next fifty years, the French were steadily extending their trade, and endeavoring to attach the remote Indian tribes to their interests. In 1687, they established a fort at Niagara, and in 1722 the English built a trading house, and in 1727 a fort at Oswego. Although England and France were during much of this time at peace, and the Governors of their colonies on terms of correspondence, there was probably no period down to the conquest of 1760 during which each of the two powers was not busy, through its agents, in endeavoring to monopolize the Indian trade, and in extending this influence with the native tribes.

INDIAN MISSION AT OSWEGATCHIE; LA PRESENTATION.—(1749.)

A considerable number of Iroquois, chiefly Onondagas, having been induced to settle on the St. Lawrence, a mission was established in 1749, at the mouth of the Oswegatchie, on the site of the present city of Ogdensburg. This mission was named La Presentation, and its founder was Francis Picquet, a Sulpician. During the first season he built a storehouse and a small fort, but before the end of the year his settlement was attacked by a band of Mohawks, who burned two vessels loaded with hay, and the palisades of the fort. After this, some soldiers were stationed here for protection. The station progressed rapidly, and in 1751 a saw mill was begun.

The English who had built a trading house and a fort at Oswego many years before, naturally looked with jealousy upon this establishment by the French. Word was brought to them by the Indians, concerning their posts lately erected on the Ohio, and the informant said "he heard a bird sing that a great many Indians from his castle, and others from the Five Nations, were gone to Swegage."

In June, 1754, the celebrated Congress of

Representatives from the English Colonies, met at Albany, to consider a Plan of Union for their common defense, and on this occasion these encroachments were fully discussed.

In the war which followed, La Presentation became a point of outfit and rendezvous for many of the war parties that laid waste the frontier settlements of the English, from which they usually returned bringing prisoners and scalps. Many of these expeditions were led by Picquet himself. Thomas Mante, in his history of the French war, says:

"As to the Abbé Picquet, who distinguished himself so much by his brutal zeal, as he did not expose himself to any danger, he received no injury; and he yet lives, justly despised to such a degree by every one who knows anything of his past conduct in America, that scarce any officer will admit him to his table. However repugnant it must be to every idea of honor and humanity, not to give quarter to an enemy, when subdued, it must be infinitely more so not to spare women and children. Yet such had often been the objects of the Abbé Picquet's cruel advice, enforced by the most barbarous examples, especially in the English settlements on the back of Virginia and Pennsylvania."

He returned to France, where he died July 15, 1781. He was succeeded at La Presentation (Ogdensburg) by La Garde, a Sulpician, and the mission was continued until broken up in 1760. The Oswegatchies continued to live on the south shore and on the islands at the head of the Rapids until 1806, when the proprietor of the lands caused their removal, a part going to St. Regis, and others returning to Onondaga. Some years since, the corner-stone of a building erected near the site of the present light-house, at the entrance of the harbor at Ogdensburg, was found in taking down the building. It may now be seen over the door of a building erected for a State arsenal in that city, and bears the following inscription:

In nomine + Dei Omnipotentis
Huic habitationi initia dedit
Frans Picquet. 1749.

These premises remained standing when settlement began under title from the State, in 1796, and until long afterwards. They were fitted up for a store and for dwellings until better could be built, and the site of the foundations may still be traced.

OPERATIONS IN 1755-6: CAPTURE OF OSWEGO.

The war, which ended in the conquest of Canada, is without incident so far as relates to the Thousand Islands; but many events occurred upon this frontier, which became the thoroughfare of large armies, the only communication then known being by the river, between the settled parts of Canada and the upper lakes.

In the summer of 1755 the French were engaged in strengthening the post at Frontenac, and later in the season at Niagara. The first detachment in going up was met by a party of Indians among the Islands on the 1st of August. They had a number of scalps, and gave the first intimation received in Canada of the defeat of Braddock's army near Fort DuQuesne a fortnight before. This success of the French determined many of the Indians to take up arms against the English, and many of the cannon captured on that occasion were used by the French at Niagara and elsewhere on the northern border during the following year.

In 1756, considerable bodies of troops were sent from France, and in May, the Marquis de Montcalm, Gen. Bourlamaque, two engineers, and an army of 1,350 regulars, 1,500 Canadians and 250 Indians, ascended the river to Fort Frontenac, and M. de Villers, with 500 men, established a post of observation on Six-town Point, in the present town of Henderson, Jefferson county, the outlines of which may still be plainly traced. It was square, built of upright timbers, with bastions at the corners, and was surrounded by a ditch, and at the time hidden from view by surrounding trees and bushes. This officer, who was captain of the marine, was brave and prudent, and had greatly annoyed the English by pillaging their munitions, and obliging them to take great precautions in sending provisions to their troops at Oswego.

Montcalm left Fort Frontenac for Point Peninsula on the 5th of August, and on the 7th the French appeared before Oswego. There were at this time two forts at this place

— Fort Ontario on the east side, and Fort Pepperell on the west. The latter, then newly erected, was 120 feet square, a rampart of earth and stone, 20 feet thick, and 12 feet high, besides the parapet.

The French began their approaches on the 12th, and on the next day the English, having spiked their guns and destroyed their provisions and ammunition, withdrew to the old fort on the eastern bank. This Col. Mercer was also obliged to surrender on the 17th. The English force consisted of 2,400 men, who yielded upon terms dictated by Montcalm, with all their effects, munitions, arms and military stores.

It is stated by English historians that, notwithstanding the pledges of Montcalm, twenty of the garrison were given up to the Indians, by way of atonement for the loss of friends, and that all the sick in the hospital were scalped. At least one hundred men are said to have fallen victims to Indian ferocity after the surrender, the remainder being taken down to Montreal, where they were mostly exchanged. The French did not attempt to hold this post after surrender, but most of the provisions were sent to Niagara and the artillery to Frontenac and Montreal. According to Pouchot, the government got small returns of the booty, as it was mostly stolen or converted to private use by the commissaries, stewards and other agents of the service, who lost no opportunity of enriching themselves at the king's expense. Some of the very articles captured were sold back to the government through contractors. Two sloops were set on fire by the French and cast adrift upon the lake. The greater part of the French army returned a week afterwards to Montreal, and appeared later the same season upon Lake Champlain.

DESTRUCTION OF FORT FRONTENAC, (1758).

In August, 1758, Colonel John Bradstreet arrived at Oswego with an army of 3,340 men and crossed the lake to Fort Frontenac, which he captured with a trifling loss. After destroying the fort and securing what he could of the immense military stores there deposited, he returned without accident to Oswego. He repaired the works on the east side of the river at that place, which remained in British possession until surrendered to the United States under treaty in June, 1796.

EXPEDITION OF LORD AMHERST, (1760).

The war between the French and English in North America, which begun in 1755, had led, by the end of 1759, to the reduction of Niagara, Ticonderoga, Crown Point and Quebec. To complete the conquest, three expeditions were planned for 1760: one from Quebec, another by way of Lake Champlain, and a third by way of Oswego and the St. Lawrence river. The latter was placed under General Jeffrey Amherst, and the forces assembled at Oswego were reported on the 5th of August as consisting of the 1st and 2d battalion of Royal Highlanders, the 44th, 46th and 55th regiments, the 4th battalion of the 60th, eight companies of the 77th, five of the 80th, 597 grenadiers, an equal number of light infantry, 146 rangers, three battalions of the New York regiment, the New Jersey regiment, four battalions of the Connecticut regiment, and 157 of the Royal Artillery — amounting in all to 10,142 effective men, officers included. There were besides 706 Indian warriors under Sir William Johnson.

The first detachment of troops sailed in two vessels, the Mohawk and the Onondaga, on the 7th, to take post at the entrance of the St. Lawrence. On the 13th all had embarked, and on the evening of that day they encamped at the head of the St. Lawrence. Captain Loring, with the two vessels, who had been the first to leave Oswego, lost his way among the islands, and while endeavoring to extricate himself, the main army passed him. They, however, arrived a day or two after at Point au Baril, near the present village of Maitland, where the French the year before had built a dock, and established a fortified ship-yard. The grenadiers and row-galleys had, in the meantime, taken an advanced position at Oswegatchie, preparatory to an attack upon Fort Lévis.

This fort stood upon an island called Oraconenton by the Indians, and Ile Royale by the French,—about three miles below the mouth of the Oswegatchie, and near the middle of the channel, which it completely commanded. In modern times it is known as Chimney island, from the ruins of the French works still visible upon it. (In Canada.)

The works upon this island were begun under the direction of the Chevalier de Lévis in the summer of 1759, and finished in 1760 by Pouchot. A map given by Mante shows that the border of the island was set with the trunks of trees having their tops still on, and firmly set in the ground, so as to present an impenetrable abatis of brush on every side but the landing at the lower end. Within this was a breastwork of earth, and behind this a deep ditch filled with water, through the middle of which there ran a stockade of strong, sharpened pickets, closely set and sloping outwards. Inside of the ditch stood the Fort proper, consisting of a timber parapet filled with earth, with a line of strong, sharpened pickets sloping out over the ditch, and platforms for cannon, and in the center of the works the magazines and quarters. The lower point of the island was not included within the ditch and parapet, but had defensive works sufficient to prevent the landing of boats.

A small church stood near the head of Gallop island, a short distance below the fort, at the time when this post was taken. The English, finding a scalp displayed in the building, burned it to the ground. The outline of the foundations of this church can still be traced.

The events attending the reduction of this fort — the last that offered any resistance in Canada, may be learned from two accounts: one by Mante, an English historian of approved credit, and the other by Pouchot, the French officer who defended the fort, and afterwards wrote a history of the war, that was published after his death.

The loss of the English was twenty-one killed and nineteen wounded. The first shot from the English battery killed the French officer of artillery. Eleven more were killed afterwards, and about forty wounded. The garrison, except the pilots, for the sake of whom chiefly the place had been attacked, were sent to New York; and the general named the fort FORT WILLIAM AUGUSTUS.

OSWEGATCHIE UNDER THE ENGLISH.

The English continued to occupy Oswegatchie as a trading post until 1796, and during the Revolution it was a point of some importance as a place for the storage of supplies, and the transfer of freight from boats to vessels. Although the St. Lawrence river had been declared the boundary by the Treaty of 1783, the British held possession of the whole line of posts on the northern frontier to secure, as they claimed, the rights of certain British subjects. In the absence of authority to prevent it, the owners of land under purchase from the State suffered great damages from timber thieves, who operated extensively and without the least restraint. A mill on the Oswegatchie owned by one Verne Francis Lorimer, a half-pay captain, did an extensive business in this line, but the remonstrances of proprietors obtained no relief. The usual plea when these complaints were brought to the attention of officials was that they had no jurisdiction in the matter, and that relief should be sought in some higher authority.

According to the terms of "Jay's Treaty," all the posts within the United States were to be given up on or before June 1, 1796. Mr. Nathan Ford, agent of Samuel Ogden the proprietor, took possession, and at once began improvements with an energy that could not fail of success. During his absence the first winter the Canadians came over, held a town meeting, elected civil and military officers and opened a land office for selling and settling his lands; but he made short work with these squatters and their title, and the settlement grew rapidly until its prosperity was checked for a time by the embargo of 1812 and the war.

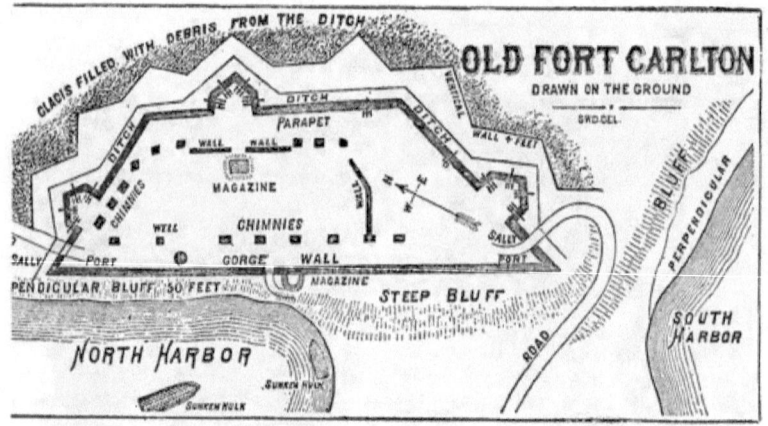

CARLTON ISLAND IN THE REVOLUTION.

FOR more than eighty years the traveller on the river St. Lawrence by way of the American channel, could scarcely have failed to notice a group of stone chimneys standing on the bluff at the head of Carlton Island. Inquiry or examination disclosed the fact that these old chimney stacks stood within an elaborately fortified enclosure of which the outlines are not only distinct, but in a degree quite perfect, so that the plan is readily determined, the system identified, its armament approximately adjudged, its magazines and barracks located, and, in short, its whole scope, object and intent made reasonably plain.

It will be remembered that the head of Carlton Island consists of a comparatively low peninsula, connected by a neck of land with the main island. On each side of this neck or isthmus is a bay, one arm of which is called South bay and the other North bay. Back of the two bays the island rises abruptly in a steep bluff to a height of about sixty feet above the water, and upon this bluff the fort was constructed.

The work occupied three-eighths of an octagon, extending from edge to edge of the cliff on which it was built, which faces to the southwest. The rear, or landward side, was protected by a strong earth-work, a ditch, an out-work and glacis of stone and a strong abatis. The ditch was cut in the limestone rock. In the center of each face of the ramparts, and midway between the salients, was a strong bastion, constructed for four guns, two of which in each bastion could enfilade corresponding angles of the ditch, which was cut to a depth of nearly five feet, with an average width of twenty-four feet. The scarp was vertical and protected by a cheveaux-de-frise of cedar logs, sharpened at the outer ends, and extending beyond the berme; these were held in place by the earth of the parapet. The counterscarp was also vertical, and beyond it extended a couvert way of about the same average width as the ditch. There were also bomb-proof magazines and barracks erected, and a well sunk to a level of or below the water in North bay. On the 10th of June, 1793, there still remained in the fort ten eighteen-pounders, five twelve-pounders, two nine-pounders and two six-pounders. In 1783, ten years previous, six eighteens and

RUINS OF FORT HALDIMAND, CARLTON ISLAND.

five twelves had been taken from the armament of the fort and placed upon vessels; so that the complete armament must have been sixteen eighteens, ten twelves, two nines and two sixes; in all, thirty guns.

As early as 1774, Carlton Island, then known as Buck, or Deer Island, became a trading post of much importance for Quebec merchants who were dealing with the Indian tribes. In 1775-6 the British government had located a military and naval supply department on the island, but it was not until August, 1778, that any attempt at fortifying it was made. The reasons for so doing may be very briefly stated. At the breaking out of the War of the Revolution, the British held Niagara, Oswego, Fort Frontenac (now Kingston), and undisputed sway of the lakes and of the river St. Lawrence. Sir Guy Carlton was governor of the Canadas, and commander-in-chief of his Majesty's forces therein. A campaign against the colonies was planned early in the war, and its management entrusted to Gen. John Burgoyne, instead of Sir Guy Carlton. The plan was well laid. Burgoyne was to move on Albany by way of Lake Champlain; Col. Barry St. Leger was to proceed up the St. Lawrence to Oswego and thence to Fort Stanwix (Rome), and, reducing that, reach Albany by way of the Mohawk, and form a junction with Burgoyne; while Sir Henry Clinton was to move up the Hudson River to the same point. But Burgoyne was defeated at Saratoga, St. Leger was forced to raise the siege of Fort Stanwix, and Clinton failed to reach Albany — so the well-laid plan was defeated. Thinking himself aggrieved by the appointment of Burgoyne, Sir Guy Carlton resigned his position and returned to England; and Sir Frederick Haldimand was appointed to his place.

In July, 1778, Gen. Haldimand issued an order to Lieut. William Twiss of the Engineers, Lieut. Schank of the Navy, and Capt. Aubrey of the 47th Regiment, to proceed to the upper St. Lawrence and there select such a place as in their judgment was best suited to establish a ship-yard and all its necessary requirements. After a careful examination of several points they pitched on Deer Island. Capt. Schank had a force of artificers, and Capt. Aubrey his own company and a detachment of Sir John Johnson's "Royal Greens." Lieut. Twiss drew the plans for the fort, and named it Fort Haldimand, in honor of the new commander, and the three officers changed the name of the island from "Deer" to "Carlton," in honor of their former commander, Sir Guy Carlton. The fort was never fully completed, work being discontinued by order of Gen. Haldimand in 1783.

During the War of the Revolution, Carlton Island was the most important post above Montreal. Many vessels of war and gunboats were built in the North Bay, and the place was the great depot of military and naval supplies for the Northwest. It was the place of refuge for the Tories of New York, Pennsylvania and New Jersey. Thayendanagea, the great chief of the Six Nations, made this his headquarters. Large numbers of those tribes encamped on Carlton and Wolfe islands. The bloody massacres of the Cedars, Wyoming, Cherry Valley, and Stony Arabia, were planned here, and executed by forces which went from here.

What a contrast between the Carlton Island of 117 years ago, and now. Then all was bustle. Vessels of war were building, a fort in construction; the drums beat the reveille, and the roar of the evening gun startled the echoes amid the dense forests on island and mainland. The notes of the bugle rang shrill and clear across the crystal waters of the St. Lawrence, while the war-whoop of the painted Iroquois boded death and disaster to the frontier settler. To-day, all is quiet. Where the artificers of the Revolution built their vessels of war, the artificers of to-day are completing the finest cottage on the St. Lawrence river. The land earned by his service in the Continental army, and granted to a soldier of the Revolution, now belongs to a gallant soldier of a later Revolution, which established as a permanent fact that which the first Revolution only inaugurated as an experiment — "The Union, one and inseparable."

HON. THOMAS G. ALVORD'S FISHING EXPERIENCES

UPON THE RIVER, EARLY IN THE FORTIES.

WHEN I first resolved to proceed with the preparation of this Souvenir, my mind conceived the idea of asking some one of the early frequenters of the Great River to write up his early experiences. I knew that Silas Wright, and Preston King, and Martin Van Buren and his son Prince John, and Dr. Bethune, and Dr. Holland, as well as the hundreds of later men of equal ability, including Grant and Sherman and Sheridan, had all passed away — their names now only a memory — their presence never more to be recognized by the great nation that delighted to honor them when living. Casting about for some aged one, yet spared, we thought of Lieut. Gov. Thomas G. Alvord, of Syracuse, and he has graciously complied with our request. Without further introduction we give his admirable letter; preceding it, however, by saying that he was for many years the owner and occupant of what is known as "Governor's Island," now the property of Mr. Emery. It is the first island above the one upon which Mr. C. G. Emery built a beautiful villa, which he has lately enlarged and greatly improved. Mr. Alvord's long connection with the political history of the State has made his name most familiar to our people under the cognomen of "Old Salt," a name earned in the Legislature by his persistent adherence to the fortunes of Syracuse where the well-known Onondaga Salt Springs have been so long a source of profit to the State, as well as the source of very much of the earlier wealth and importance of that city.

SYRACUSE, February 25, 1895.

JNO. A. HADDOCK, ESQ.:

MY DEAR SIR. — I am in receipt of your pleasant letter of request that I dot down something of a history of my early experiences as an amateur fisherman on the glorious and lordly St. Lawrence. To this request I cheerfully accede, and leave to you the decision and final judgment whether or not it shall find its way into your contemplated history of the St. Lawrence and its 1,000 islands.

I first began my piscatorial career in the waters of the Hudson river, nine miles above Albany, when I was young enough to be without discretion, but old enough to hook a sunfish, and consequently came near, on one occasion, being drowned by falling from the dock into the river. My love for the sport followed me into my college life, and as often as possible I explored the waters of Long Island Sound for its black-fish, porgies, etc. I carried the taste with me to the Berkshire Hills, and in a sojourn of two years explored all the trout streams and pickerel and bass ponds within reach of a day's journey from Pittsfield, Massachusetts. I divided my time for two years between Blackstone and my trout-rod, on the edge and over the line between wilderness and semi-civilization at Keeseville in Clinton county, and, when a full-fledged lawyer in Salt Point, I had a right to stick out my sign as "Atty. at Law," there was quite often added at the bottom a temporary postscript, "P. S. Gone fishing."

From time to time I would hear about the beauties of the St. Lawrence and its many islands in conjunction with its unequalled excellence as a hunting ground for ducks, and its great abundance of the gamiest fish to be found in fresh waters. I had a long-time acquaintance with a Mr. Dutton, a noted music dealer of Utica, who as early as in the later forties, was in the habit of spending a portion of the year with his sons fishing on the river; so finally, in 1852, I proposed to a brother-in-law visiting me from Indiana, an excursion to Alexandria Bay via Oswego. Accordingly, one September morning we landed there from the old "Cataract," whose bones have but very lately disappeared from the waters of the lower bay at Clayton, where she had enjoyed a rest for many years after she ceased to be a floating passenger transport. At that time Alexandria Bay was the Mecca of fishermen, and Clayton the headquarters of square-timber cutting, and no boatman for fisher-folk hailed from there until some years thereafter. Old man Crossmon kept the only caravansarie at Alexandria Bay, and his then small establishment on the rocks was hardly ever found unable to accommodate all comers. The enormous charge of $1.00 per day also included sufficient lunch for the noon-day meal of both sportsman and guide, taken "al fresco," on some opportune island; the food furnished was well prepared, and the more delicate accessions, now considered almost necessities, were provided under the careful watch of the hostess. It was always neat, abundant and palatable.

The boats of that day were but the crude prototypes of the present exquisite ones, which have no superiors on the globe in form, finish or perfect adaptability, with their well-matched oars, center boards, cushioned chairs, and other requisites, superior in all respects for the uses to which they are put. Then, under the command of Commodore Ned Patterson, still living and still a guide (octogenarian sure, if not centenarian), I embarked on my first fishing excursion in a boat made of pine (not piano finished), sharp at each end, not more than 14 feet long, low-sided, with naked wooden boards, without back-rests for seats. Loaded down almost invariably on the return from a day's fishing with their human cargo and catch of fish, the gunwales would be perilously near the level of the water of the river. The remembered oarsmen or guides of that day were old man Griffin, Ned Patterson, Alph and Tom Comstock, the last named being my favorite, and after my first visit invariably my guide until some time after Alexandria Bay was abandoned for Clayton as the nearer point for the more desirable fishing grounds. Not knowing the outfit best adapted to the river in the matter of fishing-tackle, and being advised that the boatman furnished all that was necessary in that regard, we took none with us, but used the native tools. These were crude in very deed, the poles were home-made; the lines were rough and the spoon for trolling was literally the bowl of an iron or pewter spoon with a single big coarse hook, brazed on the lower end, and attached to the line without swivel, and did not rotate but simply wobbled in the water; live bait for bass was not then thought of, but a supply of worms accompanied each boat. The Duttons were there with their more artistic appliances, consisting of spoons with swivels, and of various colors, and fairly smooth laid-lines and jointed bamboo rods; but with all their fancy rigs they very seldom succeeded in beating our catch with the homelier tools. Rev. Dr. Bethune was there; he was the donor of the Stone Church in the village, in which, much to the gratification of the natives and visitors, he always officiated on Sundays when in town. He was a bass fisherman and used a fly as a lure. After leaving Utica for New York he still occasionally was to be met in the season at his favorite resort luring the bass with the delusive fly during the week, and tempting men and women on Sundays, by his powerful pulpit eloquence, to a better and purer life. There and then I first met Seth Green, and then commenced a warm friendship which ended only with his death. He never failed for years to supply me, "unsolicited on my part," with an abundance of his own-make of flies, both single and in gang, and whenever we met he always gave me a learned lecture on the progress in piscatorial science and art. He was at that time and for many years thereafter the only fisher dweller on any of the beautiful islands of the St. Lawrence Archipelago, making the now renowned Manhattan Island his home where his house may still be seen, though remodeled [see frontispiece]. His memory will be "Green" in the recollection of many to whom his example and teachings have imparted a love for a sport and pastime compelling them to commune with nature where dressed in her most enticing garb and to drink in the pure air of heaven, bearing to them a healthful cure — restoring body and soul to a perfect health and vigor, and sending one back to battle with the world with not only renewed and restored bodily strength but with a mind attuned to a higher and purer conception of duty to themselves and others.

The recital of the surroundings of my first visit to the St. Lawrence would be incomplete if I did not dot down my impressions of the natural beauties of the scene afforded by the river and its many island gems. I am a natural fisherman; given intensely, whenever opportunity permits, to entice and ensnare the cunning water dwellers. I have been a visitor to the St. Lawrence, with but two exceptions, each returning season, for over forty years; and during that period I have again and again traversed in its widest extent every nook and corner, islet and island, and mainland as well, every shoal and deep of the St. Lawrence, from Chippewa on the north to the deep indentation at the head of Long or Wolfe Island, stretching up into Lake Ontario, called Reed's Bay. I have never been any day upon the water, when my line has not been neglected for hours in order to drink in the invigorating and health-laden air and the wondrous, indescribable beauty and (may I say it?) sublimity of diversified island and encircling water.

I am not going to prolong this screed by a recital of my wonderful exploits as a fisherman. I leave that task to time, and, perhaps, in the distant future I may be deified as the great "American Fisherman," and my reported deeds almost match with those wonderful tales rehearsed at camp fire, or where'er the jolly fishermen congregate.

Suffice it to say that I generally captured all the fish I was entitled to, but, what was far better, I took in annually a load of health which has prolonged my life and made me retain the feelings of youth in spite of the increasing number of years added to my roll-call.

An article on the 1,000 islands of the St. Lawrence would be incomplete unless a full description of one of their noted features, "The Boatman, or Guide," was given. Both by an experience and observation of 40 years I have carefully noted and studied them, and can safely claim for them a deservedly proud position; in the main, browned by their constant exposure and wearing the rough habiliments necessary for their calling, they are, with rare exception, Gentlemen in the truest acceptation of the word; accomplished oarsmen and sailors. Though not learned in books, they read the weather more correctly than do the trained signal-service men of the Government; they are perfect masters in the knowledge of the ways of the errant fishes; under their care, gentle woman and careless child are safe from all harm or danger. They are enthusiastic sportsmen, they never strike for an eight-hour day, but urge the lazy fisherman to an early breakfast and sunrise-start; and, oftener than their employer, insist upon one more circle or cast, so as to add another to the well-filled fish box, even if the shades of night are deepening around them. In all the time I have known the river I have never heard of the loss of the life of a fisherman or visitor by the carelessness of the Guide. Without apparent fatigue, they ply the oar for more than twenty miles, to be repeated each recurring day. They teach the tyro the gentle art, they cook you a noon-day meal the gods might envy; never sulking, always anxious to do all they can for your comfort and success. The Boatman of the 1,000 islands is easily the peer of that great army who contribute to the innocent enjoyment of others.

THOMAS G. ALVORD.

Syracuse, February, 1895.

THOUSAND ISLAND PARK.

THIS park seems to have been an outgrowth of that wave of religious sentiment which swept over the country about 1874 — the result, perhaps, of the reaction in men's minds which usually follows great financial depression. Its contemporary developments are visible at Asbury Park and Ocean Grove, two grand summer resorts upon the seaboard of New Jersey, and the latter manifestation of the same sentiment at Chautauqua, in Western New York. All of these movements towards summer residences bore a distinctly religious character, and were the outgrowth of a sincere desire to glorify God, and yet, in doing so, to make summer homes where families could receive the benefit of change of scene and of air and perhaps in their manner of living.

The manifestation of this impulse at Thousand Island Park is due to the efforts of Rev. J. F. Dayan, a well-known Methodist minister, now on the retired list. He conceived the idea that the Methodist denomination would gladly support such a resort, and he selected the southwesterly end of Wellsley Island as the most eligible spot. The selection was judicious, and his efforts were soon appreciated. The needed lands were mainly purchased (1,000 acres) from Capt. Throop, whose title was only the third remove from the State itself. Success crowned the Association's efforts, $22,000 worth of lots having been sold in a single day. Men struggled to secure the most desirable sites. It was unfortunate for the young town, however, that the extreme religious element so far prevailed that illy-considered restrictions were imposed as to entrance fee, etc., but in time these peculiar views have given way to more liberal ideas. To this day, however, no steamer is allowed to land at their dock on the Sabbath, the present management adhering to the original plan that the Sabbath should be not only a day of rest but of religious observance. The Thousand Island Park is now, as it was at the beginning, a place where a man can leave his wife and children and feel sure that they will not be exposed to any harmful influence of any nature — a place where "the assassins of society" would have no inducement whatever to come.

The situation of the park is superior. Back from the river-front plateau rises a rocky mound, nearly 200 feet in height, which afforded a permanent and accessible locality for a water reservoir with pressure enough to flood the highest buildings. The soil is productive, resting upon the moraine of this region, the result of glacial action. The second-growth of timber is mainly oak and elm, remarkably straight and vigorous, and the lot-owners are only called upon to decide what tree should be felled, and not what they should plant. It is difficult to conceive of a finer location. With man's intelligent supervision the place may be made the most delightful in America. Other resorts have the ocean, with its drifting sands, its fogs, its storms — this park has the great St. Lawrence, whose waters come sweeping down from the far Northwest, pure as the melting snow can make them, fresh as the breath of spring, placid as Nature itself. To live in such a spot is a benediction for man; there he forgets his cares, and grows into a life of contentment and thankfulness.

At the Thousand Islands there is a perceptible odor of ozone in the atmosphere. By some it is called a "sulphurous," by others a fishy smell. But there is a difference. Ozone is of itself an energetic chemical agent. It is a preservative, not a putrifying influence. In this it differs widely from oxygen, the principle in the air which assists in decay. There seems to be a reason for the belief that the beneficial effects produced upon many invalids from a residence among the Thousand Islands

The original trustees were: Chancellor E. D. Haven, D. D., President; Willard Ives, Vice-President; Col. Albert D. Shaw, John F. Moffett, J. F. Dayan, E. C. Curtis, E. Remington, Hon. James Johnson, M. D. Kinney.

Mr. Dayan continued a member of the board and as secretary and general manager until 1881. Chancellor Haven resigned in 1881, having been made one of the Bishops of the church at the preceding General Con-

THE COLUMBIA HOTEL AT THOUSAND ISLAND PARK.

or upon the sea-shore, is due largely to the ozone discernible in those localities.

The casual reader, like the author of this book, may ask to know more about "ozone." He has been told that the term is used to designate the life-giving principle which permeates the air we breathe.

The original capital of the Association was fixed at $15,000, of which $7,100 was paid in cash. On January 11th, 1876, the indebtedness of the Association was $24,647.81 and the assets $57,300.94. The capital was afterwards increased to $50,000.

ference. He was succeeded by Rev. I. S. Bingham, D. D., who, in 1883, gave place to Rev. M. D. Kinney, A. M., who had been a member of the board of trustees from the first. Under his energetic management many improvements were perfected, and there came a period of decided growth. He continued as President for seven years, and the Park owes much to his management, and to the fact that he has been of financial aid at many times.

The present trustees are: George P. Folts, President; George C. Sawyer, Vice-President; Dr. A. W. Goodale, 2d Vice-President and Secretary; W. R. Fitch, Treasurer. Trustees: George P. Foltz, F. G. Weeks, George C. Sawyer, W. R. Fitch, Walter Brown, Dr. A. W. Goodale, James P. Lewis, A. Gurnee, B. M. Britton; Jas. Smith, Superintendent. celebrated preachers in the United States and Canada, and the reputation of the Park in this respect has been admirably sustained. Rev. Dr. J. E. C. Sawyer, editor of the Northern Christian Advocate, delivered two sermons there on July 22, 1894, that were the

THE LATE CHARLES CROSSMON,
The First Summer Hotel-keeper upon the St. Lawrence.

The reader will recognize among these the names of prominent and influential citizens.

From the very first the design of the Association has been to secure the best native talent for religious services, and also bringing from abroad men of established reputation and ability. In this way the noble Tabernacle has had under its roof some of the most finished and stirring the writer has ever listened to. The influences that have gone out from that Tabernacle have been peculiarly inspiring and noble, and its services have done much to popularize the Park. The auditorium has a natural slope, the acoustics are admirable, and the sight most unique and interesting when the vast place is filled with the sea of upturned faces confronting the speaker. Situated in a fine growth of oak, with great curtains at the sides, which can be raised or lowered as desired, the people are brought face to face with nature, whence they are inspired to look up to nature's God.

It should not be forgotten that the Park as well as the Islands partake of an international character to a great extent, and the Union Jack floats in close proximity to our own beloved Stars and Stripes, and that prayers ascend for the noble Queen from the same desk as the petition for our honored President.

The population of Thousand Island Park is somewhat of a floating one, as regards its permanence, but there can be no doubt as to its pre-eminent respectability. It numbers 800 to 6,000 souls. Indeed the only occasion for fear in these established popular resorts is that they may become exclusively the summer abodes of the rich alone. At this place, however, there are ample accommodations for people of every class in point of material wealth, the hotel charges being $3.00 per day for the best, $1.00 per day for a cheaper but really comfortable place, and board in private cottages at even less rates. It is pre-eminently a democratic place, and friendliness is cultivated as not an altogether obsolete sentiment. The trustees and officers are capable men, composed of persons who have made their way from small beginnings and have always been in sympathy with plain and home-like methods. The cottages are numerous, all of them attractive, some beautiful. We give views of a few of the plain cottages as well as of some of the more elegant structures. A traveler upon any of the steamers which thread their way among the islands will observe that more people get on and off at Thousand Island Park than all the other resorts put together. The plotted ground for cottages occupies about 100 acres. The Association has sold off 200 acres for farming, and about 700 acres are left, devoted to dairying.

The pumping engines of the Association, their system of sewerage, water supply and electric lights are superior and unexcelled. Their dynamo plant and the beautiful machinery there (of the Watertown Steam Engine Company) are models of mechanical skill.

It would be, perhaps, an indication of negligence were we to fail in giving especial notice to the very large and wholly first-class hotel erected by the Association to take the place of the building destroyed by fire several years since. The new hotel is in the shape of a Greek cross, enabling every room in the house to have an outward look, the larger part facing the noble river. The rooms are all *en suite*, enabling them to be used singly or double; the ceilings are high; the furniture in keeping with the building. The closets and bath-rooms are of modern construction and appointment; the lights all electric — not a lamp being used in the whole building. The reception room and office, as well as the large ladies' parlor, and the commodious dining-room have each the patent steel ceilings admitting of fine effects in fresco and painting, as well as immunity from fire.

Taking into consideration its size, the outward view from every room, the purity of the water used, the separation of the kitchen from the hotel proper, the perfect system of sewage, and the desirability of location, it may be said that the Columbian is the finest hotel upon the St. Lawrence above Montreal. To this may be added its almost perfect safety from accident by fire.

The trustees felt that they were to a certain extent building for the future by authorizing so extensive a structure, but as the Park increases in importance every year, it is plainly seen that they acted wisely in erecting an hotel that would add to the character of the Park, where so many city people crowd during the heat of summer, and demand the best of everything.

There are other hotels and boarding places at the Park, but not owned by the Association. Mr. Billings, on Garden avenue, has five neat cottages where he accommodates very many people each summer, and his customers usually come again, for he is a very pleasant gentleman

AN INTERNATIONAL PARK.

THE popular scheme of establishing an international park, embracing the Thousand islands of the St. Lawrence river, which was discussed at length last year by American and Canadian authorities, seems almost certain of early fulfillment. A meeting was held at Ottawa in February, 1896, to promote the enterprise, and both the American and Canadian representatives present manifested much enthusiasm. The committee of Americans appointed to confer with the Canadian authorities, consisted of Hon Elon R. Brown of Watertown, chairman; Henry R. Heath of Brooklyn, and R. D. Grant of Clayton. They were met at Ottawa, by Hon George Taylor, M. P., for Canada; Hon. John Costigan, minister of marine and fisheries; Hon. Horton Reed, minister of Indian affairs; and Sir Charles Tupper, acting minister of the interior. The conference was held in Mr. Costigan's office.

As a result of this conference an agreement was made to make the opening and closure laws of both countries uniform, the closed season to extend from January 1, to June 9. Netting is to be totally prohibited on both sides of the river. The policing of the river is to be in uniform, the guards of both sides co-operating in all waters of the river.

The territory covered by the agreement extends from Ogdensburg on the American side and Prescott, on the Canadian side, to points four miles above Cape Vincent and Kingston. The Canadian government is to set aside certain islands for public parks, where those who do not own property on the river can pitch their camps. Similar parks are expected to be established on the American side.

The government of this great international park is to be vested in an international commission and is to be carried on after the plan adopted for the international park at Niagara Falls. The commissioners named on the part of New York State are Elon R. Brown, Henry R. Heath and President Mead, of the forest commission.

The thousands of people who annually find recreation and pleasure at the great watering places on the St. Lawrence will heartily approve of this plan to preserve for the whole people the beauties of the river. It is a plan that has been contemplated and one that will benefit those whose homes are in the St. Lawrence region even more than summer visitors, for the food fishes will be protected from wholesale slaughter and eventual extermination, and thus all classes of our people will be benefited.

THE RED CROSS.

RESIDENTS and voyageurs upon the St. Lawrence, when nearly opposite Alexandria Bay, have noticed upon the western bank of the river, above the fine residence of Mr. Browning and just adjoining the summer residence of Rev. Mr. Pullman (whose son is Miss Barton's financial and active secretary), a red cross emblazoned upon a white flag. That has been for two seasons past the summer home of Miss Clara Barton, the President of what is known as the Red Cross in America. We have been permitted to make extracts from an address made by Miss Barton in 1888, and by her delineation the reader will be able to get a fair idea of the Red Cross organization. For a fair representation of this wonderful woman we refer the reader to her portrait given in connection with a sketch of her life in another place in this volume. [See page 230.]

We give, in brief, much that she said at Washington before the International Council of Women in 1888.

The organization of the Red Cross is the result of an international treaty known among nations as the "Treaty of Geneva," and has for its object the amelioration of the conditions of that class of persons who, in accordance with the customs of mankind from the earliest history to the present, have been called to maintain the boundaries of nations, and even national existence itself, by human warfare.

Whether well or ill, needful or needless, that nations and boundaries be so preserved, is not a question for me here to consider. That they have been, and mainly are so preserved, that no better method is yet consummated, and that, in the progress of humanity, the existing countries of the civilized world have seen fit to enter into an international treaty for the betterment of the conditions of those subjects or citizens, who, by their laws, are called to the performance of this duty, are facts which I am here to state. This international treaty of 1864 commences with the neutralizing of all parties in their efforts at relief. It brings to the aid of the medical and hospital departments of armies the direct, organized and protected help of the people. It goes through the entire category of military medical *regime*, as practiced up to its date; makes war upon and plucks out its old-time barbarities, its needless restrictions and cruelties, and, finally, in effect, ends by teaching war to make war upon itself.

By its international code all military hospitals under its flag become neutral, and can be neither attacked nor captured. All sick and wounded within them remain unmolested. Surgeons, nurses, chaplains, attendants and all non-combatants on a field, wearing the accredited insignia of the Red Cross, are protected from capture. Badly wounded prisoners lying upon a captured field are delivered up to their own army if desired. All supplies designed for the use of the sick or wounded of either army, and bearing the sign of the Red Cross, are protected and held sacred to their use. All convoys of wounded or prisoners in exchange are safely protected in transit and, if attacked from ambush or otherwise harmed, an international treaty is broken. All persons residing in the vicinity of a battle about to take place shall be notified by the generals commanding both armies, and full protection, with a guard, assured each house which shall open its doors to the care of the wounded from either army; thus each house becomes a furnished field-hospital and its inmates nurses.

Each nation, upon its accession to the treaty, establishes a national society, or committee, through which it will act internationally in its various relations.

This body corporate adopts a constitution, in the formation of which it seeks the best methods for serving humanity in general, together with the interests of its own people, in the direction of its legitimate efforts.

The formers of the National Constitution of the Red Cross of America foresaw that the great woes of its people would not be confined to human warfare; that the elements raging, unchained, would wage us wars and face us in battles; that as our vast territory became populated, and people, in the place of prairies and forests, should lie in their track, these natural agents might prove scarcely less destructive and more relentless than human enemies; that fire, flood, famine, pestilence, drouth, earthquake and tornado would call for the prompt help of the people no less than war, and while organizing for the latter they also included the former.

It remains to name some of the things accomplished and the changes which have taken place in consequence of this treaty during its life of a short quarter of a century, and up to 1888.

Previous to the war of the Crimea civil help for military necessities was unknown. Florence Nightingale trod a pathless field. In the wars which followed, till 1866, even this example was not heeded, and the wars of Napoleon III. in Northern Italy were types of military cruelty, medical insufficiency, and needless suffering which shocked the world. Out of the smouldering ashes of these memories rose the clear, steady flame of the Red Cross; so bright and beautiful that it drew the gaze of all mankind; so broad that it reached the farthest bound of the horizon: so peaceful, wise, harmless and fraternal that all nations and sects, the Christian and the Jew, the Protestant and the Catholic, the soldier and the philanthropist, the war-maker and the peacemaker, could meet in its softened rays, and, by its calm, holy light, reveal to each other their difficulties, compare their views, study methods of humanity, and, from time to time, learn from and teach to each other, things better than they had known.

Our own terrible war which freed 4,000,000 slaves and gave to us the "Battle Hymn of the Republic" had no ray of this fraternal light. We "read the righteous sentence by dim and flaring lamps," and in darkness and inhumanity, sorrow and doubt "our souls went marching on."

But the great Commissions rose and performed a work of relief hitherto unknown, yet from lack of military recognition their best efforts comparatively failed; and from lack of permanent organization their future possibilities were lost to the world.

With the Franco-German war of '70-'71 commenced the opportunities for the practical application of the principles of the treaty. Both nations were in compact. There was perfect accord between the military and the Red Cross Relief. There was neither medical nor hospital work save through and under the treaty of Geneva. The Red Cross brassard flashed on the arm of every agent of relief, from the medical director at the headquarters of the king to the little boy carrying water to his wounded lieutenant; from the noble Empress Augusta and her court, and poor Eugenie, while she had one, to the patient, tired nurse in the lowliest hospital or tent by the wayside.

No record of needless inhumanity or cruelty to wounded or sick, stains the annals of that war.

I walked its hospitals day and night. I served in its camps, I marched with its men, and I know whereof I speak. The German, the Frenchman, the Italian, the Arab, the Turko, and the Zouave were gathered tenderly alike, and lay side by side in the Red Cross palace hospitals of Germany. The royal women, who to-day mourn their own dead, mourned then the dead of friend and foe.

Since that day no war between nations within the treaty has taken place in which the Red Cross did not stand at its post, at the field, and the generous gifts of neutral nations have filled its hands.

The treaty has brought the war-making powers to know each other. Four times it has called the heads of thirty to forty nations to meet through appointed delegates, and confer upon national neutrality and relief in war. It has created and established one common sign for all military medical relief the world over, and made all under that sign safe and sacred. It has established one military hospital flag for all nations. It has given to the people the recognized right to reach out and succor their wounded on the field. It has rendered impossible any insufficiency of supplies, either medical or nutritive, for wounded or prisoners which human sympathy and power can reach. It has given the best inventions known to science for the proper handling of mutilated persons, whether soldiers or civilians. The most approved portable hospitals in the world are of the Red Cross. It has frowned upon all old time modes of cruelty in destructive warfare; poisoned and explosive bullets are no longer popular. Antiseptic dressings and electric light at battlefields are established facts, and the ambulance and stretcher-bearers move in the rear ranks of every army. These isolated facts are only the mountain peaks which I point out to you. The great Alpine range of humanity and activity below can not be shown in fifteen minutes.

So much for human warfare and the legitimate dispensation of the treaty.

The public, in general, to a large extent is coming to the use of the Red Cross as a medium of conveyance and distribution for its contributions. The National Association, with its headquarters at Washington, has a field-agent, who visits, in person, every scene where aid is rendered. Commencing with the "forest fires" of Michigan in 1881, there has fallen to its hands a share of the relief-work in the overflow of the Mississippi river in 1882; of the Ohio in 1883; of the Mississippi cyclone the same year; the overflow of both the Ohio and Mississippi in 1884; the representation of the United States Government at the International Conference of Geneva, Switzerland, in 1884; the exhibition of "woman's work" in the Red Cross, both foreign and American, at the Exposition at New Orleans in 1885; the drouth in Texas in 1886; the Charleston earthquake in 1886; the representation of the United States Government again at the court of their Royal Highness, the Grand Duke and Duchess of Baden, at Carlsruhe, Germany, in 1887, and the relief of the sufferers from the Mt. Vernon cyclone, 1888.*

In further explanation we may say that the Red Cross was chosen out of compliment to the Swiss Republic, where the first convention was held, and in which the Central Commission has its headquarters. The Swiss colors being a white cross on a red ground, the badge chosen was these colors reversed. There are no "members of the Red Cross," but only members of societies whose sign it is. There is no "Order of the Red Cross." The relief societies use, each according to its convenience, whatever methods seem best suited to prepare in times of peace for the necessities of sanitary service in times of war. They gather and store gifts of money and supplies, arrange hospitals, ambulances, methods of transportation of wounded men, bureaus of information, correspondence, etc. All that the most ingenious philanthropy could devise and execute has been attempted in this direction. This society had its inception in the mind of Monsieur Henri Dunant, a Swiss gentleman, who was ably seconded in his views by Monsieur Gustave Moynier and Dr. Louis Appia, of Geneva.

The movements of Miss Barton, since her efforts to benefit the Armenians, has been fol-

---

* The last five years have added to the relief and labors of the above list. The yellow fever epidemic of Florida in 1888; the Johnstown disaster in 1889; the Russian famine in 1891-92; the Fifth International Conference at Rome, 1892, and the hurricane and tidal wave of the South Carolina sea-island coast of 1893-94.

In the overflow of the rivers in 1884 the Government appropriated $150,000 for distribution through the war department and magnificently and faithfully was that distribution made; an honor to any nation.

The Red Cross, with no appropriation and no treasury, received from the public, and personally distributed in the space of four months, money and material at the moderately estimated value of $175,000; an honor to any people.

lowed by the whole civilized world with the most eager interest. The annexed newspaper extract will be read with genuine satisfaction:

PERMISSION GRANTED

MISS CLARA BARTON AND HER ASSISTANTS WILL BE ALLOWED TO DISTRIBUTE RELIEF TO THE SUFFERING ARMENIANS.

WASHINGTON, Feb. 18, 1896.—A dispatch received at the State Department this afternoon from Mr. Alex. W. Terrell, United States Minister to Turkey, dated at Pera, the European quarter of Constantinople, contained the intelligence that the efforts of Miss Clara Barton, president of the American National Red Cross society, to obtain the permission of the Turkish government to distribute relief to the suffering Armenians has been successful. The decision of the Sublime Porte not to allow relief measures to be extended by the Red Cross as an organization, or by its officers as such, made it doubtful whether Miss Barton and her party would succeed in their object. It appears from Mr. Terrell's dispatch that Miss Barton had been presented by the minister to the Porte, and had received renewed assurance of full protection, and aid for her agents in dispensing charity. Her assistants, says Mr. Terrell, go at once to the interior. Miss Barton's headquarters will be at Pera.

CAPTAIN SIMON G. JOHNSTON.

IT is fortunate for the historian of the St. Lawrence Archipelago that there are yet a few men living who have been connected with that section from the time long before any attempt was made to improve it. One of the best known, most intelligent and companionable of these is Capt. Simon Johnston. We have importuned him until he has been prevailed upon to prepare a sketch of his life, which has been a long and active one, as he was born in 1821, being two years older than the author of this book. We think it best to tell his story as 'twas told to us. (For his portrait see plates of vessel captains.)

When a boy of nine years, in the year 1830, I left Ogdensburg, with my mother, for Sacket's Harbor. In those days steamboats were slow and the fares high, so my mother, with her four children, took passage on a vessel called the "Phoenix" Such sailing vessels or "packets," as they were then called, were fitted up with accommodations for passengers. We left with a fair wind, and all went well till we reached Gravelly Point, now Cape Vincent, when we were headed off, the wind coming down the Lake. The captain up helm and ran back to Hinckley's Flats, where we came to anchor. During the storm the vessel dragged anchor and went ashore on the head of Carlton Island. The mate got a long plank to reach the shore, and we all landed. Here we had to stay about three weeks before getting off, but finally reached Sacket's Harbor all right. At this time both banks of the St. Lawrence river were in a state of utter wilderness, with scarcely an inhabitant.

My father ran the first saw mill, one now built at Sacket's Harbor, owned by Col. Elisha Camp. This was about the time the colonel got a canal through from Black River. Here were also built two saw mills, one grist mill, one paper mill, one plaster mill, and a furnace. But the canal, not paying, was eventually abandoned.

One would laugh now at such steamboats as they had then, especially at the boilers and engines They burned wood for fuel, and when they came into port, instead of closing a damper as they now do, the half-burned wood was pulled out of the fire chamber and thrown overboard, to keep down steam. Then when they were ready to leave port a fresh fire was built. A boat like this, afterwards used on the river, was built at Brownville, N. Y., and passed through a lock at Fish Island (now Dexter). She was burned to the water's edge the first trip; was bought by Daniel Griffin of Sacket's Harbor, hauled out, lengthened and rebuilt, and called the "William Avery." I was on board on her trial trip to Henderson Harbor, which was in 1834 or '35. The steamer "Charles Carroll" was built at Sacket's Harbor about this time.

In 1839 I went to Kingston, Ontario, and shipped as horse-boy on the schooner "Brittania," Capt. Alex. Muer, in Calvin, Cook & Counter's employ at Garden Island, Ontario. In 1840 I was deck hand on the steamer "Telegraph." She ran between Ogdensburg and Oswego. At this time there were no lighthouses between Ogdensburg and Cape Vincent. They ran day and night, by ranges from point to point or from island to island.

In 1841 I was made wheelsman on the "Telegraph," under Capt. Geo. Mason, and we ran between Ogdensburg and Oswego, stopping at Morristown, Brockville, Alexandria Bay. French Creek (now Clayton), Kingston, and Sacket's Harbor. Kingston was the only market for surplus hogs, sheep, cattle, fish, butter, etc. Sometimes we would have a full load of sheep and calves, and the Kanucks would say, "There comes the Yankee Band," when they heard the calves bleat.

In 1842 I went with the late Capt. Thos. Collins to learn ship-building. He built vessels in the winter and sailed them in the summer. He built the first propeller that ran the rapids. She was named the "Precursor," and was launched in 1842. He sailed her in 1843, and that year I was with him as mate. Our run was between Montreal and Toronto. We went down the St. Lawrence through all the rapids to Montreal. There was no canal then except the Lachine. We came up through that, then up the Ottawa and Rideau to Kingston, then up Lake Ontario to Toronto. We made nine trips that season, running all the rapids, and had some close shaves to clear rock and shoal. The first thing the Indian pilot would do, just before entering the rapids, would be to drop on his knees, say his prayers, count his beads, cross himself, and then take the tiller, while he kept his eyes peeled for the breakers. Just as soon as we were through them he would dive for the cabin for something to eat. What a change from these days to what it was then. (See article on "How the Indians Learned the Rapids.")

In 1844 I was at Rice Lake, Ontario, building a small vessel to run on that lake. In 1845 was at Portsmouth, Ontario, working on the first vessel that went to England via the St. Lawrence river. She was called "The Lily," and was about 400 tons. In 1846 I built the schooner Odd Fellow and sailed her as master, trading between Picton and Jones Creek, Ontario.

From 1848 to 1850 I was in the employ of Calvin & Breck, at Garden Island. I sailed the schooner "Dexter Calvin" for them in 1850. Made one trip with her to Quebec in the fall, running all the rapids except the Lachine. We were in tow of a tug, and the strain on the hawser at times, when in the rapids, would make one's eyes stick out, for it seemed that we might strike some island or rock any moment while running them.

I left Garden Island in January for Hamilton, Ontario, to put timber ports in a vessel named "British Queen," for Jno. McPherson of the firm of McPherson, Cram & Co., of Kingston.

In April, 1851, I went to Erie, Pa., to put timber ports in a vessel called the "Baltic." From there I went back to Garden Island and built the yacht "Janet;" this boat 40 feet keel, 12 feet beam, and 6 feet in the hold. She had about seven tons of ballast in her. She left Kingston with a party of 45 men and women on board, bound for Clayton; they stopped at the foot of Wolf Island and had dinner, then started for Clayton; but when they got over into the American channel a white squall struck the yacht, which knocked her on her beam's end, filled the cock-pit with water, and threw most of the women into the mainsail — Capt. Hiram Hitchcock was master, and he called out to "let go the jib sheet," but some one let go the main sheet instead. This let the main boom drag, and kept her on her side. As the cock-pit was water-tight, they thought she would right up as soon as the squall was over; but some one had previously taken out the valve to pump her out, and had neglected to put it back; so she filled slowly and sunk in 40 feet of water. There were 19 drowned, 17 women and two men, all from Kingston. Many of them I knew.

Some thought that the yacht was to blame because improperly built, but they changed their minds, when they afterwards saw her working up the river in a gale of wind. She went from Clayton to Kingston, when it blew so hard that the "Ontario," Capt. Throop, would not land there.

When this happened I was building a steamboat at Keene, Ont., for Short, Kemp & Co., to run from Petersboro to Creek's Rapids, through Rice Lake. She was called the "Otonobee."

In February, 1852, I came to Clayton to work as foreman for Jno. Oades. He was doing all Fowler & Esselstyn's work. He built for them the steamers "Niagara," "Cataract," "Ontario," "British Queen," "British Empire," "Bay State" and "New York." He also built quite a number of sailing vessels. I was with him two years, and then started business for myself in Clayton. I first built the "Gray Hound," and sailed her in 1854, running between Ogdensburg and Oswego. She was a fast sailer, making a round trip a week, for eleven weeks, and bringing us home every Sunday. I learned more of the navigation of the river in this vessel than I did in all others.

The 7th of September, 1854, I was married to Emmeline H. Oades, youngest sister of John Oades, she being twenty-four and I thirty-one years old. On the 11th of September, or four days later, I left for Colburn, Ont., to build two vessels for J. M. Grover, one of which was called "Mary Grover," and the other "Alice Grover." I built these two in one year, coming back to Clayton in the fall of 1855, and that winter built the "Eagle Wing" for John Oades and myself. Oades, at that time, was building for Messrs. Merick & Co. I was master of the "Eagle Wing" in 1856, sold her in 1857, and built the schooner "Watchful." Sailed her in 1858, and in 1859 went to Dresden and built a steamboat to run on Seneca Lake. There I was taken sick and came home, where I was laid up for two years. In 1861 I sold the "Watchful" and built the "Mediator." In 1862 sold one-half of her to A. F. Barker and John Johnston, of Clayton. In 1863 I sold her out and built the "Senator" and "Snow-Bird." Sold them both in 1864, and built the "Brooklyn," which I chartered to Merick, Fowler & Esselstyne, to carry timber for two years at $100 (in gold) per 1,000 per cubic feet. She unloaded at one time when gold was $2.80.

In 1865 Mr. Oades went to Detroit to build for Campbell, Owen & Co., Mr. M. F. Merick being the company. They wanted a man to take Mr. Oades' place at Clayton and sent for me. I have never forgotten what Mr. Merick said to me. First he inquired if I "had tools to build a vessel," to which I replied "yes;" second, "can you build a good one?" I said "yes, you know, Mr. Merick, what kind I have been building, and I had to pick up my timber through the country, and when you have all the timber of the best kind delivered to you, one ought to build second to none." He then asked what wages I wanted, and I said three dollars a day. He said, "We don't want you by the day, we want you by the year." I then told him we might not suit each other, and if I was hired by the day he could let me go at any time. He said, "Name your price for a year—you will do." Mr. Henry Esselslyn being present, I told them that if I took charge of the ship-yard, I wished to hire all the men, set the wages for each and discharge any one who did not do his duty—the men to be paid every Saturday night. This would throw the responsibility on me, and when I failed to do what was right to discharge me. "Very well," said Mr. Merick. I then said $1,000 a year. He asked when I could commence, and I said "tomorrow." "Very well." he said, "I think we will have no trouble; but we have always had the best of vessels and don't want any others. Full canal size vessels and of the best stock is what we want." I never worked for a company that I liked as well as Merick, Fowler & Esselslyn. I built for them the "Montpelier," "Montcalm," "Mont Blanc," "Montgomery," "Montmorenci" and others, besides rebuilding several.

The second year they raised my salary to $1,600 and offered me $2,500 to go to Detroit to work for them there. But with my home in Clayton, and wife and children with good friends and neighbors, I decided not to go. They then wished me to buy the ship yard, which I did. This was in 1867, and I did their work until 1870, when they took their fleet of some 20 vessels to Detroit.

Since then I built the "Hoboken," in 1868, for A. F. Barker; the "L. B. Stone" for G. M. Read, Sacket's Harbor, and the "Scud" for Mr. Rogers of Rochester.

In 1869, built the schooner "Irene"; in 1870, the sloop "Dashing Wave"; in 1871, the schooner "Wm. Home"; in 1872, the "Hattie L. Johnson," and in 1874, the steamer "T. S. Faxton," for A. F. Barker, Capt. Holt and myself. In 1877, I built the steamer "Island Belle." Mr. T. H. Camp, of Watertown, N. Y., wanted me to build this boat to run in connection with the R. W. & O. R. R., from Cape Vincent to Alexandria Bay. She was a good one and a favorite on the river.

I built the steamer "S. H. Johnson," for James Johnson, of Clayton. Also the "Henry Folger" for the Folgers, of Kingston, and myself. I built the "Black Diamond," and many yachts, both sail and steam.

In 1883, I built the steamer "St. Lawrence," for Folger Bros., Kingston, Ont. She was built and launched at Clayton, May 24, 1884, and finished at Kingston. In August, 1886, I built the steam yacht "Sirius," for Capt. Henry S. Johnston. She was a fast boat and is now owned at Alexandria Bay.

In 1890, I built the steamer "Nightingale," for myself, to run on the Clayton and Fine View route. She has admirably filled the bill and by good management and prompt service has come to be a general favorite among the cottagers and Islanders on all the Parks, as well as the general travelling public.

In 1894, I built the steamer "Island Belle," (No. 2) for the Alexandria Bay Steamboat Co. She is a day boat running between Clayton and Ogdensburg, and has done admirable service.

CAPT. ALDRIDGE KENDALL,

Now in command of the steamer "Islander," is one of the best known and most popular navigators of the St. Lawrence river For thirty-two years of his life he has been a sailor on Lakes Ontario, Erie, Huron and Michigan, and the rivers connecting that great chain of lakes from Chicago to Ogdensburg.

By keen observation, and close attention to duty, he soon acquired a thorough knowledge of navigation; and at the age of twenty-two years he had distinguished himself sufficiently to become the efficient commander of the commodious passenger steamer "T. S. Faxton."

For twenty-one years he has been a commander of vessels and during that time has had under his control some of the finest steamers on the river.

For twelve years he has ran a steamer in

connection with the R. W. & O. R. R. system, and during that time has only failed in connecting with two trains. Good judgment is always exercised by him, proven by the facts that he has never lost a passenger or one of his crew, and has never been in collision with another craft, and the total damage to the boats he has commanded for twenty-one years would not amount to $200. There are few commanders who can show so clean a record as this. This good fortune is the result of constant vigilance and scrupulous regard for the safety of passengers and valuable property intrusted to his care. In addition to Capt. Kendall's ability as commander, he is an experienced river pilot, and has located channels and buoys at many difficult places on the river. Like many others of Clayton's vessel masters he began at the bottom. He was born in the town of Orleans, 1851, and came to Clayton when an infant, grew up like other boys of that time, attending school winters and working summers.

He is universally regarded as a "lucky man," but this is accounted for by his superior judgment and watchfulness.

CAPT. ELI KENDALL,

WHOSE strong and handsome face is shown among the collection of river men, was born in Clayton, and that town has always been his home. He received the benefits of the common schools in that town until the age of fourteen years, when he decided to become a sailor, and sixteen years of experience as such was passed on the "great lakes," Ontario, Erie, Huron, Michigan and Superior. He has passed through many dangers, being twice wrecked. November 8, 1878, he was a sailor on the ill-fated schooner "Monteray," lost on Sturgeon Point, Lake Huron; also on the schooner "Prince Alfred," lost in Georgian Bay, Lake Huron. From 1860 to 1876 he followed the St. Lawrence and lakes, and from 1876 to 1896 has been in different steamers on the river. During those years he has commanded the best river boats, and his vigilance and untiring industry have brought him through without mishap. He is considered one of the best pilots between Ogdensburg and Chicago. Captain "Eli," as he is familiarly called, has an unusually pleasant and agreeable character — courteous, and consequently popular. He is no exception to the Folger Bros.' officers, who have the reputation of being the ablest navigators on the river, and the millions their boats have carried without losing a man is the best evidence that this reputation is deserved, as well as affording a hopeful promise for the future.

CHAS. H. KENDALL,

COMMANDER of the steamer Jessie Bain, in childhood manifested a love for navigation. His experience began when a mere boy and covers nearly twenty years. He has a knowledge of the St. Lawrence river and Lake Ontario unrivalled by no other commander of the river crafts. His courage is dauntless, and his self-command unequalled in danger. He was born in Clayton in 1863, and since twenty years of age has commanded sail or steam crafts. His career as a commander has been brilliant, unmarred by serious accidents. By his cheerful attentiveness to business and pleasant demeanor he has acquired the title of "Genial Captain Charlie," a designation well deserved.

SOME OLDER CAPTAINS.

TRAVELLERS who were upon the river forty to fifty years ago will not forget to recall the large American boats then running upon its waters; and the names of the men who commanded these vessels will rise up in memory. Captain Throop, Captain Chapman, Captain Ledyard, Captain Estes and others but dimly remembered, have all passed away. They were an extraordinarily able body of men — probably not more so than those now upon the river, but the steamers they commanded were much larger than the Folger boats, if we except the Empire State. Peace be to the souls of those old-time commanders. They are not forgotten.

SAMUEL B. GRENNELL.

IT would be difficult to find a face more familiar to the thousands who visit the islands, or one of more interest than is the dignified representation of Samuel B. Grennell. He was born in Adams, Jefferson county, N. Y., Nov. 10, 1818. His ancestors were among the earliest settlers of the country, and they followed in succession the occupation of farming, in which Samuel himself passed the early years of his life. He surmounted the difficulties in the way of acquiring an education, and had such benefits as the Antwerp school of early days afforded. In 1840 he married Miss Lucy M. Jenison, of Watertown, N. Y., who bore him five children, only one of whom (a son, Myron W. of Luddington, Mich.) survives. In 1844 he came to La Fargeville and began hotel life. "Uncle Sam" was noted far and near for his hospitality, which was carried into extravagance. Misfortune pursued him, and, unseen and unanticipated, fell upon him. In a few short months he realized the fact that all he once possessed by honest gain was lost. Undismayed by this failure, and with a keener knowledge of the "hotel business," in 1860 a new scene began to open which gave a fresh turn to his enterprising spirit. Visiting that portion of the river above the Park, and having a prophetic sense of future value, he purchased eight islands for a small sum, and on the principal one ("Stewart's" Island, later known as "Jeffers") he erected a small house, hanging over the front door the name "Tavern," and again commenced hotel life. "Grennell's Tavern" was hailed with enthusiasm by the sparce population of the islands, and was regarded as a wonderful enterprise. The fame of the landlord spread and the "Tavern" was the scene of many a festive occasion. Thither flocked youth and maiden, and unfortunate, indeed, were the newly wed not within walking or rowing distance of the "Tavern," as it was the one place to spend the honeymoon. Years passed on. The fame of the Thousand Islands became known, and brought many visitors from all parts of the land. The old "Tavern" has been changed to a modern hotel of beauty and convenience, and many whom the nation has honored have been the guests and received the meritorious service of "Uncle Sam." After thirty years of struggle and success Mr. Grennell retired from hotel life, and in 1890 sold the beautiful site, now occupied by the "Pullman," to J. I. Sales, of Rome, N. Y. The eight islands purchased in 1860 have been converted into pretty summer homes, and Jeffers' Island is the beautiful spot known as "Grennell Park," where Mr. and Mrs. Grennell still reside in peaceful seclusion. By marked industry Mr. Grennell has made a comfortable fortune, but he still retains the spirit and activity of youth, and during the summer he continues a flourishing mercantile business, and also has charge of the post-office. Although seventy-six years of age he has not yet yielded to the decrepitude of age, but is never better pleased than when relating experiences. N. M. K.

HOWARD S. FOLGER.

AMONG the river men who have come to the front within the past few years, and who now fill a position of great responsibility, is by its prompt service to the public, and its remarkable freedom from accidents or carelessness. We show elsewhere portraits of the

HOWARD S. FOLGER.

Mr. Howard S Folger, the General Manager of the Thousand Island Steamboat Company, popularly known as the "White Squadron," which embraces the palatial steamers Empire State, America, St. Lawrence, Islander, and Jessie Bain, which carry without accident more than half a million of passengers each season. That this fleet is well managed is evidenced commanders of these vessels, and they are "able seamen" in every respect, careful, able, and discreet gentlemen.

"Howard," as he is everywhere called, to distinguish him from the numerous class of Folgers, is the son of Mr. Henry Folger, of Folger Brothers, bankers, steamboat owners, brokers, etc., of Kingston, Ontario. Howard was born in 1868, and up to the time he took charge of the large business of the company he was a student. He earned the degree of A. B. from Queen's College, Kingston, in 1889. The next fall he entered Columbia College, New York City, and after spending two years there in the Law Department, was graduated with the degree of LL. B. in the spring of 1891. The object in taking this course was to fit him more completely for the position he was to fill by becoming well grounded in a knowledge of the general principles of law. In 1891 he took charge of the business of the company, and since then he has devoted himself most perseveringly to its interests, as well as to those of the New York Central Railroad Company, with which the steamboat company is closely allied.

The Folgers are Americans, even though their business interests are so largely in Canada. We say this because rivals upon the river have designated them as foreigners. They are descended from a long line of sea captains whose operations were around Cape Cod and Massachusetts Bay from 1775 to 1850. This family are directly related to that of Benjamin Franklin, whose mother was a Folger. No family in this section can trace its ancestry back to a more patriotic and honorable beginning. The sons and daughters of the Folger family would be admitted any day to become sons or daughters of purely American societies organized in this country to perpetuate the memory of the American Revolution.

Mr. Howard S. Folger has always shown himself a worthy scion of this patriotic stock. He has exhibited remarkable business ability in the several positions he has been called upon to fill, and the popularity of the boats of the White Squadron is very much due to his executive ability. A person intimately acquainted with the travel upon the river, which, some days, calls for the handling of 20,000 people, with car loads of baggage, express, mail, etc., can understand that the demands upon the general manager are sometimes imperative, and are always laborious, calling for forethought, prompt action, and a careful consideration of the safety of passengers. The low water on the St. Lawrence during 1895 developed many new dangers, but the White Squadron got through the season without any serious mishap, a fact that is the highest compliment to the skill of Mr. Folger and all his numerous subordinates, and enhanced the already enviable reputation of that company for handling safely the precious lives and the property committed to their charge. This is an enviable record, well earned.

MR. FRANCIS M. HUGO.

EVERY traveller upon the Folger boats (and they carry about 70 per cent of all those who frequent the St. Lawrence archipelago), will have no trouble in recognizing the portrait we present on the next page, that of Mr. Hugo, the former purser, but now the assistant-general manager of the T. I. S. B. Co., and a genial, accommodating, pleasant gentleman, whom it is a pleasure to know. He has a watchful eye for business, and it is said he would not pass his own mother at the gangway unless she could produce a proper ticket. Be that as it may, he is ever attentive to passengers, and is popularly known as the right bower of the steamboat magnates. the Folger Bros.

He is Canadian born, though now a citizen of Watertown, N. Y. He graduated from Queen's College, Kingston, in the class of '92, and bears with dignity the degrees, M. A. and LL. B., and when not engaged in summer on the river, is studying law with the well known attorneys, Purcell & Carlisle, in Watertown. His ancestry is English, and he has the peculiar healthful brawn and vigor of that remarkable people. He promises to become a distinguished lawyer, and though the recipient of much flattery, his head has not yet swelled observably. Take him all in all, although reserved in manner, he is the most popular young man upon the river, a distinc-

MR. FRANCIS M. HUGO.

tion he has earned by politeness, kindly feeling and by an unswerving attention to his own business. Frank is now twenty-five, having been born in 1870, at Kingston, Ont.

CAPTAIN C. HINCKLEY,

WHOSE classical features are shown among our unusually good-looking river men, was born at Cape Vincent, in 1842, making him now fifty-four years of age. He has commanded steamers since 1861, and has always followed the water since his early youth. He now commands the fine steamer "America," the newest and one of the finest of the Folger boats, in which capacity he is unusually popular.

Captain Hinckley's modesty has prevented our procuring as extended a sketch of his life as we had desired.

CAPTAIN H. C. HUDSON.

THE popular and persevering commander of the "New Island Wanderer," one of the fastest and promptest boats on the river, was born in Clayton, in 1855. He had the usual advantage of the common schools and became possessor of a fine constitution by the labor incident to farm life. At fifteen he concluded to plough water instead of land, and in 1870, began to serve under Capt. W. E. Williams. For seven years he sailed the great lakes in the employ of the Northern Transportation Company, and then two years in the service of the Whiting Company of Detroit. For two years he commanded the steamer "Juniata," and for five years the "J. F. Maynard," which was consigned to the bone-yard last fall. For five years he also commanded the "Ontario," one of Captain Sweet's boats. He has commanded the "New Island Wanderer" for four years, and the public will find him on deck on that fine steamer during 1896. His young son accompanies Capt. Hudson on the "Wanderer," a very bright, active lad, promising to become as good a sailor as his father. The Captain was married to Miss Philena Hart, of Clayton, in 1877, and they have two children born to them. The youngest (Ross C.) is an infant, but the eldest (Chester E.) sails with his father on the Wanderer, and though only fifteen years of age is proving a reliable and eager participant in the affairs of the vessel, having charge of the book-stand. But few things transpire on that boat unknown to young Hudson, who only needs years to make him a full fledged sailor able to command. He is already a fair business man.

CAPTAIN CHESTER W. REESE

Is the son of William Reese, of Clayton, where the captain was born in 1867. He had the advantage of the excellent common schools of the town and early manifested a love for the water. His first experience upon the river was upon the "Island Belle" in his 14th year, where he served as a deck hand, learning to become a pilot and navigator. Prompt, active, industrious and energetic, he rose from one position to another, until at last he became a full-fledged captain commanding the Folger Bros.' steamer "J. F. Maynard," then the "New Island Wanderer," then the "Islander," and now commands the most reliable, well-managed and every-way successful Folger steamer, the "St. Lawrence."

Captain Reese has proved himself emphatically the "right man in the right place," and is one of the most successful and popular of the Folger employés. His boat is always on time, and by his bravery, forethought and pleasant address Captain Chet. Reese has won his way to the very front rank among the river navigators. His aged parents still survive him, and his home is with them in the village of Clayton, which we may truthfully designate "the sailors' snug harbor." Our Souvenir shows the faces of many of her seamen.

CAPTAIN HENRY T. JOHNSTON.

COMMANDING steamer "Nightingale," was born in Clayton in 1863. Naturally, when not at school he spent most of his time on or near the water. His father, Captain S. G. Johnston, then, and for years after, carried on an extensive business in ship-building. The son early learned all about boats, and later learned to draft and build them, and soon mastered all the details of that business. In 1883 he passed the examination before the government steamboat inspectors and received his first license as pilot. Seeing an opening on the river for a fast pleasure steam yacht for parties to charter, Capt. Johnston, senior, with his son, built the well-kown steam yacht "Sirius." The son sailed her for five seasons among the Thousand Islands, the foot of Lake Ontario and the Bay of Quinte, thereby acquiring a knowledge of the river that could not be learned on the large steamers in years —

a complete knowledge of the fishing grounds, shoals and beautiful narrow channels that are so numerous among these wonderful islands. Selling the "Sirius," the son built the "Alert" and commanded her for two seasons, and used her in the same capacity as the "Sirius." The river business increasing now so rapidly, and the different parks gaining so fast in summer population, the now well-known steamer "Nightingale" was built and made her appearance among the river crafts. Becoming interested in her, the young captain was given command and established his well-known ferry-route between Clayton and Thousand Island Park. The popularity she at once met with can be seen by the favor shown her by the public in her passenger traffic between the places named. Having seen the grand old St. Lawrence spring into world-wide fame and popularity in so short a time as a summer resort, and the wildest islands, as if by magic, transformed into the finest of summer homes and parks, who would venture to predict what the future holds for this most beautiful and grandest watering place on the continent of America?

CATHERINE—KNOWN IN HISTORY AS "KATE" JOHNSTON,

WAS born in Sackets Harbor, Sept. 11, 1818. Her parents were William and Ann Johnston, and she was sister to two men well and favorably known in Clayton, Hon. John Johnston, a member of the Assembly, as well as having held many other offices — now a banker, and Stephen Decatur Johnston, for many years proprietor of the Walton House,

THE DEVIL'S OVEN.

and that fine property is yet held by his widow and managed by his son-in-law.

Kate Johnston came first into more or less public notice through her efforts to aid her father, over whose head a reward was suspended because he had been an active participant in what is still denominated "The Patriot War," though what particular patriotism was displayed during the continuance and ignoble ending of that remarkable episode, we have never been able to ascertain. Her father being forced to go into hiding, she became his companion, adviser and real support,

"KATE" JOHNSTON.

for she kept him supplied with provisions, clothing and news of the efforts his enemies were making towards his capture. In this work she was busy for over a year, and at last had the good fortune to see her father a free man, and holding the position of light-house keeper upon the great river which had been his hiding place for so long a time. He received a free pardon for whatever he had done in violation of international law. His daughter earned a wide reputation for her devotion to her father and thus became an important historical character. She married Charles L. Hawes, a brother of Mrs. John Johnston, of Clayton, and they reared five children. She died at the home of her brother, Hon. John Johnston, Clayton, N. Y., on March 14, 1878, in her 60th year, leaving a name indissolubly interwoven into the legendary remembrances of the St. Lawrence, because she proved herself a brave daughter and a local heroine.

CAPTAIN E. F. FORRESTER

WAS born on the St. Lawrence, near what is known as "Forrester Dock," August 16, 1842, and was never out of sight of the river excepting for one year. During the rebellion he enlisted in Co. B, 142d N. Y. Infantry, and served one year. After coming home was out of health for a year or two, and so concluded to try the water for a while. His first sailing was on an old scow, on which he made one trip to Oswego. That made him a sailor, so he struck for more wages and shipped on a small schooner. There he served a couple of seasons, and then went into the employ of what was known as the Northern Transportation Company, running propellers between Ogdensburg and Chicago. Here he stayed eleven years, commencing as wheelsman, and afterwards filled first and second officers' positions. Finally he got tired of the great lakes and concluded to stay on the old St. Lawrence. So when Capt. Visger built the "Island Wanderer" he bought the steamer "Cygnet," that built up the route among the Islands, since so popular with the tourist, and run her on the Ogdensburg and Alexandria Bay route for five years; then sold out and commanded the steamer "Rawson" for two seasons, then took the "Lotus" one year; then the "Stranger" one year, and then he commanded the "Island Wanderer" for six seasons between Alexandria Bay and Ogdensburg, and last season commanded the "Island Belle" between Clayton and Ogdensburg, making sixteen seasons he has been on the river routes. He has carried many thousands of passengers, 12,500 last year, and has always had his share of business on the river. Captain Forrester enjoys the respect and confidence of all who know him as a competent commander and kind gentleman.

CAPTAIN ELISHA W. VISGER

WAS born in the town of Orleans, which has a wide frontage upon the St. Lawrence, and has ever afforded extraordinary opportunities for making sailors of its young men. Capt. Visger had the advantages of the common schools of that day, and put in his time working on the farm winters and attending school summers. In his 43d year he bought the steamer "Cygnet," and in 1876 began to make the first trips ever known among the Islands, an industry which has since developed into great importance, and has become a leading feature upon the river. He ran the "Cygnet" three years, and then he built the "Island Wanderer" (now the "Island Belle"), which he ran until 1888, and for nine years this proved the most celebrated excursion steamer on the river. During the winter of 1887 he formed a stock company and built the steamer "New Island Wanderer," which came out in

CALUMET ISLAND, THE SUMMER HOME OF CHARLES G. EMERY, NEW YORK.

CALUMET ISLAND.—THE SUMMER HOME OF CHARLES G. EMERY, OF NEW YORK.

THE FINE STEAM YACHT "SOPHIA," CAPT. H. W. VISGER.
[E.]

THE FIDDLER'S ELBOW, CANADIAN CHANNEL.
[H]

THE OLD SETH GREEN HOUSE ON MANHATTAN ISLAND (AS REBUILT), SUMMER RESIDENCE OF THE LATE MR. HASBROUCK, OF NEW YORK.

IN THE RIFT — SHOWING CANADA UPON ONE SIDE AND THE UNITED STATES UPON THE OTHER.

BIG MASCOLUNGE — 45 POUNDS.
[L.]

YACHTING ON THE ST. LAWRENCE. [SEE PAGES 79 AND 247.]

CAPT. E. KENDALL, OF THE "ISLANDER."
APT. FORRESTER, OF "ISLAND BELLE."
CAPT. HUDSON, OF "NEW ISLA WANDERER."
CAPT. JOHNSTON, OF "NIGHTINGA
CAPT. S. G. JOHNSTON, BOAT BUILDER.
CAPT. TAYLOR, ORIGINAL PROPRIETOR OF HEMLOCK ISLAND.
[All these have Biographical Sketches, which see.]

STEAMER EMPIRE STATE.

July, 1888. This boat Capt. Visger managed two years, then he acted as pilot upon the river until 1894, when he again managed the "Island Wanderer." Since then he has been the assistant to his son upon the "Captain Visger." Captain Visger, senior, is now in his 63d year, as young as at 35, and is in many respects a remarkably well preserved man, one of the pioneers in steamboating, a man respected by everybody, and looked up to as one of those who originated these excursion routes which have proved such an attraction to visitors.

CAPTAIN WALTER L. VISGER

WAS born in St. Lawrence county in 1864, attended the common schools and completed his education at a business college in Rochester. His father having been for many years a navigator upon the river, naturally led his son into the same business, and in 1875 he became an assistant to his father upon the yacht "Cygnet." He remained upon that boat for three years, and then took a position upon the "Island Wanderer," now the "Island Belle." Here he remained until 1887, when the "New Island Wanderer" came out in 1888, which was commanded by his father, Capt. Elisha Visger. Here Captain Walter L. remained a year. After several years of varied employment, in the spring of 1895 he built and assumed command of the "Captain Visger," which has proved the most popular yacht upon the river, thus continuing the business conducted for twenty years by his father, who was the first man to make the passage through the Lost Channel.

The beautiful yacht "Captain Visger" is being overhauled for 1896, and it is the purpose of the commander to show his passengers every island, both American and Canadian, from three miles below Alexandria bay to Clayton. The trips will include nine-tenths of all the islands, improved and unimproved, in the St. Lawrence River, and are to be three hours in length, and will become a leading feature in the St. Lawrence river excursion business for the season of 1896, as well as for other seasons, as the "Captain Visger" has attained a popularity that will not soon be eclipsed by any rival, large or small. A picture of this fine boat is given elsewhere.

CAPTAIN FRANK KENDALL.

UPON our composite plates of the river captains we present to the reader Captain Frank Kendall, commander of one of the Thousand Island Steamboat Company's steamers.

He was born on one of the Thousand Islands of the old St. Lawrence, October 20, 1858. His earliest desire was to navigate that grand stream, and he began to carry out this inclination while a mere lad, and his early boyhood found him a sailor in summer and attending school during the winter. Thus it was he laid the foundation of a knowledge which enabled him to hold so high a position of trust. He is a thorough gentleman as well as an efficient pilot. Long before he was twenty-one, the age required before receiving a pilot's license, he was thoroughly qualified to hold such a position.

Among other crafts which he commanded in his early days were some of the steamers owned and managed by Mr. A. F. Barker, so that when the present Thousand Island Steamboat Company was organized, Captain Frank Kendall's ability and worth were not overlooked, and he was assigned to command a steamer in "the White Squadron." The Folgers soon recognized the fact that he was one of the most thorough and successful of their employés, he never having had an accident. It is but fair to add that Capt. Kendall still enjoys the high esteem of the company and is still in their employ.

A more thorough and competent gentleman cannot be found anywhere. He is familiar with every point of interest on the river. This with his pleasant and affable manner, his conscientious adherence to the truth in even the most trivial matters, makes him one of the most interesting and entertaining gentlemen a stranger on the river could meet, and these agreeable attributes have made him hosts of friends at home and abroad.

CAPTAIN JAMES A. TAYLOR.

GAMALIAL TAYLOR, the grandfather of James A. Taylor, was a native of Rhode Island, and fought under General Greene in the Revolutionary war. In 1778 was married to a Miss Lacy, and settled at or near Poughkeepsie, N. Y., where Benjamin B. Taylor, the father of James A., was born April 18, 1779, and served in the war of 1812 under General McCombs. He removed to Canada with his parents in 1818, and settled near the Bay of Quinte, twenty miles above Kingston. In 1819 he married Sarah Bosback, and had two children, James A., born October 3, 1824, and Benjamin Taylor, born September 5, 1827. This one joined the 186th N. Y. Vol. Inf., and was shot in the rebel works before Petersburg, April 2, 1865. Benjamin B. Taylor, the father, died in 1830, and Sarah Taylor, the mother, married D. R. Maxon, a former resident of Brownville, N. Y., September 25, 1833; they reared three girls and three boys. (Marshman and Malcom Maxon served in the 2d Michigan Cavalry, and Matthew in the 186th N. Y. Vol. Inf.) The family removed to New York State May 6, 1838, and settled in the town of Orleans, on the St. Lawrence, directly opposite to where the "Sir Robert Peel" was burned, which occurred May 29, 1838, and the family saw it burn and "Bill" Johnson leave the wreck.

The subject of this sketch then followed a sailor's life until 1846, when, in company with his step-father, he built a steam saw-mill and went into the lumber trade, which occupation he followed until 1862, when he joined the 10th N. Y. Artillery as a private at its organization, August 7, 1862, at Sacket's Harbor, serving in company K, Capt. B. B. Taggart.

James A. Taylor was ordered by the War Department to take charge of a recruiting party and proceed to Jefferson county, where he located in Watertown and Alexandria Bay. He received his commission as First Lieutenant May 9, 1863, and was assigned to company I, Capt. H. O. Gilmore. On May 28, 1863, he relieved Capt. Standring, 5th N. Y. Artillery, and took command of Fort Greble with half of company I, and a company of California cavalry, until relieved by Capt. Greene. He returned to his company, and resigned September 19, 1863. Re-enlisted August 22, 1864, joining the 186th as a private. January 14, 1865, commissioned as Second Lieutenant and assigned to company B, commanded by Capt. Jay D. McWayne. He took part with the regiment in the following engagements: Hatcher's Run, Fort Stedman, and at the fall of Petersburg, April 2, 1865, and was at Appomattox when Lee surrendered April 9, 1865. He was mustered out with the regiment June 2, 1865, near Alexandria, Va.

He returned home, and the same year bought Hemlock Island, now Murray Hill Park, for $100, part cash and the balance in trade. About the year 1870, in company with Sisson & Fox, of Alexandria Bay, bought the Fuller mill and what was called Potash Point, now a part of the village of Alexandria Bay, and engaged in the lumber trade. In 1873, in company with John F. and Chas. Walton, bought the steamer "Shoecraft," of Buffalo, being the first yacht brought on the river for pleasure parties, and for exploring the islands and the various intricate channels of the river. In 1875 the "Needle Gun" was added, owned by E. N. Robinson, of the well-known firm of Robinson & Drew, of New York city. This gentleman gave our hero the name of "Captain Jack," by which name he has since been familiarly known on the river. He was appointed deputy collector of customs at Thousand Island Park in 1890, and the same year assisted in the formation of the "Thousand Island Investment Co.," with A. Corbin, Jr., of Gouverneur, N. Y., as President; J. A. Taylor, Vice-President; J. C. Lee, Secretary and Treasurer. This company is located at Murray Hill Park, with capital stock of $100,000, fully paid and non-assessable. The company sold in fourteen months lots to the value of $63,000. It paid to stockholders four 5-per cent dividends, and is still a large owner of stock in said company, besides owner of Palisade Park and various points on the river. Captain Taylor's immediate family contributed five recruits to the Union army.

CAPTAIN GEORGE SWEET

WAS born in Schuyler, Herkimer county, N. Y., in 1825. He had the advantages of the common school of that era, attending it winters and working on his father's farm in summer. His first experiences away from home were upon the Erie canal, and that gave him an inclination for life upon the water. In 1850 he was married to Miss Catherine Fults, and they have reared three children, two girls and one son, Vernon. Leaving the Erie canal, he came to Carthage in 1858, that place being the foot of navigation upon the Black River canal, then recently constructed, and there he was one of those who started the Carthage, Lowville and New York freight lines. They transported the greater part of the outgoing produce from Jefferson and Lewis counties to the east, the railroads not then being built. In 1860 he launched the "Gallagher" for towing, and built several other boats for Black River service, including, in 1865, a passenger boat which made regular trips from Carthage to Lyons Falls. This boat was named the "F. G. Connell," and continued in service on the river until the Black River road was completed to Carthage.

In 1872 Captain Sweet went to Rochester and built the "James H. Kelly," to run on the Genesee river between Charlotte and Rochester. In the spring of 1873 this boat was transferred to Cape Vincent for service upon the St. Lawrence between Cape Vincent and Alexandria Bay, connecting with the trains of the Rome and Watertown Railroad. This service employed the captain for three years, and the boat was used afterward for eleven years in the service of the Utica and Black River road after completion to Clayton. In this connection it may be said that Captain Sweet was the first person to present to the Rev. J. F. Dayan the possibilities of Wellsley Island as the locality for a permanent Methodist camp-meeting ground. That was the beginning of the now celebrated Thousand Island Park.

About 1876 Captain Sweet built the steamer "J. F. Maynard," so long known on the river between Cape Vincent, Clayton and Alexandria Bay. Having lengthened the "Kelly" some 30 feet, and had her registered as the "John Thorne," the captain had two boats upon the river, travel having increased very considerably. In 1886 he sold his boats to the Folger Bros. and purchased the "Ontario," using her as an excursion boat from Charlotte to points near that locality, but she was soon put on the route to Alexandria Bay. She was, at a later day, put upon the regular route from Oswego to Alexandria Bay, in connection with the Delaware, Lackawana and Western Railroad, and thus continued until 1891. In 1892 the captain put a steamer on Lake Canandarago, at Richfield Springs, and in 1893 he built a steamer at Old Forge, upon the Fulton Chain, in the Adirondacks. He retains this boat (the "C. L. Stowell") at the present time.

The captain has been a popular and efficient

navigator, and has always made friends wherever his lot has been cast. He is well remembered upon the St. Lawrence as one of the most agreeable and fortunate steamboat men, and as one of the first to build up and popularize the local passenger traffic, which has now become so profitable and important. Since 1858 he has been a resident of Carthage, N. Y., where he is recognized as a leading and influential citizen.

Vernon Sweet, the captain's only son, was also a river captain, having commanded the "John Thorne" for a number of years, and took the "Ontario" down the St. Lawrence and around to New York harbor, whence she was despatched to the Caribbean Sea for duty there. His sudden and unfortunate death occurred in June, 1895, at Fulton Chain, and created extended sympathy. There was an amount of mystery about his death that has not yet been cleared up satisfactorily. [See Vernon's portrait on another page.]

THE ST. LAWRENCE RIVER AND INLAND NAVIGATION.

SEVERAL years ago there appeared in one of New York's illustrated newspapers three curious pictures. The first represented fifty men carrying a large block of stone. The men were arranged in four files and each file carried on their shoulders a stout pole. By means of other poles and ropes the block of stone was suspended in the middle of the group of men, and with much strain and labor they were staggering along with their great load. The second picture represented the same stone placed in a rude cart and drawn by a pair of oxen with much difficulty over a sandy road. The third picture represented the same stone placed upon a hand-car and pushed along the railroad track by one man.

This first picture represented animal power used in the most wasteful manner. In the second picture the simpler principles of mechanics were applied in a rude way to assist the oxen, who could not carry the stone or lift it from the ground, but when it was placed upon the cart they were able to carry it a much longer distance than was possible for the fifty men. In the third picture the mechanical advantage was utilized to the utmost by employing a better vehicle and placing it upon a smooth track. So great was the gain that one man did the work of fifty, and could propel the stone thirty miles a day, whereas the fifty men could barely carry it six miles a day with their utmost effort.

It may be said that these pictures were highly instructive but incomplete, because a railroad was used as the means of swiftest and least laborious method of transporting the stone; whereas, if applied to transportation by water, the resulting power, speed and saving would have been enormously increased. If, instead of one block of stone, five such blocks as the one shown had been placed upon a boat and poled upon a river or canal, one man could have been seen doing the work of five times fifty men. The same effect would have been observed if, instead of poling the boat, one man had towed her along by means of a line in his hand, he travelling along a beaten path. The four pictures would then tell more than the first three, and they would together make a graphic detail of some of the factors of the most important commercial questions of the day, and it would be clearly shown the great superiority of rivers or other waterways over railroads for the transportation of freights. These word-pictures may be called illustrations of the primitive methods of moving freights.

Fifty years ago the St. Lawrence was just beginning to be appreciated as one of the great waterways of the Western world, and people in the East began to understand that along this great artery freights could be moved with reasonable celerity for half the rates charged by the railroads.

In "Scribner's Magazine" an able article appeared a few years since, entitled "The Water Route from Chicago to the Ocean," by

Capt. C. C. ROGERS, U. S. N. The whole article is too long to be given here, but it is so admirably written that we transcribe that portion taking in Lake Ontario, the 1,000 Island Archipelago, as well as the lower river below Ogdensburg and Prescott. In this connection the author of this Souvenir declares his intention, if spared, to prepare and publish a book which shall give a complete history of every port upon the river, from Kingston to Quebec,

Captain ROGERS, in his article in Scribner's, says:

Lake Ontario, the smallest of the great lakes, is 190 miles long and more than 50 miles wide; its mean depth exceeds 400 feet, and its elevation above the sea is 234 feet. It seldom freezes, except near the shore. Oswego and Rochester are its principal ports on the south. The former has been in direct communication with the Hudson since 1822, by means of a small canal as far as Syracuse, and thence by the Erie Canal to Troy and Albany. Four railways con-

A SAFE DAY FOR THE FISH, BUT A GOOD DAY FOR THE LOVERS.

profusely illustrated. Indeed, he was preparing for such a book, and had expended over $3,000 upon it, when the money panic of 1873 occurred, and from that cause he was unable to proceed with the work. Such a book would, of necessity, be expensive, but it seems even now to be demanded by the travelling public as well as by the progressive people who have come into this unique St. Lawrence river section.

verge here, and steamers ply daily to the eastern and western ports. Large quantities of grain are received, and twenty or more mills make it one of the largest flour manufacturing cities in the Union. There are also several foundries, machine shops and shipyards.

Rochester, though seven miles from the lake, receives a large quota of shipping through Charlotte, its port. From Charlotte the steamer "Bon Voyage," whose picture is shown in this book, makes tri-weekly trips to Alexandria Bay; and it has two important channels of trade in the Erie and Genesee

Valley Canals, the latter here uniting with the former. Its elevation above the lake is 226 feet, and its situation on the Genesee River secures the immense water power due to its falls, and thus makes it naturally a manufacturing city. Though ranking as one of the greatest flour-producers in the world, its manufactures in clothing, iron, glass and rubber are extensive. It is connected by rail with every city of importance in this country and Canada.

On the Canadian side, Toronto is the largest city of this and of all the great lakes. Entered by six railways, possessing a good harbor, situated in the centre of a rich agricultural district, and being at once the religious, educational, political, literary, legal and commercial centre of the most populous province of Canada, it has advanced with great rapidity. Its population is about 160,000. To the English people of Canada, Toronto is what Quebec is to the French inhabitants. Quebec is French; Montreal, as the meeting place of all, is cosmopolitan; and Toronto is English. It has several foundries and engine works, car-shops, rolling-mills, breweries, a mammoth distillery, and many other varieties of manufacture.

The Richelieu & Ontario Navigation Company runs a daily line of steamers between this city, Montreal, Quebec, the Saguenay, and intermediate ports; it owns twenty-five vessels, the largest being nearly 300 feet long and having a stated speed of twenty miles an hour. It has virtually a monopoly of the steam traffic over its itinerary.

Hamilton, at the extreme west end of the lake, is the second city of Ontario in population, and the first in manufacturing industry. Its railways furnish communication with the principal points of the Dominion and of the United States. It is often styled the Birmingham of Canada, and, though the comparison is presumptuous, it is not altogether unwarranted. Its factories are equipped with modern plant and the latest labor-saving devices, and maintain a daily output of metal, wood, and leather products, textile fabrics, glassware, engines, and boilers. The capital invested in industrial operations is about one-thirtieth of the entire capital invested in manufacturing industries throughout the Dominion, and the proportion of goods is in nearly the same ratio.

Cobourg, though small, boasts of a university, and ships annually to the United States 30,000,000 feet of lumber, 30,000 tons of iron ore, and 150,000 bushels of grain. Daily steamers run to Charlotte; and after leaving here, eastward-bound vessels pass well out into the lake, to avoid the great peninsular county of Prince Edward.

Kingston, at the foot of the lake, has 16,000 inhabitants, is the seat of the Royal Military Academy of Canada, and ranks as a fortress next to Quebec and Halifax. Its bay is broad, deep, and well sheltered, and in war it would become an extensive naval depot. Being the port of trans-shipment for Montreal of three-fourths of the grain arriving from the upper lakes, it is a city of some commercial importance; the grain is sent down the St. Lawrence in barges, the cost of such transfer being about one-half cent per bushel. Kingston is also the south terminus of the Rideau Canal, which connects it with Ottawa. There are manufactories of iron castings, machinery, locomotives, marine engines, and leather; boat-building is carried on to a great extent, and vessels for lake and river navigation are built and fitted out.

From Lake Ontario to Montreal the distance is 183 miles. Just below Kingston, the lake contracts into the funnel-shaped head of the St. Lawrence River, enclosing the Thousand Islands. In reality they number 1,692 and extend forty miles, with a width in some places of seven miles. The descent of the river through them is made in well-defined channels, which, with their extensions, are so deep that vessels of the greatest draught can pass readily between the lake and Ogdensburg. As early as 1673, the waters of this archipelago were traversed by a flotilla of two-gun barges and one hundred and twenty canoes, led by Frontenac, Governor of Canada, attended by the celebrated Abbé de Fénélon. Steamers ply between Cape Vincent, Clayton, and Alexandria Bay, on the arrival of trains at the two former places, and, in addition to the Folger steamers, which connect with the trains, there are other good boats constantly plying up and down between Clayton, Alexandria Bay and Ogdensburg.

Overlooking the islands, on the Canadian side, is Brockville, of 6,000 inhabitants, a railway junction, and below which the Thousand Islands are left, and the open river, two miles wide, is entered. Thirteen miles farther lies Prescott, a stone-built town, whose chief business is done by a great distillery and brewery, and two iron foundries. The bastions of Fort Wellington are seen on the east. The Grand Trunk railway is nearly one mile from the town, and the St. Lawrence and Ottawa railway begins at the river side. The river is a mile wide here, and opposite stands Ogdensburg, with two miles of wharves and extensive flour and lumber mills. It is the terminus of three railways; and its situation at the foot of sloop navigation on the lakes gives it peculiar commercial advantages. Ten million bushels of western grain pass this point annually; in 1892, 16,000 tons were transhipped here for Montreal — a new departure, for up to 1890 such transfers were made only at Kingston.

About seven miles below Prescott begins the chain of the St. Lawrence canals proper, constructed to overcome the rapids which they flank, with a total rise of 206½ feet, and locks enabling lake vessels to descend and exchange cargoes with the sea-going ships at Montreal. They are, in order of descent, the Galop, Rapide Plat, Farran's Point, Cornwall, Beauharnois, and Lachine canals. Their combined length is 43½ miles, the distance between Prescott increased size of vessels, the Canadian government decided in 1871 to make a navigable depth of 12 feet through all the canals and river-shallows, which soon after was changed to 14 feet. Since then work has been carried on with this object in view, but it has not been completed. Two new locks of the Corn-

A GOOD PLACE FOR BASS.

and Montreal being 119 miles. The first three are also styled the Williamsburg canals. The Galop formerly comprised two distinct channels, known as the Iroquois and the Galop canals; they were joined and now form one line.

Originally, this system of canals was designed for a depth of 9 feet, but the fluctuations in the stage of the river rendered it difficult to maintain; at times it falls to 6 feet seven inches. On account of the wall canal are of the standard dimensions (Welland size); and the Lachine canal has been completed for 12 feet navigation, with locks and bridges adapted for 14 feet navigation, the untouched work in it consisting of the excavation of the canal prism to a further depth of two feet for more than six miles of its length.

The river channel has been cleared of obstacles to 14 feet navigation from the head of Galop Rapids to the Cornwall canal; from the foot of the latter to the Beauharnois canal it is navigable by the largest vessels; and a depth of 14 feet again exists through Lake St. Louis, excepting the lower four miles, in which the channel must be deepened and widened at a number of places.

The Cornwall canal overcomes the Long Sault Rapids; at St. Regis, near the foot, the forty-fifth parallel intersects the St. Lawrence, which now becomes exclusively Canadian. It is also interesting to observe the small width of the river near this point, and that the narrowest width between the United States and Canadian territory is about 600 feet, measured between the northwest side of Croil's Island and the canal bank. The St. Lawrence now expands into Lake St. Francis, 25 miles long and 5 miles in maximum breadth, and dotted with inlets at its lower end.

The Beauharnois canal lies on the south side of the river and overcomes the Cascades, Cedar, and Coteau Rapids. Surveys for a new route have been made on the northern bank. It connects Lakes St. Francis and St. Louis, the latter in turn being connected with Montreal harbor by the Lachine canal.

The latter consists of one channel with two distinct systems of locks, the old and the enlarged, both of which are in use. On its banks are the canal and Grand Trunk offices and sheds, occupying a point of land on which the celebrated Victoria bridge finds its terminus. Opposite the upper entrance is the Indian village of Caughnawaga, the terminus of the Montreal and New York railway, with which the Grand Trunk connects by ferry; a railroad from Montreal to Lachine borders the northern bank of the canal. Sea-going vessels can now pass into the basins between the lower locks with coal, sugar, and plaster for the factories in this part of the city and for the Grand Trunk works. They can also reload at the same points, where there is ample dock room.

After leaving Lake St. Louis, the St. Lawrence dashes wildly down the Lachine Rapids, a descent of forty-two feet in two miles; and eight miles farther on, after passing beneath the twenty-five spans of the Victoria bridge, one and three-quarter miles long, reaches the quays of Montreal.

The purposes had in view by the Canadian government in determining upon a depth of fourteen feet, were to enable the largest class of lake vessels at that time to carry their cargoes direct to Montreal without breaking bulk; to secure for Canada all the advantages which the possession of this magnificent waterway ought to give it; to make the St. Lawrence in its whole length the highway by which the surplus products of the West would seek an outlet to the sea; and to put it into a position to compete successfully for the export trade of the continent with the several lines of communication on our side of the boundary.

The total expenditure on the Welland and St. Lawrence Canals is about $41,250,000; it will require $12,750,000 more to complete the work, or $54,000,000 in all. The construction of the lock at Sault Ste. Marie and other necessary improvements will swell this sum to $60,000,000, the final result being a navigable depth of fourteen feet between Lake Superior and Montreal.

The history of marine architecture does not furnish another instance of so rapid and complete a revolution in the material and structure of floating equipment as has taken place on the great lakes since 1886. In that year the total valuation of the vessels by Lloyd was about $30,600,000. In 1889, sixty new steamers and eleven sailing vessels, aggregating 70,000 tons, and valued at $6,650,000, were added to the fleet. During the four winters of 1886-1890, the tonnage of the lakes was nearly doubled; 206 vessels, measuring 399,975 tons, were turned out of the shipyards with a valuation of $27,389,000. During the same time, the number of steamers of more than 1,500 net register tons increased from 21 to 110. The two valuations of the fleet already presented differ by more than $9,000,000; but either one emphasizes the fact of the very recent and extraordinary growth of this commerce, and renders it difficult to predict the increase in the tonnage and in the size of vessels upon the lakes during the four years that remain till the opening of the next century.

More than one-half of the vessels on the great lakes are assigned to Chicago, Port Huron, Detroit, Milwaukee, Grand Haven, Cleveland, and Buffalo.

The number of Canadian vessels on the lakes is 647; tonnage, 132,971; valuation, $3,989,130. For further comparison, it may be stated that the total of coast and inland shipping registered in Canada is 7,153 vessels, of 1,040,481 register tons, valued at $31,213,430.

The increase in population of the lake ports indicates the great increase that must follow, necessarily, in the business of the lakes and also of the railways tributary to them. Buffalo has increased from about 42,000 in 1850 to 255,000 in 1890; Cleveland, from 17,000 in 1860 to 262,000 in 1890; Chicago, from 30,000 in 1850 to 1,100,000 in 1890; while Detroit and Milwaukee exhibit a remarkable parallelism in growth, the former having increased from 116,340 to 205,876 during the last ten years, and the latter from 115,587 to 204,468.

The simplicity of lake commerce is one of its chief characteristics. Coal, iron ore, and lumber comprise three-fourths of the total cargo tonnage of the lakes: add to these corn, wheat, and mill products, and nine-tenths of the total traffic will be accounted for.

The sailing vessel has almost disappeared from the lakes. The square-rigged ship is no longer seen, and only a few of the great cargo-carrying schooners are left. The sailing fleet was succeeded by the propeller, as it is known locally, with its tow of one or more consorts; and it in turn is giving way to the modern steamer, maintained at little more than one-half the cost while having a carrying capacity quite as great, a speed double that of the propeller and consort, and making two or three round trips for one of the tow.

The rapid growth, too, of steam transportation, and the competition of lake lines with the railways, have caused continual reductions in the cost of transportation. The cost per ton per mile of carrying freight an average distance of eight hundred miles, was one and one-half mills in 1889. The value of all the cargoes—27,500,000 tons—carried on the lakes during that year was over $305,000,000. Had this been carried at railway rates, Mr. E. L. Corthell, of the Society of Engineers, estimates that the cost to the public would have been over $143,-000,000; by the lake rates it was about $23,000,000 only; so that transportation on the lakes saved to the public about $120,000,000 in one year. A large part of the heavy freight has been carried for less than one and one-half mills per ton per mile. Anthracite coal is carried from Buffalo to Duluth, 1,000 miles, for 30 cents per ton. The water-rates from Chicago to Buffalo, on wheat, were two and one-half cents per bushel in 1890.

The average distance for which freight on the lakes is carried is 566 miles. From this, the Census Bureau estimates the ton mileage for the season of 1889 to be 15,515,360,000 ton miles. The aggregate ton mileage of railways for the year ending June 30, 1889, was 68,727,223,146; which shows that the ton mileage of the lakes is nearly one-fourth of the total ton mileage of railways in the United States. In no other way could the relative importance of lake commerce be more effectively shown.

The ship builders of the lakes are progressive, and keep pace with all improvements in marine architecture. Steel vessels are built with double bottoms, water-tight compartments, triple-expansion engines, and modern electrical and steam appliances. The structural strength may be realized from the fact that a large proportion are built for the trade in iron ore. At a time trial in Escanaba, during the summer of 1887, a steamer was loaded with over 2,000 tons of ore, and steamed away from the dock in forty-five minutes after being placed under the chutes. The record shows that another vessel was loaded with 2,800 tons of coal in one hour and fifty minutes, 300 tons for fuel were put on board in another hour, so that in two hours and fifty minutes after opening the hatches, the vessel was loaded and coaled. That ordinary sea-going ships will not stand the strains of this traffic is demonstrated by the fact that four steel steamers, built on the Clyde for Canadian owners, had to be repaired and strengthened throughout, after one season's work, to fit them for further service. These vessels steamed across the Atlantic, were cut into halves on the lower St. Lawrence, the sections being then towed through the canals and put together on the lakes. Two more were built on the Clyde, with the benefits of this experience and of the builders' visits to our Northwestern ship-yards.

The wharves for the unloading of ships at Montreal are ten feet below the level of a revêtement wall, which extends along the entire river-front of the city; so that one standing upon the wall may see the shipping of the port spread out before him. Near the Lachine canal are the basins for the Allan steamers to Glasgow and Liverpool; then follow steamers from the Maritime Provinces and European ports, then sailing ships and the sheds of the London Line and of the Dominion Line from Liverpool; next are the river boats plying between Quebec and Montreal; then succeed the smaller river steamers, barges, and finally sailing vessels and steamers as far as Hochelaga. Here, nearly 1,000 miles inland from the Atlantic, are vessels from all parts of the world; from England, with iron, dry goods, and general goods; from the Mediterranean, with wines and groceries; from Germany, with glass and general goods; from China with tea—alongside of vessels loading with return cargoes of grain, cattle, lumber, mineral phosphates, and other products of Canada. The wharves are not disfigured by unsightly ware-houses, but the river-street is as clear as a Parisian quay.

Leaving Montreal, the steamer glides swiftly down the St. Mary current, leaving on the right St. Helen's Island, a prettily wooded spot, named after Helen Boulié, the young wife of Champlain, who charmed the wild Hurons in 1620 with her gentle manners. Still further to the right opens out Longueil Bay, exhibiting in the tinned steeple and steep roof of its village church the characteristic picture of the lower St. Lawrence in parish after parish. The river flows through a wide alluvial plain, the Laurentian Mountains far on the north, and on the south the Green Mountains; everywhere long stretches of arable land, broken only where the Lombardy poplar rears its formal shape against the sky.

Below Longueil the Ottawa joins its flood finally with the St. Lawrence, hiding its union in a cluster of low islands. Opposite Berthier, on the right bank, the Richelieu falls into the St. Lawrence, after draining Lakes Champlain and George. On its eastern bank stands Sorel, where most of the steamers on the river have been built. The Richelieu is rendered navigable to Lake Champlain by a small lock twelve miles above Sorel, and by the Chambly Canal, thirty-two miles further up-stream; these give a navigable depth of seven feet, and accommodate vessels 114 feet long and 23 feet wide.

The St. Lawrence now opens out to a width of nine miles; and for twenty-five miles the steamer passes

THE STEAMER "ALGERIAN" RUNNING THE LONG SAULT RAPIDS.

through Lake St. Peter, a vast expanse of flats through which a ship channel has been dredged. At several places between Montreal and Quebec, there were formerly shoal places, preventing large vessels from reaching the former city. Their aggregate length was nearly forty miles, divided between twenty different places, the widest being in Lake St. Peter. The work of dredging the channel here began in 1844, and continued with the increase in trade and size of ocean steamers, till, at the end of 1885, a depth of 27½ feet was reached, the total cost being $3,503,870. This channel varies from 300 to 450 feet in width. As a consequence of these river improvements, the size of vessel able to ascend to Montreal has increased from 1,045 tons and 12 feet draught, in 1856, to 3,211 tons and 23 feet draught in 1878; and now that the works are completed, ships of 4,000 tons or even more can navigate the St. Lawrence with safety.

East of the lake lies Three Rivers, the third city of importance on the lower St. Lawrence. Here the river first meets the tide; the St. Maurice falls in from the north, after a course of 300 miles through an important lumber region. Further east, and running parallel to it, is the St. Anne, twenty miles below which, in the St. Lawrence, occur the Richelieu Rapids, where large ships usually wait for high tide before passing, as the rocks are dangerous. The scenery now begins to lose its flatness, and in the distance the mountains around Quebec can be seen, blue and dim. On the right, near the city, is the mouth of the Chaudière River; and gliding on, past ships, rafts, and booms, the steamer sweeps under Cape Diamond, into the basin of Quebec, shadowed by precipitous cliffs from which the Queen of the St. Lawrence looks down in all her quaint beauty upon a scene rarely equalled in the new world.

The lower town of Quebec is built on reclaimed land, around the base of the cape, one of its sides being washed by the St. Charles, which here flows into the St. Lawrence. At the mouth of the St. Charles is the Princess Louise Embankment, enclosing a tidal basin of twenty acres, which is 24 feet deep at low water; connected with it is a wet dock, of 27 feet depth, and forty acres area. On the opposite side, at point Levis, is the Lorne Dry Dock, 500 feet long, 100 feet wide, and 25½ feet deep on the sills. The commerce of this city began with the fur trade, and this remains an important element.

Enormous transactions in lumber go on here annually. The whole lower valley of the St. Lawrence and the northern lumber regions draw their merchandise from this center.

On leaving Quebec, far off to the left is the Montmorenci, whose white foam shines out from the green hillside. As the steamer moves across the basin, beautiful views are afforded on all sides, including a fine retrospect of the citadel, towering over the river. The fine island of Orleans is soon reached on the left, with its village of St. Laurent, where the expedition under Wolfe landed in 1759.

ning to approach nearer, and while watching the ever-changing views, the Traverse is reached, where the river is thirteen miles wide, but the only channel available for large ships is not more than 1,400 yards across. The Isle-aux-Coudres and two large shoals obstruct its navigation, the bottom is irregular, and currents run in all directions.

The traveller's interest is now apt to pass from the water and the mountain heights to the seigniory of Les Éboulements, remarkable as an earthquake centre. Jesuit tradition relates that in 1663 the mountains were thrown down and the face of the

STEAMER "CORSICAN" RUNNING LACHINE RAPIDS.

An intervening island hides St. Anne, a pretty village to which pilgrimages are made, and where the patron saint has worked as many miracles as any in Europe. Thirty miles below Quebec is Grosse Isle, the quarantine station, and about which linger the memories of 1807, when the famine-stricken Irish poured into Canada, and 6,000 are said to have been buried here in one long grave. Opposite rises Cape Tourmente, 1,800 feet high, the north shore now being wild and mountainous, and rising so boldly from the river as to permit no roadway along its base, and so rocky and desolate as to prevent habitation for many miles; while the south side for more than 100 miles is a continuous settlement. Yet far off in the latter direction, the mountains are begin-

country was changed as far as the Saguenay. Ice was thrown up in great heaps, the river ran of a changed color, a mountain was cast into the sea and became an island, the piety of the inhabitants grew more earnest, and there were never so many confessions or conversions; even liquor-dealers saw the error of their ways and repented.

A short run brings the steamer to a wharf where passengers land for Rivière du Loup and for Cacouna, the paradise of fair Quebeckers and famous for dancing and flirting. Nearly opposite enters the Saguenay, cleft through the mountains and nearly 900 feet deep for many miles. In the little harbor at its entrance died Chauvin, the enterprising Huguenot, who induced Champlain to visit Canada.

Perched high above it on the cliffs, is a quaint little chapel, evincing the zeal of its founders, in a wilderness of cliffs where roads are impossible.

Bic Island is the next point of interest; it is the last anchorage in the river, where outward bound vessels leave their pilots and many ships are found during the summer. Here in December, 1861, a Cunard steamer landed a regiment of the Guards during the crises of the Trent affair. Finally, Rimouski is reached; the Intercolonial Railway to Halifax passes through it, and ocean steamers receive passengers and mails for the last time. The town is two miles from the wharf, and is the most important settlement in the province east of Quebec.

The south bank now rapidly becomes bold and grand: the mountains have receded from the north shore, so that all the scenery is on this side. At Point des Monts, the Gulf of St. Lawrence is entered; the left shore trends rapidly to the north; little fishing stations only are seen at the base of the steep hills. Anticosti becomes quickly visible in the distance, with a flora indicating a subarctic climate; while opposite, near the western shore, are the Seven Islands, green with turf and flowers, and forming a beautiful land-locked bay where the largest fleets could ride in safety. Whittier has made them the scene of a touching ballad, in which he aptly styles them "the last outpost of summer upon the dreary coast." All along to Belle Isle are deep nords, broad bays crowded with rocky islets, salmon streams without number, and myriad inlets, the haunts of innumerable aquatic birds from these forbidding shores, whose cold waters teem with fish in inconceivable numbers, greater wealth has been carried than from the mines of Potosi. Nor has time deprived them of a place in romance, as the steamer bids adieu to St. Lawrence waters, the eye has a final glimpse of the pretty island of Meccatina, where Roberval, the stern Huguenot, abandoned his niece, Lady Margaret, and her duenna, when her love became evident. Her lover jumped overboard and swam to the island to share her fate. The duenna died, and the lover died; and after two years of solitary struggle, the lady was rescued by a passing vessel and carried to her home across the ocean while she was trying to forget what she had endured.

HOW THE INDIANS LEARNED THE RAPIDS.

CAPT. JOHNSTON, OF CLAYTON, TELLS ABOUT THE FIRST STEAMER THAT RAN THE ST. LAWRENCE RAPIDS.

AMONG the ablest of those river-men who have made their impression upon the era in which they have lived, is Captain SIMON G. JOHNSTON, of Clayton, for many years foreman in Merrick, Fowler & Esselstyn's large shipyard at that place, where they built the finest steamers that ever ploughed the waters of the St. Lawrence, the "New York," "Northerner," "Bay State," and "Niagara." The captain is now owner, with his son, of the steamer "Nightingale," which forms an independent line upon the river.

In a late conference with Captain Johnston we were much impressed with his knowledge of river incidents, and we let him tell his story in his own unique manner:

A great deal of steamboat talk has been going the rounds of the press lately, and some of it is far from true.

I have been on Lake Ontario and the St. Lawrence river sixty years. In 1840 I was on the steamer "Telegraph" as wheelsman, and since 1844 I have been in the vessel or steamboat business. I was on the propeller Western, running between Montreal and Toronto and west, in 1843, and in those days we ran all the rapids, for there was no canal but the Lachine. We came up through the Lachine, thence up by the way of the Ottawa (then called "Bytown") and thence to Kingston on the Rideau. I am stating these facts to explain what I mean.

Now the first large boat to run the rapids was a boat built at Niagara, called the "Ontario," which came out in 1839 or 1840, and proved to be a very fast boat for those days. On her trial trip she broke one of her shafts thirty or forty miles below Toronto. It happened that the steamer "Coburg" came along and asked if the "Ontario" needed assistance, and the latter's captain replied, "No, I thank you." He then caused the boiler on that side of the boat to be filled with water, moved all the ballast over to that side, and started with one wheel. Running under these difficulties, the "Ontario" beat the "Coburg" into Toronto. This went the rounds of the press so that parties from Montreal came up, bought her and took her to Montreal to run between Montreal and Quebec as a mail boat. She carried the mail in 1843 and was called the "Lord Sydenham." She was the first steamer to run the rapids.

She was piloted by Indians, "Old Jock" and "Old Pete" being chief pilots. As no boat had run the Lachine rapids before that, it was quite a risk for the owners as well as for the Indians. The pilots were to have $1,000 each if she was landed safely at Montreal, which was done.

First a crib was made forty feet square with pine floats ten feet apart, with stakes ten feet long driven in each square, projecting downward. When all was ready some Indians were sent to the foot of the rapids and some were stationed in the trees on the side of the rapids. Several Indians towed the crib to the head of the rapids with their canoes and let go of it. Then every Indian watched the course it took as the crib sped on its way with the current of the stream. When it reached the foot of the rapids the crib was turned over and it was found that none of the stakes were broken. That was a positive indication that there was water enough to run the "Ontario" through. The Indians then boarded the steamer. Each Indian piloted the "Ontario" as far as he had observed the crib's course. The only white man on board was the engineer, who also, I was told, received $2,000. This story I got from "Old Jock," who used to pilot us and who ran us through the Lachine rapids nine times without a mishap.

As Mr. James Mooney takes exception to the statement in connection with Captain Chapman, of Ogdensburg, I likewise take exception to what he says, though he is right as to the "Canada" and "America" running the rapids before the "New York." The "Canada" and "America" were modeled in New York and built at Niagara by Louis Sichaluna, and the joiner work, cabins, etc., were done by A. B. Wright, of New York

A PICNIC IN THE RIFT, LA RUE ISLAND.

city. They were built for the Great Western railroad, and ran between Hamilton and Cape Vincent. They were about 1,100 tons each, 275 feet keel, and fitted and furnished with all conveniences in the way of state rooms, etc. The boats did not pay and were sold to some company to run on a river in the south. They were taken through the rapids in 1858 or 1859.

The "New York" was built at Clayton by John Oades, and never belonged to the same line that the "Canada" and "America" did, though she ran with them in 1856 and made better time than they could, and was acknowledged to be the fastest boat on the lake and river. She was 255 feet keel and of 995 tons.

Her joiner work was done by A. B. Wright, of New York city, and she was finished complete at Clayton. Captain Chapman came out in her with William Gardner, of Ogdensburg, as chief engineer in 1852. On her trial trip, with machinery and everything new, she made eighteen miles per hour. She made a record, from Cape Vincent via the north side of Carlton Island to Rock Island light, of sixty minutes. We have no boats now that can do that in seventy-five minutes.

The "New York" belonged to the Ontario and St. Lawrence Steamboat Company, and hailed from the port of Ogdensburg. This company owned the steamer "Northerner" of 905 tons, and Captain Chapman was a large stockholder in them. These two boats, in 1859 and 1860, ran an express line between Lewiston, Toronto and Ogdensburg, making a daily line and stopping at Cape Vincent, Clayton, Alexandria Bay, and Brockville.

In 1861 and 1862 they were sold to the United States government, and Captain Chapman took them both to Montreal. William Gardner was engineer of both boats. After the government bought them the "Northerner's" name was changed, but the "New York's" was not. She was the flag of truce boat at Fortress Monroe during the war. One year ago she was still running at Cape Breton. The "New York" and the "Northerner" were run through the Lachine rapids by Indians. I never knew but one white man to run the Lachine rapids, and his name was Robuck.

THE FRONTENAC HOTEL AND ROUND ISLAND.

THE conspicuous location of Round Island has given the ideal summer community which adorns its shores, and the handsome hotel at this point, the advantage of a wide

MR. H. VAN WAGENEN'S COTTAGE, ROUND ISLAND.

reputation. It is the first stopping place for travel-laden steamers which pass down the river from Cape Vincent or Clayton.

Round Island was bought about seventeen years since by an association of gentlemen, largely from Central and Northern New York, who proposed to found a resort connected with the Baptist church. Many prominent people purchased lots in picturesque sites and built handsome cottages.

The island has always been popular, and the hotel, in the course of time, became too small to accommodate the many families who made it their usual summer home. Six years ago the charter of the association and its property were acquired by a number of wealthy cottagers and others resident there, and a large amount of money was expended in building wings to the hotel, remodelling its interior and in refurnishing and equipping the house throughout, and at the present time it enjoys a reputation with the best class of the travelling public second to none upon the river.

Round Island is now entirely unsectarian. No cheap excursions are permitted to land there. The island, with its beautiful rambles, walks and vistas, is maintained for the pleasure of the hotel guests and the inmates of its seventy cottages.

The Frontenac Hotel is conducted by Mr. E D. Dickinson, of Syracuse, a veteran and most popular host. Kapp's excellent orchestra, of Syracuse, is engaged each season.

The Frontenac is provided with a handsome elevator, sideboard in the café, billiards, pool, ten-pins, tennis field, base-ball grounds, boat livery, telegraph and express offices, in fact, every convenience of a thorough modern hotel.

The voyageur down the river approaching the head of Round Island is interested in the handsome summer homes half hidden among its verdure. Those upon the head, showing large expenditure of money in their construction and environment, are owned by Mr. Jacob Hayes and Mr. Hubert Van Wagenen, of New York, and Hon. J. J. Belden, of Syracuse. Dr. Geo. D. Whedon, of Syracuse, owns "Ethelridge" upon the point. Along the channel are the cottages of Dr. F. H. Stephenson, of Syracuse; A. B. Schrueder, of Syracuse; E. M. Henderson, of Weedsport; W. B. Kirk, of Syracuse; Mrs. T. B. Kirk, of Syracuse; Mrs. George Harbottle, of Auburn; Mrs. H. A. Foster, of Syracuse; H. S. Barbour, of Watertown; J. D. Squires, of New York; D. H. Murray, of Syracuse; N. A. St. John, Binghamton; Chas. E. Best, Jordan, N. Y.; Fred O. Lloyd, of Syracuse; Geo. L. Crandall, of Binghamton; R. E. Rindge, of Norwich, N. Y.; Mrs. S. R. Francis, of Carthage, N. Y.; J. N. Cloyes, of Utica; Mrs. J. H. Harris, of Syracuse; Mrs. J. G. Harbottle, of Watertown; C. C. Laidlaw, of Gouverneur, N. Y.; E. D. Sherwood, of Camillus, N. Y.; Geo. M. Barnes, of Syracuse; E. L. Heminway, of Watertown; Anthony Lamb, of Syracuse; Fred Frazer, of Syracuse; E. M. Allewelt, of Syracuse; Estate of Dr. Edward Bright, of New York; N. H. Burhans, of Syracuse; L. V. Rathbun, of Rochester; Mrs. L. T. Sawyer, of Watertown; Mrs. Jas. Eaton, of Syracuse; N. H. Bulloch, of Fisher's Landing (below the wharf); Mrs. I. G. Morehouse, of Syracuse; C. H. Rose, of New York; and S. V. R. Van Heusen, of Syracuse. At the immediate foot of the island are the handsome and picturesque properties of John Dunfee, of Syracuse; Chas. A. Johnson, of New York, and Frank H. Taylor, of Philadelphia.

Fronting upon the east channel are the pretty cottages built by B. W. Wrenn, of Savannah, and those of A. E. Kilby, of Carthage; E. H. Myers, of Carthage; C. W. Sikes, of Philadelphia, N. Y.; A. J. Chester, of Albany; Mrs. Samuel Branaugh, of Carthage; Mrs. E. A. Perrine, of New York; Mrs. H. H. Mills, of Syracuse, and Mrs. Mary D. Kinmouth, of Hamilton, N. Y.

C. S. Ball, of Syracuse, Robert Andress, Mrs. Denny, of Watertown, and some others, have cottages upon the inland avenues of the island.

The association controlling Round Island and the Frontenac Hotel is composed of A. C. Belden, President; Chas. A. Johnson, Vice-President; Chas. A. Myers, Secretary. These gentlemen are trustees, together with Hubert Van Wagenen, Jacob Hays, E. D. Dickinson and Frank H. Taylor.

THE CHIPPEWA YACHT CLUB.

WAS organized in 1895. Its location is indicated by its name, and its races and sailing bouts are usually held in Chippewa Bay, some ten miles below Alexandria Bay, a region fast coming into favorable notice. Many fine improvements have been made there, and more are in contemplation. The officers of this yacht club for 1895 are: Commodore, Hon. George Hall; Vice-Commodore, James G. Knap; Secretary and Treasurer, John E. Bell; Measurers, S. Gilbert Averell, A. R. Porte, W. H. Post. The Executive Committee are the Commodore, Vice-Commodore, the Secretary-Treasurer, A. R. Porte and John C. Howard. The Regatta Committee are D. H. Lyon, Frank Chapman and E. L. Strong.

LIST OF MEMBERS.—Hon. George Hall, James G. Knap, John E. Bell, S. Gilbert Averell, A. R. Porte, Capt. Frank Chapman, D. H. Lyon, Edward L.

Strong, Wm. H. Post, Charles P. Lyon, John C. Howard, J. Y. Chapin, A. K. Strong, Dr. J. R. Dickson, Geo. B. Shepard, T. F. Strong, Dr. J. H. Brownlow, Chas. O. R. Bell, John A. Seely, Dr. Willard N. Bell, G. S. Dorwin, S. W. Wilson, E. C. J. Smith, Louis Hasbrouck, A. R. Herriman, George F. Darrow, S. H. Gardinier, H. A. Lord, E. F. Seymour, H. F. James, Levi Hasbrouck, Col. E. C. James, Mrs. R. A. Chapman, Dr. S. E. Brown, Jas. R. Bill, Philip B. Hasbrouck, all of Ogdensburg; Ford Jones, Brockville, Ont.; Elmer S. Jones, Brockville, Ont.; George Clayes, Brockville, Ont.; Frank Clayes, Brockville, Ont.; E. H. Bisset, Brockville, Ont.; R. W. Travers, Brockville, Ont.; N Gilbert, Brockville, Ont.; J. P. Wiser, Prescott, Ont.; Wm. L. Webster, New York; W. H. Hutchinson, New York; H. A. McGruer, New York; Lewis Wallace, New York; Lester Wallace, New York; John McGruer, New York; W. W. Jackson, New York; M. V. Brokaw, New York; C. M. Englis, New York; Wm. Taylor, New York; Joseph M. Knap, New York; Edgar D. Knap, New York; J. Day Knap, New York; Henry Chapman, Morristown, N. Y.; W. F. Sudds, Gouverneur, N. Y.; J. B. Preston, Gouverneur, N. Y.; Henry Sudds, Gouverneur, N. Y.; C. B. Orcutt, Elizabeth, N. J.; Clinton McKenzie, Elizabeth, N. J.; Mrs. Clinton McKenzie, Elizabeth, N. J.; Percy McKenzie, Elizabeth, N. J.; S. S. Thompson, Elizabeth, N. J.; Dr. F. R. Bailey, Elizabeth, N.J.; Dr. W.J. Herriman, Rochester, N.Y.

COOPER'S "PATHFINDER" AND STATION ISLAND.

THE reader has probably read Cooper's thrilling tale of "The Pathfinder." He locates the main incidents of the tale at what he calls "Station Island," but does not attempt to locate the exact spot, save that it was among the islands of the St. Lawrence archipelago. But he relates some historical facts connected with his island, and leaves but little doubt that it was one of those now designated as the "Admiralty Group" situated in the Canada channel, above Gananoque.

The time described was during the French and English war of 1755-60. At that time the English held Oswego, while the French had control of the lakes, with a strong fort at Frontenac, now Kingston, and a detachment at Gananoque. The French received their supplies from Montreal in batteaux, which came up the river in detachments, numbering ten or more batteaux each. The English kept spies on the lookout for the arrival of these convoys of stores and provisions with a view to their capture. To that end "Station Island" had been fixed upon as a suitable place for a rendezvous from which to waylay the expected fleet of batteaux.

Now what are the historical facts? First, the French posts were supplied from Montreal by means of batteaux; second, the British troops attempted to, and did at various times, capture some of these batteaux, with their stores; third, that the British had some hiding place among the islands, from which they sallied forth and made their captures, if possible. Now it is evident that this very group of islands would be the one chosen for such a hiding place for several reasons. First, it was nearer Oswego; second, the chances of recapture were lessened; third, the opportunity of watching the approach of a fleet of batteaux unseen. If the hiding place had been chosen in the Lower or Naval group, the chances of a recapture would have been materially increased. Now how was "Station Island" situated? So that a lookout could be kept on the river below; so that the French post on the main land could be watched; so that the island itself could hardly be distinguished from those by which it was surrounded. One island in this group fulfills the conditions, and there is not another among all the Thousand Islands that does; and hence the presumption that the island is here, and that it borders on Bostwick channel. It is not possible to locate the exact island, but all considerations point to one of the Admiralty group as the one designated by Cooper, and it was certainly in the Canadian channel.

THE BEAUTIFUL STEAM YACHT CAPTAIN VISGER, WITH PORTRAIT OF HER COMMANDER.

ISLAND KATE, THE PROPERTY OF G. W. LASCELL, OF LYNN, MASS.

JUDGE SPENCER'S RESIDENCE, EASTERLY SIDE OF MANHATTAN.

NAPTHA LAUNCH, OWNED BY PROF. BLANDNER, AT WESTMINSTER PARK.

VIEW IN THOUSAND ISLAND PARK.

FRIENDLY ISLAND, RESIDENCE OF W. E. DEWEY, ESQ., OPPOSITE ALEXANDRIA BAY.

THE FRONTENAC, ROUND ISLAND, STR. ST. LAWRENCE MAKING A LANDING.

THOUSAND ISLAND HOUSE, ALEXANDRIA BAY, N. Y.

[Aa]

VIEW IN GANANOQUE, SHOWING WATER-POWER.

[Cc]

RESIDENCE OF W. C. BROWNING.
[Ff]

A GLANCE AT CLAYTON.

FROM an unimportant village for many years, Clayton, through its being the river terminus of the R. W. & O. R. R. system, has become a town of frequent mention, and its history must surely be interwoven into any story that treats of the St. Lawrence archipelago — for it stands directly in the midst of the best fishing grounds, fronting the river at a spot of peculiar loveliness, and right in the eye of the beholder looms up the most beautiful chateau upon the whole stream — a spot of such natural beauty as well as of artistic adornment that its superior is not often met with in this country — actually rivaling some of the most renowned villas upon the "wide and winding Rhine." The magnificent St. Lawrence here appears more like a lake, with wooded shores and far-away vistas which reveal other beauties. Here the "rush and dash from Niagara's leap" and Ontario's wide expanse are subdued to narrower limits, inviting, entrancing, complete.

Clayton has excellent schools, fine churches, an unusually enlightened and "up to date" population, superior hotels — one of them, the Walton, a very old and always well-kept establishment — a fair local trade that calls for good stores and the usual accommodations of a river town, including boat-building facilities and good wharves for handling freight and passengers. Less than an hundred years ago the site where Clayton stands was an unbroken wilderness — a region too insignificant to possess even a name. A creek and bay form a natural boundary, and in the year 1802 a Mr. Bartlett built a log house for himself and family about half a mile from the mouth of the creek. The place selected was near a precipitous bluff that attains in one place an altitude of nearly 100 feet. This was the first building in what is now the town of Clayton.

One year later a French Canadian erected a rude hut on the opposite side of the creek, which he occupied alone. He subsisted wholly by hunting and trapping on the creek, which then abounded in game. During the

MRS. CARLISLE'S COTTAGE, GRENNELL PARK.

winter of the same year a severe storm came on. As no smoke arose from the lone hut on the other side of the creek, the Bartletts made a search, but no trace of the Frenchman could be found. The following spring his body was found and buried beneath the dark cedars that lined the banks of the creek. The Frenchman gave his name to the locality, which was called "French creek" for many years.

Time passed on, nothing breaking the silence of the woods until the commencement of hostilities in the war of 1812.

At that time the whole line of frontier, from Oswego to St. Regis, a distance of over 250 miles, was placed under the military command of Jacob Brown. One November afternoon in 1813, when an American force with a small flotilla were nearing French Creek, they were attacked by the British. Capt. McPherson, of the American company, took possession of

THE OLD BRIDGE AT CLAYTON.

the high bluff near Bartlett's clearing, and returned the enemy's fire with American spirit, quickly repulsing them. A second attempt was made by the British, but with no better result. Three new-made graves indicated the burial places of the martyrs of the fight, and the place was named "Bartlett's Point."

A few years later a number of families located on the bay at the mouth of French creek, forming a small settlement.

In 1823 a mail service was established, and the name of "Cornelia" was given the post-office.

In 1831 the present township was set off from the towns of Orleans and Lyme and named Clayton, in honor of J. M. Clayton, United States Senator from Delaware, a devoted Whig.

The village had scarcely began to develop when it was regarded as possessed of facilities for an important business center.

The rafting business was started by Jesse Smith and E. G. Merick. Shortly afterwards Merick & Fowler engaged in the business of ship building under the management of John Oades. Some of the finest boats on the great lakes and river were constructed in the old shipyard at Clayton.

This was a great "boom" for the little town. Streets were laid out and buildings sprang up on both sides of French creek. A rude stone bridge was constructed at its mouth to meet the demands of travel and trade. Enterprise was the prevailing spirit, and the interests of the town grew stronger with each returning year.

A school was in progress, and an exhorter once a week warned the people against covetousness. When the little town emerged into the forties it could boast of thirty-two families, three stores, a school house, and post office. Thus we draw an accurate view of Clayton in its infancy, and from the present we may observe the fruits of its developement.

The changing years have brought new interests and rapid growth. The elegant residences of the town speak of refined taste, and its excellent school and five beautiful churches, indicate an intellectual people. As a place to permanently settle, it is unsurpassed for business facilities. The modern business blocks and suitable stores testify to a good patronage. The town has two reliable banks, the First National Bank and the Exchange Bank.

Among the popular business people we name the following: H. F. Barker, C. E. Reese, James Johnston, Chas. Ellis, Wm. Clark, Jas. Hayes, H. F. Dewey, E. A. Burlingame, G. M. Hungerford, D. C. Porter, A. G. Holstein, G. E. & J. O. Thibault, W. H. Consaul, John Foley, W. H. Thorpe, A. E. Wood, S. E. Howard, Mrs. A. Locklin, F. L. Hall, W. W. Hawes, A. Williams, J. F. Graves, M. Atwood, S. Breslow, Thos. Esselstyne, G. W. McCombs.

H. S. Barker's and G. H. McKinley's business blocks are among the best in town; and Mr. McComb's novelty store is superior to any of its kind in Northern New York. One of the best bakeries in the county is managed by John Ross—a very active business man, a one-armed veteran. A very successful business man is G. M. Skinner, manufacturer of his trolling spoon, which is of national reputation.

Capt. S. G. Johnston, ship builder, has been owner and builder of some of the most successful steam yachts on the river. The firm of Strough & Brooks, lumber merchants and contractors, carry on an extensive business. Both are reliable, active men, and their business is unusually prosperous.

Wilbur & Wheelock are noted for modeling the daintiest and most artistic skiffs on the river, and they also keep a boat livery.

As a summer resort Clayton ranks among the first. This is due to its beautiful situation, the health-giving properties of its air, easy access to all points, and its being in the midst of the Thousand Islands. Its popularity increases every year.

Among its first-class hotels are the Walton House, with its enviable reputation of lavish comfort and generous fare, and the Hubbard House, lately rebuilt. The spacious new Windsor, with its pleasant apartments and well-furnished tables, is first-class in all respects. Mr. and Mrs. Hawes are making new friends every year.

The Hayes House and Pastime have excellent tables and home-like comforts.

Much more might be written, and Clayton really deserves a more extended description. But we must leave it, crowning its beauty with lovely Calumet, the elegant summer home of Chas. G. Emery, one of New York's millionaires, whose benevolence has deservedly given him the name of Clayton's benefactor.

N. M. E.

STEAM YACHTS FOR HIRE.

INDEPENDENT of the many private yachts upon the river, doing service among the islands forming the St. Lawrence archipelago, we name the following in service at the close of 1895:

The CAPTAIN VISGER, Capt. Walter L. Visger; The CRESCENT, Capt. John Bolton; The SOPHIA, Capt. H W. Visger; The SPRY, Capt. Dingman; The IONE, Capt. Gifford Benson; The MASSENA, Capt. Dana; The ADA B., Capt. G. R. Brown; The PASTIME, Capt. Bertrand; The H. P. BIGELOW, Capt. Thos. Comstock; The EDITH MAY, Grand View Park Ferry; The EDGEWOOD FERRY, by Andrew Thompson; The SIRIUS, Capt. Derian; The F. S. LAYNG, Capt. D. Wagoner; The VALLETTA, Capt. John Comstock; The GEN. W. B. FRANKLIN, Capt. Fitz Hunt; The JUNIATA, Capt. A. C. Dukelin; The MINNIE, Capt. Wm. Westcott; The NETTIE, Capt. W. E. Smith; The CLAUDE S., Capt. S. Griffin; The OLIVIA, Capt. C. Hunt; The ALERT, Capt. G. Wilson; The E. A. VAN HORN, Capt. Jasper Ellis; The JUNITA, Capt. Rattray; The LITTLE MACK, Capt. Hudson; WESTMINSTER PARK FERRY, Capt. S. Reed.

Besides the above, which run for hire, there are many very fine steam yachts owned by wealthy private parties. Among the finest of these is the yacht owned by Mr. Hayden, at Fairy Land, built by Herreshoff, doubtless the most costly yacht on the river. The LOTUS SEEKER, owned by Mr. Holden, at Thousand Island Park, is also a beautiful boat, and claimed to be the fastest on the river. The CAPTAIN VISGER and the SOPHIA are both beautiful models, and are very fast.

CAPT. ANDREW H. MILLER.

Captain Miller, commanding the "Empire State," the largest steamer of the Thousand Island Steamboat Company, is one of the ablest and most highly respected of the steamer captains on the St. Lawrence. He was born at Cape Vincent May 9, 1844, and when 14 years of age began sailing with Capt. Colman Hinckley, Sr. From the river Capt. Miller went upon the lakes in the service of the Northern Transportation Company, of Cleveland, O., and continued in their employ seven years. When the civil war broke out he enlisted in the 20th N. Y. Cavalry, which went into the field under the command of Col. Newton B. Lord. In 1865, at the close of the war, and having been honorably discharged with his company, Capt. Miller returned to his home and was in the employ of the Merchants' Union Express Company for two years, 1866–67. He then again returned to his home and became once more a sailor on the great lakes until 1872, when he began to command one of the Thousand Island Steamboat Company's boats, and has been in the employ of that company as a commander for the past 22 years.

This fact is an honorable test of Captain Miller's ability as a navigator, as well as of his integrity as a man. He is a careful sailor, takes no risks, and knows the Thousand Island archipelago as one knows his own bedroom. He has been remarkably successful and stands at the head of his profession. He puts on no "airs," but he is a wholesome man to know, and has earned a fine reputation upon the river for his ability and steadfastness. In his 53d year, he is as active as at 30, and nothing happens upon the "Empire State" that escapes his watchful attention. He is a model commander, and popular with the travelling public. His permanent home is in Kingston, Ont.

CAPT. H. W. VISGER.

This young sailor, commanding the steam-yacht "Sophia," is the son of the veteran river captain, E. W. Visger, so long and favorably known among the Thousand Islands, and the first to make excursions among them, in fact the one who first attempted to navigate what is known as the "Lost Channel."

H. W. Visger was born at Richville, St. Lawrence county, N. Y., in 1857. His first steamboat experience was as engineer on the "Cygnet." He was captain of the "Island Wanderer" (now the "Island Belle") during 1879-80-81-82. He bought the steamer "R. P. Flower" in 1883, and ran her successfully as a charter packet for several seasons. Disposing of her, he purchased the "C. M. Crossman," which he sold in 1893 to Mr. H. R. Redfield, the wealthy Hartford banker. With an honorable ambition to keep pace with the times, and to show his visitors what could be done on the St. Lawrence, he built the steam-yacht "Sophia," conceded by all to be the finest boat for hire that sails the waters of the Thousand Island archipelago. This has proved a good venture, for the "Sophia," like her consort, the "Captain Visger," has sprung into a deserved popularity, being roomy, fast and new. The Visger family are thus demonstrating their superiority as navigators, as well as showing that the finest yachts can be built at Alexandria Bay. They deserve their success, for they have served the travelling public faithfully, and demonstrated their ability as builders.

MISS NELLIE M. KENDALL.

Those who read our descriptions of the St. Lawrence steamer captains will not fail to note that Clayton seems to be the natural habitat for sailors, and that four of these vessel captains are named Kendall—all good and honest river-men. We do not pretend to vouch for the reason, but wherever you find sailors you find literary people. The lamented Dr. Holland was never so happy as when he was gathering inspiration for his grand literary efforts by listening to the talk of the sailormen and oarsmen at Alexandria Bay. He loved them well enough to start a fine library for their benefit, which was burned in

MISS NELLIE M. KENDALL,
Clayton, N. Y.

the great fire at that place in 1894, and has never been replaced. At Clayton we have Mr. George H. Strough, a fine writer, but with his soul immersed in lumber; and Mr. C. A. Shaver, the noted school superintendent, who handles a facile and graceful pen, but fools away part of his time on local politics. These are men—plain, unpretending men, and for further illustration of these and their traits we refer the historical student to Haddock's Centennial History of Jefferson County, a work ably written, which cost two years of the author's valuable time, besides leaving him $2,000 in debt.

But all this prelude is foreign to our purpose when we sat down to write. What we desired to say was that at Clayton may be found quite a natural growth of literary and artistic excellence as well as so much sailor ability. This literary taste we have found illustrated in Miss Nellie M. Kendall, sister to the handsome Kendall boys. She was born on Point Pleasant, in Clayton some twenty years ago, received the benefits of the excellent Clayton public schools, and as she belonged in a "nest of brothers with a sister in it," she was spared the trials and hardships which came to them. She had the fields to roam in, the river to row over, the golden sunsets to admire, the beautiful and romantic scenery of the St. Lawrence to enjoy. What wonder that from nature she looked up to Nature's God and received into her soul the inspiration to love all things good and beautiful. As years passed on, in a distant city she was permitted to enjoy associations with some of the best minds and purest hearts, and learned that there is no such thing as "cornering" the market of intelligence—that literature is a well where all who are athirst may come and drink freely. Under such inspiring influences she learned to write easily and well, and so when the author of this book called for some one to write up Clayton and many of the individuals named herein, she came readily into the work and has done it well. We give a view of her face, which does not do her justice, for her countenance is full of expression, as her form is full of grace and modesty. She is a native Clayton girl, and that is saying a good deal, for that vicinity has always been noted for its pretty girls and handsome sailors. We leave her in her pleasant home,

"Near meadows white, where daisies grow,
Near where St. Lawrence whispers low;
Near sylvan dells, where Nature smiles,
Earth's paradise, the Thousand Isles."

J. A. H.

ON HISTORIC GROUND.

(From the Congregationalist, Sept. 27, 1894.)

SHOULD an American Walter Scott arise he would find ample material for a new series of Waverly novels in the historic associations of the River St. Lawrence. He would find here mighty fortresses built by no human hands, castles made more secure by natural bulwarks than moat or barbican could make them, hidden bays in which a fleet might hide, channels three hundred feet deep winding between wooded islands and secluded waterways. Ellen's Isle, made famous by the Wizard of the North, is reproduced here in a hundred forms, and Loch Katrine has scores of rivals at our very door.

We have our legends of battle and carnage, of valiant deeds by souls as heroic as those who wore the tartan and the plaid. We can point out a cavern hidden away beneath precipitous rock on a secluded island, which has its romance of a maiden's devotion to her father hiding from bitter enemies seeking his life. To-day this Devil's Oven, if not as famous as the little island among the Trossach's, is often visited by thousands, and the heroism of the maiden recalled.

The night attack on Deerfield, Mass., in 1704, for the rescue of the Bell, and the terrible massacre of Wyoming, were planned on one of these islands. Many of them have their tales of terror connected with the French and English and Indian wars.

The name of Bonaparte is perpetuated by a charming lake not far away. The story of Joseph, the brother of the great Napoleon, and his career in Northern New York is as romantic as any in its history.

Not far away, too, is the childhood home of the famous singer, Antoinette Sterling, the beauty of whose Christian character has not been exaggerated. We could go on with these illustrations *ad libitum*, but space forbids.

THE MEN I HAVE MET UPON THE GREAT RIVER.

BY THOS. G. ALVORD, EX-LIEUT.-GOV. OF NEW YORK.

A FRIEND has suggested that I could write a very interesting human history of the river's rapid growth as a sportsman's paradise, a health-bearing, exhilarating, joy-inspiring refuge for tired and invalid humanity. It will be readily conceded that in the performance of my task I must omit mention of many — for the many I have met are legion in number. And again, looking back over a period of more than forty years, I must unavoidably fail to recall many, the mention of whose names would be of great interest. In order to do justice to my own city and to scores of other cities and towns, I would need but strike a few names from their annual directories, and then append the corrected lists to this article, to enumerate "The Men I Have Met upon the Great River." But to accomplish the undertaking in some acceptable way and within reasonable limits, I must cease apology and explanations, and proceed with my projected work, or I shall never finish it.

I have already, in another chapter in this Souvenir, had something to say of my first experience on the noble river, and I beg again to introduce to your notice the REV. DR. BETHUNE, the original fly-caster of the St. Lawrence. Need I say that his profound learning, his acknowledged preëminence as a pulpit orator, and withal his kindly, openhearted, Christian benevolence will remain a pleasant remembrance so long as the waters of his beloved river flow from the lakes to the sea.

The DUTTONS, father and sons, who gave us the silken line and the polished rotating spoon, will be remembered as giving as much of music and harmony to their beloved pastime as did their unequaled collection of drum and fife, cymbal and hautboy, fiddle and flute to their music-loving neighbors in "the pent up city," where their memory is ever green.

Is it necessary to make aught of explanation in bringing SETH GREEN to your notice? Not learned in schools, but an untiring, bright student of nature, he read as from an open book all the secrets of the finny tribe, over whom, by the consent of fishes and men, he was the sole and undisputed ruler. Educated in the school of Nature, he was Nature's nobleman, with a heart beating kindly toward all things animate.

Another noted individual is mixed in with my earliest recollections of the river. It is true I had never met him there, for he had visited the bay for the first and only time the year before my first arrival, but every time (and that was often) I tried the then super-excellent fishing-ground near the foot of Grenadier, I was very emphatically told where he had lunched when fishing, and he had lunched there so often that the natives, taking advantage of the fact that the much-lunched island lacked a name, solemnly decreed that from that time and forever thereafter it should be known as "VAN BUREN'S ISLAND." It may be that the man is forgotten, but I believe that it is a matter of history that he was in the cloudy and distant past once President of the United States; but, not being reëlected, he went—fishing. But once I did come near to fishing in his company. Having given up his "job" at Washington and retired to the Lindenwold shades of sleepy Kinderhook he, after "cradeling his buckwheat," would hie to the lovely Hudson, a short two miles away, to fish. I happened one day to be the guest of a gentleman who lived on the bay where "Matty" was wont to fish; and on that day, he at one end and I at the other of the bay—both "Matty and myself—bobbed for white perch; each, I am happy to say, with great success.

In the later days of my periodical sojourn with old man Crossman, there came thither two of our country's most distinguished men on their way to the haunts of the princely salmon of the Saugnenay, pausing here for a few days to tempt the springy, cunning, sportcreating bass of the St. Lawrence. Theirs was a friendship at that time (somewhat clouded in later years) like that of Damon and Pythias. Utterly unlike in temperament, manners and action, they were both, I sincerely believe, a unit in their unselfish, powerful devotion to the best interests of their country in her hour of sorest trial and direst need. If in ROSCOE CONKLING, that stubborn, selfwill, uncontrollable temper, never-dying enmity to all who dared oppose his will, had been tempered and softened by the suave, courtly and conciliatory manners and tact of CHESTER A. ARTHUR—in fine, if the better qualities of each had been used to neutralize the failings of both, it would have added increased weight to their great deeds patriotically done to save the Nation's life. Humanity is frail, never perfect; but in the world's picture of great men the heads of CONKLING and ARTHUR will loom up as did that of Saul among the prophets.

In the last year of my annually recurring stay at Alexandria Bay I met and fraternized with WILLIAM J. SKINNER, GEN. BENJAMIN F. BRUCE and FRANKLIN A. ALBERGER, the three Canal Commissioners of the State, and in their company NATHANIEL S. BENTON, then and for twelve years Auditor of the Canal Department, who had also during his long and busy life well and worthily discharged the duties of Surrogate, State Senator, United States Attorney for ten years, County Judge and Secretary of State. While they were ostensibly fishing, they were really weighing and measuring the probabilities of the success of an attempt of the mighty river to deflect to its own channel on its way to the ocean, the rapidly growing tonnage of the boundless

West, and to steal it away from our canals—those magnificent artificial waterways, alike the glory of the State and the wonder of the world, then under their official care. SKINNER proposed that above where the Great River took its primal leap in its heedless flight o'er rocky barrier and through mountain gorge in its mad haste to meet the sea, to swerve the mighty flow of its great body of waters to the valley of that other Great River the incomparable Hudson; but BRUCE and ALBERGER, with the potent aid of BENTON, rolled the mighty cloud-piercing peaks of the Adirondacks in his pathway, and sadly and reluctantly SKINNER abandoned the attempt. They finally departed with the satisfying belief that Nature had reared insurmountable barriers to the accomplishment of the river's dream of victory. Charon's boat has long since ferried them all across the dark stream, all too soon for them to know that men of their own blood pull down mountains and fill up seas with nature's forces tamed to their bidding. Already that growing city standing at the head of the greatest body of inland waters known to the world, demands and will have an unbroken waterway to the earth-encircling oceans. PROCTOR KNOTT, with burning eloquence, intentionally sarcastic, but truly prophetic, has made enduring fame for Duluth, its own great opportunities, coupled with its determined push and energy, compliment—aye, accentuate his unintentioned prediction. Our blood cousins and friendly rivals over the border, unstintedly aided from the overflowing coffers of the grand old Mother across the sea, are already deeping and widening the channel and curbing the rush of the mighty river, building with its own stone and filling with its own water the gigantic steps overcoming the elevation from the Atlantic to the Great Lakes, and soon shall we view floating easily past our shores the mammonth freight-bearing ships of the world, laden with cargoes at the elevator-docks of Duluth, 2,000 miles inland from the western shore of the Atlantic, to be discharged unbroken at the distant ports of Europe, another 3,000 miles away from where inland flow and ocean tide meet to greet its coming.

In company with the Commissioners, and often thereafter, we joyfully welcomed the pleasant companion, skilled angler and accomplished clerk of Mr. SKINNER, Mr. HOPKINS, of Little Falls, occasionally accompanied by his worthy brothers in unity, BIRCH and LADUE, whose names and merited fame in those olden days scorned to be bound by the narrow valley of the bloody Mohawk. WRIGHT, the story teller of Geneva, the Jefferson county wit, and WALRATH, the terrible joker of Oneida, both good men and true, sometime Division Commanders on the Erie, have been met sounding the depth and measuring the breadth of its giant rival, the St. Lawrence.

In 1866 I changed my base, for at this time the habitat of the desirable game-fish seemed to have moved up stream, so that the boys of the Burg had to pull against the current of Wellesly Island in order to successfully compete with their Clayton rivals; at Clayton there were then two notable caravanseries, the Hubbard and the Walton, and without premeditation I dropped into the Hubbard, where for eleven years I was a summer fixture. Permit me to say here that both houses had good and well-deserved reputations, enhanced by the fact that the genial hosts were friends not rivals, and in its best sense friends of the guests of both; a favor (often offered) asked by the guest of one at the hands of the other, was met and granted promptly and cordially. I but voice the sincerely deep regret of their army of friends at their untimely taking off, and bespeak for their brave widows the kindly and bounteous support of all those who knew and esteemed their departed husbands. Mrs. JOHNSON is yet actively engaged in the care of the Walton, the grand property left her by her husband; and one who has seen her and recalls the fact that she was a neice of General WILLIAM H. ANGEL, the broadest man Clayton ever knew, will not fail to gladly come within the charmed circle of her kindly care and elegant personality.

About this period began the idea of island ownership and summer cottage; among the first to adventure was a broker from New York, EUGENE A. ROBINSON, who expended money

THOMAS G. ALVORD.

freely on his island in grading and docking and the erection of a commodious and roomy mansion. He flourished for a time, an erratic meteor athwart the island sky, but at last the gravitation of his own errors brought him, burnt out and exhausted, down to earth.

One of my esteemed colleagues in the halls of legislation, and later, an honored representative of his district in Congress, E. KIRK HART, of Orleans, built himself at an early day, an imposing mansion facing Alexandria.

I have sailed and angled on the water and often lunched on the green-sward of an island in the company of the world-renowned sculptor, R. H. PARK. His more recently reported social standing, if true, leaves his artist fame his only claim for recollection.

I must occasionally bunch the men I have met on the river, and generalize their good points, else I will be unable to enumerate a tithe of the most worthy; so permit me to say that at Albany "as colleagues," and on the noble stream that marks the northwestern bounds of their county "as friends" I have met Hon. WILLIAM DEWEY, Hon. WILLIAM BUTTERFIELD, JAMES JOHNSTON, Col. W. W. ENOS, Hon. GEORGE E. YOST, HON. CHAS. R. SKINNER, Hon. HENRY SPICER, Hon. WILLIAM M. THOMSON and Hon. JOHN D. ELLIS, representatives of the County of Jefferson. In the rôle of law-makers of the State, I pronounce them all to have been faithful, capable and honest in the discharge of their official duties. We always meet with smiles of welcome and with hearty handshake. Some of them have been called, and have not been found wanting in the faithful and worthy discharge of other public duties.

It would seem proper in this connection to mention others of my fellow-legislators who renewed and strengthened the friendship begun at Albany by kindly greeting and mingled pleasures on the peaceful islands of the St. Lawrence: VAN HORN, VAN VALKENBURGH and LOW followed down, from Niagara's colossal leap, her angry waters, until, peaceful and quiet, they gently laved the shores of the many island-gems of the Great River; BURNS and DUGUID, of Onondaga, the "TWO CHARLIES," BAKER, of Monroe, and CHICKERING, of Lewis; WARNER MILLER, of Herkimer; CONGDON, of Cattaraugus; A. X. PARKER, of St. Lawrence; A. B. HEPBURN, of the same county; MOOERS, of Clinton, and KERN, of Madison. All these may well be proud of their public records. They have each enjoyed with me innocent sport in the balmy air of the River of Rivers.

A prominent figure on the river for many years was THEODORE S. FAXTON. I first knew him in my boyhood-days, as one of that coterie of brainy men — PARKER, BUTTERFIELD, CHILDS and FAXTON — controlling in the office or from the driver's box those wonderful lines of post-coaches which radiated from Utica, reaching East, West, North and South, the uttermost parts of our noble State, just then emerging from a state of nature into an active, thriving, energetic Commonwealth of civilization and progress. THEODORE S. FAXTON was a prominent factor in this march of progress, keeping pace with the onward step; from the position of an humble stage-driver, he reached the higher rounds of life's ladder, dying universally honored and deeply mourned.

In marked contrast, there was another well-known Utican, a frequent and ever-welcome visitor; few in the State are ignorant of the name and fame of AMMI D. BARBOUR. For many years, as soon as the halls of legislation were opened to the annual inrush of the people's servants, BARBOUR, seeking no certificate from an avowed constituency, followed in their wake and quietly, from choice, took his stand "outside but close up to the bulwarks" — a cool, level-headed mind-reader, with a persuasively eloquent tongue and a well-lined pocket, he forced upon the ignorant or lucre-loving representative the course which, not perhaps leading to glory, would certainly be to the "material" profit of the legislator; active and efficient in the ranks, he was early made his chief of staff by General Tweed, and finally became the undisputed King of the Lobby. Apart from his discreditable calling, BARBOUR was a man entertaining and interesting; he was the best posted of all others on the political history of parties as well as the inner character of politicians, and he had the rare faculty of an easy and pleasant recital. Above all else, in private life he was respected and esteemed by his neighbors as upright, honest and correct in his family and social relations and business dealings. He was an enthusiastic angler, but never wooed the finny people except his worthy wife and favorite grandson enhanced his enjoyment by their presence and participation.

I have met, with great pleasure and intellectual profit, Judges of every grade, who, hailing their vacation with the hilarity and abandon of the school boy, have hastened to doff the ermine, and donning the well-worn habiliments of secular days, concealing the dignified brow beneath the broad-brimmed palm-leaf, have sought the balmy air and cool waters of the Great River to recuperate their jaded minds and weary bodies. First, in strict compliance with legal rule, and in due order of judicial precedents, we welcome, marching forward, hand clasped in hand, those two inseparable disciples of Walton, Chief Judges ANDREWS and RUGER, whose names are written on a more enduring scroll than this fleeting note. I refrain from marring, by any attempt of mine, to laud their fame. We have met the pleasant countenances of CALVIN E PRATT and his able and eccentric namesake, DANIEL. They each worthily represent the honor, dignity and learning of the Supreme Court, but they are boys again as they dart in and out, around and about, the rock-bound and grass-covered islands of the Great River.

I must not forget that there resides in the Summer days, in his tasteful cottage erected on consecrated ground — he would select no other — my fellow townsman and friend, GEORGE N. KENNEDY. He needs no eulogy at my hands, for he is proving for himself, by his untiring industry and acknowledged pre-eminence at the bar, the folly of that legislative dictum, "that a man's ability and power for intellectual work and honorable toil ceases at the age of seventy years."

I recall two other gentlemen of this grade of judges — one still in harness — both in deserved public esteem, whose pleasant smile and friendly grip have been seen and felt on the waters of the St. Lawrence, CHARLES MASON and PARDON C. WILLIAMS. It was here that PETER B. MCLENNAN acquired that calm mind and sound judgment marking his course on the bench to-day.

As County Judge and a colleague in the Constitutional Convention of '67-8, Member of Congress, Secretary of State and State Senator, the mere recital of his official honors stamp HOMER A. NELSON, of Dutchess, as an able and trusted public man, and I can testify that he was a keen and successful angler, and, by natural sequence, a polished gentleman. JEROME FULLER, of Monroe, was another fellow member in the Convention of '67-8, and the recital of his official positions, all filled ably and well, are sufficient testimony of his acknowledged worth and character. He has filled the additional positions of County Judge of Monroe, Territorial Judge of Minnesota, Member of Assembly and State Senator, as well as that of successful angler on the bonny St. Lawrence. The legal learning, sound judgment and righteous administration of justice which marked the judicial lives of Judges VAN VORST, of New York, and SMITH, of Cortland, were never lessened by their keen appreciation and enjoyment of the unequaled attraction of our summer paradise.

Last, but not least, comes the beaming face of that true hearted and broad minded son of Madison, once its honored Judge, CHAS. L. KENNEDY.

I had firmly resolved early in my life on the river that whenever the opportunity offered to suit my taste and not wholly empty my pocket, I would

"Be monarch of all I surveyed,
With none my right to dispute;
From the center all around to the sea,
The lord of the fowl and the brute"—

in the shape of an island in the St. Lawrence. My eye always rested lovingly and hopefully on an island in the broad channel immediately opposite to and about one-half mile distant from the docks of Clayton. In the "native directory" it had been christened "Shot Bag" to keep company with a near-by island and islet called respectively "Powder Horn" and "Cap Box," each so designated from its fancied resemblance to one of these necessary appendages to the shot gun. I early became acquainted with the owner, a gentleman by the name of LAWRENCE, a successful hat, cap and fur dealer in the city of New York. By the way, it might as well be noted right here, that he was an accomplished fly-caster, his daily catch of beauties being seldom second in number in the friendly struggle of the jovial anglers for preëminence. A pleasant, genial companion, he is gone never to return, but he is not forgotten. To return to my island. For a number of years I was advised that it was not for sale, and other spots were urged upon my attention, but I still hoped for my first choice, and finally declining health induced my friend to make me a proposition to part with it at the price of $400. At length, confirmed in his own belief by the judgment of others whom he considered experts, that the island would measure at least four acres, he closed the deal with myself and son-in-law, JAMES A. CHENEY, at $100 per acre; and when the survey demonstrated that $170 paid for 1 70-100 of an acre (the area of the island), with great disappointment, somewhat forcibly expressed, but with unhesitating adherence to his pledged word, the owner executed the deed of transfer. In family convention — from which I was carefully excluded — the name of "Shot Bag" was dropped, and the newly-acquired summer home was rechristened "Governor's Island." It was never under any "government," but the denizens, adults and children alike, took in health, happiness and all edibles within reach. There the cannon roared, the flags waved, the beacons shone, not with hostile intent, but as a cordial welcome to the coming, and a kindly farewell to the departing friend. These pleasant days covered seventeen joyous summers. That island is one of the brightest gems that adorn the water-encircled diadem of the Great River. It has now fallen under the dominion of one who, with rare taste and skill combined with a judicious expenditure of wealth, is constantly adding new attractions to the wonderful beauties of America's peerless summer resort. A hearty welcome to CHARLES G. EMERY. Others have met him on the Great River, and we all trust that many happy summers still await him on its restful bosom.

We have not deserted the river of our love and our pride; but, a little nearer its source, on a projecting point on old Grindstone — its primary rocks still showing the deep scars of the Glacial Period —"Lindenwold" displays its unmatched beauties, and the old starry flag of "Governor's Island," undimmed, waves over it, and the doors of the same modest but roomy cottage, stand wide open to all friends. Excuse this apparently wide departure from the original text. It was partly necessitated as a means by which to bring into deserved notice my friends LAWRENCE and EMERY, and partly to authorize the use of my well-filled cottage registry, containing the names of "men I had met upon the Great River," thus rejuvenating a failing memory and rescuing from oblivion the river history of many who should not be forgotten.

The REV. DR. REESE, of Albany, was first met on the river, on the inside of St. John's Island, fighting manfully for and rejoicing over the capture of his first muskalonge, a beauty of over thirty pounds in weight; the occasion made us fellows, and began (for me) a pleasant acquaintance, renewed almost yearly for many summers past. This eloquent divine is ever welcome to Clayton, for he never fails to interest crowded audiences from the local pulpit on the appointed rest-days from secular labor. The Doctor is, like all good anglers, wholesouled, genial and an exceedingly interesting raconteur.

The REV. DR. CALTHROP, hailing from the Central City, fulfilling strictly and conscientiously his clerical duties, figures also as astronomer, expert, and peerless billiardist and chess-player, and excels in each. While at home he (rather too often) reads from the Sun, dire storm, destructive blizzard, drenching rain or parching drouth, his presence in the valley of the St. Lawrence always insures us beautiful sun-shine, placid waters, and abounding game for the angler.

Once upon a time there came into the legislative halls from the home of Conkling, a worthy, honest man, who answered equally and readily to either of the familiar names of "UNCLE DAVID" or "APPLE BARREL" GRAY. His heart was set upon the passage of his only bill; it was a bill "To regulate the size of Apple Barrels." Passing through the ordeal of the appropriate committee, it came before the full body of the Assembly for discussion and amendment. The naughty boys of that body offered and adopted so many incomprehensible and inconsistent amendments, that soon the honest old man did not know "where he was at." He appealed to me — to whom he had somehow been attracted—to solve the difficulty; I undertook the task, and soon the chairman announced, that "what was left of the bill was ordered to be engrossed for a third and final reading;" with bulging eyes and bated breath, Uncle DAVID asked "what was left?" He was blandly informed, that the title was intact, but that the staves, hoops and heads of the barrel were missing. He was at first somewhat inclined to blame me for the catastrophy, but he was persuaded to visit me in my summer home, where the Lethean effect of the "pellucid" waters, and the electric shock transmitted to his body by the strike of the bass through the line attached to his submerged hook, cured him of all suspicion, and he became, and still is, one of my warmest friends; but I have occasionally heard him, when overcome with sleep, after a heavy lunch on a grass-covered island, mutter "My next Apple Barrel Bill shall have the hoops nailed on, and the heads nailed in, *and I will attend to it myself.*"

On the river for many years the most marked man to be met was a Mr. SELLECK, from Newburgh. He was evidently a well educated person, and as a conversationalist, entertaining and instructive. Though totally blind he went everywhere without a guide, with a firm and assured step. He would walk from the hotel to the landing, and enter his boat without aid, and he seldom returned at nightfall with a smaller catch of the finny tribe than a full average of the return captures of the day. Report said that in his business as designer and manufacturer of artistic and decorated furniture, he had but few equals and no superiors.

I must not omit the military arm of the Nation. My register records their presence singly and in squads, veteran corps, and regiments, Kentucky colonels and "high privates," with waving banners and martial music. They were peacefully inclined, however; the bivouac and battle-field were memories. They march erect and step proudly to the beat of the drum, save when tempting forage was uncovered; then "double quick" and rapid rush broke down all lines, and discipline was ignored. From the many (few can be named "Facile Princeps"), stands forth the gallant SLOCUM. Not on the battle field, but when white-robed peace smiled on the beloved country he fought to save, he laid him down to die. History will keep ever green the sacred memory of this patriot soldier.

Make way for the heroic SNIFER, leading to the peaceful banks and enticing islands of the Great River the few remaining veterans of that noble regiment, which—when three of its gallant number had fallen with the flag they died to save, raising that starry emblem from the dying hands of its last defender, bearing it proudly forward—he rallied to victory; the sods of the valley now press upon his breathless form, but in the memory of the multitude who but knew him to love him, the patriotic deeds of General GUSTAVUS SNIPER will endure forever.

The name of General DAVIES stands high on the roll of fame among the noted cavalry leaders in the late Civil War, his clarion voice and flashing sabre gave victory to his gallant troopers in many a well fought fray; he is the same general on the waters of the Great river; cool, determined, untiring, he strikes for the royal muskalonge, and the trophies that adorn his wigwam are large in size and great in number.

The erect and noble form of the "Hero of

Fort Fisher" looms above the waves of his native river; General in war, he is now guardian in peaceful days, of that ark of safety, the Constitution of our fathers, he so bravely helped to rescue from destruction, and stands as St. Lawrence's sentinel on the ramparts of the Nation's capitol. Though an eye was cheerfully lost amid the scenes of battle, he still, with one, single to his duty, fights bravely to protect and perpetuate for his country the rights so nobly defended on many a bloody field. All honor and praise to General NEWTON MARTIN CURTIS.

There is a "WYLIE" man, whose countenance is a familar one on the long reaches and deep bays. Do not be deceived by surmising that the " D. D." which the name carries with it stands for " Doctor of Divinity." He is too wily and a little too wicked for that; but he was a good soldier and loyal man when the nation needed good soldiers and loyal men to compel and perpetuate an unbroken Union, and he is well entitled to be called "General." The only bad mark on his character ever discovered was his attempt to carry off, on a wager, a basket of champagne, as the reward of the superiority of his catch (with his own unaided rod and reel), in the number of lawfully sized bass by one day's fishing, over that of an antagonist (bound by the same requirements). He apparently won the match by a very narrow margin, and announced the victory to his shouting comrades with wilder shouts than theirs. But a few hours of sober reflection brought swift repentance, and on bended knee he humbly confessed that a brother conspirator from one boat and a venal guide from another, with no regard for lawful weight, had tumbled into his craft the larger number of his reputed victims, and he tearfully, but manfully, rolled into the cottage-door of his competitor, the coveted prize. He has been forgiven, and hopes are strong that by continued repentance of past deeds of wickedness and firm resolve of an honest future he may yet be allowed to write "D. D." as well in rear as in front of his patronymic, and thus wipe out forever any sinister meaning to the honored name of " Wylie."

Seventeen years have passed away since WILLIAM H. VANDERBILT and the lamented WEBSTER WAGNER came here to spy out the land. Both have passed to the " beyond." but their keen business eyes — we have reason to know — took in all the beauties and possibilities of the grand panorama spread before their vision, and the fruits of that visit are clearly noticeable in the increased comfort and ease of access hither from all parts of the Union, and under the wise and able management of their successors this will not be abated, but improved and amplified.

Not clothed in trappings of war but in the habiliments of peace, we look on the face and admire the soldierly bearing of one of the elite of that crack regiment, New York's only 7th, CHRIS WOLF, an island-dweller and ever a welcome comrade. The quiet, unobtrusive HICKS, with pleasant wife and daughter, not only guards, but makes, with cow and chicken, homelike and enviable, the upper gate of our archipelago.

Scarcely fifty years ago 1,500 of the Thousand Islands of this great river lay upon its glassy waters in the garb of Nature's clothing, save where, on the larger ones, blackened stumps marked the incipient effort of the husbandman or the ruthless swath of the wood-devouring steamer, then first invading the peaceful waters. To-day, in quiet bower and shady nook, on bold promontory or widespread lawn, in single sites and in varying groups, from lower Grenadier to upper Wolf, reaching as an outlying sentinel beyond the line where lake and river join, tiny cottage and palatial mansion mark an almost continuous city of grandeur and beauty — the imposing Crossmon at one extremity, and the towering Frontenac midway to the deep Ontario, inclose many other gorgeous resting places as homes for the flitting sojourner. As the swift-darting inhabitants below the water's surface, so on its bosom in almost equal numbers shoot hither and thither the ever-restless steamers — many at stated intervals on regular duty bound, many with banners flying and gladsome music, laden with the people from deserted town and village, breathing the balmy air and drinking in the gorgeous beauties of the Great River, as with twinkling feet and glad shout they greet its glories. The trim-built, lavishly-furnished, flag-enveloped, swift-running yachts, alive with their crews of summer residents, add to the wild carnival of pleasure and happiness, and human shout, shrill whistle, sharp-clanging bell and barbaric music drive the rightful owners of the waters, frightened and alarmed, to the lowest depths and darkest caves of their watery kingdom.

Now many of these many men (and lovely women, too, God bless them!) "I have met upon the Great River." Time and space alike forbid a mere recital of their names; I must, therefore, be content with a brief notice of a few others who have been foremost, and who have not yet ceased their loving labors in adding to Nature's wonderful work on this unequaled river.

The widely-known and sincerely lamented scholar and scribe, the late DR. HOLLAND, is with us no longer; but his warm love for his "Bonny Castle" has descended to his surviving family, who still enjoy, and each returning season make more beautiful, the delightful spot he loved so well.

The HAYDENS, PULLMAN, the large-hearted BROWNING, the coal king of the Lehigh valley, the denizens of Westminster Park, and many others, still intent upon gilding the refined gold of their incomparable Bay, all bear faces I have met upon the beautiful River. I have met many of the men who summer in assured safety and peaceful comfort under the Christian banner of the itinerant Methodists; among them my home neighbors, none of whom need go from their Central City to find witnesses to their worthy and Christian character. (Judge KENNEDY I have already named) WEEKS, HOLDEN, PENN, LEE, SPRAGUE, and scores of others, are men I am proud to say "I have met upon the Great River."

I even own up that I knew SAM GRINNELL, when he pastured his cow on his island, now studded with many beautiful cottages, and joyously welcomed the thirsty dwellers on Prohibition-1,000-Island-Park to his choice dispensary of contraband whisky.

Round Island is peopled with many worthy of notable mention. Across its head, facing the on-coming waters, stand four dwellings: First, the modest villa of DR. WHEDEN, the pioneer of the island-dwellers, followed by Messrs. HAYES, VAN WAGONEN, and JAMES J. BELDEN, ex-mayor and congressman, who, applying well-earned wealth with sound judgment and artistic taste to their work of pleasure, have erected houses of comfort and delight, the very embodiment of the poet and the painter's dream of loveliness. Another chief of the Central City, WM. B. KIRK, has applied a portion of his wealth to the adornment of this beautiful island, and these have found willing comrades to aid in making this cosy hamlet a beauty spot on the Great River.

As I pen these lines so many faces crowd upon my reviving memory, that my task must be abruptly closed or it will become endless. A few more of the multitude of those who deserve recognition and I have done.

No one who frequents the river can fail to know that always hilarious crowd, hailing from Albany, headed by JIM STORY, JOHN H. QUINBY, and CHARLIE GAY. At home, staid, steady, model business men. On the river—never offensive—but full to the brim, of fun and frolic, good anglers and genial companions.

There comes periodically to the river a quiet, unobtrusive but worthy and interesting gentleman. It is said that "Good wine needs no Bush," but a troll on the water and a lunch on the shore are made more enjoyable and satisfying whenever MR. "BUSH," of Buffalo counts as one of the party.

We entreat LUCIUS MOSES to bring back to the river himself with his delightful family; we yearn to hear once more the swish of his wonderful cast, as the fly tempts the bass to strike "twenty yards away."

In writing the name of MR. BROWNING, of New York, there came back to me the remembrance of his brother-in-law, MR. SCOTT, who is an annual visitor, seldom failing a yearly return. Although a city man, he is old fashioned in dress and manners, though never other than a gentleman. Though easily approachable, he is naturally taciturn; an untiring angler, wind and wave never staying him. One day near the head of Hemlock, he was at anchor still-fishing for bass; a good sized perch was hooked, and he rapidly drew him up, and was rendered almost helpless by the onrush of a thirty-pound muskalonge, striking for his dangling perch. The big fellow landed with the perch, in the boat, and with the aid of the guide was killed. After a few moments delay, S., recovered sufficiently to ejaculate "GREAT SCOTT," the only words (the guide avers) that he uttered until he reached the dock at Clayton, three miles away.

Clustered on and around the hoary head of old Grindstone, the MORGANS and the LOVELLS, of New York, have brought refinement and artistic skill to adorn their summer homes, and in themselves have added acknowledged worth to the goodly society of our Summer City.

It would be very wrong and unjust if the men and women who dwell in inclement winter as well as in gentle summer on the banks of this world-famed stream were not recorded among the throng of those "I have met upon the Great River." In all ranks and conditions among them, they are the hosts and helpers of their welcome summer visitors; kind, considerate, helpful, never exacting or mercenary, they are always ready and obliging. Their character and conduct are in marked contrast with the reported greed, venality and robbery at other noted places of summer resort. I am glad to proclaim that I have met and have learned to respect and honor these constant dwellers in the valley of the Great River.

If life and health are spared, I trust to meet many old and to greet many new faces in the coming years, enjoying renovated health and needed relaxation from the ilis and cares of busy life amid the scenes of grandeur and beauty nowhere so sure to be found as " Upon the Great River."

THOMAS G. ALVORD.

SYRACUSE, March, 1895.

We think no man or woman can rise up after reading Governor ALVORD'S unique and entirely unapproachable remarks upon the people he has met, without a better feeling towards all mankind, and a most grateful sense of appreciation of this honored man, whose green old age has met with no blight, and whose frosted head bears no possible indication of any frost of heart. With thousands who love him and revere his matchless ability, we reëcho his own wish that he may yet be spared for many years to visit the Great River.

THE RIVER CAPTAINS.

BY reference to the pages in this book devoted to pictures of men whom we have thought should be shown, the reader will find many captains of St. Lawrence steamers. We have tried to give portraits of them all, for they are a peculiarly deserving set of men, good sailors, mild in manner, and accommodating in disposition. These pictures have been procured from some of them unwillingly, and the short sketches of their lives we have worried out of them, sometimes by extreme urgency. They are really too modest for this progressive age, but we give them as they appear in every-day life, and we think them a fine looking lot of men.

A BONAPARTE IN NORTHERN NEW YORK.

[THE following excellent article is not exactly history, though germain, and its insertion in this volume is considered proper and instructive because most of the people named were long ago residents of Cape Vincent, a town of many memories, which stands at the very head of those islands we are attempting to describe and to give their histories, as well as to make brief mention of those superior men who first settled on and near them, and were certainly the first to sound their praise and introduce them to the attention and knowledge of the American people.]

THE advent of Joseph Bonaparte, or Count de Survilliers (as he desired to be known), into Northern New York and upon the St. Lawrence, is scarcely explainable without some reference by way of introduction to Count James Donatien Le Ray de Chaumont, who was the son of Count Donatien Le Ray, the intimate friend of Franklin and Adams, and Morris, and a devoted adherent to the fortunes of the United States, who in a time of the utmost need imperiled his great fortune by coming to our assistance. He it was who sent a shipload of powder to Boston; who furnished clothing for La Fayette's army, and fitted out three vessels of war to join the fleet under Commodore Jean Paul Jones.

Previous to the elevation of Joseph Bonaparte to the thrones, first of Naples and then of Spain, he and young Le Ray were students at the celebrated school of Juilly, near Paris; here their acquaintance ripened into an intimacy which, although interrupted by succeeding events, did not wholly cease, and so we find it renewed at a time when the friendship of a Le Ray was not to be despised, even by a Bonaparte, though twice a king. The young Le Ray, intimate at his father's house with such men as Franklin, Adams and Morris, had early learned lessons of Republican wisdom, and understood how to sympathize with the infant States in their struggle for freedom. His intercourse with these gifted statesmen did much to perfect a character naturally superior, and of which an intimate acquaintance wrote in after years as follows: " He had a strong mind, great penetration, sound judgment, a warm and affectionate heart, and a noble soul. He was guided through life by a high and chivalrous integrity." It was related that on one occasion a difference arose between the elder Le Ray and Robert Morris, then at the court of France. An umpire was to be chosen, and Robert Morris at once selected Mr. Le Ray's own son; the case was stated, and a decision in favor of Mr. Morris was the result. The citizens of Jefferson and Lewis counties, N. Y., owe much of their prosperity to his enlightened and liberal management; and by the citizens of Jefferson county especially he is affectionately remembered for his public-spirited improvements, his dignified and courteous demeanor, and the sympathy he never failed to express, not only in words, but practically, for whatever concerned the public welfare. He fully sympathized with all that his father did to aid the colonies in their struggle with Great Britain, and upon him it finally devolved to effect a settlement with them. It was a task of great difficulty. The depreciation of paper money, and the differing currencies of the States, were obstacles almost insurmountable. Tearing himself from the seductions of the most elegant court in Europe, and from the near prospect of a brilliant marriage, he sailed for the United States, to distinguished citizens of which Franklin had given him letters; and yet, notwithstanding his talents and energy, strengthened by all the influence of Franklin, and Morris, and Adams, it was not until 1780 that a settlement was effected; just in time to save his father from a humiliating bankruptcy.

While in the United States he became acquainted with two men who largely influenced his subsequent career,—Gouverneur Morris and Count de La Foret, Consul-General of France,—who induced him to make heavy purchases of land. In company with the latter, he purchased a large tract in Otsego county, and established as his agent there Judge Cooper, father of the great novelist. With the former he made extensive purchases in Northern New York, and by reason of these purchases it was that Joseph Bonaparte came upon the scene. In 1790, young Le Ray became a naturalized citizen of the United States, and married the daughter of Charles Coxe, Esq., of New Jersey, returning to France the same year. Between that and 1810, he had several times visited the United States; returning to France in that year, he settled upon his estates in Touraine, and busied himself in settling his affairs in Northern New York. The last meeting for more than a decade between young Le Ray and Joseph Bonaparte, was on the occasion of the signing of the treaty between France and the United States at Morte Fontaine, September 30, 1800, at which time they dined together. Fifteen years later came the downfall of Napoleon, and with him that of his family. Hearing that Joseph was at Blois, M' Le Ray hastened to offer his friendship. He was warmly welcomed, and the intimacy of former years was renewed.

One day while at dinner, a train of wagons passed the window near which they were sitting. Joseph, turning to M. Le Ray, said: "Mon ami, I remember that you have spoken to me of your large possessions in the United States. Do you still hold them? If so, I should like to exchange for a part of them some of the silver that I have in those wagons, which may be pillaged at any moment. Take four or five hundred thousand francs, and give me the equivalent in land." This M' Le Ray declined, saying: "It is impossible to make a bargain where I alone know the facts. "Oh," said Joseph, "I know you well, and I rely more upon your word than upon my own judgment."

A bargain was soon entered into, the terms of which were, that for 200,000 francs the elder Le Ray would give Joseph Bonaparte a letter to his son Vincent, then in the United States, instructing him to show to the ex-king a certain tract; when, if approved of by him after seeing it, the sale would be confirmed. If not approved, the money was to be returned. The bargain was consummated with a slight change in the terms of payment.

Some writers have asserted that Joseph Bonaparte's farewell to France was an escapade; but whether true or not, he reached the United States in 1815, and Northern New York in 1818. Of his career in New Jersey and elsewhere, this account has nothing to do, as it proposes to deal with his affairs in Northern New York and not elsewhere, unless it may be incidentally. On arriving in the United States he assumed the title of Count de Survilliers, by which name and title only he desired to be known. His purchase included the greater part of the town of Diana, in Lewis county, together with portions of several towns in Jefferson county, lying principally in the valley of the Black River and on the shores of Lake Ontario and the St. Lawrence river; the whole amounting to 150,000 acres, which was paid for in diamonds and silver. Subsequently, owing to the fact that diamonds had fallen to half their former value in market, other arrangements were entered into, and in 1820 the count accepted a tract of 26,840 acres, for which he paid $40,260.

He now memorialized the Legislature of New York to grant him the privilege of holding titles in his own name. In his memorial, he says: "Not being of the number of those who would wish to abandon this land of hospitality, where the best rights of man prevail, I am nevertheless bound to my own country by ties which misfortunes render sacred." The privilege solicited was granted by a special act, bearing date March 31, 1825. Having acquired his titles, the ex-king began to explore his possessions; and it is told of him that whenever it was possible, he traveled in great state. Under any circumstances, his private secretary, M. Carot, his cook, butler, valet and page constituted his suite; these, with the servants of his guests, of whom he usually entertained several, made up a train, which, in the eyes of the simple backwoodsmen of those days, formed a pageant long to be remembered. Those were the times when the old country tavern was in the ascendant; and how to dispose of such a retinue, became at times a problem too intricate for the rural host to solve.

On one occasion, when on his way to spend the winter in New York and Philadelphia, his train was unusually large, having for his guests, Count Pierre François Real, who was Chef de Police under the Emperor, and who then lived at Cape Vincent, Jefferson county; Emmanuel Count de Grouchy and General Desfurneaux, who, with their attendants, were also going to the metropolis, together with several distinguished gentlemen from Albany, who had been guests of Count Survilliers at Bonaparte lake. They halted in the evening at a well-known hostelry in the Mohawk valley, kept by a sturdy old Dutchman. As was by no means uncommon among those who were in company with Count Survilliers, a night of revelry followed; a kingly revel, where the guests were served on silver by Parisian waiters. The choicest vintages were served in Venetian-cut glass, and the costliest teas and coffees in Sevres china. First, drinking to the idol of their hearts, him who was even then breaking his heart against the bars of St. Helena, and whom they seldom for a moment forgot, they gave way to amusement and hilarity. Song and story followed in rapid succession, witticisms sparkled like the bead upon their champagne, while the worthy host, called here and there, often two ways at the same moment, was half crazed, and wholly bewildered. In the morning M. Carot, the Count's private secretary, called upon the landlord to present his bill. This was a poser; never before in that house, had a bill of items been asked for, but the crisis had come, and it must be met; and so the worthy Boniface, groaning over the unwonted mental exertion required, set slowly about his task. Aided by the "good frouw," whose qualifications as an accountant, were, if possible, fewer than his own, he finally, with much mental travail, produced a bill which seemed to meet the requirements; and with some trepidation in his manner, he presented it to M. Carot. It was a bill for $200. The astute secretary detected the exorbitant charges at a glance, and looked with dismay upon the final footing, the manifest result of an attempt to divide a large sum total among a few items only; the house as a matter of fact, having contributed but very little toward the entertainment.

Noticing the look upon his secretary's face, Count Survilliers demanded to see the bill. It was handed to him, and thence ran the guantlet of the merry company, who, shouting with laughter at Mynheer's unique specimen of bookkeeping, nevertheless protested against his outrageous charges; which, allowing him the highest possible prices for labor and supplies, would scarcely amount to $50. The bill was returned to the landlord, and the exorbitant charges pointed out; in process of time an amended bill was brought in, which contained a very fairly itemized account amounting to $50, after which followed the crowning entry: "To making in mine house one d——d fuss, $150,"—thus triumphantly sustaining the original grand total. Saying "cheap enough, too," the ex-king ordered M. Carot, to settle the bill. For many years thereafter that same bill was in the possession of one of Albany's most distinguished citizens, who frequently exhibited it to his friends as a "model Mohawk-valley tavern bill."

Count Survilliers made a number of improvements in various parts of his domain, and expended money with a princely liberality, thereby benefiting many a poor man, who in those days would otherwise have handled money but rarely. At Natural Bridge, he erected a large framed house, with all the convenient accessories of a gentleman's summer residence and furnished it elegantly at a great expense. Here, for several seasons, the ex-king kept open house, and was visited at times by some of those whom, in his days of regal pomp and power, he had entertained at court in Naples and in Madrid. Among the more constant of his guests, however, were Count Real; the Peugnet brothers, Louis, Hyacinthe and Theophilus; Louis, having been a captain in the Emperor's body guard, an officer of the corps d'elite; still wore the cross of the Legion d'Honneur, placed upon his breast by the Emperor's own hand; General Rolland, Count Real's son-in-law Col. Jermoux, Camille Armand, and others, all living at Cape Vincent, where M. Le Ray had founded a prosperous village and erected a stately mansion, now the property of Mrs. Beaufort, and her sister, Miss Emeline Peugnet, daughters of Captain Louis Peugnet; estimable, refined ladies are they, well known far beyond the bounds of their village-home.

There are many circumstances which render it probable that these re-unions, in which M. Le Ray was by no means the least honored guest, and which he often reciprocated by gathering the entire company under his own roof, either in his stately chateau at Le Raysville, or in his house at Cape Vincent, were for the purpose of discussing matters of much greater importance than disquisitions on matters piscatorial, or the art of living; although hunting and fishing was the ostensible object. The woods abounded in game, and the streams and the lakes with fish. A beautiful lake of some 1200 acres area, abounding in the choicest varieties of fish, and forming a part of the Count's domain, was but a few miles from his mansion, at Natural Bridge, N. Y. It is a beautiful sheet of water, with bold and rocky shores, its surface sprinkled with island gems,—an archipelago in minature. On an eminence overlooking its shores the Count erected a commodious hunting lodge, and opened a road from the old State Turnpike to the lake, on which boats were launched and every possible convenience provided for both hunting and fishing, of which sports the Count was extremly fond; and yet, to use the phraseology of a man who worked on the building mentioned, and who is yet living at Natural Bridge: "They didn't seem to hunt and fish much a'ter all." This charming lake (Bonaparte, now named) is now the property of Hon. Joseph Pahud, a superior and most interesting gentleman, and he has erected a neat hotel there, a very paradise for anyone desiring rest, combined with fish and game.

That a scheme was formed to rescue the Emperor from the custody of Sir Hudson Lowe, and spirit him away to the United States, there can now be no doubt. The French residents of Cape Vincent, after the news of Napoleon's death was received, did not hesitate to avow that such had been their purpose. A well-known American naval commander, whose reputation for courage, skill and daring, even to recklessness at times, could not be questioned, was to have aided the scheme; and with his help, they hoped to succeed. It is also highly probable that, in some way, the exiles on St. Helena were made aware of the efforts on foot to secure their liberation. A letter written by Count Bertrand to Joseph Bonaparte on the death of the Emperor, after announcing the sad event, says of him: "The hope of leaving this dreadful country often presented itself to his imagination. Some newspaper articles added to, and excited our expectations. We sometimes fancied that we were on the eve of starting for America; we read travels; we made plans; we arrived at your house; we wandered over that great country, where alone we might hope to enjoy liberty. Vain hopes! Vain projects! which only made us doubly feel our misfortunes."

That Count Real erected a house at Cape Vincent for the reception of his adored Chief, is so well known in that locality that it "goes without saying;" and also that during its erection, Count Survilliers was oftener a visitor at Cape Vincent than at any other time. Then, too, his constant communication with this band of enthusiastic imperialists, and especially with Professor Pigeon, who was Private Secretary to Count Real, and who, no doubt, wrote every letter and every communication of whatever nature relating to their secret plans.

It was Prof. Pigeon who took a vow never to cover his head while Napoleon was a prisoner; and notwithstanding the severity of the winters in Northern New York, he steadfastly adhered to his resolution until the death of the Emperor released him from his vow.

During Joseph Bonaparte's last visit to Bonaparte Lake, a tragedy occurred that, for some time, threw a gloom over his daily life, which seemed impossible for him to shake off. Not far from Bonaparte Lake is Green Lake, a body of water not half the size of Bonaparte Lake, and as dismal, gloomy and repulsive as the other is delightful. Its shores are bold and rocky; and owing to a mass of fallen timber, which forms an almost impenetrable cheveaux de frieze around it, it is very difficult of access. Not far from the water's edge, at a point where the rocky wall almost reaches it, is a cave so dark and dismal that it became known as the "Cave of the Sepulchre," a name which a subsequent occurrence served to establish more completely, if possible, than it was before.

Among the attendants of the count, was a young Frenchman named Jean Vallois, who paid marked attention to the daughter of a French settler living in the vicinity. She was a beautiful girl, and it was not long before they were almost inseparable. It was especially their delight to take a boat and row away together among the islands, or climb the rocks to find some new view on which to feast their eyes. Count Survilliers was himself too fond of the fair sex to put any restraint on the loves of his followers, and so the liaison went on uninterrupted until it became apparent to all that a climax was not far distant. One day the young people announced their intention to visit Green Lake, which was but a short distance away. They were never seen again. Days lengthened into weeks, and weeks into months, and yet no trace of them was found. The woods were scoured far and wide in every direction, and the waters of Green Lake dragged in vain. Years sped on, and finally the old Frenchman and his wife died, and gradually the occurrence faded from recollection. In 1850 a party of hunters conceived the idea of exploring the Cave of the Sepulcher. Providing themselves with an abundance of material for lights and whatever else they deemed necessary, the exploration was made. Among the rubbish in the bottom of the cave some bones were found, which were thought to be those of an animal. One of the party, however, in looking closer, discovered a human skull, and further search revealed another; then some little trinkets were found; and finally a Spanish gold coin, on one side of which was stamped the head of Joseph Bonaparte. When these facts became known, it was remembered that Count Survilliers had often presented similar pieces to members of his suite, and to particular friends as souvenirs of some special occasion. This fact coupled with the medical testimony, that one of the skulls found belonged to a male and the other to a female, made the conclusion almost irresistible that these were none other than the remains of Jean Vallois and the French maiden so soon to become a mother. Whether it was deliberate suicide on the part of both, or whether they fell victims to a beast of prey, will never be known so far as human knowledge is concerned.

The author considers himself fortunate in having interviewed Mr. Joseph Blanchard, of Natural Bridge, N. Y., before his death in 1895, he having then reached his 88th year. His recollection of Joseph Bonaparte was distinct and special, and being a man of great intelligence as well as wholly truthful, Mr. Blanchard's description of the ex-King of Spain became very interesting. He describes Joseph as having been suave in manner, very kind to the settlers and easily approached. At times, to relieve the monotony of life in that far-away forest, he would don a workman's blouse and aid in the work of building his house. This was in 1828. The Hon. Lotus Ingalls, the veteran Watertown editor, well remembers the ex-king as a jolly Frenchman, who would sit in front of his dwelling of a summer evening and scatter small coins among the expectant boys who would struggle for the prizes.

An examination of his dwelling at Natural Bridge gave rise to many peculiar sensations. Here dwelt one who had tasted every earthly pleasure, and had reigned as king over one of the proudest and oldest countries of modern times. Did he hope to obtain forgetfulness of the past by intercourse with the common people of a back settlement, or by living close to nature; did he hope to rejuvenate a constitution doubtless worn by high living and the excitements that surround a throne? Be that as it may, he tarried not long at Natural Bridge, returning to Bordentown, N. J., in 1829.

There are several dwellings in different parts of Jefferson county which were built by Joseph Bonaparte for residences or offices. Not more than one or two of these are standing. He built a large stone house on the shore of Perch Lake, in the town of Pamelia, N. Y. This was very richly furnished throughout; the fireplaces were fitted with marble mantels, and the whole house was finished to correspond. This was intended for a winter residence, being within easy reach of his friends at Cape Vincent, and of the chateau of M. de Le Ray, at Le Raysville. This part of his domain was afterward sold to John La Farge, another French émigré, but now scarcely one stone stands upon another to mark what was once the dwelling of royalty. A nephew of Count Survilliers, Joachim Murat, was a frequent guest of his uncle, who presented him with a tract of land lying between the present villages of Antwerp and Theresa. Here the young man began business on a large scale. He caused a canal to be dug, a dam was built on Indian river, and a mill erected, a storehouse and dwellings put up, a town laid out on a grand scale, and every preparation made for a city in the wilderness, but it failed to materialize. While the young Murat possessed all the natural proclivities which constitute the modern "boomer," he was half a century in advance of the times; settlers failed to come, the development of the country was slow, the locality was off the natural lines of communication, so that after the expenditure of a fortune, he was forced to abandon the enterprise, and now but little remains to indicate the spot where he fondly hoped to rear the flourishing city of "Joachim."

In 1833, or it may be in the spring of 1834, Joseph Bonaparte returned to France, and Northern New York knew him no more. In 1835 his agent, Judge Joseph Boyer, sold all his remaining lands in Jefferson and Lewis counties to John La Farge. At this time, political events in France apparently favored a reinstatement of the Bonaparte family, and Count Survilliers, hopeful that the next turn of the political wheel would bring the Bonapartes to the surface, was anxious to be where his greatest interests lay, and where his personal efforts might be of some avail. With the sale of his landed estates, his interests in a country where, to use his own expression, "The best rights of man prevail," entirely ceased. Some three or four old men are yet alive, who, in the capacity of guides or laborers for the ex-king, can relate some anecdote of him; but of his real life while in Northern New York, scarce anything is publicly known beyond what is embodied in this brief sketch. Of one who was king of Naples, who sat on the throne of Spain, whose brother was an emperor, and wore the diadem of the Cæsars, and whose acts have filled more pages of history than did those of Alexander the Great, it seems trifling indeed.

THE MYSTERY OF MAPLE ISLAND.

BY AN AMATEUR HISTORIAN.

Oh, that I were a painter! who could a picture make,
A fitting guide to be, into this Island mystery.

MAPLE ISLAND, on which the tragedy which I am about to relate took place, lies a little beyond the main steamboat channel on the American side, almost in front of, and in plain view from the balconies of the "Frontenac" on Round Island. It has an area of about six acres, and a high ridge extends across it from east to west, or nearly so, which is inclined to be precipitous on the north and north-west. For the most part, the island is covered by a thick undergrowth with here and there a few larger trees, excepting on the south side of the dividing ridge, where the timber has been cut away, leaving a triangular shaped clearing with its apex at the top of the ridge. There is nothing about it to attract especial attention.

Some time since, while glancing through the columns of Clayton's newsy weekly, On the St. Lawrence, I lighted upon a brief article which at once engrossed my attention. At this date I cannot give more than the substance of the sketch, having mislaid the clipping made at the time; but if my memory serves me it was headed: "The Tragedy of Maple Island;" at all events, if not this in exact terms, it conveyed the idea so forcibly that I read and re-read the article, vainly trying to recall something that I had read before, which in a vague, shadowy way seemed connected with it. The substance of the article in question is as follows:

In the summer of 1865, in the early part of June, a stranger made his appearance at the hotel in the little hamlet of Fisher's Landing, on the east bank of the St. Lawrence river, below Round Island, and opposite Thousand Island Park, which at that time had no existence. It was a singular fact that although he gave a name, which is not now remembered, he never signed the hotel register.

He was a broad-shouldered, dark-haired man, moustache and goatee, genteelly dressed, evidently not more than twenty-five years of age, probably less; of very agreeable manners, but very reticent, and with the characteristics of a Southerner. He spent his time chiefly in looking about the country, visiting, at times, the little village of Omar, and rowing in a skiff among the adjoining islands. He finally announced his intention of erecting a cabin on one of the islands, the better to enjoy his favorite pastime of fishing. He selected Maple Island as his place of residence, and at Clayton he purchased lumber and all the necessary materials for the structure, hired them transported to the island, engaged workmen to build it, bought a skiff with its outfit, and the furniture necessary for housekeeping, and in a short time occupied his island domicile. His food supplies — bread, butter, eggs, milk and vegetables — were obtained from farmers on Grindstone Island, and his groceries from Clayton. He made no intimate acquaintances, though, if a chance caller visited him, which was but seldom, he was treated courteously, but never invited to repeat the call. He was known to have quite a store of books, and to amuse himself by playing upon the violin, as the strains of one were often heard proceeding from his cabin, which stood in a dense thicket against a wall of rock, and so hidden that it could not be seen from a passing skiff. The summer months sped away, and so quiet and undemonstrative was the stranger that he would have been almost entirely forgotten but for his semi-occasional visits to Clayton for supplies.

Very early in the autumn, and it may have been during the last days of August, several strangers made their appearance on the river, stopping for a time at Alexandria Bay, at Fisher's Landing, and at Clayton. As it was nothing unusual to see strangers at these places, no especial notice was taken of them further than that they all seemed to be Southerners. But for subsequent events, this would not have been remarked, as it was by no means an unusual thing for Southerners to visit the Thousand Islands, prominent even then as a resort for those who affected the rod and gun.

But an event took place which arrested the attention and aroused the sympathy of the people; a bloody mystery, which to-day is almost as great a mystery as ever, and one which will, in all probability, never be fully solved, until the day when all mysteries shall be made clear.

It was in September; the loveliest month on the St. Lawrence. As the poet Reade, sings:—

"The season where the light of dreams
Around the year in golden glory lies;—
The heavens are full of floating mysteries,
And down the lake the veiled splendor beams!
Like hidden poets lie the hazy streams,
Mantled with mysteries of their own romance,
While scarce a breath disturbs their drowsy trance."

It was on such an evening that a bright light was seen by residents of Clayton, on Maple Island. It was conjectured at once that the Hermit's cabin had caught fire, but as it was impossible to reach him in time to be of any assistance, and apprehending no personal danger to him, but little thought was given to the occurrence; further than that he was expected to come ashore for lodgings at a hotel; but as he did not come within a reasonable time, it was thought that he had rowed over to Grindstone Island, or down to Grenell's tavern, which stood where the Pullman Hotel now stands, and so nothing more was thought of the matter that night.

The next morning, some fishermen went ashore on Maple Island, and visited the spot where the cabin stood. They saw at once that something unusual had occurred. The ground was tramped as with many feet. Evidences of a desperate struggle were on every hand. Traces of blood were found on the bushes, and then robbery and murder was suspected. A careful search was instituted, and finally the body of the unfortunate occupant was found near the water's edge, on the lower end of the island. His throat was cut from ear to ear, and a knife thrust had nearly severed the heart. There was no clothing on the body except a pair of drawers, and across the breast three crosses were cut in a triangle, one cross forming its apex, and two its base. To the discovers of the body, these had no especial significance. They saw nothing beyond plain murder and robbery. It might have been stated before, that the deceased was known to have plenty of money. He had always been a prompt and liberal paymaster, and whenever it had been necessary, owing to a lack of American money, he had offered English gold in payment for his purchases; and so, that he was murdered solely for his money, was the prevailing idea, and no significance attached to the crosses; and yet, these and these alone, furnished the clew which has nearly succeeded in tracing out the mystery.

The coroner was summoned, and after a patient examination, the principal facts as above stated were brought out, and a verdict rendered accordingly. The body was decently buried, the occurrence created a "nine day's wonder," and then passed out of mind; and but for the meager statement in the newspaper referred to, it would have never been revived, as there is to-day but one or two persons living who had an actual knowledge of the facts above stated. It must not be supposed that the newspaper article contained a tenth part of what is already related. It was by close and persistent search and careful inquiry, that these additional facts were gleaned, and they are presented here as a reason for, and an introduction to, what follows:

It was the month of April, 1865. The nation was jubilant. The long and bloody conflict had closed, and joy reigned triumphant everywhere. The country was ablaze with bonfires, and grand illuminations turned night into day. The evening splendors of the National Capital were unsurpassed, and the grand illuminations were made still more gorgeous by the display of fireworks. Bands of music serenaded the President, whose congratulatory speeches it seemed to many were tinged with a shade of melancholy. But a day was at hand; a day of gloom, and of darkness, and of woe, unparalleled in the history of the world. Were it not necessary, by reason of their being an important factor in this narrative, the sad events which plunged a nation into mourning and lamentation would not be here rehearsed. The inexpressible sadness which pervaded every countenance at the news of the assassination of Abraham Lincoln, was an index to the heartfelt pain within; and even now, though thirty years have rolled into the dim and misty past, I am unable to recall the terrible event, much less to transcribe, however briefly, its salient features, without experiencing again that fearful shock, which, like an electric current laden with woe and draped with disaster, ran from man to man and from camp to camp throughout our lines at Raleigh, where the corps to which the writer belonged was stationed. It was the same everywhere. All nature seemed clad in the habiliments of woe.

On the evening of the 14th day of April, 1865, the play "Our American Cousin" was in progress at Ford's Theater, on Tenth street, just above E street, Washington, D. C.; a large, plain brick edifice, now converted into a museum of war relics. In honor of the occasion and of the day's rejoicing, because the folds of the Nation's Flag had that day been once again flung to the breeze above the shattered ramparts of Fort Sumter, President Lincoln was to occupy the "Presidential box," which consisted of the two upper boxes on the left of the stage thrown into one. The box on that memorable evening was occupied by the President and Mrs. Lincoln, Major R. H. Rathbone and Miss Clara H. Harris. The house, holding nearly three thousand people, was filled with the wealth and fashion of the city.

At about 10 o'clock, when the second scene of the third act was on, a stranger worked his way into the proscenium box occupied by the Presidential party, and leveling a pistol close to the head of Mr. Lincoln, he fired; then drawing a knife he inflicted a severe wound upon Major Rathbone, who had seized him, and breaking away he sprang down upon the stage, flourished his knife and shouted: "Sic Semper Tyrannis!" and before the real position of affairs could be comprehended, he dashed across the stage, mounted a fleet horse, which was in waiting in the alley in the rear of the theater, and escaped.

That man was John Wilkes Booth, notoriously a rebel, an actor of some merit, but now an escaping murderer.

As soon as the audience realized the fact that the President was shot, the wildest excitement prevailed, and shouts of Hang him! Hang him! resounded from every part of the house. The dying President was borne to a private house — Mr. Peterson's, across the street — and prominent physicians and surgeons were summoned at once. It was soon discovered that there was no hope. Members of the cabinet assembled, together with other distinguished men, and stood mournfully grouped about the couch of the unconscious chief magistrate. An eye witness wrote thus: "The scene was one of extraordinary solemnity. The history of the world furnishes no parallel. Breathing his life serenely away, sensible to no pain and unconscious of all around, the Great Man of the nineteenth century lay, passing away to that immortality accorded by Providence to few of earth."

All the long, weary night the watchers stood around the couch. Day came at length, and at twenty-two minutes past seven o'clock on Saturday morning, April 15th, 1865, the spirit of Abraham Lincoln, freed from its earthly tenement, went to God who gave it, and the nation went into mourning.

It had been remarked that Secretary Seward was not among the members of the Cabinet who rallied around the bedside of their dying Chief; but when Surgeon-General Barnes reached the house, the reason was made clear. In substance, this is what happened to Surgeon-General Barnes: He was met in front of Willard's Hotel by an officer, on the night of the assassination, who informed him that the President was shot. Supposing that the deed had been done at the presidential mansion, he hurried to the surgeon-general's office to give orders for assistance, and there he found a summons to the bedside of Secretary Seward, who had also been attacked by an assassin. Believing that this occurrence was what gave rise to the story that the President was shot, he immediately hurried to the chamber of Mr. Seward. He found him lying upon the bed with one cheek cut open, and the flesh lying over on the pillow. The room presented a horrible appearance. Blood bespattered everything. The attendants were huddled into corners, frightened and helpless. No one seemed capable of giving a single detail of the terrible occurrence. Dr. Barnes immediately gave his attention to Mr. Seward, but shortly Dr. Norris came, and turning Mr. Seward over to his care, the surgeon-general proceeded to look after the assistant secretary, Mr. Frederick Seward, who was lying wounded and insensible in an adjoining room. Soon after, other surgeons came in, and from them he learned the distressing facts regarding the assassination of the President, and went at once to his bedside.

However strange it may seem to us of to-day, as we read the various and voluminous accounts of those occurrences, yet it is a fact, that not for several days afterward, did any one seem to grasp the idea that it was a preconcerted scheme of assassination — a concerted plot to take not only the life of the President, but of other prominent men also.

The one great overshadowing crime seemed to literally draw all attention to itself. Other transactions were dwarfed by it. Even the history of nations could produce no equal. True, Brutus slew Cæsar in the Roman Senate chamber, and Charlotte Corday murdered Murat in his bath; but neither instance paralleled this unheard of atrocity.

Gradually, however, as events began to unfold themselves, and the horizon of disturbance to clear, it was seen that the assassination was a part of a well-devised scheme, the only part, which, owing to some cause or causes unknown, had been carried into full effect. It soon became known also that the Metropolitan police had long been aware that a society called the Knights of the "Blue Gauntlet," the same in all essentials as that of the "Knights of the Golden Circle," existed in Washington; and they not only knew its place of meeting, but the names of many of the members. Not deeming it at all dangerous, but little attention had been paid to it, because the secrets of the "Knights of the Golden Circle," or rather the "Sons of Liberty," that being the real name of the organization, had become known, through the address of Timothy Webster, one of the most daring and skillful members of the secret service ever in the employ of the United States government; and who was captured in Richmond, tried, convicted and hanged as a spy by the orders of Gen. Winder, April 29, 1862.

A brief account of Webster's initiation into the secret society of the "Sons of Liberty" in the city of Baltimore, in 1861, may be given here as an illustration of the general character of the secret societies of that time, whose object was to aid the cause of the South, no matter under what name they masqueraded. Webster, it should be understood, had so ingratiated himself into the good graces of leading secessionists in Baltimore, that there was not the slightest suspicion afloat regarding him. On the contrary, he was so implicitly trusted that he visited unquestioned all parts of the South, making long visits to Richmond, where he was "Hail fellow, well met!" with prominent rebels, and their trusted agent in Washington, where they frequently sent him with important dispatches, the answers to which were to be delivered to the authorities in Richmond; but which, it is needless to say, reached other hands than those of Judah P. Benjamin, the rebel Secretary of War, for whom many of them were intended. Among other prominent rebels in Baltimore was one Sloan, a noted rebel, with whom Webster was on the most intimate terms. During Webster's absence on one of his southern trips, certain secessionists of Baltimore organized a secret society of which they were very desirous that he should become a member, and to Sloan, because he was an intimate friend, was delegated the duty of soliciting him to join. Seizing a favorable opportunity on Webster's return to the city, Sloan guardedly broached the subject.

"The fact is," said Sloan, "after you went away we formed a secret society."

"A secret society?"

"Yes; and we have held several meetings."

"Is it a success?"

"A perfect success. Some of the best in the town are among our members. We may be forced to keep silent, but they can't compel us to remain idle. We are well organized, and we mean undying opposition to a tyrannical government. I tell you, Webster, we will not down!"

"Never!" responded Webster, imitating the boastful tone and bearing of his friend Sloan. "It does not lie in the power of those white-livered Yankees to make slaves of Southern men! I should like to become a member of your society, Sloan."

"They all want you," said Sloan, eagerly. "We passed a resolution to that effect at our last meeting. We want the benefit of your counsel and influence."

"What is the name of your society?"

"The Sons of Liberty."

"When will your next meeting be held?"

"To-night."

"So soon?"

"Yes; and you are expected to attend. Have you any objections?"

"None whatever. But how will I get there?"

"I am delegated to be your escort."

"What is your hour of meeting?"

"Twelve o'clock."

"Ah! A midnight affair. All right, Sloan, you will find me waiting at the hotel."

Promptly at eleven o'clock Sloan appeared at the hotel, whence he and Webster proceeded toward the place of meeting. It was a dark and stormy night, and, as Webster thought, just the right sort of a night for concocting hellish plots and the performance of evil deeds. As Robert Burns says:

"That night, a chiel might understand,
The Deil had business on his hand."

Sloan led the way to a remote quarter of the city, and into a street which bore a particularly bad reputation. Stopping, he said:

"I must blindfold you, Webster, before proceeding any further. This is a rule of the order, which, under any circumstance, cannot be departed from."

Webster quietly submitted, and a thick bandage was placed over his eyes and securely fastened. Then Sloan took him by the arm and led him forward. Blindfolded as he was, Webster knew that they turned suddenly into an alley and passed through a gate which Sloan shut behind them. He also knew that they were in a paved court, probably in the rear of some building. Just then Sloan whispered:

"Come this way and make no noise."

The next moment he knocked in a peculiar manner against a door, and Webster knew it to be a signal. Immediately a guarded voice asked:

"Are you white?"

Sloan responded: "Down with the blacks."

A chain clanked inside, a bolt was withdrawn, the door creaked slightly on its rusty hinges, and they entered; immediately they began to climb a thickly carpeted stair, at the head of which they were challenged:

"Halt! Who comes there?"

"Long live Jeff Davis," answered Sloan.

Passing through another door, they entered an apartment in which there seemed to be several persons. A voice, meant to be impressive, demanded:

"Whom have we here?"

"A friend, Most Noble Chief, who wishes to become a member of this worthy league."

"His name?"

"Timothy Webster."

"Have the objects of this league been fully explained to him?"

"Most Noble Chief, they have."

"Mr. Webster, is it your desire to become a member of this knightly band?"

"It is."

Then came the ring of swords leaping from scabbards, and their clank as they met in an arch of steel above his head; and then the Noble Chief continued:

"You will now kneel upon your right knee, place your right hand upon your heart, and repeat after me the obligation of our brotherhood."

"I, Timothy Webster, a citizen of Baltimore, having been fully informed of the objects of this Association, and being in full sympathy and accord with the cause it seeks to advance, do solemnly declare and affirm, upon my sacred honor, that I will keep forever secret all that I may see or hear, in consequence of being a member of this league; that I will implicitly obey all orders, and faithfully discharge all duties assigned to me, no matter of what nature or character they may be; and that life or death will be held subordinate to the success and advancement of the cause of the Confederacy, and of the defeat of the bloody tyrants who are striving to rule by oppression and terrorism. Should I fail in the proper performance of any task imposed upon me, or should I prove unfaithful to the obligations I now assume, may I suffer the severest penalty awarded for treason and cowardice, and the odium belonging thereto, as well as the scorn and contempt of all true brother knights."

Again the swords clanked as they were returned to their scabbards, and the newly obligated member was commanded to arise. He obeyed, and the bandage was removed. At first he was blinded by the sudden light, but as his eyes became accustomed to it, he found himself surrounded by several stalwart men, all of whom wore dark cloaks and black masks.

"Mr. Webster," said the Chief, "I now pronounce you a Son of Liberty."

The masks were now removed, and to his relief, Webster discovered that the faces were all familiar. A cordial grasp of the hand was given by each in turn, and then they entered the principal council chamber, and Webster was escorted to a seat. In a few minutes the clock struck twelve, when every door was locked, and the real work of the order begun. There were some forty men present, and Webster noticed that they were from among the best citizens of Baltimore, the rowdy element not being represented. He was now instructed in the passes, signs and grips of the order, and especially in the rallying sign, which was three crosses, disposed in a triangle.

It is not necessary to say more under this head, our only design being to give the reader a brief sketch of the so often denied secret society of the South, which in time, by the aid of Clement L. Vallandingham, of Ohio, permeated the entire North, and which, but for a fortunate circumstance that took place in the city of Indianapolis in 1863, would have resulted in fire and bloodshed throughout several of the Northern States, and which years later found an individual culmination in a bloody tragedy on an obscure island in the Great River St. Lawrence.

Suffice it to say that in this case Webster listened to the schemes which were in preparation to destroy our National Capital, learned the names of the plotters and sympathizers in Washington, and in process of time so managed matters that this particular camp of the Sons of Liberty found itself immured behind the bars of the Old Capitol Prison.

As a further instance, it may be interesting to know that a shrewd detective, who is yet living, and whose name it is unnecessary to mention here, was sent from Cincinnati to Louisville, Kentucky, by order of Gen. George B. McClellan, for the purpose of uniting with the Brotherhood, in order that he might learn its secrets, methods of work, designs and plans, which he fully accomplished, being initiated, as a comparison of dates shows, at Louisville, only two nights later than was Webster at Baltimore. The initiatory ceremonies, grips, signs, passes and signals were found to be identical.

The Knights of the "Blue Gauntlet" had no names. The individual members were known only by numbers; and any order or direction from the Chief was always sent to a number and not to a name. With this, and a few other minor differences, the Sons of Liberty and the Knights of the Blue Gauntlet were the same. All this was known to the police, but never for a moment was there the slightest danger apprehended, so powerless for any real harm did the organization appear. That it was not more closely investigated, and entirely broken up, was a fatal mistake; realized when too late to be remedied. In fact, it had been but little more than a year since these secret meetings had been revived, and then more as a political factor than any thing else. To prevent the nomination and re-election of Abraham Lincoln was a consummation ardently desired by the friends of the Confederacy. With him no longer at the head of the government, a compromise would be effected, the war ended, and virtually victory would perch upon the flag of the South.

But from this semi-passive political position to one more pronounced was easy. All that was wanted was a leader. A man who, within himself, combined all the elements,— a strong will, unlimited zeal, unbounded enthusiasm, a strong personal magnetism, and a blind, unreasoning devotion to a cause whether right or wrong, coupled with an overwhelming desire for notoriety. Such a leader they found in John Wilkes Booth. . As affording a slight insight into his character, an extract of a letter to the Washington Chronicle, written after the assassination, by A. D. Doty, of Albany, a soldier then in Carver hospital, Washington, is here given. He says: "At the commencement of the war, J. Wilkes Booth was playing an engagement at the Gayety Theater in Albany, N. Y., which city attested in action more eloquent than words its love for the old flag by displaying it from every roof and window, when the news came of the unholy attack on Fort Sumter. Booth, at that time, openly and boldly avowed his admiration for the rebels and their deeds, which he characterized as the most heroic of modern times; and he boasted loudly that the Southern leaders knew how to defend their rights, and that they would never submit to oppression. So vehement and incautious was he in his expressions, that the people became incensed and threatened him with personal violence, and he was compelled to make a hasty departure from the city. Before leaving, he attempted the life of an actress of whom he had become jealous. Finding his way to her room at midnight, he assaulted her with a dagger, fortunately inflicting but a slight wound. With the fury of a tigress she sprang upon him, and wrenching the weapon from his hand, in turn wounded him."

These episodes show that he was not only a virulent rebel, but was at heart an assassin. Not only was Booth a murderer, but he was a mercenary one. While he was willing to assassinate the President, he wanted pay for doing it. Notoriety it would bring, but with it he wanted gold.

All along during the war, and especially in the years 1863 and 1864, Canada's principal cities swarmed with Southerners. St. Catharines, Toronto, Kingston, Ottawa and Montreal, were especially favored by these gentlemen; some of whom were accredited agents of the Confederacy, while they were all engaged in plotting against the North, and setting schemes on foot worthy the palmiest days of Diabolus, for the destruction of our lake cities in the absence of their defenders who were fighting against treason and rebellion on Southern soil.

It has been already hinted that the secret order of the Knights of the Golden Circle had found a lodgement in some of the Northern States, especially in the States of New York, Indiana and Illinois; though Pennsylvania and Ohio were largely represented in their councils. In Michigan, Wisconsin and Iowa, the lodges were but few and far between. It was in Indiana and Illinois, that their great strength lay. In the former State there were 100,000 armed and organized knights, ready to do the bidding of their chiefs. These were in constant communication with the Southern emissaries who, under the protection of Canada, plotted treason, laid plans to capture steamers on the lakes and on the St. Lawrence river, fill them with armed men, and simultaneously descend upon Rochester, Buffalo, Detroit, Cleveland and Chicago, and firing them, rob, pillage, and murder, escaping to Canada as a place of safety. It was among the Confederate residents of Canada that the diabolical scheme was set on foot to scatter small pox throughout the cities of the North by means of infected rags.

While Indiana, under the magnetic inspiration of that greatest among the great war Governors, Oliver P. Morton, responded with alacrity to every demand upon her for troops, to an extent far beyond her quotas, sending to the front, as a matter of fact, more men in proportion to her population than any other State in the Union, she was also cursed to a much greater extent with that abhorred product of the rebellion, the "Copperhead;" who was also, whenever the opportunity offered, a Knight of the Golden Circle. It has been already stated that they numbered a hundred thousand. It is no wild statement. It can be verified by the muster rolls of the order, captured in Indianapolis, and now preserved in the archives of the State. A brief allusion to the facts, will refresh the memory of many of our readers, while the incident may be of some interest.

In 1863-4, Indianapolis was a great military camp. Sentries were stationed everywhere. The air was rife with rumors of an uprising in various portions of the State. The camps around the city were more closely guarded than ever. Emissaries of those inimical to the government had secretly poisoned the minds of many of the soldiers, and desertions were frequent. These were concealed in almost inaccessible places and carefully guarded against recapture. Bands of Southern sympathizers drilled openly in the fields. United States marshals were set upon by infuriated mobs, maltreated and murdered. Every citizen went armed. Fearful rumors of an impending outbreak permeated the community, but when, or how, or from what source the blow was to come, none could tell. Surmise was the only certainty. A sentry on duty at the Union depot was watching the unloading from a car a mass of boxes. They were consigned to Dodd & Co., merchants, at whose store was the "Repository of the American Bible Society," and these boxes were supposed to contain Bibles for distribution among the soldiers. One of the boxes was slightly shattered by the rough handling it received at the hands of those who were unloading the freight. A bit of metal gleaming through a crevice in the broken box attracted the soldier's attention.

"Nice lot of books them," he said to himself. "Silver plated Bibles, I reckon. Pretty durn tony them tract peddlers is gittin. Guess I'll have a look at one of 'em, anyhow."

A brief investigation revealed to the soldier the startling fact that the box contained revolvers. It suddenly occurred to him that he had heard that the firm of Dodd & Co. were suspected of being rebel sympathizers, though by no means outspoken. Unlearned, but with a shrewdness worth more in a case like this than all the diplomas ever issued from college halls, he at once decided how to act. Not a word did he breathe to his sergeant, nor to the officer of the guard. He saw clearly that it was a case requiring judgment, and yet promptness. Calling a comrade, he was about to send him to the General's headquarters with a note, when fortunately the General and two or three members of his staff came riding down Illinois avenue. As they neared his post, he saluted and then called to the General. In a few words he made known his discovery. The General dismounted and made a personal examination, satisfying himself that the statement was true. Sending for the officer of the guard, he ordered him to count the boxes and affix a private mark to each one, and then note carefully who came for them. Mounting his horse, he returned to headquarters.

By and by draymen came for the boxes, and, strangely enough, with every dray load that moved away, there loitered along on the opposite side of the street a lazy unconcerned looking citizen who always had business in the same direction the dray was going. The goods were unloaded in the rear of Dodd & Co.'s store, transferred to an elevator and sent above. Over this store, and three stores adjoining, in the third story, was an immense empty chamber which had never been utilized. It was one vast unfinished garret, as every one supposed.

There were times when early in the morning bits of paper, on which three crosses in a triangular form had been printed, were found pasted to fences, trees and tree boxes, or scattered loosely about; and so often did this occur that it was accepted as a sign — but a sign of what?

The next morning after the boxes were hoisted to the upper story of Dodd & Co.'s store, those triangular emblems were more numerous than ever before. So were the lazy men in citizen's clothes. They were disreputable men, too, because they were frequently seen to gather, two or three at a time, in the alley in the rear of the store, and drink from a bottle and then disappear. That night was a great business night for Dodd & Co. The store was thronged and never before were clerks so busy. Even the lazy citizen was there, having overcome his indolence so far as to make some slight purchases. Not having anything himself to do, he noticed what others were doing; and, among other things, he noticed that instead of going out the way they came in, that is to say, by the front door, they went out at the back door; slipped out, so to speak, singly; and, it seemed to him, as if desirous of not being observed. It also seemed to him that he could hear the noise of the elevator at work. A careful investigation showed that it was at work, and that the customers were going into the story above, probably to complete their purchases!

Be that as it may, a couple of hours later, all the lower part of the store was filled with soldiers, both front and rear, and squad after squad went up in the elevator, and then came the grand climax. The boxes of Bibles consigned to Dodd & Co. were found as marked and numbered. They were packed with navy revolvers and ammunition. But this was the least important of the capture. This turned out to be the general headquarters of the order for the State. In this room the Adjutant-General had his office. The rolls and reports of the order were found. The names of the members of every camp of the Knights of the Golden Circle in the State were there. It was a revelation. Men against whom not a breath of suspicion had ever found utterance, here stood revealed as officials high in the secret councils of treason. Correspondence with Jacob Thompson, Clement C. Clay and Larry McDonald, then in Canada as accredited agents of the Confederacy, was discovered; but over and above everything else, a plot to burn the cities already mentioned, and the time when a general rising was to take place, all was revealed. The conspirators stood aghast, with no word of excuse to offer. Under a strong guard they were marched away to the jail and to the military prison, and by early morning two Major-Generals of the order, one in La Fayette, and another in Evansville, together with several Brigadiers and Colonels, a score or more, were under arrest, and on their way by the first trains to the Capital City. Dodd, Horsey and Mulligan, the Bible operators, were tried among the rest, and in a few weeks there were no spare casemates in Fort La Fayette, and the Dry Tortugas was crowded. From that time a great fear fell upon the Knights of the Golden Circle in Indiana. Their collapse was as complete as it was sudden. Here and there in the strongest copperhead localities, an attempt was made to revive the order under new names, but it was a signal failure. It is a pleasure to be able to record the fact that the soldier who first discovered the "silver plated Bibles" was promptly promoted. His coolness and self-command at the time of the discovery made the detection of the conspirators certain. Had he been less shrewd, and informed his sergeant or lieutenant, the chances are that the find would have been known throughout the city in an hour; the evening paper would have displayed glaring headlines, and the chance to entrap the Knights of the Golden Circle would have been lost.

In the meantime, Chicago, Cleveland, Buffalo and other lake and river cities were warned, and had taken measures for their own safety. The Confederate plotters in Canada saw at a glance that the game was up. The chances of capturing steamers on the lakes, and transforming them into quasi vessels of war, were utterly destroyed; and so they turned themselves to the consideration of new schemes. They began to despair of conquering the North, and as a recompense for defeat they nourished revenge. Gradually this desire grew into a discussion as to ways and means, and finally led to the consideration of a method of relief for the South, which, could it be carried into effect, would be the crowning scheme of all. This was the assassination of Lincoln, Johnson, Seward, Grant, Sherman and Sheridan, and as many other prominent officers and men of affairs as could be reached and struck down at the same hour, through concerted action. This done, the South must be victorious. Visions of place and power in the future to those who could conceive and execute this daring scheme fired their ambition, and personal aggrandizement, more than pro patria, urged them on. But a tool must be found, and they had not far to look.

John Wilkes Booth was starring in Canada, and to him they instinctively turned. During his engagement in Toronto, a meeting took place at the Queen's Hotel. Booth knew enough about these men and some others then in Canada, not to be surprised at any scheme they might propose. Already they had perpetrated acts of villainy that if even half punished, would expatriate them for life. On the other hand they knew the man before them. They had fathomed his inordinate vanity, and well knew his sordid ambition. They ministered to the one, and made promises which, if fulfilled, would abundantly gratify the other. They assured him that the success of the scheme depended upon himself alone. That, if successful, unbounded wealth and fame to gratify the most ambitious would be his.

At first, Booth hesitated at the idea of wholesale murder. Another scheme had entered his fertile brain, and until that failed, there should be no murder; but if it failed, then— The plan was to kidnap the President and as many others as could be taken, gag them, convey them to a safe retreat, and when an opportunity offered, transfer them to the rebel capital. All these facts are substantiated by evidence on file in the government archives at Washington, among which is a letter written by Booth which reveals the entire scheme. The discovery of a house on —— street in Washington, with furnished underground apartments provided with manacles, and all the accessories of solitary confinement, is evidence indisputable. In an upper room of the same building the Knights of the Blue Gauntlet held their secret meetings, and finally plotted murder.

Throughout all his base designs the dramatic element in Booth was always uppermost. He planned a triumphal starring trip throughout the South. Full of this idea, he shipped his theatrical wardrobe from Canada, and when his plans had been successfully carried out, he would don the buskin once more, and become a theatrical star of the first magnitude, though his crime rather than his ability as an actor, should prove the drawing card. If assassination, which he now began to seriously contemplate, should be the final outcome of all this damnable plotting, what a Brutus he would become. That immortal creation of Shakspeare, Julius Cæsar, should be so modified, that Washington would become Rome, and Abraham Lincoln, Cæsar. Payne, and Atzeroth, and Surratt, and Harold, and half a score of others of a like character should be the grand conspirators, while he, the chief conspirator of all, the head, the director, the murderer par excellence, would be the Brutus. How realistic it would all be. A great Shaksperean tragedy, only modified in some particulars to adapt it to time and circumstance, played by a troupe whose leading characters were real assassins! What a triumph of the Thespian art! What a modern histrionic success! One thing only was lacking. Were it but possible to assassinate a veritable Lincoln at every presentation of the play, nothing more could be desired.

Booth soon discovered that his scheme of kidnapping could not be carried out. It was deemed too rash. He could find no one who would engage in the hazardous undertaking. Something must be done to satisfy, first, his own egotistic ambition, and, second, to earn the guerdon of blood, an earnest of which, in English gold, he had already received at the hands of his employers, the Confederate agents of the South.

Now he began to plan in earnest the villainous scheme of assassination. Furnished with abundant funds, he dropped an anchor to windward by depositing four hundred and fifty-five dollars, his own money, in the Bank of Ontario, at Montreal. This, with date of entry, was shown by his bank book, which was captured with Atzeroth.

Then came a search for the proper tools. Along the eastern boundary of Kentucky, bordering on Virginia, in a region of hills and mountains almost inaccessible, is a section of country which, for years, has been the home of family feuds, which have resulted in numerous murders, and, consequently in the growth of a class of men who held life very cheap, and to whom a bloody vendetta was but a recreation. In the midst of such associations, seven brothers, named Payne, had grown up. They were outlaws born, robbers by profession, and murderers from choice, though the sons of a Christian minister. So bold had they become, and so bloody their raids, especially on the homes of those mountaineers suspected of favoring the Union, that at length troops were sent into their neighborhood with instructions to kill or capture them. It was a cavalry force under the lead of an officer only too well disposed to carry out his instructions. The father was captured and imprisoned, and the sons made their escape. Three of them went to South America, and four of them to Florida, and thence to Canada. Two of them were engaged in the St. Albans raid, one escaped, and the other, Lewis Payne, under the assumed name of Wood, and by the direction of the Confederate agents in Canada, reported to Booth in Washington, where, later on, he was joined by John A. Payne, one of his brothers, whom he had left in Canada. Here, then, is a list of conspirators, all of whom have joined the Knights of the Blue Gauntlet—Booth, the two Paynes, one of whom was known as Wood, John H. Surratt, Sam Arnold, McLaughlin, Harold, John Lloyd, and several others, who took the alarm and escaped in time to avoid arrest.

The assassination of Murat by Charlotte Corday, of Normandy, is one of the conspicuous instances on record, that a woman may become an assassin; and even though we may applaud and justify her act, yet it was assassination; and because it was at the hands of a woman, its dramatic effect was increased tenfold. Keeping the dramatic effect in view, Booth determined to have a woman in this case, and it was not long before he became acquainted with the very person he needed.

Ten miles from Washington, in Prince George's county, Maryland, was a little cross-roads hamlet called Surrattsville. The principal property there was a hotel; one of the fine old Southern hostelries which, when in the right hands, was as complete a home as a temporary stopping place can be made to be. The owner gave his name to the village and his property to his wife, and died peaceably, as a good landlord should. The wife carried on the hotel business for a while and then rented the property to one John Lloyd, removing with her son and several daughters to Washington. Early in the conflict, Surrattsville became a rebel post-office, and Mrs. Surratt a post-mistress. When she removed to Washington, John Lloyd looked after the mails. In renting her hotel, Mrs. Surratt reserved apartments for her own use whenever she chose to visit Surrattsville. Mrs. Surratt was a large, masculine woman, always self-possessed, and in her way, as dangerous a rebel as was ever Belle Boyd or Rose Greenhow. John Wilkes Booth could not have found a fitter agent in all Washington, and at her house in the city and her rooms in the country tavern Booth was ever welcome, and there treason took definite shape.

After the preliminaries had all been settled, a plan of escape was to be devised. To this end, Booth took a trip on horseback through lower Maryland as far as Leonardstown, professing to purchase land, but in reality to mark on his map every spot and place, and every road and crossing which might in the near future become useful. He had provided himself with one of the maps which was published for the rebel government by a copperhead firm in Buffalo, N. Y., but which was not full enough for his purposes, and so he made the needed corrections after personal examination.

The conspiracy made no undue haste. All the influence thereto was absorbed by Booth and Mrs. Surratt. He was the chief plotter and she his main stay. Even among the principals, assassination, though agreed upon, was never referred to except by implication. To have openly spoken of murder among themselves and in their most secret consultations, would not have been tolerated for a moment. It was against the canons of polite society. In this society Booth was at home; he was supreme; cool, vigilant and plausible; the chief command was easily accorded him, and he felt himself great in intellectual stature. Mrs. Surratt was too shrewd to embroil any member of her family in the conspiracy; and so it happened that young Surratt, though fully cognizant of everything, was sent north by his mother a day before the assassination. For a year or more he had been employed as a clerk in the office of the Commissary-General of Prisoners. He was a prominent member of the Knights of the Blue Gauntlet, and treasurer of the camp.

An extract or two from a letter of his to a cousin residing in New York, may be of interest:

"OFFICE OF THE COMMISSARY-GENERAL OF PRISONERS,
WASHINGTON, D. C., Feb. 6, 1865.

'MISS BELLE SEAMAN:

"DEAR COUSIN,—I received your letter, and not being quite so selfish as you are, I will answer it in what I call a reasonable time. I am happy to say that we are all well and in fine spirits. We have been looking for you to come on, with a great deal of impatience. Do come, won't you? Just to think, I have never yet seen one of my cousins. But never fear, I will probably see you all sooner than you expect. Next week I leave for Europe, and may give you a call, as I go to New York. * * * I have just taken a peep in the parlor. Would you like to know what I saw there? Well, Ma was sitting on the sofa, nodding first to one chair, then another, and then the piano. Anna is sitting in a corner, dreaming, I expect, of J. W. Booth. Who is J. W. Booth? Well, she can answer that question. * * * But hark, the door-bell rings, and Mr. J. W. Booth, is announced. Just listen to the scampering. Such brushing and fixing. We all send love to you and family.

"Your Cousin,
"J. HARRISON SURRATT,
"541 H Street, between 6th and 7th streets."

Matters were now approaching a crisis. It was at first intended that the assassination should take place during the inauguration ceremonies, but it was finally decided to be too risky. When it became known that the President would appear in public at Ford's Theatre, the time for definite action was plain.

Booth's principal actors were now assigned their parts. John Harrison Surratt was to go north into Canada, and on hearing of the result, if all was right, he was to repair at once to Toronto and there claim the promised gold and make his way to Richmond. Atzeroth was to murder the Vice-president, Andrew Jackson; Lewis Payne, or Wood as he called himself, was to look after Seward; Sam Arnold and McLaughlin, were each to kill a cabinet officer, and John Lloyd, a general. John A. Payne, with two confederates, had gone to North Carolina to look after Sherman. Harold was the stage manager, and looked after the properties. Horses and arms were provided, and every possible avenue of escape cleared, even to cutting the telegraph wires around the city. On the very afternoon of the murder Mrs. Surratt visited Surrattsville and told John Lloyd to have the carbines which young Surratt had placed in his care, ready for immediate use, as they would be needed that night. Lloyd had sent his wife away on a visit. Three weeks before the murder, Harold told some friends that the next time they heard of him he would be in Spain; adding that there was "no extradition treaty with that country." John Lloyd told friends at Surrattsville that he would "make a barrel of money or that his neck would stretch." Atzeroth said in Port Tobacco, that if he "ever visited that place again he would be rich enough to buy it."

On that fateful Friday night Ford's Theater was crowded. Long before the curtain rose, the "Standing room only" card was displayed at the ticket office window. Near the door, the lobby was crowded. Booth went on the stage, and from behind the scenes looked searchingly over the audience. Suddenly near the door, a voice was heard. It said:

"Nine o'clock and forty-five minutes!"

The words were repeated by other voices until they reached the sidewalk. While people wondered, the voice said again:

"Nine o'clock and fifty minutes!"

This also passed on as before, and then — after an interval —

"Nine o'clock and fifty-five minutes!"

The life of the President was growing shorter by intervals of five minutes each. The bells in the clock towers tolled out ten o'clock. Why, they knew not, but a shudder crept through the audience.

"Ten o'clock and five minutes!"

Another interval. Then:

"Ten o'clock and ten minutes!"

At this instant Booth entered the door of the theater, and the men who had so faithfully repeated the murder-laden minutes scattered as though a messenger of Death had approached. Five minutes more and the deed was done.

At the same moment Payne was scattering blood from room to room in Secretary Seward's home. Having murdered Mr. Seward, as he thought, and but for Robinson, the nurse, it would have been an accomplished fact, he mounted his horse and attempted to find Booth and Harold, but the selfishness of crime was uppermost, and they had gone and left him to his fate. The city was alarmed, and he fled to the open country; when near Port Lincoln, on the Baltimore pike, his horse stumbled and threw him headlong. Half stunned and bewildered, he arose and resolving to return to the city, attempted to disguise himself.

He threw away his bloody coat, which was afterward found, and from a sleeve of his woolen undershirt he fashioned a rude cap, and then, plentifully daubing himself with mud and clay, and shouldering a pick which he found in the intrenchments near by, he started for Washington.

He reached Mrs. Surratt's door just as the officers were arresting her. He was taken into custody. He had come, he said, to dig a ditch for Mrs. Surratt, who had hired him. With all the effrontery of crime, Mrs. Surratt protested that she had never before seen the man, and that she had no ditch to dig. The officers washed Payne's hands and found them to be soft and tender as a woman's. In his pockets they found tooth and nail brushes, and a delicate pocket knife. Unusual toilet implements to be found on the person of a digger of ditches.

Atzeroth's room at the Kirkwood was directly over that of Vice-President Johnson. He was there to do murder, but the opportunity failed, and his courage also. He fled in such haste that he left his weapons, a bowie knife and revolver, between the mattresses of his bed. Booth's coat was found in his room, and in the pockets were riding gauntlets, boxes of cartridges, a map of Maryland, published in Buffalo, and corrected by his own hand, a spur, and a handkerchief marked with his mother's name. Atzeroth fled alone, and when captured was at the house of his uncle in Montgomery county, Maryland. Sam Arnold and McLaughlin grew faint hearted and ran away, without making the slightest attempt to carry out their part of the programme.

It was not until Thursday night that the real intentions of Booth became fully known to the Knights of the Blue Gauntlet. John H. Surratt, before leaving the city on Thursday morning, confided the facts to a brother Knight. Confusion and terror ensued, and many of the band hurriedly fled from the city, and those who remained kept themselves in seclusion. Booth, with his accustomed duplicity, had kept them in ignorance, leading them to believe that the plan of abduction was the one to be pursued. So frightened were they that the lodge room, with its paraphernalia, was left undisturbed, and with it the cells in the basement still furnished, in which condition they were found by officers later on. Canada was a refuge for Southern rebeldom, and thither they fled.

Booth and Harold met immediately after the murder, and sped away at a gallop past the Patent Office, up and over Capitol hill, and away to the bridge which crossed the Eastern branch at Uniontown, and at midnight they drew rein at Surrattsville. Harold dismounted, and entering the bar procured a bottle of whisky which he handed to Booth, and then rushing up stairs he brought down one of the carbines which had been left there by John H. Surratt. One only was taken. The other, left in the hall, was found by the officers. As they started off, Booth said to Lloyd: "We have murdered the President of the United States and the Secretary of State." Before sunrise on Saturday morning they reached the house of Dr. Mudd. Here Booth's injured leg, one of the bones of which was broken when he jumped down upon the stage at the theatre, was set. A link in the chain of evidence was left here; Booth's riding boot had to be cut to get it from his foot, and his name was written in the inside of the leg on the lining. It was not noticed, and so it remained there until found by the officers in pursuit; one of the clews which revealed the route of the fugitives. They were concealed at Dr. Mudd's during the day, but at night, mounting their horses, they rode away in the direction of Allen's Fresh. It was to Allen's Fresh that Lloyd had sent his wife on a visit to get her out of the way. By the aid of a negro, to whom they gave five dollars, they reached the house of one Sam Coxe, at midnight. Coxe was a notorious rebel, and though the fact could not be fully established, enough was learned to convince all who heard his examination that he was well aware of the conspiracy.

The negro, whose name was Swan, remained at Coxe's until they were ready to go, when he was to pilot them further on their road. Notwithstanding the fact that Swan had seen them eating and drinking, the refugees when they left the house swore bitterly at Coxe for his lack of hospitality. This was to blind the negro; for after they had ridden about five miles, they told him that they now knew the road, and would no longer have need of his services; and giving him five dollars more they rode on. But Swan was a shrewd negro, and so he watched them until he saw them turn back to Coxe's again, where they were harbored from Sunday until the next Thursday.

The next move of the fugitives was to cross the Potomac. This was a move of some danger. Friday evening a white man was seen to bring a canoe to the shore and anchor it with a stone. Between seven and eight o'clock the next morning it disappeared, and in the afternoon some workmen saw two men land in a canoe on the south side of the Potomac, and strike across a ploughed field toward King George Court House. One of the men walked with a crutch. Booth was provided with a crutch at the house of Dr. Mudd. They were next heard of at the Port Royal Ferry, and then at Garrett's house. Now, the long-persecuted Unionists of Lower Maryland began to come forward and give important testimony, which under threats and intimidation they never before dared to whisper. They told of the meetings of the conspirators at Lloyd's Hotel in Surrattsville, and then Lloyd was arrested, Booth's carbine found, and three days later Lloyd confessed. A little party of detectives under the untiring Lovett overhauled the residence of Dr. Mudd, where they found Booth's boots. This was before Lloyd confessed, and was the first positive evidence the officers had that they were upon the trail of the murderers. Much of the after success of the pursuit was due to the careful work done by this little squad of detectives.

A second party, under the charge of Major O'Beirne, now took the field. Through these the hiding place of Atzeroth was discovered, and he was arrested. With this party was Captain Beckwith, Gen. Grant's chief cipher operator, who tapped the wire at Point Lookout, and thus put the War Department in momentary communication with the theater of events. By this time the troops were assembling in various parts of the country in considerable numbers. Seven hundred men of the Eighth Illinois Cavalry, six hundred men of the Twenty-second Colored Volunteers and one hundred of the Sixteenth New York were patrolling the country by detachments, while Major O'Beirne and Col. Wells, with a force of cavalry and infantry, swept the entire peninsula with a line of skirmishers deployed in close intervals. Major O'Beirne, with his detectives, then crossed the Potomac and found where the fugitives had landed from the canoe on Boone's farm. This was another link in the chain which gave a clew to their route.

Now comes the chief of the secret service, Col. Lafayette Baker, on the scene. Absent from Washington at the time of the murder, he returned three days after, by order of Secretary Stanton, and engaged at once in the search for Booth. He possessed himself of all the War Department knew regarding the matter, and then acted. His first find was a negro who saw Booth and Harold when they crossed the Potomac.

Sending to General Hancock for twenty-five cavalrymen and an officer, Lieutenant Edward P. Doherty, he sat down to his maps to decide upon the probable route of the fugitives. He knew that they would not keep close to the coast owing to the difficulty in crossing swamps and rivers, nor would they take any direction leading east of Richmond, where they were likely at any time to strike our lines. He soon decided that they would be most likely to pass through Port Royal, and there he hoped to intercept them. The little force of cavalry detailed from Company G, 16th N. Y., under the command of Lieutenant Doherty, having reported, he placed them under the command of Lieutenant-Colonel Conger, of Ohio, and Lieutenant L. B. Baker, of New York, and sent them direct to Belle Plain, on the lower Potomac, from thence to scour the whole country north of Port Royal. Here they found a negro who had driven two men, in his wagon, a short distance toward Bowling Green. These men answered the description of the fugitives. The ferryman who took the party across the Rappahannock gave them information of the utmost importance, though wrung from him by threats. They learned that the two men were at that moment lying at the house of one Garrett, which they had passed some time before. Retracing their steps, the nearly exhausted cavalrymen reached Garrett's at two o'clock in the morning. It was a pale moonlight night. The plain old farmhouse was dimly seen through a locust grove. It stood about three hundred yards from the road, and behind it an old weather-beaten barn, some long corn cribs, and a cattle shed.

Entering the roadside gate, the troops rode up to the house. Lieutenant Doherty picketed the premises, and then rode up to a side entrance and rapped. An old man in his night clothes, with a candle in his hand, made his appearance. It was Garret.

"Where are the men who are staying with you?" asked Doherty.

"They are gone," he said. "They went to the woods this afternoon."

In the meantime a lad, John M. Garrett, had been found by one of Doherty's men in a corncrib. Questioned in earnest, he saw that evasion would not do, and at once revealed the fact that Booth and Harrold were asleep in the barn. Doherty had already threatened to search the house, and the women were up and dressed, but this news changed the programme.

The troops were dismounted and the barn surrounded. Baker hailed the persons inside, who could now be heard stirring.

Lieut. Baker called to them: "We are about to send in the son of the man in whose custody you are found. Surrender your arms to him, and give yourselves up or we will fire the place."

There was no answer. The door was opened and young Garret pushed inside, appealed to them to surrender. With an oath Booth said: "Get out of here. You have betrayed us." The boy slipped out again as the door was slightly opened, and reported that his errand had failed.

The summons was repeated by Baker. "You must surrender! Give up your arms and come out! There is no chance for escape. We give you ten minutes to make up your minds."

Then came the demand: "Who are you, and what do you want with us?"

Baker again said: "We want you to deliver up your arms and become our prisoners."

After a lapse of some minutes, Baker hailed again: "Well, we have waited long enough; come out and surrender, or we'll fire the barn."

Booth answered: "I am a cripple, a one-legged man. Withdraw your forces twenty-five paces from the door, and I will come. Give me a chance for my life. I will never be taken alive."

"We did not come here to fight, but to capture you. Surrender, or the barn will be fired," said Doherty.

"Well, then, my brave boys, prepare a stretcher for me," cried Booth.

Then there was a pause, during which a discussion between Booth and his companion was heard. Booth said, "Get away from me. You're a —— coward, and want to leave me in my distress; but go — go! I don't want you to stay — I won't have you stay!" Then he shouted: "There's a man inside here who wants to surrender."

Then Harold rattled at the door, and begged to be let out, saying, "I want to surrender."

"Hand out your arms, then," said Doherty.

"I have none."

"You are the man who carried the carbine yesterday; bring it out."

"I haven't got any." In a whining tone.

Booth then said: "On the word and honor of a man and a gentleman, he has no arms with him. They are mine, and I have them."

Harold came to the door, was seized and pulled out by Doherty, handcuffed and turned over to Corporal Newgarten.

Booth then made his last appeal. "Captain, give me a chance. Draw off your men and I will fight them singly. I could have killed you six times to-night, but I believe you to be a brave man, and would not murder you. Give a lame man a show."

It was too late for further parley. Before he had ceased to speak Colonel Conger slipped around to the rear of the barn, and drawing some loose straws through a crack set them on fire. They were dry and soon in a blaze lighting up every part of the great barn. At sight of the fire Booth dropped his crutch and carbine and crept on his hands and knees to the spot hoping to see the incendiary and shoot him down. Then he turned upon the fire as if to leap upon and extinguish it; but it had gained too much headway. Turning, he made for the door, resolved not to die alone, when Sergeant Boston Corbett, thinking that he was about to shoot Lieutenant Doherty, fired with the intention of hitting him in the arm, but instead of the arm the bullet struck him in the head, barely an inch from the spot where the assassin's bullet struck the murdered President.

It was first thought that he had shot himself. He fell into the arms of Lieutenant Doherty, who brought him out of the burning barn and laid him upon the grass. Water was brought and dashed upon his face, and he revived. He was then carried to the porch of the house and laid upon a mattress. Brandy and water was given him, and when able to speak he said: "Useless, useless." The soldiers extinguished the fire. Booth muttered "Kill me! Kill me!" Brandy was given him every minute, and the doctor who lived six miles away, arrived but could do nothing. Booth asked to have his hands raised so that he could see them; his arms were paralyzed, so that he knew not where they were. When they were shown him, he muttered: "Useless, useless!" They were his last words; applicable not only to his hands, but to his whole life. "Useless." And so he died. His remains were sewed up in a saddle blanket, placed in a rickety old wagon drawn by an ancient relic of a horse, and the march to Washington was begun. The arms found with him were a knife, a repeating carbine and a pair of revolvers. A diary, bills of exchange and Canada money were found on his person. Harold was mounted on a horse, his legs tied to the stirrups, and placed in charge of four men, and the cortege of retributive justice moved on.

"Though the mills of God grind slowly,
Yet they grind exceeding small;
Though with patience He stands waiting,
With exactness grinds He all."

Ferrying once more at Port Royal they pushed on for Belle Plain, reaching there about three o'clock in the afternoon, when they embarked for Washington, where a few only were permitted to see the corpse for the purpose of identification. That this should be complete, the Secretary of War directed Col. Baker to summon a number of witnesses residing in Washington who had previously known Booth. Six witnesses, who had for years known him intimately, were examined, and identified the remains. Surgeon-General Barnes cut from the neck about two inches of the spinal column through which the bullet had passed. This is in the Government Medical Museum in Washington, and is the only relic of the assassin's body in existence. No further mutilation of the remains took place in the slightest degree. Following the further instructions of the Secretary of War as to the disposition of the body, it was taken directly from the gunboat to the old penitentiary building adjoining the arsenal grounds, and there in a cell a large flat stone was raised from the floor, a rude grave dug, the body dropped in, and so ended the funeral obsequies of John Wilkes Booth, the assassin.

Atzeroth, Payne, Harold and Mrs. Surratt were tried, convicted and hanged. The execution took place on the 9th of July, 1865.

Others, no doubt equally guilty in intent, escaped; and the movements of some of these will be set forth in this narrative. Into the details of the trial and execution, I need not enter. Complete accounts may be had from other sources, no doubt well known to the reader. From this point the narrative will press steadily on toward the "Mystery of Maple Island."

Much of what is yet to be said is but a compilation of existing records, published and unpublished, some of which have been kindly loaned to the author of this chapter. The reader will remember that John A. Payne was sent to North Carolina to look after General Sherman, and the first clue to his whereabouts at the time of the assassination, is found in the following correspondence, which we give entire.

"MOORHEAD CITY, NORTH CAROLINA,
May 5, 1865.

"Hon. WILLIAM H. SEWARD, Secretary of State:

SIR:—Enclosed you will find a letter which I found floating in the river by the new Government wharf, at this place, on the evening of the 2d inst. It was not until late last night that I succeeded in learning its purport, it being in cipher. Having learned its nature, I lose no time in transmitting it to you. I also send a copy of the letter as translated. The letter evidently had not been opened when thrown in the river. I think the fiend was here awaiting the arrival of General Sherman, but learning that he had gone by way of Wilmington, and being pressed by detectives, threw it overboard.

CHAS. DENET.

"P. S.—If the letter should lead to anything of importance, so that it would be necessary that I should be seen, I can be found at 126 South H st., between 6th and 4½ sts. I am at present engaged in the Construction Corps, Railroad Department, at this place. Will be in Washington in a few days."

The following is a translation of the cipher letter. It was one of those ciphers which are readily translatable when the key is known, and even that is not so very difficult to discover. The government experts were familiar with it, having often seen the same cipher in captured rebel correspondence. Hence it was easy to see that Mr. Denet's ingenuity had given him the key to the true meaning of the epistle.

[Translation.]

"WASHINGTON, April 15, 1865.

"DEAR JOHN — I am happy to inform you that Pet. has done his work well. He is safe and old Abe is in hell. Now, sir, all eyes are on you — you must bring Sherman. Grant is in the hands of Old Gray ere this. Red Shoes showed lack of nerve in Seward's case, but fell back in good order. Johnson must come. Old Crook has him in charge. Mind well the Brother's Oath, and you will have no difficulty. All will be safe, and we will enjoy the fruit of our labors. We had a large meeting last night — all were bent on carrying out the programme to the letter. The rails are laid for safe exit. Old — always behind — lost the pass at City Point. Now, I say again:— The lives of our brave officers and the life of the South depends upon the carrying this programme into effect. No. 2 will give you this. It is ordered that no more letters be sent by mail. When you write again, sign no real name, and send by some of our friends who are coming home. We want you to write us how the news was received there. We receive great encouragement from all quarters. I hope there will be no getting weak in the knees. I was in Baltimore yesterday. Pet. has not got there yet. Don't lose your nerve.

"NO. FIVE."

O. B.

That this delicious bit of treasonable correspondence was sent to John A Payne there is little or no doubt. From it we also learn that "Pet." was John Wilkes Booth; "Red Shoes." Wood, alias Lewis Payne, and "Old Crook," Atzeroth. The letter was evidently written early on the morning after the assassination, and placed in the hands of No. 2, to convey to Payne. It further shows that there was a meeting of the Brotherhood of the Blue Gauntlet on the very night of the assassination; or, if not of them as a camp, of some of them as a band of conspirators.

General Sherman's change of route threw Payne out in his calculations. The ordinary route from Raleigh, where Gen. Sherman's headquarters were at the time, to Washington, was by rail via Goldsborough and New Bern to Moorhead City, thence by steamer to Washington. There is no doubt, as Mr. Denet suggests, that Payne was on the watch at Moorhead City, but, learning that Sherman had gone to Washington via Wilmington, and hearing, as he could not fail to hear, the result of the assassination, he lost heart, rid himself of every thing of a suspicious nature, and fled.

We will probably strike his trail again before our narrative closes. The following letter, dated at Buffalo, N. Y., is of no little interest, because it verifies in a degree what has already been stated.

"BUFFALO, N. Y., April 18, 1865.

"Hon. E. M. STANTON, Secretary of War, Washington, D. C.:— My Dear Sir:— Business has called me to Toronto, C. W., several times within the past two months; and while there, I have seen and heard some things which may be of service to the government.

"About five weeks ago, I saw at the Queen's Hotel, Toronto, a letter written by the late John Y. Beale, just previous to his execution, which, after speaking of his mock trial, unjust sentence, the judicial murder that was to be perpetrated by his execution, etc., called upon Jacob Thompson to vindicate his character before his countrymen of the South, and expressed his belief that his death would be speedily and terribly avenged. The letter itself was addressed to Colonel J. Thompson, Confederate Commissioner at Toronto, but the superscription on the envelope, which was in a different handwriting. read simply, J. Thompson, Toronto, Canada. This circumstance caused it to be delivered to a Mr. Thompson for whom it was not intended. I was permitted to peruse, but not to copy, the letter. I was informed, at that time, that the friends of Beale were banded together for the double purpose of avenging his death, and aiding the rebel government. I have heard the same statement repeated many times since, and have been frequently told by citizens of Toronto that some great mischief was being plotted by refugees in Canada. For more than a month General Dix's name was mentioned in my hearing in connection with the threatened vengeance. Regarding all such stories as idle tales, I never repeated them. Last Friday evening, while sitting in the office of the Queen's Hotel, I overheard a conversation between some persons sitting near me, which convinced me that the plot to murder the President was known to them. The party was mourning over the late rebel reverses, commenting upon the execution of Beale, the extradition of Bueley, etc., and then they cheered themselves after this fashion: "We'll make the damned Yankees howl yet." "Boys, I'll bet that we'll get better news in forty-eight hours." "We'll have something from Washington that will make people stare." Their words at the time seemed to me to be simply vulgar and profane, and implying idle threats which could never be executed. The next morning (Saturday, April 15), when I heard of the assassination, I could not help feeling that the party were implicated in the act. On Saturday, I met two of them in company with Ben Young, and one or two others of the St. Albans raiders, in the bar-room at the Queen's. One said, "Good news for us this morning," and another, "Damn well done, but not enough of it." Raising their glasses, one said, "Here's to Andy Johnson's turn next, to which another responded, "Yes, damn his soul." On relating this circumstance to Hon. E. G. Spaulding and others, they were of the opinion that I should communicate them to your Department. For my own part, I beg to refer to Hon. Ira Harris, of the Senate, and Hon. John A. Griswold, of the House."

"I am, my dear sir, very truly yours,
G. C."

Mr. C. is a respectable lawyer in this city, and his statements are entitled to credit.

E. G. S.
BUFFALO, N. Y.

The letter speaks for itself, and needs no comment. The only criticism to offer is not upon the letter, but upon the writer. Had he been possessed of the shrewdness which the average lawyer ought to possess, he would have written to the War Department long before. Written at the time it was, it only showed how great was the lack of detective ability which every great lawyer possesses in some degree. In the writer, it only verified the old adage about "locking the stable after the horse is stolen."

The next letter in evidence throws a ray of light on the trail of John Harrison Surratt, and also, from the description, of John A. Payne. It is from one of the many detectives which were sent into Canada on a hunt for the escaped conspirators. It is dated at Montreal on the 27th of April. Its great length precludes its insertion in full, but we give the salient portions; those relating directly to the subject in hand. Just here, it may be well to note that a prominent Englishman in Montreal, who, previous to the assassination of the President, was a strong sympathizer with the South, and was well acquainted with the Confederate agents in Canada, and fully informed of their plans and movements, said that the murder of the President was too much for him; and he told Alderman Lyman, of that city, that the Southern agents had heard from the party who murdered the President, and that they expected him in Montreal within forty-eight hours; and if not the principal, one closely connected with the assassination. This information the agents received on the 20th of April. The reader will bear the date in mind, as he reads the extracts from the detective's letter:

"MONTREAL, April 27, 1865.
"COLONEL L. C. BAKER:

"Dear Sir — While in Burlington (Vt.), I obtained a white linen handkerchief, which was dropped in the Vermont Central Depot, on Thursday evening April 20, by one of three strange men who slept in the depot all Thursday night. These men came from the steamer Canada, Capt. Flagg. She was very late that evening, and did not connect with the train north, to Montreal, which leaves at 7 o'clock, P. M. They came into the depot between seven and a half and eight o'clock, after the night watchman went on duty. They had no baggage. They were all rather poorly dressed, and looked hard, worn out, and tired. The watchman asked them which way they were going; they said "to Montreal." When told that they could not go that night, they said that they knew it. He asked them if they wanted a hotel; they said no, that they were going to stay in the depot. They did not seem to have much to say or do with each other. They curled up on seats in different parts of the room, and went to sleep, and remained quiet all night. The watchman awakened them about 4 o'clock in the morning to take the train, which they did. After they left he picked up two dirty pocket handkerchiefs where they had slept. While looking them over, he found the name of J. H. Surratt No. 2, on one of them. B., the watchman, got his mother to wash the handkerchiefs, and on Saturday he went to the city, and told the circumstance of finding them. Detective G. C. got the handkerchief from B., and I got it from him. Enclosed you will find it. B. said that one of the men was tall and the others short. He identifies the likeness of Surratt, as being one of the men. I then found the conductor who ran the train to Essex Junction that morning, and he too, fully identified Surratt's likeness as being one of the men. I next found C. T. Hobart, who runs the through train to St. Albans, Vermont. He gave a description of two men only who boarded his train at Essex Junction on Friday morning, April 21, at 5.05 o'clock. One was a tall man, broad shoulders, otherwise slim, straight as an arrow, did not look like a laborer, though dressed rather poor; had on a loose sack coat, cassimere shirt, light colored pants, and a tight fitting skull cap. His hair was black as jet and straight; no beard; was young, not more than twenty-one or twenty two. The other man was not much over five feet, thick set, short neck, full face,

sandy complexion, sandy chin whiskers and no other beard. He wore a soft black-felt hat, dark-colored sack coat, light-colored pants, and a reddish-colored flannel shirt. He had but little to say; let the tall man do the talking. They both got off the train at St. Albans. He felt as if they were a pair of assassins, and in speaking to a friend about the matter, he gave vent to his suspicions. He fully identified Surratt's picture as that of the tall one, and said that he would know him anywhere. * * * There is no doubt that Surratt is in this province, together with some others, but whom I cannot tell. Enclosed I send you a likeness of one of the Paynes, of whom there are seven brothers, all Kentuckians. Three of them are said to be in South America, one is in jail at St. Albans, and the others are here unless you have them with you. The picture is marked on the back. If of no use, please send it back to the owner. I am going out along that portion of Canada bordering on Maine, Vermont and New York. Many rebels are in there. Young Saunders and others are there now. Porterfield, a dangerous rebel, is making preparations to go to Nashville; ought not to be allowed. Trowbridge, another, has gone to Detroit. "Respectfully, etc.,
———— ————."

It was that very picture of "one of the Paynes," which fully revealed the identity of the man Wood, who attempted the assassination of Secretary Seward. It was, in fact, his own portrait taken in Montreal, some time previous to starting for Washington to report to John Wilkes Booth. The next communication is addressed to Secretary Stanton. It was dated at Montreal on the 29th of April, 1865. We append an extract or two:

"HON. E. M. STANTON, Secretary of War:

"Dear Sir.—There is no doubt that J. H. Surratt and John A. Payne were in the city yesterday, and that they left last night in company with Clement C. Clay and others probably for Toronto. I am a private detective here, without authority to act for your government. I looked the city over for G., one of Baker's men, but found that he left for the border townships yesterday morning, so I failed to see him. * * * I am not at all certain that they went to Toronto; it is only my opinion. They may have gone to Three Rivers, as there are a great many Southern refugees there, or to Tanner, where it is said that John A. Payne has heretofore spent a great deal of his time, together with three of his brothers. "Respectfully, etc.,
———— ————."

About this time a letter was received at Washington, post-marked Detroit, but written at Tanner, Canada, by one John P. H. Hall, of that place, and directed: "To Andrew Johnson, President of the United States, or other authority." Its contents are as follows:

"With certainty I state to you that John A. Payne, and thirteen others, are sworn to murder Andrew Johnson, E. M. Stanton, L. S. Fisher, and others, within thirty days from April 23d, 1865. The arrangements are all made and in progress toward execution. I do not know where John A. Payne is now. He was at Montreal when this plot was projected. His brother (whose name I do not recollect) is implicated. Seven of the plotters are at Washington, four at Bedford, Pennsylvania, and the thirteenth is with Payne. These are plain facts. Do not reveal this, but arrest John A. Payne and his brother. I send this to Detroit to avoid suspicion.
'Yours, etc.,
"———— ————."

The Montreal private detective was right in his opinion, at least so far as Clement C. Clay was concerned; because, among many other names registered at the Queen's Hotel, Toronto, on the evening of April 29, 1865, was that of C. C. Clay. Whether Surratt and Payne were in his company remains to be seen. Jacob Thompson and Larry McDonald were already there.

So far, the testimony as to the whereabouts of John H. Surratt is fairly complete. In the absence of direct and absolute proof, it may, at all events, be accepted as strong circumstantial evidence. We now present yet another letter, written by a colored man, which, though anonymous, and as such not entitled to take rank as evidence, yet it harmonizes so well with what has been already learned that it seems worthy of some credence. At all events, it is here given place, and left to the judgment of the reader.

The letter is postmarked "Niagara Falls," and is dated "Monday, May 2nd, 1865," and directed "To the Secretary of War, Washington, D. C." The writer says:

"I beg of you not to let any one see this letter. I dare not sign it for fear that my name may somehow come out. I send you my name and business on a separate paper so that you may judge whether I have an opportunity to learn what I tell you. Be sure to destroy it. I send this to be mailed at Niagara Falls, because a letter directed to you and dropped into this post-office, would be read by Jake Thompson before it was sent out, if it was ever sent at all. What I want you to know is that there is an awful nest of rebels here at this time. Clay, Surratt and John A. Payne are here. They came Saturday with a lot of others. Surratt and Payne skipped out last night and now there is the very devil to pay. It seems that Surratt was the treasurer of some society that was hired to murder President Lincoln and a lot of others, and that Jake Thompson took the gold out of the bank here and paid it over to him and Payne, and that they were to divide it among the others; but they skipped out and now they can't find hide nor hair of them. I wouldn't like to be in their shoes if the gang gets them, and they are going in pursuit. They are plotting now to murder a lot more in revenge for the killing of Booth, and if Payne and the rest are hung they say that they will burn Washington. You can't tell how much I hear, and of course I don't hear it all, as I am only in the room when I take liquor to them, which is pretty often though, but one of the girls hears heaps and tells me all about it. Anyway, you folks in Washington ought to look out. I hope you will catch and hang every one of them, especially Jake Thompson. I hate him. That is all I can write now.

"———— ————."

But little more remains to be said, and that is scarcely more than conjecture. This much is positively known. A sharp lookout for J. H. Surratt and John A. Payne, was kept at St. Catharines, Canada, for some time. That city was a great place of resort for Southern rebels, among whose citizens they found a welcome, especially among a certain class. Then, too, Col. Beverly Robinson, of Virginia, was the proprietor of a fashionable hotel there, which became a noted resort for Southerners and Southern sympathizers, and where rebellion against the Government of the United States was as openly discussed as it ever was in Charleston, South Carolina, where it originated. But the rebellion went down with a crash and so did Beverly Robinson's hotel business, to the sorrow of several capitalists of St. Catharines, whose only security for heavy loans was a life insurance policy, and the "honah, sah," of Col. Beverly Robinson, one of Virginia's F. F. V.'s, on neither of which as late as 1881, had they ever realized a cent. Whether the indebtedness has since been canceled, this deponent saith not.

But John H. Surratt and John A. Payne were too shrewd to visit St. Catharines. The former made his way to Three Rivers, Quebec, where he was protected for a time by Father Boucher, a Catholic priest. He went thence to Italy, enlisted in the Papal Zouaves, was exposed by another Papal soldier by the name of Massie, extradited, tried and acquitted in Washington in 1868, and now lives in Baltimore. A man bearing the description of John A. Payne, was seen in the vicinity of Sharbot and Rideau lakes, Ont., and at Smith's Falls during the latter part of May, 1865, and shortly afterward at Gananoque, where he stayed for a day or two, and then settling his hotel bill, in payment of which he offered a gold piece of English coinage, he left, no one knew whither. Was it John A. Payne who made his appearance at Fisher's Landing? The description and the time tally well. It may with some show of reason be asked: If he wanted to hide himself effectually among the islands, why did he not choose some spot among the myriad islands of the Admiralty group near Gananoque, or in the Navy group below? Evidently he was a shrewd observer. He well knew that the defrauded Brotherhood would hunt him to the death, but he also knew that they would be unlikely to venture to the American side of the St. Lawrence; while they would search every island in the Canadian Channel. He knew, too, that Baker's government detectives, would never think of looking for him on the United States side of the line. Besides, had he located in either of the island groups mentioned, the Admiralty, for instance, his supplies would necessarily be drawn from Gananoque, a dangerous point for him to visit. If in the Navy group, it was not easy to procure needed supplies, without travelling some distance. Then, too, the main channels of steamboat travel at that time, especially for the Canadian steamers, passed through those groups.

Locating where he did — if indeed it was him, showed great shrewdness. Maple Island is at some distance from any of the regular lines of steamboat travel, and from any of the channels taken by excursion steamers, which, at that time, were few and far between; and while the island is by no means hidden, that fact of itself was an element of safety; because no one would think of searching an island so open to the view of every one. That a party of five or six men made their appearance in Gananoque in the month of August, 1865, making inquiries about a man who answered the description of John A. Payne, already given, is a fact that may be easily substantiated. They affirmed that they all belonged to a party of workmen who had been employed near Montreal, and that the man for whom they were looking drew the pay for them, and then ran away. They had followed him to Smith's Falls, and from there could get no further trace of him.

There is some significance, too, in the fact that after the burning of the cabin on Maple Island, nothing more was seen of the party of supposed Southerners, who had for some days previous sojourned at the Hubbard and Walton Houses in Clayton.

But of yet greater significance is the fact that the fateful sign of the three crosses was cut upon the breast of the murdered hermit. That of itself is almost positive evidence that he met his doom at the hands of the Brotherhood, and that not robbery only, but revenge, was a prime factor in the assassination.

Scores of instances can be produced where the bodies of those who fell victims to the relentless oaths of the secret Brotherhoods of the South during the rebellion were marked in like manner. Even the "Ku Klux Klans" of 1866, '67 and '68, during the reconstruction period, left in many instances the same bloody sign upon the breasts of their murdered victims.

Reader, the testimony is all in; whatever may be its value as evidence, it is wholly a matter of record, accessible to those who care to investigate. The writer has sought far and wide for additional proofs, but they could not be found by him; and now the judgment remains with you; for with this paragraph, he submits for your decision THE MYSTERY OF MAPLE ISLAND.

"LITTLE FRAUD," BELOW FAIRY LAND.

THE "NEW ISLAND WANDERER."

ongs to the Alexandria Bay Steamboat Company, making daily excursions up and down the River and among the Islands. Steamer "Island of same line, makes daily trips to Ogdensburg.

H. WALTER WEBB.

SOME writer for a New York newspaper, under date of August 18, 1894, lets himself loose in the following style:

"While Dr. Chauncey M. Depew is dividing his time in Europe between talking horse and diplomacy with Lord Roseberry, Rhine wine and yachts with the German Kaiser and anarchy and politics with President Casimir-Perier, of France, his job, as the president of the New York Central Railroad and authority on almost everything pertaining to railroads, is being held down by a young man who is not so well known as he, but who is thought by men who know, to be an altogether better president of railroads than the talented Dr. Depew. Dr. Depew's 'sub' is about twenty-five years younger than himself, and he can probably outrun and outbox his superior and do a lot of things that the doctor's stiffened joints would not possibly permit him to undertake. He is very much quieter than the doctor, and while he may not have as many friends, those who talk with him every day say that he can give his chief points in the line of 'hustling.' Although he was not altogether unknown four years ago, it was not until then that his genius as a railroad manager brought him prominently before the public. Mr. Depew was then, as now, in Europe hobnobbing with the big guns over there, while Cornelius Vanderbilt, who owns most of the New York Central Road and who hires Mr. Depew at a fancy salary, was somewhere in Africa."

This screed reads well, and desiring to know more of this man who has proven himself able to "hold down" the great Chauncey's seat, we have taken some pains to make inquiries about him. We are told that in the spring of 1890 the directors of the New York Central Railroad determined to make some changes in the organization — changes which involved promotion of some of the abler officers of the road. Among other things which they voted to do was the creation of a new department, the head of which was to be elected third vice-president of the system, and to have supreme direction of the traffic of the road, both passenger and freight. He was to be held, in short, responsible for the management of such business as was offered to the company. The choice for this responsible office fell upon H. Walter Webb, and only a few weeks later this young man found himself face to face with a strike which was more threatening than any that had occurred upon the road, perhaps in its existence, certainly since the great strike year of 1877.

Two years later Vice-President Webb was called to face another emergency of the same sort, and these two experiences fixed attention upon him as one of the great railway managers of the United States. Men who do not know Major Webb are asking one another something about his personality and his intellectual qualities, as the generalship he displays not only in strike crises, but in those more silent but in some respects equally desperate battles which railroad companies as competitors of other railroad companies are constantly fighting.

In New York Major Webb is well known, but elsewhere, although he has gained wide repute, there is little knowledge of the manner of man he is. The story of his career contains much that is instructive and interesting.

Major Webb is one of the sons of that distinguished politician and editor of the time when the Whig party was fighting its battles, Gen. James Watson Webb. Great as were Gen. Webb's achievements in the political world, when he came to old age he took greater pride in the promise which was already beginning to be fulfilled, of raising a family of boys who would gain distinction, perhaps, equal to that which was gained by the famous Field, or Washburn, or Wolcott families.

Walter Webb, in his youth, showed some taste for engineering, and he was placed in the Columbia College School of Mines, which is the scientific department of that institution, and was at the head of his class some twenty years ago. After graduation, however, young Webb felt some inclination toward a career at the bar. He gratified it to the extent of studying, being admitted, and hanging out his shingle for a brief time. His legal education was of value to him, though only in other achievements toward which he began to drift soon after he opened his office. An opportunity was presented for him to go into the banking and brokerage business, and for some years he was busy in studying the mysteries of Wall street, and in learning the market value of the securities there dealt in.

Almost incidentally he drifted into the railway business. His brother, Dr. Seward Webb, who married one of the daughters of William H. Vanderbilt, became interested in the Palace Car Company which the Vanderbilts controlled, and when Webster Wagner, the president of that company, met his sudden death, having been crushed between two of his own cars in a railway collision, Dr. Webb became president of the company, and invited his brother to accept an official post in connection with it. Walter Webb had not been in the railway business a month before both he and his employers discovered that he had peculiar qualifications for this business. It seemed to fascinate him. He was no pompous official, fond of sitting in richly carpeted rooms and issuing orders with heavy dignity. He was everywhere. He studied the science of railway car building; he skirmished around among the shops; he was not afraid of dirt, nor of putting on a jumper and a pair of overalls, if necessary, and as a consequence he soon had not only mastered those duties he was employed to perform, but being full of suggestions and devoted to his avocation, he was rapidly promoted. He served, while an officer, really an apprenticeship, working harder than any other employé, never thinking about hours or salary, but only bent on learning the business.

In the railway business such a person moves rapidly toward the top. The history of railway corporations in the United States furnishes many such instances. Social influence, political pulls, as they are called, family prestige, count for nothing in the development of railway men. Nothing but fidelity and capacity have any influence with directors in the selection of executive officers. Any other course would be perilous.

Therefore, when the time came for this corporation, one of the greatest in the world in railway management, to place a competent man at the head of its traffic business, Major Webb was selected, and so thoroughly has he justified that choice that at the time when President Chauncey M. Depew was considering the invitation of President Harrison to become the successor of Mr. Blaine, as Secretary of State, it was understood in railway circles that Major Webb would be chosen president of the New York Central, in case Depew resigned that office.

Chief among Major Webb's qualifications for this work is his devotion to business. His college training as an engineer has served him well, and his legal knowledge has been of great value to him in the two great emergencies which he was called of a sudden to face, when many of the employés of the road went out on strike. He lives not five minutes' walk from his office, and he is frequently there as early as 7 o'clock in the morning. In the summer, when he is at his country place, he takes the first train into the city, while the bankers and brokers and professional men who live near him, do not follow until two or three hours later. He rarely leaves his office before 6 o'clock, and sometimes is there until late at night. His office is a place of comfort, but not of luxury. Major Webb is democratic in his relations with men, and none of the red tape which prevails in some of the great corporation offices annoys visitors who desire to see him. If a delegation from the engineers or switchmen, or from any of the other employés call, Major Webb receives them in a manner which does not lower their self-respect. There is neither condescension nor haughtiness in his relations with them. Major Webb will receive hard-handed employés, and within an hour be in association with a group of millionaires, fellow-directors of his in the great bank which is located near his office, and his manner is the same in each case. He treats everybody in a business-like way. He is quick-spoken, prompt, decisive, without being curt or brusque.

As a railroad man, he is what is called a flyer. Like William H. Vanderbilt, he is fond of going fast, and when business calls him to a remote point, he will order a locomotive attached to his special car, and within half an hour after the decision is taken, will be flying over the rails at the rate of a mile a minute. He is absolutely fearless in his travels, as William H. Vanderbilt was. Business men may see him in the afternoon of one day, and hear of him the next morning at Buffalo, 450 miles away. This does not indicate restlessness, but energy. Major Webb is one of the most quiet, self-contained and serene-mannered of all our railway managers.

When, just after he became vice-president, he was called upon to face a most dangerous strike, railway men said that he had been put to the test too early, and some of them feared that he would not be equal to the responsibility. Depew was in Europe. Cornelius Vanderbilt in Newport, and members of the executive board scattered here and there. Major Webb immediately made of his office a campaign-place. He collected his staff about him. The strikers had control of the approaches to New York city, and traffic was paralyzed. He first took pains to discover how many of the men were out, and also to learn what their precise grievance was. If it was a question of time or wages or any other thing over which there had been misunderstanding or business disagreement, he believed that the trouble could be speedily settled. He found, instead, that it was a matter of discipline, that the men protested against certain rules which the subordinate officers had found necessary, as they believed, in order to maintain discipline. The strikers objected to the discharge of certain men who were reported disobedient or incompetent, and when Major Webb heard this, he said, in a quiet way, to his staff: "This is a point this company cannot yield. The stockholders must retain the right to manage, in their own way, this property."

Then he called upon his resources. He sent agents to procure men to take the places of the strikers. He called upon the police force of New York for protection, and got it. Night and day for seventy-two hours he left his office for only a few moments at a time. He caught catnaps, and two nights did not sleep a wink. And, when the railway men connected with other lines found out what he was doing, they said: "There is a young general in command at the Grand Central Station."

In his conferences with leaders of labor associations, Major Webb's legal knowledge was of great service to him, and Mr. Powderly himself, who met him in conference several times, was greatly impressed by his tact, coolness, good temper, and his firmness as well.

When Mr. Depew returned from Europe, not a sign of the strike appeared. Cornelius Vanderbilt, constantly informed over the wire at his Newport home of what was going on, deemed it unnecessary to come to the city.

At the first mutterings of the strike in Buffalo, information of which was sent to Major Webb by telegraph, he touched his electric bell, the messenger who answered received an order which was taken to the proper authority, and within half an hour Major Webb was aboard his private car, speeding over the tracks at the rate of fifty miles an hour; and before dawn next morning he was in Buffalo. His part in that convulsion is a matter of recent history, and unnecessary to describe here.

In physical appearance, as his photogravure picture shows, Major Webb does not at all suggest the typical railway manager. He is of slight figure, medium stature, erect in carriage. He cares nothing for social pleasures of the fashionable set. His home and his office are his life. He is not a club man. He takes no conspicuous part in politics, although he has strong political views; but it is safe to say that not a dozen men employed by his company know whether he is a Republican or a Democrat. He is a strong churchman, being a vestryman, and one of the most active members of one of the New York uptown Episcopal churches; and if the millionaires contributed sums proportionate to their wealth as great as those he gives for church work, his church would have an enormous income. Major Webb is a great believer in the future possibilities of fast railway travel. He has studied this development with great care, and with such results that he is now running daily the fastest railway train in the world, making nearly a mile a minute consecutively for 450 miles. His experiments have shown that the old idea that very fast traveling does not pay, is an error, but he says that in order to make it pay, the cars must be light but strong, the service sufficient but not luxurious, and the carrying capacity limited, so that an engine will not be compelled to draw too heavy a train.

Chauncey M. Depew has the reputation of being the most accessible to newspaper men of all the distinguished men in New York, yet he is not more so than Major Webb. Any respectable newspaper man is welcome to his office at all times, and he treats such callers as though they were men, and like one who respects their calling. The reporter has yet to be found who has got of Major Webb a suggestion that a puff or a bit of praise would be pleasing. He will not talk about himself, but will cheerfully give all the news which he has, provided it is consistent with the policy of the road to make publication of it. If it is not consistent, he says frankly: "That is something I cannot talk to you about just now. Perhaps I may be able to do so to-morrow."

Perhaps this disposition is partly due to his recollection of the fact that his father was a newspaper man who always treated the humblest of reporters with great respect. At the time Gen. Webb was approaching death, and the various newspapers of New York sent reporters to his home, so that immediate information of his death might be obtained, Gen. Webb used to say to his sons: "Are you taking good care of the newspaper men? If any of them have to wait long, show them some hospitality. Give them a glass of Madeira and a sandwich or biscuit, and do not forget that the newspaper reporters as a class are hard-working, fair-minded, intelligent men, who should be treated exactly as any other business man is, who comes to you on business matters." Whether this injunction accounts for the treatment the Major and his brothers give newspaper men or not, the fact remains that they all are thus minded when they receive representatives of the press.

The general impression in railway circles is, that when President Depew retires from official connection with the New York Central, Major Webb will be his successor.

HIS CONNECTION WITH THE ROADS OF NORTHERN NEW YORK.

What we have thus far said relates to Mr. Webb's connection with the main lines of the Central corporation, the extent of which all our readers understand, for that system is one of the largest in the world, and is managed with a degree of judgment and practical capacity that has elicited the wonder of travellers who are familiar with the great lines both in Europe and America. But it is in Major Webb's connection with our own northern line that he has been brought more directly into official relations with our own people. When the New York Central, on March 14, 1891, leased the lines of the R. W. & O. Road, Major Webb was placed in complete control of that entire system, and became the managing officer, the supreme executive head. Almost from the very week he assumed control, the beneficence of his management has made itself manifest. He began the great work of raising the newly-acquired property to the high standard of the trunk line. This necessitated new bridges, new rails, and the accomplishment of almost a process of new construction — entirely so in some localities. The outlay for these improvements has been enormous, reaching $2,000,000 of which $600,000 has been expended in the construction of new bridges, built of steel and iron. The bridges upon the whole line are now as good as any in the country.

The entire road-bed has been re-ballasted, and in most of it new ties have been placed, and the number of the same per mile has been increased. New steel rails have been laid, weighing 70 and 72 pounds to the lineal yard, and the equipment has been correspondingly improved by the addition of standard locomotives of the heaviest pattern, which could not be run over the old R. W. & O., but which now, under the new improvements — steel rails, perfect road-bed, and strong bridges — are allowed to run at high speed, and haul heavy trains. New passenger cars have been added; in fact, the road has been virtually re-constructed. Freight rates have been reduced, and the general conditions have been greatly improved. Among other things, several enterprises in Northern New York have been assisted; and all this has been done by hard work, and under the plans made and supervised by Mr. Webb.

For such labors, so well done, too much praise cannot be given this young man, who might have chosen ease, but prefers work. All that he touches he benefits. He has raised the old R., W. & O. R. R. system from a decaying condition, with worn material and weak bridges, to become a grand roadway in itself, the natural ally of the great trunk system with which it makes close connections, with vestibuled trains, and in summer with its steady-running "flyers" that cross the country at forty miles an hour in entire safety. The value of such a system, so connected, adds to the value of every acre of land in Northern New York, and is of interest to the poorest man as well as to the richest. The remarkable freedom from personal accidents to passengers during the year 1894 affords the best possible guaranty that the system is well and safely managed. Speed and comfort are two conditions demanded by modern travellers; but the perfect combination is a rare one. On most American railroads, high speed is only possible at the expense of danger and discomfort. To combine comfort and safety with the greatest speed, perfect equipment and absence of sharp curves are necessary. This is certainly the case with the R., W. & O. system. Its great eastern and western outlets, the New York Central and Hudson River Roads, hold the world's championship for long distance fast trains, won by recent improvements in equipment and locomotive-building, that fairly mark an epoch in railroading; and its hundred-ton engines, borne on massive rails weighing 120 pounds per yard, now skim with perfect safety around curves at the rate of fifty-five miles an hour. The solidest of road-beds is needed to withstand this marvelous speed, and to bear the enormous locomotives and trains; what it does with safety is impossible to other railroads of inferior equipment, or built with sharp curves. Excepting the Great Western of Canada, which has one air-line reach of 100 miles, the New York Central straight tracks exceed those of any other railroad in the world.

J. A. H.

THEODORE BUTTERFIELD.

MR. BUTTERFIELD comes into the transportation system of Northern New York by what may be called "natural inheritance." His grandfather, the Honorable John Butterfield, of Utica, was the originator of the American Express Company, which was started under the firm of Wells, Butterfield & Company. He also raised the money and built the first Western Union Telegraph Line, which was called the Morse Line Telegraph at that time, and was a director in the New York Central in its early stages, and one of the promoters and capitalists who built the Utica and Black River road, which started in opposition to the Rome and Watertown road, because they could not agree on a starting point, as the capitalists of Northern New York wanted to start from Herkimer; the Utica people would not hear to that, and were bound to start from Utica; so the other people started from Rome, and the Utica people, not to be outdone, started their road from Utica, which was built up to Boonville, and finally extended to Ogdensburgh, Clayton and Sackets Harbor. John Butterfield also started and owned the famous Pony Express or Overland Mail, which was the precursor of the Pacific railroads.

Theodore Butterfield's uncle, Major-General Daniel Butterfield, was the first general superintendent of the American Express Company, and also was chief of staff of the various commanders of the Army of the Potomac, and gave the celebrated order, by direction of General Meade, to the corps commanders to fight Lee at Gettysburg, the battle that nearly broke the back of the Confederacy.

Mr. Butterfield has been connected with the railroads of Northern New York for 20 years. He began as chief clerk in the accounting department of the old Utica & Black River railroad, at Utica, and was soon after made general ticket agent, and then general passenger agent of that road; and, as the road grew, he was made general freight and passenger agent. He remained in that position until the consolidation with the Rome, Watertown & Ogdensburg railroad, when he was appointed general passenger agent of the R., W. & O. R. R., and has held that position under the consolidation of that system with the New York Central & Hudson River R. R.'s. When first appointed he was the youngest general ticket agent in the United States. His experience as assistant to the general superintendent, and in the operating department of the Utica & Black River railroad, made him familiar with all departments of railroading, and that is the secret of his success in the passenger business, as he thoroughly understands the details in railroading, and has in addition rare executive ability. He is the originator of the long-distance excursions, such as the New York, Washington and Chicago excursions; and the idea of attaching sleeping-cars and drawing-room cars to excursion trains, now generally adopted, originated with him.

At the time of his appointment he was the youngest general passenger agent in the United States. He is beyond all doubt the most popular railroad man in Northern New York, the best known and most appreciated. With a clear head and ample knowledge of all railroad matters, his suggestions at the meetings of the passenger agents of the whole country are always listened to with the closest attention, and usually adopted.

THEODORE BUTTERFIELD.

COL. ZEBULON HOWELL BENTON.

COLONEL ZEBULON HOWELL BENTON.
[Copied from Wallace's Guide to the Adirondacks.]

THERE was probably no more romantic, picturesque or conspicuous figure connected with the chronicles of Lake Bonaparte than Colonel Zebulon H. Benton. The accompanying engraving faithfully represents his appearance in daily life. He invariably dressed with the nicest regard to minute particulars, in peaked felt hat, long black coat and ruffled shirt — every article faultlessly neat. With his fresh, ruddy complexion, clean-shaven face, rich growth of snow-white hair, graceful carriage, and form almost as lithe and perfect, at the ripe age of 82, as if in the flower of youth and strength, he seemed the embodiment of a gentleman of the old regime.

Colonel Benton was born in Apulia, N. Y., January 27, 1811, and the details of his checkered life would fill a book. We can only briefly allude to the following facts: He was a cousin of Thomas Hart Benton, the great Missouri statesman, and consequently a kinsman of his daughter, Jessie Benton Fremont, the noted wife of the famous "Pathfinder." In the war of the Rebellion he received an appointment on the staff of General Fremont, but before he could arrange to take the position the general was suspended. He was also a relative of the eminent novelist, James Fenimore Cooper. From his very boyhood he led an extremely active life, and before he was fairly out of his teens he was entrusted by his employers with commissions of the utmost importance, which he brought to successful consummation. He was engaged from time to time in great enterprises, especially those of land, mining and railroading. The capital invested in these sometimes exceeded a million dollars. His ventures, often gigantic, were not confined to Lewis and St. Lawrence counties, but extended into the Canadas, to the Gulf of Mexico, and even into South America. The mines at Rossie, Clifton, Jayville and Alpine are examples of these operations. We are convinced that the Carthage & Adirondack Railway owes its existence to Colonel Benton and to Hon. Joseph Pahud, of Harrisville, N. Y., as they were unceasing in their efforts to establish that line to the Jayville mines.

From the Carthage Republican, Philadelphia Press and other reliable sources, we glean the following interesting information: Soon after the arrival of Joseph Bonaparte in this country, he met and loved a beautiful Quakeress, by the name of Annette Savage, a member of a family of high respectability, residing in Philadelphia, descendants of the celebrated Indian princess, Pocahontas. They were subsequently married in private by a justice of the peace in that city. Two daughters were the fruit of this union, one of whom died in infancy. The other was christened Charlotte C. Soon after arriving at maturity, she became the wife of Colonel Benton. Their marriage resulted in seven children. The five surviving bear the appropriate names of Josephine Charlotte, Zenaide Bonaparte, Louis Joseph, Zebulon Napoleon and Thomas Hart.

Mrs. Benton, having obtained a letter of introduction from General Grant to Hon. Elihu B. Washburn, United States Minister to France, and one also from Dr. J. DeHaven White, the eminent Philadelphia dentist, to his former pupil, Dr. Evans, the dental surgeon of Louis Napoleon, repaired to Paris in 1869. She obtained audience with the Emperor, and received immediate recognition as the daughter of Joseph Bonaparte; and by his imperial will and the laws of France, the union of her parents was confirmed and her legitimacy established. Honored by an invitation to attend the French court, she and two of her children were there kindly and cordially entertained by the Emperor and Empress, who presented her with valuable souvenirs upon the occasion. Napoleon often expressed great regret that he did not know his cousin earlier, so that he might the sooner have bestowed upon her children the places to which, by birth, they were entitled. He presented her with her father's palace; but this was lost through the downfall of the empire and of that ill-fated royal family. Mrs. Benton attended Napoleon during his imprisonment in Germany, and a short time afterward (1871) returned to America. She was a woman of remarkable beauty and talent, and of most lovely characteristics. Her eyes were large, dark and lustrous, and, like the Colonel's, never dimmed by age. Receiving a fine education, in Europe and in this country, she early developed great versatility in writing. Many brilliant articles in various papers and magazines were the productions of her pen, and she was the author of a book of rare merit, entitled "France and her People." She died December 25, 1890, at Richfield Springs. Her husband, the subject of this sketch, died May 16, 1893, closing an unique, interesting and wonderfully romantic life.

BURNING OF THE STEAMER "SIR ROBERT PEEL."
[See Article on Patriot War.]

ON the 29th day of December, 1837, the steamer Caroline, an American steamboat, while lying tied to the wharf at Schlosser, a port on the Niagara river below Buffalo, was boarded by a band of Canadians, robbed, set fire to, cut loose from her moorings, and sent burning over Niagara Falls. This caused great indignation throughout the country, and added much to the excitement consequent on the breaking out of the so-called Patriot war, which was a weak rebellion on the part of some dissatisfied Canadians, with which a number of United States citizens very foolishly took sides. The steamer Sir Robert Peel was new and stanch, built at Brockville only the year before, and owned by both Canadian and American citizens. She was sailed by Capt. John B. Armstrong. Starting from Prescott on the afternoon of the 29th of May, 1838, she touched at Brockville on her way to Toronto, having on board a cargo and nineteen passengers. She arrived at McDonnell's wharf at midnight to take on wood. It had been hinted to the captain before leaving Brockville that there was danger ahead, but he disregarded the warning. The passengers were asleep in the cabin, and the crew had almost finished their labor of taking on wood, when a party of twenty-two men, disguised and painted like Indians and armed with muskets and bayonets, rushed on board, yelling like savages, and shouting, "Remember the Caroline!" They drove the passengers and crew ashore, allowing but little time for the removal of baggage belonging to them, the most of which was lost. The steamer was fired in several places, and the party left in two boats, steering for Abel's Island, about four miles away, which they reached at sunrise. The ill-fated steamer sunk in mid-channel but a short distance below the wharf where she was captured, and there she now lies twenty fathoms deep, while we sail to and fro directly over her wreck.

The leader of this party was William Johnston, better known to fame, or notoriety rather, as "Bill Johnston," a Canadian outlaw, around whose career, and that of his daughter Kate, the once famous novelist, "Ned Buntline" (E. Z. C. Judson), threw a halo of mystery and romance. Bill Johnston was born at Three Rivers, Lower Canada, February 1, 1782. His parents removed to Kingston in 1784, and at the breaking out of the war of 1812, he was a grocer in Kingston, and a member of a military company. For an act of insubordination, it is said, though what was its nature is not now apparent, he was tried by a court-martial, lodged in jail, and his property confiscated. Escaping thence he came to the States, and became the bitterest and most vindictive foe Canada ever had. He acted as a spy for the Americans during the war of 1812-15, robbed the British mails, and committed every depredation possible upon Canada and Canadians. After the burning of the Sir Robert Peel, he was outlawed by both the United States and Canadian governments, who tried in every way possible to effect his capture; but his hiding places were so numerous, and so many were his personal friends, that, with the aid of his daughter Kate, who kept him supplied with food, which she took to him in the dead of night in her skiff alone, and with news of his enemies, also, that they succeeded in capturing him but twice, both of which times he escaped; though if the stories told of his hair-breadth escapes, whether true or not, were written down, they would fill a book. Finally, when matters became quiet, he returned to his home in Clayton, and in time was appointed keeper of the Rock Island light, whose rays illumine the very spot over which once shone the light of the burning steamer Sir Robert Peel.

The descendants of Johnston are now residents of Clayton, where they have been for years honorable and efficient citizens. The original William was a "good hater," as shown by his bitter denunciation of everything British.

But stepping aside from the mere personalities concerned in such an affair as the burning of the "Peel," and the other burning and murder which precedes that episode, to-wit, the burning of the "Caroline" at Schlosser landing in the Niagara River — it is disheartening to consider how strongly such unlawful acts appeal to the sympathy of the reckless characters to be found in every community, and that from such small beginnings wars are sometimes begun among great nations. The affair of 1837, the lawless efforts of a few invading marauders upon the soil of Canada, came near precipitating England and the United States into a conflict of arms which would have been deplorable even if our cause were just. But at that time the prejudices of the American masses were all wrong, and it is curious reading at this day to go over the newspapers of that era, nearly all of them sympathizing with the invaders, who were honored by being called "patriots." Robbers would have been a more appropriate designation. But the fate of the poor fellows who were sent to the then penal colony of Van Dieman's land, now Australia, will probably have a weakening effect upon any future undertaking of that kind.

GENERAL WILLIAM H. ANGELL

WAS long prominently connected with the interests of the St. Lawrence, and legitimately belongs with those who are entitled to prominent remembrance in any history of the Upper St. Lawrence and of the Thousand Islands. He is remembered with pleasure by the older citizens of Clayton and of Jefferson county, for he was a man of great business capacity and force. Many buildings in Watertown bear silent witness of his manner of construction — notably the Taggart Bros'. mill at the lower falls, and the water-reservoir, now over forty years in use. He was born in Burlington, Otsego county, N. Y., in 1797, one of a family of ten children. When only ten years of age he left home, and thenceforward earned not only his own living, but helped to care for the less able members of the family. At fourteen he gave his father $200 for his "time" — that is, for the time he would be a minor, and his father would, therefore, be legally entitled to his earnings. The General came into Jefferson county about 1815. He first located at Smithville, where he went into business with old-time Jesse Smith. When less than twenty years of age he bought over $5,000 worth of goods, and from Smithville, went to Clayton. Several years later (about 1834) he was at Sackets Harbor. In 1824 he had married Miss Harriet Warner. Seven children were born to this union, four of whom are still living. While at Sackets Harbor the General became associated in the management of the Sackets Harbor Bank, which was later merged into the Bank of Watertown, of which, about 1842, General Angell became sole owner. In 1858 his beloved wife died — a lady well remembered in Watertown for her devotion to charity and Christian works. The deserving poor never had a better friend, for what she gave was given with a grace and gentleness that made the action doubly endearing.

In 1860, General Angell married Miss M. Louise Judson, cousin of the late Gen. R. W. Judson, of Ogdensburg. She was an accomplished lady, the pattern for a kind, dutiful wife. In 1861, at the beginning of the civil war, the General removed to New York, where he become interested in several city contracts, and in 1862 he removed his family to that city, which was thenceforth his home. By nature he was too active to relish a life of idleness, and he took up several means of acquiring wealth, among others extending the circulation of his bank from $29,000 to $80,000. He was also largely interested in the Continental Steel Works at Maspeth, Long Island. In 1863 the imposition of a tax of ten per cent upon the circulation of State Banks, drove them out of business. In 1871, General Angell had accumulated enough means to make home comfortable, and in that year he removed to Geneseo, expecting to spend there several years in the enjoyment of needed rest and a release from the cares of business. But his hopes were to be disappointed. On the 1st of July, 1872, he was his home early in life, instead of Watertown, he would have taken rank with George Law and the elder Vanderbilt, for he was their superior in shrewdness of management, in perspicuity, in ability to predict the rise or fall of cereals or articles of general consump-

GENERAL WILLIAM H. ANGELL.

taken ill, and after great suffering, died at Geneseo on November 26, 1872.

Viewed in the light of his varied and eventful career, General Angell was a character difficult to reproduce. He had a noble soul, which scorned little things. He was undoubtedly superior to the average able business men of his day—and had he made New York city tion. He was a firm friend, and he had many friends, for he was a friendly man, democratic in his ways, easily approached, never elated by success, nor intimidated by adversity. From 1820 to 1861, he was a conspicuous figure in Jefferson county, and his removal was a source of sincere regret.

J. A. H.

THE WHITTLESEY AFFAIR.

IN giving an extended notice of this Whittlesey episode, we are perhaps open to the criticism of making a great deal out of a comparatively unimportant matter; but there is so much of tragedy in the story, and it affords so striking an illustration of the soul-destroying influence of a dishonest greed for money, that the tale rises above a mere relation, and becomes a great moral lesson. In that light we present it as a legitimate chapter of history.

Samuel Whittlesey, originally from Tolland, Ct., had removed, about 1808, to Watertown, and engaged in business as a lawyer. On the 12th of February, 1811, he received the appointment of district attorney for the territory comprised in Lewis, Jefferson and St. Lawrence counties, and on the 6th of February, 1813, he was superseded by the appointment of Amos Benedict, who had preceded him. Events connected with this, led to some sympathy for him, and the office of brigade paymaster, which had been tendered to Mr. Jason Fairbanks, was by him declined in favor of Whittlesey, and he, with Perley Keyes, became security for the honest discharge of the duties of the office. At the close of the war a large amount of money being due to the drafted militia, for services on the frontier, Whittlesey went to New York, accompanied by his wife, to obtain the money, and received at the Merchants' Bank in that city $30,000, in one, two, three, five and ten-dollar bills, with which he started to return. At Schenectady, as was afterwards learned, his wife reported themselves robbed of $8,700, an occurrence which greatly distressed and alarmed him, but she advised him not to make it public at that moment, as they might thereby better take steps that might lead to its recovery, and on the way home, she in an artful and gradual manner persuaded him that "if they should report the robbery of a part of the money, no one would believe it, as a thief would take the whole, if any. In short (to use a homely proverb), she urged that they might as well "die for an old sheep as a lamb," and keep the rest, as they would inevitably be accused of taking a part. Her artifice, enforced by the necessities of the case, took effect, and he suffered himself to become the dupe of his wife, who was doubtless the chief contriver of the movements which followed. Accordingly, on his return, he gave out word that his money had been procured, and would be paid over as soon as the necessary papers and pay-roll could be prepared. In a few days, having settled his arrangements, he started for Trenton on horseback, with his portmanteau filled, stopping at various places on his way, to announce that on a given day he would return, to pay to those entitled, their dues, and in several instances evinced a carelessness about the custody of his baggage that excited remark from inn-keepers and others. On arriving at Billings' tavern at Trenton, he assembled several persons to whom money was due, and proceeded to pay them, but upon opening his portmanteau, he, to the dismay of himself and others, found that they had been ripped open, and that the money was gone! With a pitiable lamentation and well-affected sorrow, he bewailed the robbery, instantly despatched messengers in quest of the thief, offered $2,000 reward for his apprehension, and advertised in staring handbills throughout the country, in hopes of gaining some clew that would enable him to recover his treasure. In this anxiety he was joined by hundreds of others, who had been thus indefinitely delayed in the receipt of their needed and rightful dues, but although there was no lack of zeal in these efforts, yet nothing occurred upon which to settle suspicion, and with a heavy heart, and many a sigh and tear, he returned home, and related to his family and friends his ruin. As a natural consequence, the event became at once the absorbing theme of the country, for great numbers were affected in their pecuniary concerns by it, and none more than the two endorsers of the sureties of Whittlesey. These gentlemen, who were shrewd, practical and very observing men, immediately began to interrogate him, singly and alone, into the circumstance of the journey and the robbery, and Fairbanks in particular, whose trade as a saddler led him to be minutely observant of the qualities and appearances of leather, made a careful examination of the incisions in the portmonteau, of which there were two, tracing upon paper their exact size and shape, and upon close examination, noticed pin holes in the margin, as if they had been mended up. Upon comparing the accounts which each had separately obtained in a long and searching conversation, these men became convinced that the money had not been stolen in the manner alleged, but that it was still in the possession of Whittlesey and his wife. To get possession of this money was their next care, and, after long consultation, it was agreed that the only way to do this, was to gain the confidence of the family, and defend them manfully against the insinuations that came from all quarters that the money was still in town. In this they succeeded admirably, and from the declarations which they made in public and in private, which found their way directly back to the family, the latter were convinced that, although the whole world were against them in their misfortunes, yet they had the satisfaction to know that the two men who were the most interested were still by their side. To gain some fact that would lead to a knowledge of the place of deposit, Messrs. Fairbanks and Keyes agreed to listen at the window of the sleeping room of those suspected, which was in a chamber, and overlooked the roof of a piazza. Accordingly, after dark, one would call upon the family and detain them in conversation, while the other mounted a ladder and placed himself where he could overhear what was said within, and although they thus became convinced that the money was still in their possession, no opinion could be formed about the hiding place. Security upon their real estate was demanded, and readily given.

A son of the family held a commission in the navy, and was on the point of sailing for the Mediterranean, and it was suspected that the money might thus have been sent off, to ascertain which, Mr. Fairbanks, under pretext of taking a criminal to the State Prison, went to New York, made inquiries which satisfied him that the son was innocent of any knowledge of the affair, and ascertained at the bank the size of the packages taken. He had been told by Whittlesey that these had not been opened when stolen, and by making experiments with blocks of wood of the same dimensions, they readily ascertained that bundles of that size could not be got through an aperture of the size reported, and that instead of a seven it required an eighteen-inch slit in the leather to allow of their being extracted. Some facts were gleaned at Albany that shed further light, among which it was noticed that Mrs. Whittlesey at her late visit (although very penurious in her trade) had been very profuse in her expenses. After a ten-days' absence Mr. Fairbanks returned; his partner having listened nights meanwhile, and the intelligence gained by eves-dropping, although it failed to disclose the locality of the lost money, confirmed their suspicions. As goods were being boxed up at Whittlesey's house at a late hour in the night, and the daughters had already been sent on to Sackets Harbor, it was feared that the family would soon leave; decisive measures were resolved upon to recover the money, the ingenuity and boldness of which evince the sagacity and energy of the parties. Some method to decoy Whittlesey from home, and frighten him by threats, mutilation or torture, into a confession, was discussed, but as the latter might cause an uncontrollable hemorrhage, it was resolved to try the effect of drowning. Some experiments were made on their own persons, of the effect of submersion of the head, and Dr. Sherwood, a physician of the village, was consulted on the time life would remain under water. Having agreed upon a plan, on the evening before its execution, they repaired to a lonely place about a mile south of the village, screened from the sight of houses by a gentle rise of ground, and where a spring issued from the bank and flowed off through a miry slough, in which, a little below, they built a dam of turf that formed a shallow pool. It was arranged that Mr. Fairbanks should call upon Whittlesey, to confer with him on some means of removing the suspicions which the public had settled upon him, by obtaining certificates of character from leading citizens and officers of the army; and that the two were to repair to Mr. Keyes's house, which was not far from the spring. Mr. Keyes was to be absent repairing his fence, and to leave word with his wife that if any one inquired for him, to send them into the field where he was at work. Neither had made confidants in their suspicions or their plans, except that Mr. Keyes thought it necessary to reveal them to his son, P. Gardner Keyes, then seventeen years of age, whose assistance he might need, in keeping up appearances, and in whose sagacity and fidelity in keeping a secret he could rely.

Accordingly, on the morning of July 17th (1815), Mr. Keyes, telling his wife that the cattle had broken into his grain, shouldered his axe and went to repair the fence which was thrown down, and Mr. Fairbanks called upon Whittlesey, engaged him in conversation, as usual, and without exciting the slightest suspicion, induced him to go up to see his partner, whom they found in a distant part of the field at work. Calling him to them, they repaired as if casually to the spring, where, after some trifling remark, they explicitly charged him with the robbery, gave their reasons for thinking so, and told him that if he did not instantly disclose the locality of the money, the pool before him should be his grave. This sudden and unexpected charge frightened their victim; but with a look of innocence he exclaimed, "I know nothing of the matter." This was no sooner said than he was rudely seized by Mr. Keyes and plunged headforemost into the pool, and after some seconds withdrawn. Being again interrogated, and assured that if the money were restored, no legal proceedings would be instituted, he again protested his innocence, and was a second time plunged in, held under several moments and again withdrawn, but this time insensible, and for one or two minutes it was doubtful whether their threats had not been executed; but he soon evinced signs of life, and so far recovered as to be able to sit up and speak. Perhaps nothing but the certain knowledge of his guilt, which they possessed, would have induced them to proceed further; but they were men of firmness, and resolved to exhaust their resource of expedients, rightly judging that a guilty conscience could not long hold out against the prospect of speedy death. He was accordingly addressed by Mr. Keyes in tones and emphasis of sober earnest, and exhorted for the last time to save himself from being hurried before the tribunal of Heaven, laden with guilt—to disclose at once. In feeble tones he re-asserted his innocence, and was again collared and plunged in, but this time his body only was immersed. It had been agreed in his hearing, that Fairbanks (being without a family) should remain to accomplish the work, by treading him into the bottom of the slough, while Keyes was to retire, so that neither could be a witness of murder if apprehended; and that on a given day they were to meet in Kingston. Keyes paid over about $90 to bear expenses of travel, and was about to leave, when the wretched man, seeing these serious arrangements, and at length believing them to be an awful reality, exclaimed, "I'll tell you all about it!" Upon this, he was withdrawn, and when a little recovered, he confessed, that all but about $9,000 (which he now, for the first time, stated to have been stolen at Schenectady), would be found either under a hearth at his house, or quilted into a pair of drawers in his wife's possession. Mr. Keyes, leaving his prisoner in charge of his associate, started for the house, and was seen by his wife, coming across the fields, covered Hutchinson and John M. Canfield, the facts, and with them repaired to the house of Whittlesey. Seeing them approach, Mrs. Whittlesey fled to her chamber, and on their knocking for admission, she replied that she was changing her dress, and would meet them shortly. As it was not the time or place for the observance of etiquette, Mr. Keyes rudely burst open the door, and entering, found her reclin-

THE "BON VOYAGE" ENTERING ALEXANDRIA BAY.

with mud, and, to use the words of the latter, "looking like a murderer;" and although in feeble health, and scarcely able to walk, she met him at the door, and inquired with alarm, "What have you been doing?" He briefly replied, "We have had the old fellow under water, and made him own where the money is;" and hastily proceeding to the village, related in a few words to his friends, Dr. Paul ing on the bed. Disregarding her expostulations of impropriety, he rudely proceeded to search, and soon found between the straw and feather bed, upon which she lay, a quilted garment, when she exclaimed : "You've got it! My God, have I come to this?" The drawers bore the initials of Col. Tuttle, who had died in that house, under very suspicious circumstances; were fitted with two sets of buttons, for either the husband or wife to wear, and contained about thirty parcels of bills, labelled, "For my dear son C———, 250 of 5;" "For my dear daughter E———, 150 of 3," etc., amounting to $15,000 to her five children; the remainder being reserved for her own use. The garment also contained a most extraordinary document, which might be called Her Will, and about which she expressed the most urgent solicitude, imploring, "That you have children as well as me!" It was soon after published in the papers, and was as follows:

"It is my last and dying request, that my children shall have all the money that is contained in the papers which have their names on, which is $3,000 for each; and let there be pains and caution, and a great length of time taken to exchange it in. God and my own heart knows the misery I have suffered in consequence of it, and that it was much against my will that it should be done. I have put all that is in the same bank by it, that I had from prudence, and a great number of years been gathering up; and when I used to meet with a bill on that bank in your possession, or when I could, I used to exchange others for them, as I supposed it was the best, and would be the most permanent bank. You know the reason of your taking this was, that we supposed that from the lock of the small trunk being broken, and the large one being all loose, and the nails out, that we were robbed on the road of $8,700. You know that I always told you, that I believed it was done in the yard, where you, as I told you then, put the wagon imprudently in Schenectady. Oh! how much misery am I born to see, through all your improper conduct, which I am forced to conceal from the view of the world, for the sake of my beloved offsprings' credit, and whereby I have got enemies undeservedly, while the public opinion was in your favor! But it fully evinces what false judgments the world makes. Oh! the God who tries the hearts, and searches the veins of the children of men, knows that the kind of misery which I have suffered, and which has riled and soured my temper, and has made me appear cross and morose to the public eye, has all proceeded from you, and fixed in my countenance the mark of an ill-natured disposition, which was naturally formed for loves, friendships, and other refined sensations. How have I falsified the truth, that you might appear to every advantage, at the risk and ill-opinion of the sensible world towards myself, when my conscience was telling me I was doing wrong; and which, with everything else that I have suffered since I have been a married woman, has worn me down and kept me out of health; and now, oh! now, this last act is bringing me to my grave fast. I consented because you had placed me in the situation you did. In the first place you were delinquent in the payment to the government of eighteen or nineteen hundred dollars. Then this almost $9,000 missing, I found when you came to settle, that you never could make it good without sacrificing me and my children, was the reason I consented to the proposal. I did you the justice to believe that the last sum had not been missing, that you would not have done as you did; but I am miserable! God grant that my dear children may never fall into the like error that their father has, and their poor unfortunate mother consented to! May the Almighty forgive us both, for I freely forgive you all you have made me suffer."

The money being counted, and to their surprise found to embrace a part of the sum supposed to be stolen, Mr. Keyes went back to release Whittlesey. The latter, meanwhile, had related the circumstances of the robbery, and anxiously inquired whether, if the whole was not found, they would still execute their purpose; to which Mr. Fairbanks replied in a manner truly characteristic, "that will depend on circumstances." No one was more surprised than Whittlesey himself, to learn that most of the money was found, and that he had been robbed at Schenectady by his own wife. He begged hard to be released on the spot, but it was feared he would commit suicide, and he was told that he must be delivered up to the public as sound as he was taken, and was led home. The fame of this discovery soon spread, and it was with difficulty the villagers were restrained from evincing their joy by the discharge of cannon. Mr. Whittlesey was led home and placed with a guard in the room with his wife, until further search; and here the most bitter criminations were exchanged, each charging the other with the crime, and the wife upbraiding the husband with cowardice for revealing the secret. The guard being withdrawn in the confusion that ensued, Mrs. Whittlesey passed from the house, and was seen by a person at a distance to cross the cemetery of Trinity church, where, on passing the grave of a son, she paused, faltered and fell back, overwhelmed with awful emotion; but a moment after, gathering new energy, she hastened on, rushed down the high bank near the ice-cave, and plunged into the river. Her body was found floating near the lower bridge, and efforts were made to recover life, but it was extinct.

The sympathies of the public were not withheld from the children of this family, who were thus cast penniless and disgraced upon the world. Many details connected with the affair we have not given; among which were several attempts to throw suspicion upon several parties by depositing money on their premises, writing anonymous letters, etc.; which served but to aggravate the crime by betraying the existence of a depravity on the part of the chief contriver in the scheme, which has seldom or never been equaled. The marked bills amounting to $400 had been dropped on the road to Sackets Harbor, and were found by Mr. Gale, who prudently carried them to a witness, counted and sealed them and after the disclosure brought them forward. Mr. Whittlesey stated that he expected some one would find and use the money, when he could swear to the marks, and implicate the finder. Mr. Gale, upon hearing this, was affected to tears, and exclaimed: "Mr. Whittlesey, is it possible you would have been so wicked as to have sworn me to State Prison for being honest!"

Mr. Whittlesey remained in Watertown nearly a year, and then moved to Indiana, where he afterwards became a justice of the peace and a county judge, and by an exemplary life won the respect of the community; and although the details of this affair followed him, yet the censure of opinion rested upon the wife.

Congress, on the 11th of January, 1821, passed an act directing the Secretary of the Treasury to cancel and surrender the bond given by Whittlesey and endorsed by Fairbanks and Keyes, on condition of the latter giving another, payable with interest in two years, for the balance remaining unaccounted for — thus virtually closing up a business arrangement which had been a continued occasion for anxiety and trouble to them through successive years.

In speaking of the Whittlesey matter, to the author of this History, Mr. Fairbanks said:

Before we executed our plan we had positive evidence of his knowledge of the transaction and of his guilt; and, on the strength of that, we did not expect to proceed to extremities further than to frighten him until he informed us where the money was secreted. But his stubborness held out much longer than we supposed it would or could. When we put the evidence of his guilt before him in such a plain manner his looks were evidence of it. We informed him that there was no doubt about it, and I believe that there is not one case in a thousand where evidence was so palpable as in this case. But Lynch Law is a dangerous one, and I would not advise it. But with other guilty parties who have stolen from me and been detected, I believe I have used more mild and lenient measures. I have probably caught twenty persons pilfering from me, and I have always made them give me a confession in writing, and then promised them, that as they had relatives who would be disgraced by their conduct, I would keep it a profound secret until they committed the crime again, when I would prosecute them. I found this plan the surest method of reforming them.

THE "PATRIOT" WAR.

COPIED FROM HADDOCK'S HISTORY OF JEFFERSON COUNTY, N. Y.

DURING the fall of 1837 there occurred one of the most curious, and what would now be classed as inexcusable and insane, episodes that Jefferson county and the whole northern frontier had ever witnessed — nothing more nor less than a popular effort on the part of American citizens to overthrow the government of Canada by an unwarranted invasion of the frontier towns, expecting to arouse the people to immediate participation in the rebellious effort as soon as a stand should have been made. Ridiculous as this affair appears at this day, it was a popular and an enthusiastic effort at the time, drawing into its service many educated and apparently levelheaded men, and meeting with an amount of smypathy in Northern New York that was really astonishing.

There had been for some time considerable discontent in Canada, some claiming that they were virtually shut out from proper participation in the government, and their repeated efforts to obtain better legislation had been disregarded. This discontent was more pronounced in the Lower Province, where the French Canadians had great influence, and had never in their hearts yielded a loyal support to the English rule over a country which had once belonged to France. It was said at the time that the charges made by the Canadians against their rulers were greater than the causes that separated the American colonies from the English. The Reform party in Parliament of the Upper Province was led by William Lyon McKenzie, and Papenau was the leader in the Lower Province. The Home Government sustained all the alleged oppressive acts of the local government. The Reform party refused to vote supplies for the support of the government, and the Parliaments were dissolved. The excitement had become great all through the provinces, extending to the frontiers on this side. The parliament buildings at Montreal were burned. The first collision between the Reform parties and the Tories, in the Upper Province, was on Yonge street, Toronto, where several were killed. The feeling now became very intense. The reform party contained many determined and resolute men, but they desired relief from British oppression through peaceful means. They had never contemplated a resort to arms, but the feeling in both provinces was aroused to such an extent that it could not be peaceably controlled. The feeling for the "relief" of Canada seemed to pervade all classes; secret societies were formed in the principal towns on this side as well as many on the Canadian side of the river. They were called Hunter's Lodges, and had signs and pass-words by which they could recognize each other.

In the summer of 1837, William Lyon McKenzie and Gen. Van Rensselaer, with 300 men, established themselves on Navy Island in Canadian waters, between Chippewa and Grand Island, in the Niagara river. Reinforcements came to Navy Island from the American side. The little steamer "Caroline" was chartered to carry passengers and freight to the island from Buffalo. On the night of November 29, 1837, while this steamer was moored at Schlosser's wharf, a captain in the English army with a company of British soldiers, boarded her and set her on fire, and cutting the boat loose, sent her adrift over Niagara Falls. One Captain Alexander McLeod, while on a debauch at Niagara, made his boast that he was one of the gang that burned the Caroline. He was arrested for the murder of Durfee. His trial was commenced at Canandaigua, but it was considered unsafe and he was removed to Utica. His defense was that he acted under the authority of the British government. He proved an alibi and was acquitted, being defended by able Canadian lawyers. The outrage was complained of by Governor Marcy to Martin Van Buren, then President of the United States, but no demand on the British government was ever made. The President issued a proclamation forbidding all persons from aiding or assisting, in any way, the rebellious acts of any people, or collection of people who interfered with the execution of the laws of a friendly nation, declaring all such persons outlaws and not entitled to the protection of the American government.

Great preparations were soon made for an attack upon Kingston, while the St. Lawrence was bridged with ice. On the night of February 19, 1838, the arsenal at Watertown, N. Y., was broken into and 400 stand of arms were taken. The arsenals at Batavia and Elizabethtown were also plundered. On the 20th of February patriots began to flock to French Creek in large numbers with a supply of arms and ammunition, consisting of 1,000 stand of arms, twenty barrels of cartridges and a large store of provisions. It was intensely cold, and the men suffered from exposure. General Rensselaer Van Rensselaer, a son of General Van Rensselaer, of the war of 1812, was to assume the command. Either through the cowardice of the officers or the men, no man saw Canadian soil, and after much talk of bravery the men dispersed to their homes. It was reported that Colonel Bonnycastle, at the head of 1,600 men, was coming from Kingston to make an attack upon the town, and through fear and of the loved ones at home, the patriots scattered without much ceremony, leaving all their arms and ammunition behind. This flight homeward was as ridiculous as their attempt was insane.

On the night of May 30, 1838, the Canadian steamer, Sir Robert Peel, which was commanded by John B. Armstrong, on her way from Brockville to Toronto, with nineteen passengers and about £20,000 in specie for paying off the troops in the Upper Province, was taking on wood at McDonnell's wharf, in the southern channel of the St. Lawrence, above Alexandria Bay, when a company of men, led by "Bill" Johnston, the alleged hero of the Thousand Islands, disguised and painted like savages, armed with muskets and bayonets, rushed on board, shouting, "Remember the Caroline." The night was dark and rainy. The passengers (who were asleep in the cabin) together with the crew were ordered on shore. The boat was then pushed out into the river and burned. The sunken hull can be seen there to this day. Heavy rewards were offered for the apprehension of the offenders by both governments. Twelve of the band were arrested and held in the Watertown jail for about six months. On the 2d of June, Anderson was indicted and held for arson in the first degree. He was tried before John P. Cushman, one of the circuit judges, and defended by Calvin McKnight, Benjamin Wright, John Clark and Bernard Bagley. After a deliberation of two hours the jury brought in a verdict of "not guilty." After a time the others were released on their own recognizance, and were never subjected to a trial.

William Johnston was born in Lower Canada and became a confidential friend of William Lyon McKenzie. He became a leader in the Reform party, and afterwards removed to French Creek. He was a man of great energy, but bore a bad reputation. Johnston was now considered the patriotic commander, and a band under his command fortified themselves on one of the islands within the Jefferson county line. His daughter, Kate Johnston, held communication with them and furnished them with provisions and supplies. It was at this time that Johnston published the following curious manifesto — which is, so far as the writer knows, the only instance in which an outlaw had the "cheek" to declare war from his place of hiding against a friendly nation:

"I, William Johnston, a natural born citizen of Upper Canada, do hereby declare that I hold a commission in the Patriot service as commander-in-chief of the naval forces and flotilla. I commanded the expedition that captured and destroyed the Sir Robert Peel. The men under my command in that expedition were nearly all natural born English subjects. The exceptions were volunteers. My headquarters are on an island in the St. Lawrence without the line of the jurisdiction of the United States, at a place named by me Fort Wallace. I am well acquainted with the boundary line and know which of the islands do, and which do not, belong to the United States. Before I located my headquarters I referred to the decisions of the commissioner made at Utica, under the sixth article of the treaty of Ghent. I know the number of the island and know that by the division of the commissions it is British territory. I yet hold possession of the station and act under orders. The object of my movement is the independence of the Canadas. I am not at war with the commerce or property of the United States.

"Signed this 10th day of June in the year of our Lord one thousand eight hundred and thirty-eight.

"WILLIAM JOHNSTON."

The effect of this manifesto was quite important, as it was distributed through all the provinces and in all parts of the frontier States. The excitement along the frontiers grew more intense. Sir Allan McNab, the governor-general, fearing for the safety of his life, had resigned, and in returning to England passed through Watertown disguised as a laborer. He was recognized by Jason Fairbanks while sitting on a wheelbarrow in front of Gilson's tavern, waiting for the stage for Utica. Being advised by some of the leading men that he need have no fear of danger while travelling through the States, he changed his disguise and assumed his former dignity. Lord Durham succeeded him as governor-general. The secret lodges were now making large additions to their membership. It had now become evident that a stand was to be made somewhere for the threatened invasion.

On the 10th of November, two schooners, the "Charlotte," of Oswego, and the "Isabelle," of Toronto, left Oswego with arms and ammunition and about 300 men for some Canadian point on the St. Lawrence. The steamer "United States" left Oswego on the following morning for the same destination, touching at Sackets Harbor and taking on board about 100 men, besides arms and ammunition. The schooners had proceeded as far as Millen's Bay, below Cape Vincent, and the steamer "United States" coming up took them in tow, one on each side. There were now about 500 men on board the boat, all young, destined for some point known to but very few, if any, except the officers. They were fully officered, Gen. J. Ward Birge holding the appointment of commander-in-chief. He was very sanguine, but his subsequent acts made him conspicuous as a coward. These vessels being well supplied with field pieces, small arms, ammunition and provisions, started on the morning of the 17th of November, down the river. When passing Alexandria Bay, Charles Crossmon, one of these "patriots," then a young man of twenty years, full of patriotic impulses, little thought that one day at this point a beautiful tourist home should bear his name.

The boats swept down the river until abreast of Prescott. At that point the schooners were detached, and dropped down to Windmill Point, about a mile below the city, where stood an abandoned windmill. In trying to land, the schooners ran aground, one near the point and the other farther down the river. About 250 men landed from the schooners, and the greater part of the guns and ammunition, together with one twelve pounder and two brass seven pounders were brought down. They then took possession of the windmill, which they held with three other stone buildings. The schooners, after getting afloat with the balance of the men and ammunition, sailed for Ogdensburg. This looked rather discouraging to the men in the windmill, to see these schooners leave them with many of their men and nearly all of their provisions and ammunition. Colonel Worth and the United States Marshal, Garron, afterwards seized the vessels and all of their cargoes. Prospects began to darken for the Patriots. They were deserted by nearly all of their officers. General Birge wilted at the first chance of facing British bullets. It happened that among the Patriot band was a Polish exile, Niles Sobelitcki Von Schoultz, who came from Salina. He was of noble birth, his father being an officer of high rank, and he himself had been an officer in the Polish service. He had been deluded into the project of freeing Canada from "tyranny and oppression." In the emergency he was now placed in command. It had all along been understood that as soon as a stand was made by any Patriot force, the Canadians would flock to their standard. In this they now found themselves grossly deceived; not a single man came to their relief. They were looked upon as brigands and robbers. On the morning of the 18th, three Canadian steamboats, the "Coburg," the "Experiment" and the "Traveller," with about 400 regular troops from Kingston, were seen coming down the river. They landed at Prescott. It was now evident that some fighting was to be done. Von Schoultz gave great encouragement to his men, advising them to brave the British bullets and stand by each other to the last man. They agreed to follow wherever he should lead.

The British steamers were now patroling the river, and occasionally firing shots at the wind-mill. One shot was fired at the steamer "United States" while in American waters passing through her wheel house, killing the man at the wheel. The British troops, under Colonel Dundas, came marching from Prescott to annihilate the Patriots. Von Schoultz marched his men out of the building into the field. They formed in line behind a stone fence, which they used as a breast-work. The British commenced firing when about 150 yards away, and continued their firing as they advanced, without doing any injury. The "Patriots" held their fire until the

BAT-WING SAIL.

enemy had advanced to within fifteen rods, and then they got the order to fire. This broad-side resulted in killing thirty-six British soldiers, and wounding many others. The British fell back, but the firing continued on both sides. This was followed by the withdrawal of the "Patriots"—some into the wind-mill, and others occupying the outhouses, but continuing their fire at long range. The cannon shots aimed at the mill glanced off and produced no effect upon the walls. The battle raged three hours and twenty minutes, during which time six of the Patriots had been killed, and twenty-one wounded. It was estimated that seventy-five of the British lay dead upon the field, and 150 were wounded. Colonel Dundas now sent a flag of truce, asking a cessation of hostilities for an hour, that he might remove his dead and wounded, which was cheerfully granted by Von Schoultz.

The strife was watched with intense interest by a large crowd of people at Ogdensburg, directly opposite. The river now being clear, Hon. Preston King, with a few volunteers, chartered the "Paul Pry" to go over and get the Patriots away from the wind-mill. This was done probably by consent of the British forces. The boat went over, but only a few of the men chose to leave. Jonah Woodruff, the artist, afterwards the sleeping-car inventor and proprietor, was one of those who came away on the "Paul Pry." As time was precious, the night dark and the limit of the truce uncertain, the men in the mill irresolute and under poor military subjection, Mr. King and his party were forced to leave with but few, when all could have been saved.

About 10 o'clock on the third day the British regulars, reinforced with about 1,000 militia, came bearing down upon this almost defenceless band in the old mill. They had but little ammunition left, but they resolved to sell their lives as dearly as possible. The troops continued firing their cannon and volleys of musket balls, however, without perilous effect. At length Von Schoultz ordered a cannon loaded with musket balls, spikes and pieces of iron placed in the door of the mill, and at an opportune moment it was discharged, killing twenty-five of the British and wounding as many more. This threw them into confusion, and they retreated.

At length Von Schoultz saw that his men could not stand another charge, and, with much reluctance, sent out a flag of truce, the bearers of which were immediately taken prisoners. They then displayed a white flag from the top of the mill, but no notice was taken of it. Towards night Colonel Dundas sent out a flag demanding a surrender of the men at his discretion. Von Schoultz offered to surrender as prisoners of war, but Colonel Dundas would grant no conditions. Finally the little band, finding opposition hopeless, gave themselves up without terms into the hands of the British commander.

Thus ended one of the most foolish and ill-conceived expeditions that was ever undertaken. Nineteen of the patriots were killed, thirty-five were wounded and about 190 were taken prisoners. The latter were placed on board the steamers and taken to Kingston, where they were confined in Fort Henry. It was estimated that about 125 of the British were killed and 200 wounded.

The prisoners were confined in squads of fifteen to twenty in small rooms in the fort, and placed under a strong guard. Sir George Arthur had decided that they were brigands and must be tried by a court martial, to be composed of seven field officers and seven captains of the line.

The serious condition of these prisoners excited the sympathy of the people of Jefferson county as well as of their friends, and meetings were held in all the towns under great excitement, petitions being circulated far and wide and extensively signed. These were presented to Sir George Arthur, the governor-general, asking clemency for these poor deluded victims. The best legal talent in the State volunteered their aid in defence of the prisoners, and in mitigation of their condition. William H. Seward, Philo Gridley, Hiram Denio, Joshua A. Spencer, Bernard Bagley and George C. Sherman, all united and used their best efforts in appealing to the governor-general for clemency.

The court convened on the 28th of November; Daniel George being the first prisoner to be tried, pleaded not guilty. When he was taken from the steamer, papers were found in his pockets commissioning him as paymaster of the eastern division of the Patriot army. Von Schoultz was then brought before the court for trial. He employed the barrister, Sir John McDonald, to aid him in his defense. He pleaded guilty. He sent a written appeal to the governor-general, in which he stated that he was deluded into joining in the invasion of Canada by the gross misrepresentations of such men as J. Ward Birge and William Lyon McKenzie, who claimed to know the sentiment and wishes of the people of Canada, and that they would be received with open arms. Also, that the militia, when called out, would flock to their standard. All of which proved to be a base delusion. He asked for mercy at his hands. Every means of influence which could be brought to bear upon the governor-general by such men as Judge Fine, Silas Wright and a host of others, could not change his determination of executing all the officers and leaders.

Dorephus Abbey, a former newspaper editor of Watertown, was the next to be tried. He was captured while carrying a flag of truce, and was next in rank to Von Schoultz. Next was Martin Woodruff. All of these, after trial, namely : Daniel George, Nicholas Von Schoultz, Dorephus Abbey and Martin Woodruff were sentenced by Sir George Arthur to be hanged, and this sentence was carried out December 8th. Von Schoultz made his will, giving, among his many bequests, $10,000 for the benefit of the families of the British soldiers who were killed at the battle of the Windmill. He also wrote the following pathetic and farewell letter to his friend, Warren Green, of Syracuse:

"DEAR FRIEND,—When you get this letter, I shall be no more. I have been informed that my execution will take place to-morrow. May God forgive them who brought me to this untimely death. Hard as my fate is, I have made up my mind to forgive them, and do. I have been promised a lawyer to write my will — intend to appoint you my executor. If the British government permits it, I wish my body delivered to you and buried on your farm. I have no time to write more because I have great need of communicating with my Creator to prepare myself for His presence. The time allowed me for this is short. My last wish to the Americans is, that they will not think of avenging my death. Let no further blood be shed. And believe me, from what I have seen, all the stories which were told of the sufferings of the Canadian people were untrue. Give my love to your sister, and tell her that I think of her as I do of my own mother. May God reward her for her kindness. I further beg of you to take care of W. J. so that he may find honorable bread. Farewell, my dear friends. May God bless you and protect you.
"*December* 18.
"N. VON SCHOULTZ."

Joel Peeler and Sylvanus Sweet were executed, January 11, 1839. Sylvester Lawton, Duncan Anderson, Christopher Buckley, Russell Phelps and Lyman H. Lewis were sent to the scaffold, February 11. They were followed by Martin Van Slyke, William O'Neal and James Cummings. The officers now having all been dealt with, they made quick work trying the men under them. The prisoners were brought into court in squads of from ten to fifteen, and asked a few questions, and were then returned to their quarters. They all expected that their doom was sealed, and were anxiously awaiting their death warrants. But a powerful influence was brought to bear upon Governor-General Arthur, and he finally decided that there would be no more executions, and went so far as to say that a number of them would be pardoned. The court had adjourned from January 4th to February 26th. The prisoners were allowed to receive visits from their friends, but under close guard. On the 8th of April the steamer "Commodore Barry" arrived at Sackets Harbor with twenty-two prisoners, pardoned by the governor-general. And on the 27th of April, thirty-seven more pardoned prisoners arrived at the same place. All released were under twenty-one years of age. The balance of the men remained in the fort all summer, uncertain as to their fate, whether they would be pardoned or banished. On the 17th of September, 1839, orders were given to prepare for departure, and ninety-five of them were heavily ironed, placed in canal barges and taken to Montreal, and there, with another lot of prisoners, making about 150 in all, were put on board the ship "Buffalo," bound for Van Dieman's Island.

February 13, 1840, after an uneventful voyage, they landed in the harbor of Hobart Town. After the inspector had taken a description of them, the governor, Sir John Franklin, who afterwards died during a voyage of exploration to the Arctic region, came to see them, and after looking them over, read their sentence, which was banishment for life. He was happy to learn of the captain of the "Buffalo" that they had behaved remarkably well during the voyage. He also informed them that they would be placed at hard labor on the public roads with other convicts, and that with good behavior, after three years, they would be granted tickets of leave, which would give them the liberty of the island.

After three years of this service, they were granted tickets of leave, but were confined within certain limits, and obliged to report at the station every Saturday night. If they so desired, they could be changed from one district to another. The deliverance from the heavy work they had hitherto endured was a blessing, and gave them new life. A reward of a pardon and free passage to America having been offered by the governor to any of the convicts who would capture some bushrangers who were infesting the island, W. Gates, Stephen Wright, Aaron Dresser and George Brown succeeded in discovering the hiding-place and capturing two of the rangers. They were pardoned, and, after a long voyage, returned to America, having served five years of a convict's life.

In September, 1845, the governor commenced to deal out pardons of ten and fifteen at a time. He thought it not quite safe to liberate too many at once. During the year 1846, all of the Canadian prisoners had received pardons excepting some few whose behavior did not entitle them to such a reward.

Thus ended the Patriot war. It was not without some beneficent results to the Canadas, for the home government granted them a new charter, by which the provinces were united into a dominion with a parliament. The Tories were defeated in the parliament, and the Reform party, after driving them from power, assumed control of the State. Even the outlaw, William Lyon McKenzie, was restored to citizenship, and was for many years a member of parliament, and the premier of the government. A curious phase of the Patriot troubles was the effect on the political heads of National and State governments. President Van Buren and Governor Marcy were both soundly denounced by many newspapers for performing their duty in enforcing the neutrality laws, and lost many votes in the frontier States. Marcy was succeeded by Seward, and on the day the election of Harrison was announced in Washington, the boys shouted about the White House the refrain : " Van! Van ! is a used-up man." And even General Scott attributed his failure to receive the Whig nomination at the Harrisburg National Convention to the machinations of Col. Solomon Van Rensselaer, a delegate from New York, who held a spite against General Scott for having " squelched " his son, the general in command at Navy Island. J. A. H.

During the "Patriot" war, Watertown and the adjoining towns were filled with expatriated "Patriots" who had fled from Canada to avoid arrest and imprisonment for alleged treason. Watertown being the headquarters of the Canadian leaders, William Lyon McKenzie, Van Rensselaer, and others, were located at the old stone Mansion House, kept by Luther Gilson, on the site of the present Iron block. The old hostelry was crowded with the patriots. During the early winter of 1838, the then governor-general of Upper Canada, who had been recalled from his position by the British government, was ordered to return. This notable official was Sir Francis Bond-Head, an ex-officer of the British army, and thoroughly despised in Canada. Wishing to reach New York to sail for England, he undertook to make the journey by stage to Utica via Watertown. Not desirous of meeting his expatriated subjects for fear of recognition and possible insult, he determined to pass through incognito. Leaving Kingston during the night, accompanied by a prominent citizen of that city, to whom he acted the part of valet (or gentleman's gentleman), he arrived safely next morning by wagon and driver, hired as an "extra." The driver, not being informed as to the quality or rank of his passengers, drove straight to the Mansion House, and landed his man at the headquarters of his enemies. It was just after the breakfast hour, and the lobby was filled with the Patriot community, who recognized the Kingston citizen and greeted him cordially, but did not recognize the valet, who discreetly kept in the back ground. Prominent among the Patriot leaders at the hotel was Hugh Scanlon, an Irish-Canadian, a bright and shrewd fellow. After a short time, Scanlon noticed that the valet was missing, and his suspicions were aroused, so he began to hunt him up. After looking high and low and all around the public square without finding him, he continued to search elsewhere, and at last found the lost valet cosily sitting on a wheelbarrow near the stables. Walking up to the late governor-general, he recognized him at once. Introducing himself, Scanlon invited him to breakfast and to meet his late subjects, assuring him that he would be welcome, and receive every courtesy due his rank. The governor accepted the invitation and came forward. He was met by all in a courteous and friendly way, and was assisted in his arrangements for departure. He left town in a coach and four, with cheers, and without a single uncomplimentary remark.   A. J. F.

SIGNALING THE "NORTH KING," OF THE CANADIAN LINE.

AN EPISODE OF NORTHERN NEW YORK.

MAJOR JOHN A. HADDOCK'S CELEBRATED BALLOON VOYAGE WITH PROFESSOR JOHN LA MOUNTAIN.

IT is now about thirty-five years since the undersigned made the memorable balloon voyage with Professor LaMountain — a voyage intended to be short and pleasant, but which resulted in a long and most disastrous one, entailing the loss of the valuable balloon, and seriously endangering the lives of the travellers. Since then, LaMountain, after serving through the great rebellion, has made his last "voyage," and has entered upon that existence where all the secrets of the skies are as well defined and understood as are the course of rivers here on the earth.

To fully understand my reasons for making the trip, some leading facts should be presented:

1. There had been, all through the year 1859, much excitement in the public mind upon the subject of ballooning. In August of that year, I returned from Labrador, and found that the balloon Atlantic, with Wise, Hyde, Gaeger and LaMountain, had been driven across a part of Lake Ontario, while on their great trip from St. Louis to New York city, and had landed and been wrecked in Jefferson county, N. Y., and the people of that whole section were consequently in a state of considerable excitement upon the subject of navigating the air.*

2. I had heard of other newspaper editors making trips in balloons, had read their glowing accounts, and it seemed to me like a very cunning thing. Desiring to enjoy "all that was a-going," I naturally wanted a balloon ride, too, and therefore concluded to go, expecting to be absent from home not more than ten or twelve hours at the longest, and to have a good time. Being a newspaper man, and always on the alert for news, I had also a natural desire to do all in my power to add to the local interest of my journal, and for that reason felt a willingness to go through with more fatigue and hazard than men are expected to endure in ordinary business pursuits.

3. I felt safe in going, as I knew that LaMountain was an intrepid and successful æronaut, and I thought his judgment was to be depended upon. How he was misled as to distance, and how little he knew, or any man can know, of air navigation, the narrative will readily demonstrate.

* The Wise named above was the celebrated æronaut, Professor John Wise, of Lancaster, Pa.; and I may here remark that the trip made by him and his associates is by far the longest on record. Leaving St. Louis at about 4 P. M., they passed the whole night in the air, were carried across the States of Illinois, Indiana, a portion of Ohio and Michigan, over the whole northwestern breadth of Pensylvania and New York, and were at last wrecked in a huge tree-top near the shore of Lake Ontario, at about 3 P. M. the next day, escaping with severe bruises, but without broken bones, after a journey of eleven hundred miles. These adventurers did not travel as fast, nor encounter the perils that awaited us, but they made a longer voyage. It was with this same balloon Atlantic that LaMountain and myself made our trip; but it had been reduced one-third in size, and was as good as new. John Wise afterwards lost his life in a balloon, but just where he perished was never known. Gaeger was a manufacturer of crockery, and he died in Massachusetts. Hyde is publishing a newspaper in one of the western States. LaMountain died in his bed at Lansingburgh, N. Y., about 1884.

With these explanations, I will proceed with my original narrative, nearly as written out at the time.

Nearly every one in Watertown is aware that the second ascension of the balloon Atlantic was advertised for the 20th of September, 1859. The storm of that and the following day obliged the postponement of the ascension until the 22d. Every arrangement had been made for a successful inflation, and at 27 minutes before 6 P. M., the glad words "all aboard" were heard from LaMountain, and that distinguished æronaut and myself stepped into the car. Many were the friendly hands we shook—many a fervent "God bless you," and "happy voyage," were uttered — and many handkerchiefs waved their mute adieus. "Let go all," and away we soared; in an instant all minor sounds of earth had ceased, and we were lifted into a silent sphere, whose shores were without an echo, their silence equaled only by that of the grave. No feeling of trepidation was experienced; an extraordinary elation took possession of us, and fear was as far removed as though we had been sitting in our own rooms at home.

Two or three things struck me as peculiar in looking down from an altitude of half a mile: the small appearance of our village from such a height and the beautiful mechanical look which the straight fences and oblong square fields of the farmers present. As we rose into the light, fleecy clouds, they looked between us and the earth like patches of snow we see lying upon the landscape in springtime; but when we rose a little higher the clouds completely shut out the earth, and the cold, white masses below us had precisely the same look that a mountainous snow-covered country does, as you look down upon it from a higher mountain. Those who have crossed the Alps — or have stood upon one of the lofty summits of the Sierra Nevada, and gazed down upon the eternal snows below and around them, will be able to catch the idea. In six minutes we were far above all the clouds, and the sun and we were face to face. We saw the time after that when his face would have been very welcome to us. In eight minutes after leaving the earth, the thermometer showed a fall of 24 degrees. It stood at 84 when we left. The balloon rotated a good deal, proving that we were ascending with great rapidity. At 5:48 the thermometer stood at 42, and falling very fast. At 5:50 we were at least two miles high — thermometer 34.

An unpleasant ringing sensation had now become painful, and I filled both ears with cotton. At 5:52 we put on our gloves and shawls — thermometer 32. The wet sandbags now became stiff with cold — they were frozen. Ascending very rapidly. At 5:54 thermometer 28, and falling. Here we caught our last sight of the earth by daylight. I recognized the St. Lawrence to the southwest of us, which showed we were drifting nearly north. At 6 o'clock we thought we were descending a little, and LaMountain directed me to throw out about 20 pounds of ballast. This shot us up again — thermometer 26, and falling very slowly. At 6:05 thermometer 22 — my feet were very cold. The Atlantic was now full, and presented a most splendid sight. The gas began to discharge itself at the mouth, and its abominable smell, as it came down upon us, made me sick. A moment's vomiting helped my case materially. LaMountain was suffering a good deal with cold. I passed my thick shawl around his shoulders, and put the blanket over our knees and feet. At 6:10 thermometer 18. We drifted along until the sun left us, and in a short time thereafter the balloon began to descend. We must have been, before we began to descend from this height, 3½ miles high. At 6:32 thermometer 23; rising. We were now about stationary, and thought we were sailing north of east. We could, we thought, distinguish water below us, but were unable to recognize it. At 6:38 we threw over a bag of sand, making 80 pounds of ballast discharged, and leaving about 120 pounds on hand. We distinctly heard a dog bark. Thermometer 28 — and rising rapidly. At 6:45 the thermometer stood at 33.

At 6:50 it was dark, and I could make no

more memoranda. I put up my note book, pencil and watch, and settled down in the basket, feeling quite contented. From this point until next morning I give my experience from memory only. The figures given were made at the time indicated, and the thermometric variations can be depended on as quite accurate.

We heard, soon after that, a locomotive whistle, and occasionally could hear wagons rumbling over the ground or a bridge, while the farmers' dogs kept up a continual baying, as if conscious there was something unusual in the sky. We sailed along, contented and chatty, until about half-past eight o'clock, when we distinctly saw lights below us, and heard the roaring of a mighty water-fall. We descended into a valley near a very high mountain, but, as the place appeared rather forbidding, we concluded to go up again. Over with 30 pounds of ballast, and sky-ward we sailed. In about 20 minutes we again descended, but this time no friendly light greeted us. We seemed to be over a dense wilderness, and the balloon was settling down into a small lake. We had our life-preservers ready for use, but got up again by throwing out all our ballast, except perhaps 20 pounds. LaMountain now declared it was folly to stay up any longer, that we were over a great wilderness, and the sooner we descended the better. We concluded to settle down by the side of some tall tree, tie up, and wait until morning. In a moment we were near the earth, and as we gently descended I grasped the extreme top of a high spruce, which stopped the balloon's momentum, and we were soon lashed to the tree by our large drag-rope.

We rolled ourselves up in our blankets, patiently waiting for the morning. The cold rain spouted down upon us in rivulets from the great balloon that lazily rolled from side to side over our heads, and we were soon drenched and uncomfortable as men could be. After a night passed in great apprehension and unrest, we were right glad to see the first faint rays of coming light. Cold and rainy the morning at last broke, the typical precursor of other dismal mornings to be spent in that uninhabited wilderness. We waited until 6 o'clock in hopes the rain would cease, and that the rays of the sun, by warming and thereby expanding the gas in the balloon, would give us ascending power sufficient to get up again, for the purpose of obtaining a view of the country into which we had descended. The rain did not cease, and we concluded to throw over all we had in the balloon, except a coat for each, the life-preservers, the anchor and the compass. Overboard, then, they went — good shawls and blankets, bottles of ale and a flask of cordial, ropes and traps of all kinds. The Atlantic, relieved of this wet load, rose majestically with us, and we were able to behold the country below. It was an unbroken wilderness of lakes and spruce — and I began then to fully realize that we had, indeed, gone too far, through a miscalculation of the velocity of the balloon. As the current was still driving us towards the north, we dare not stay up, as we were drifting still farther and farther into trouble. LaMountain seized the valve-cord and discharged the gas, and we descended in safety to the solid earth. Making the Atlantic fast by her anchor, we considered what was to be done.

We had not a mouthful to eat, no protection at night from the wet ground, were distant we knew not how far from any habitation, were hungry to start with, had no possible expectation of making a fire, and no definite or satisfactory idea as to where we were. We had not even a respectable pocket knife, nor a pin to make a fish hook of — indeed, we were about as well equipped for forest life as were the babes in the woods.

After a protracted discussion, in which all our ingenuity was brought to bear upon the question of our whereabouts, we settled in our minds (mainly from the character of the timber around us), that we were either in John Brown's tract, or in that wilderness lying between Ottawa City and Prescott, Canada. If this were so, then we knew that a course south by east would take us out if we had strength enough to travel the distance.

TRAMPING IN THE WOODS.

Acting upon our conclusion, we started through the woods towards the south-east. After travelling about a mile we came to the bank of a small stream flowing from the west, and were agreeably surprised to find that some human being had been there before us, for we found the stumps of several small trees and the head of a half-barrel, which had contained pork. I eagerly examined the inspection-stamp; it read:

"MESS PORK."
" P. M."
"MONTREAL."

This settled the question that we were in Canada, as I very well knew that no Montreal inspection of pork ever found its way into the State of New York. Although the course we had adopted was to be a south-easterly one, we yet concluded to follow this creek to the westward, and all day Friday we travelled up its banks — crossing it about noon on a floating log, and striking on the southern shore, a "blazed" path, which led to a deserted lumber road, and it in turn bring us to a log shanty on the opposite bank. We had hoped this lumber road would lead us out into a clearing or a settlement, but a careful examination satisfied us that the road ended here, its objective point evidently being the shanty on the other bank. We concluded to cross the creek to the shanty, and stay there all night. Collecting some small timbers for a raft, LaMountain crossed over safely, shoving the raft back to me. But my weight was greater than my companion's, and the frail structure sank under me, precipitating me into the water. I went in all over, but swam out, though it took all my strength to do so. On reaching the bank I found myself so chilled as scarcely to be able to stand. I took off all my clothes and wrung them as dry as I could. We then proceeded to the shanty, where we found some refuse straw, but it was dry, and under a pile of it we crawled — pulling it over our heads and faces, in the hope that our breath might aid in warming our chilled bodies. I think the most revengeful, stony heart would have pitied our condition then. I will not attempt to describe our thoughts as we lay there; home, children, wife, parents, friends, with their sad and anxious faces, rose up reproachfully before us as we tried to sleep. But the weary hours of night at last wore away, and at daylight we held a new council. It was evident, we argued, that the creek we were upon was used by the lumbermen for "driving" their logs in the spring freshets. If, then, we followed it to its confluence with the Ottawa or some stream which emptied into the Ottawa, we would eventually get out the same way the timber went out. The roof of the shanty was covered with the halves of hollow logs, scooped out in a manner familiar to all woodsmen. These were dry and light, and would make us an excellent raft. Why not, then, take four of these, tie them to cross-pieces by wythes and such odd things as we could find around the shanty, and pole the craft down stream to that civilization which even a saw-log appeared able to reach. Such, then, was the plan adopted, although it involved the retracing of all the steps hitherto taken, and an apparent departure from the course we had concluded would lead us out.

Without delay, then, we dragged the hollow logs down to the creek, and LaMountain proceeded to tie them together, as he was more of a sailor than myself. We at last got under way, and, as we pushed off, a miserable crow set up a dismal cawing — an inauspicious sign. We poled down the stream about a mile, when we came abruptly upon a large pine tree which had fallen across the current, and completely blocking the passage of the raft. No other course was left us but to untie the raft, and push the pieces through under the log. This was at last accomplished, when we tied our craft together again, and poled down the stream. To-day each of us ate a raw frog (all we could find), and began to realize that we were hungry. Yet there was no complaining — our talk was of the hopeful future, and of the home and civilization we yet expected to reach. Down the creek we went, into a lake some four miles long, and into which we of course supposed the stream to pass, with its outlet at the lower end. We followed down the northern bank, keeping always near the shore and in shallow water, so that our poles could touch the bottom, until we reached the lower extremity of the lake, where we found no outlet, and so turned back upon the southern shore in quest of one. On reaching the head of the lake, and examining the stream attentively, we found that the current of the creek turned abruptly to the right, which was the reason of our losing it. We felt happy to have found our current again, and plied our poles like heroes. We passed, late in the afternoon, the spot where we had at first struck the creek, and where we stuck up some dead branches as a landmark which might aid us in case we should, at a future time, attempt to save the Atlantic.

When night came on we did not stop, but kept the raft going down through the shades of awful forests, whose solemn stillness seemed to hide from us the unrevealed mystery of our darkening future. During the morning the rain had ceased, but about 10 o'clock at night it commenced again. We stopped the "vessel" and crawled in under some "tag" alders on the bank, where our extreme weariness enabled us to get, perhaps, half an hour's sleep. Rising again (for it was easier to pole the raft at night in the rain down an unknown stream amidst the shadows of that awful forest than to lie on the ground and freeze), we pressed on until perhaps 3 in the morning, when pure exhaustion compelled us to stop again. This time we found a spot where the clayey bank lacked a little of coming down to the water. On the mud we threw our little bundle of straw, and sat down with our feet drawn up under us, so as to present as little surface to the rain as possible. But we could not stand such an uncomfortable position long, and as the daylight of the Sabbath broke upon us, we were poling down the stream in a drizzling rain. At 8 o'clock we reached a spot at which the stream narrowed, rushing over large boulders, and between rocky shores. This was trouble, indeed. To get our raft down this place, we regarded as well-nigh hopeless. We tied up and examined the shore. Here, again, we found unmistakable marks left by the lumbermen, they having evidently camped at this point, to be handy by in the labor of getting the timber over this bad spot in the stream. The rapids were about a third of a mile long, and very turbulent. After a protracted survey we descended the bank, and thought it best to abandon our raft, and try our luck on foot again. After travelling about a mile, we found the bank so tangled and rugged, and ourselves so much exhausted, that satisfactory progress was impossible. So we concluded to go back, and if we could get the raft down, even one piece at a time, we would go on with her — if not, we would build as good a place as possible to shield us from the cold and wet, and there await with fortitude that death from starvation which was beginning to be regarded as a probability. This was our third day of earnest labor and distressing fatigue, and in all that time we had not eaten an ounce of food, nor had dry clothing upon us.

Acting upon our resolution, we at once commenced to get the raft down the rapids, and I freely confess that this was the most trying and laborious work of a whole life of labor. The pieces would not float over a rod at a time, before they would stick on some stone which the low water left above the surface, and then you must pry the stick over in some way, and pass it along to the next obstruction. We were obliged to get into the stream, often up to the middle, with slippery boulders beneath our feet. Several times I fell headlong —completely using up our compass, which now frantically pointed in any direction its addled head took a fancy to. The water had unglued the case, and it was ruined. After long hours of such labor, we got the raft down, and LaMountain again tied it together. Passing on, in about an hour, we came to a large lake, about ten miles long by six broad. Around it we must of course pass, until we should find the desired outlet. So we turned up to the right, and pressed on with as much resolution as we could muster. To-day we found one clam, which I insisted LaMountain should eat, as he was much weaker than myself, and had eaten nothing on the day we went up.

Part of this day LaMountain slept upon the raft, and I was "boss and all hands." As the poor fellow lay there, completely used up, I saw that he could not be of much more assistance in getting out. Erysipelas, from which he had previously suffered, had attacked his right eye; his face was shriveled so that he looked like an old man, and his clothes were nearly torn from his body. A few tears could not be restrained, and my prayer was for speedy deliverance or speedy death. While my companion was asleep, and I busily poling the raft along, I was forced to the conclusion, after deliberately canvassing all the chances, that we were pretty sure to perish there miserably at last. But I could not cease my efforts while I had strength, and so around the lake we went, into all the indentations of the shore, keeping always in shallow water. The day at last wore away, and we stopped at night at a place we thought least exposed to the wind. We dragged the end of our raft out of the water, and laid down upon the cold ground. We were cold when we laid down, and both of us trembled by the hour, like men suffering from a severe attack of the ague. The wind had risen just at night, and the dismal surging of the waves upon the shore, formed, I thought, a fitting lullaby to our disturbed and dismal slumbers.

By this time our clothes were nearly torn off. My pantaloons were split up both legs, and the waistbands nearly gone. My boots were mere wrecks, and our mighty wrestlings in the rapids had torn the skin from ankles and hands. LaMountain's hat had disappeared; the first day out he had thrown away his woolen drawers and stockings, as they dragged him down by the weight of water they absorbed. And so we could sleep but little. It really seemed as though, during this night, we passed through the horrors of death. But at daylight we got up by degrees, first on one knee and then on the other, so stiff and weak that we could hardly stand. Again upon the silent, monotonous lake, we went—following around its shore for an outlet. About 10 o'clock we came to quite a broad northern stream, which we thought was the outlet we were seeking, and we entered it with joy, believing it would take us to our long sought Ottawa. Shortly after entering this

THE POP-CORN MAN, KNOWN AS OLD "JUST ABOUT."

stream it widened out, and began to appear like a mere lake. We poled up the westerly shore for about seven miles, but found ourselves again deceived as to the outlet — the water we were upon proving to be another lake or bayou. We had gone into this lake with the highest hopes, but when we found that all the weary miles of our morning travel had been in vain, and had to be retraced, my resolution certainly failed me for a moment. Yet we felt that our duty, as Christian men, was to press forward as long as we could stand, and leave the issue with a higher Power.

It had now been four full days since we ate a meal. All we had eaten in the meantime was a frog apiece, four clams and a few wild berries, whose acid properties and bitter taste had probably done us more harm than good. Our strength was beginning to fail very fast, and our systems were evidently undergoing an extraordinary change. I did not permit myself to think of food — the thought of a well-filled table would have been too much. My mind continually dwelt upon poor Strain's sufferings on the Isthmus of Darien (then lately published in Harper's Magazine). He, too, was paddling a raft down an unknown stream, half starved, and filled with dreadful forebodings. But I did not believe we could hold out half as long as he had. Besides, he was lost in a tropical country, where all nature is kind to man; he had fire-arms and other weapons with which to kill game. We were in a cold, inhospitable land, without arms, and utterly unable to build a fire. Strain was upon a stream which he knew would eventually bear him to the sea and to safety; while we were upon waters whose flow we positively knew nothing about, and were as much lost as though in the mountains of the moon. Yet we could not give it up so, and tried to summon up fresh courage as troubles appeared to thicken around us. So we turned the raft around, and poled it in silence back towards the place where we had entered this last lake. We had gone about a mile when we heard the sound of a gun, quickly followed by a second report. No sound was ever so sweet as that. We halloed as loud as we could, a good many times, but could get no response. We kept our poles going quite lively, and had gone about half a mile, when I called LaMountain's attention to what I thought was smoke curling up among the trees by the side of a hill. My own eyesight had begun to fail very much, and I felt afraid to trust my dull senses in a matter so vitally important. LaMountain scrutinized the shore very closely, and said he thought it was smoke, and that he believed there was also a birch canoe on the shore below. In a few moments the blue smoke rolled unmistakably above the tree tops, and we felt that

WE WERE SAVED!

Such a revulsion of feeling was almost too much. We could hardly credit our good fortune, for our many bitter disappointments had taught us not to be very sanguine. With the ends of our poles we paddled the raft across the arm of the lake, here, perhaps, three-quarters of a mile wide, steering for the canoe. It proved to be a large one, evidently an Indian's. Leaving LaMountain to guard and retain the canoe, in case the Indian proved timid and desired to escape from us, I pressed hurriedly up the bank, following the footprints I saw in the damp soil, and soon came upon the temporary shanty of a lumbering wood, from the rude chimney of which a broad volume of smoke was rising. I halloed—a noise was heard inside, and a noble-looking Indian came to the door. I eagerly asked him if he could speak French, as I grasped his outstretched hand. "Yes," he replied, "and English, too!" He drew me into the cabin, and there I saw the leader of the party, a noble-hearted Scotchman named Angus Cameron. I immediately told my story; that we had come in there with a balloon, were lost, and had been over four days without food—eagerly demanding to know where we were. Imagine my surprise when he said we were ONE HUNDRED AND EIGHTY MILES DUE NORTH OF OTTAWA, near 300 miles from Watertown, to reach which would require more than 500 miles of travel, following the streams and roads. We were in a wilderness as large as three States like New York, extending from Lake Superior on the west, to the St. Lawrence on the east, and from Ottawa, on the south, to the Arctic circle.

The party consisted of four persons — Cameron and his assistant, and a half-breed Indian (LaMab McDougal) and his son. Their savory dinner was ready. I immediately dispatched the young Indian for La-

Mountain, who soon came in, the absolute picture of wretchedness. All that the cabin contained was freely offered us, and we BEGAN TO EAT. Language is inadequate to express our feelings. Within one little hour the clouds had lifted from our sombre future, and we felt ourselves to be men once more — no longer houseless wanderers amid primeval forests, driven by chance from side to side, but inspired by the near certainty of seeing home again and mingling with our fellows once more in the busy scenes of life.

We soon learned from Cameron that the stream we had traversed with our raft was called Filliman's creek — the large lake we were then near was called the Bos-ke-tong, and drains into the Bos-ke-tong river, which in turn drains into the Gatineau. The Gatineau joins the Ottawa opposite the city of that name, the seat of government of Canada. Cameron assured us that the Bos-ke-tong and Gatineau were so rapid and broken that no set of men could get a raft down, no matter how well they knew the country, nor how much provisions they might have. He regarded our deliverance as purely providential, and many times remarked that we would certainly have perished but for seeing the smoke from his fire. He was hunting timber for his employers, Gilmour & Co., of Ottawa, and was to start in two days down the Gatineau for his headquarters at Desert. If we would stay there until he started we were welcome, he said, to food and accommodations, and he would take us down to Desert in his canoe, and at that point we could get Indians to take us further on. He also said that he had intended to look for timber on Filliman's creek, near where the balloon would be found, as near as we could describe the locality to him, and would try to look it up and make the attempt to get it to Ottawa. This would be a long and tedious operation, as the portages are very numerous between the creek and Desert—something over 20—one of them three miles long. Over these portages, of course, the silk must be carried on the backs of Indians.

After eating all I dared to, and duly cautioning LaMountain not to hurt himself by over-indulgence, I laid down to sleep. Before doing so, I had one of the men remove my boots, and when they came off, nearly the whole outer skin peeled off with the stockings. My feet had become parboiled by the continual soakings of four days and nights, and it was fully three months before they were cured.

After finishing up his business in the vicinity where we found him, on Friday morning (our ninth day from home), Cameron started on his return. We stopped, on our way up the creek, at the spot where we had erected our landmark by which to find the balloon. We struck back for the place, and in about twenty minutes found her, impaled on the tops of four smallish spruce trees, and very much torn. LaMountain concluded to abandon her. He took the valve as a memento, and I cut out the letters "TIC," which had formed part of her name, and brought the strip of silk home with me. We reached what is known as the "New Farm" on Friday night, and there ended our sleeping on the ground. Up by early dawn, and on again, through the drenching rain, reaching Desert on Saturday evening.

At Desert we were a good deal troubled to obtain Indians to take us further on. La-Mab McDougal had told his wife about the baloon, and she, being superstitous and ignorant, had gossipped with the other squaws, and told them the balloon was a "flying devil." As we had traveled in this flying devil, it did not require much of a stretch of Indian credulity to believe that if we were not the Devil's children we must at least be closely related. In this extremity we appealed to Mr. Backus[*], a kind-hearted American

---

[*] Something quite curious grew out of my naming Mr. Henry Backus as having assisted us at the mouth of the Desert river. My account was generally published throughout the country, and some ten days after our return I received a letter from a lady in Massachusetts asking me to describe to her the man Backus, as that was the name of her long-absent son, who, twenty years before, had disappeared from home, and had never afterwards been

trader, who agreed to procure us a complement of redskins, who would take us to Alexis le Beau's place (sixty miles down the river), where it was thought we could obtain horses. Sunday morning (our eleventh day from home), we started from Desert, and reached Alexis le Beau's just at night. The scenery upon this part of the route was sublime and imposing. The primeval forest stood as grand and silent as when created. Our Indians, too, surpassed anything I ever beheld, in physical vigor and endurance. In the day's run of sixty miles, there were sixteen portages to be made. On reaching one of these places, they would seize the canoe as quick as we stepped out of it, jerk it out of the water and on to their shoulders in half a minute, and start upon a dog trot as unconcernedly as though bearing no burthen. Arriving at the foot of the portage, they would toss the canoe into the stream, steady it until we were seated, then spring in and paddle away, gliding down the stream like an arrow. In the morning we traveled fifteen miles and made seven portages in one hour and forty minutes.

At Alexis le Beau we first beheld a vehicle denominated a "buckboard"—a wide, thick plank reaching from one bolster of the wagon to the other, and upon the middle of which plank the seat was placed. This sort of conveyance is often used in new countries, being very cheap, and within the reach of ordinary mechanical skill. Starting off as soon as we could get something to eat, we travelled all night through the forest, over one of the worst roads ever left unfinished, and reached Brooks' farm, a sort of frontier tavern, in the early morning, where we slept a couple of hours,

---

heard from. I answered the letter immediately, and soon after learned that the man proved to be her son, and that he had promised to come home. What had driven him away from civilization to live among the Indians, was best known to himself. But a man of his generous impulses might have been an ornament to society, and a blessing to his friends. [This note was written the next week after we escaped from the wilderness. The article following this treats of Backus' experience quite exhaustively.]

and after breakfast pressed on by the rough frontier stage towards Ottawa.

While the stage was stopping to-day to change horses, I picked up a newspaper at Her Britannic Majesty's colonial frontier post-office, and in it read an account of our ascension and positive loss, with a rather flattering obituary notice of myself. And then, for the first time, I began to comprehend the degree of concern our protracted absence had aroused in the public mind. And if the public felt this concern, what would be the degree of pain experienced by wife, children, parents, friends? These reflections spurred us forward — or rather, our money induced the drivers to hurry up their horses — and at last, on the twelfth day of our absence, at about five o'clock in the afternoon, we jumped off the stage in front of the telegraph office in the good city of Ottawa, whence, in less than five minutes, the swift lightning was speeding a message to home and friends. That was a happy moment—the happiest of all my life—when I knew that within thirty minutes my family would know of my safety.

I do not know how the people of Ottawa so soon found out who we were—but suppose the telegraph operator perhaps told some one; and that "some one" must have told the whole town, for in less than half an hour there was a tearing, excited, happy, inquisitive mass of people in front of the grand hotel there — the clerk of which, when he looked at our ragged clothes and bearded faces, at first thought he "hadn't a single room left," but who, when he found out that we were the lost balloon men, wanted us to have the whole hotel, free and above board, and had tea and supper and lunch, and "just a little private supper, you know!" following each other in rapid, yet most acceptable succession. The happy crowd in the hotel and upon the street were determined to shake hands with us every one, and nearly all wanted to give or loan us money. Pretty soon the newspaper men and some personal acquaintances began to press through the crowd, and some cried while others laughed and huzzahed. Indeed, every one acted as if they had just "found something!" And such is human nature always, when its noble sympathies are aroused for the suffering or distressed.

Although the president of the Ottawa and Prescott Railroad (Robert Bell, Esq.), volunteered to send us on by a special engine that night, we thought it best (inasmuch as our friends had been informed of our safety), to stay at Ottawa until morning. It did seem as though the generous people of that city could not do enough for us, and their kind attention and disinterested enthusiasm will never be forgotten.

hibit unmistakable evidence of the deep interest felt in our fate. At Watertown, which had been my home from boyhood, the enthusiasm had reached fever heat, and the whole town was out to greet the returning æronauts. They had out the old cannon on the Public Square, and it belched forth the loudest kind of a welcome. My family had, of course, suffered deeply by my absence. Everybody had given us up for dead, except my wife. I felt very cheap about the whole thing, and was quite certain that I had done a very foolish act. Not so the people—they thought it a big thing to have gone through with so much, and yet come out alive.

BAY IN LA RUE ISLAND, CANADIAN CHANNEL.

Well, the next morning we left Ottawa, and were quickly carried to Prescott; thence across the St. Lawrence river to Ogdensburg. Here a repetition of the same friendly greetings took place; and at last, after a hearty dinner, we left for home, now distant only seventy-five miles by rail. All along the line of the road we found enthusiastic crowds awaiting our coming, and all seemed to ex-

Several general conclusions and remarks shall terminate this narrative, already too long. "Why did you permit yourselves to go so far?" will naturally be asked. To this inquiry I reply: that the wind was exceedingly light when we ascended; that we were very soon among the clouds, and consequently unable to take cognizance of our course, or to judge how fast we were travelling. It should be distinctly understood that when you are sailing in a balloon, you are unconscious of motion and progress, unless you can see the earth. Even when you first leave the earth, you seem to be stationary, while the earth appears to drop away from you. Nor can you, when out of sight of the earth, although you may have a compass, judge of the direction you are travelling, if travelling at all. In a few words, *unless you can see the earth, you cannot tell how fast nor in what direction you are travelling.* This, perhaps, better than anything else will explain why we unconsciously drifted off to latitudes so remote. When we arose above the thick mass of clouds, before sundown, we undoubtedly struck a rapid current that carried us north-east, and after we had travelled in this current about an hour, we probably struck another current, from the variation of our altitude, which bore us off to the north-west, for the place where we landed is about thirty miles west of due north from where we ascended.

When we first descended near the earth, and saw lights and heard dogs barking, we should have landed. But we were unwilling to land at night in a deep wood, even though we knew that inhabitants were near by, and we thought it best to pick out a better place. This was our error; and it came near being a fatal one to us — it was certainly so to the balloon. In trying to find our "better place" to land, we were up longer than we supposed, and as we were travelling in a current that bore us off to the northward at the rate of 100 miles an hour, we soon reached a point beyond the confines of civilization.

THE AWAKENING OF HENRY BACKUS.

A ROMANCE OF THE BALLOON JOURNEY OF HADDOCK AND LA MOUNTAIN.

IN the preceding account of the balloon voyage made by LaMountain and Haddock into the Bos-ke-tong wilderness of Canada in September, 1859, allusion was made by the writer to one Henry Backus. The early history of this man and the peculiar manner in which he was restored to civilized society and to his mother, from whom he had foolishly separated himself twenty years before, forms a story which would be called a "romance" were it not founded upon actual facts.

LaMountain and myself made our balloon ascension from Watertown, N. Y., and were carried by a swift northerly current far beyond the bounds of civilization, landing in that immense forest in Canada, which is larger than the great States of New York, Pennsylvania and Ohio combined, and limited on the north only by Labrador and the Arctic circle. Having been rescued from starvation and probable death by the brave Cameron and his Indian guides, whom we providentially encountered, we had reached, on our way "out of the wilderness," that frontier post of the Hudson Bay Company, known as Desert, where we were detained by inability to procure Indians for the further prosecution of our journey, because one of Cameron's Indians, who lived at Desert had circulated a story among his associates that we had come into that wilderness in a "flying devil," which had fallen from the sky. Naturally superstitious and densely ignorant, these boatmen readily concluded that we were really children of the Devil himself, and undesirable people to work for, even if well paid. We were very impatient at the detention, and Cameron, who could take us no farther towards Ottawa, advised us to consult one Henry Backus, the local trader, who might be able to help us, for he sold "fire-water" to the Indians and had great influence with them. To Backus' little store, then, we went, and found him somewhat hard to approach, as if he were suspicious of any attempt at intimacy; but when we told him our trouble and urgently solicited his good offices, he appeared anxious and willing to aid us. He struck me as being too intelligent and well educated for the position he was filling, as a small trader in so remote a place, but we were too much concerned with our own plans for reaching civilization to scrutinize him very closely. He knew just how to deal with the ignorant river men, and soon had a crew selected who promised to depart with us at early daybreak, so that we might reach Alexis-le-Beau before nightfall. The promise was redeemed, and in the morning we departed, and Backus saw us no more, but from one of us he was yet to hear.

Who was Henry Backus? To answer this inquiry I must take the reader back more than fifty years, to 1837, when there lived in Western Massachusetts a family named Hancock, consisting of the parents and two daughters, sixteen and eighteen years of age, the elder named Mabel, the youngest Harriet. It is with Mabel we have more particularly to deal. She was above the average in beauty of person, bright and engaging, and, like most of her sex, well aware of her good points, and not by any means unmindful of the admiration she elicited from the young men of her neighborhood. As a result, she was often invited to the merry-makings of that section, accompanied sometimes by one, sometimes by another young gentleman — but for a long time she gave none of her admirers any special preference. In her twentieth year, when the heart is apt to be the most susceptible, she had two admirers who had distanced her hitherto numerous gallants, and whenever she went to church or to the country parties, one or the other of these was always her attendant. Henry Backus, one of these young men, was rather a silent and reserved, but really handsome young man of twenty-two, well-educated in the country schools, active and enterprising, the comfort of his mother, who was a widow and the owner of a good farm, left her by her husband. Henry was somewhat in appearance like an Indian, tall and dark-skinned, and there was a tradition that the Backus family, a hundred years before, had been crossed by Narraganset blood.

Be that as it may, Henry was observant but silent, seldom gay and never frivolous, but he was popular among his companions, who gave him their full confidence, for they knew he meant all he said, and that his word was as good as most other men's bond. His competitor in Mabel's good graces was equally regarded, but in a different way. Witty, agreeable, full of vivacity and animal spirits, James Atwell was the life of every social gathering, greatly admired by the girls, and welcome in every circle. Although a year older than Henry Backus, he had not yet settled down to any serious pursuit, which, in his case, was thought to be a necessity, as his father had never accumulated more than a mere subsistence. James had twice left home, and had spent a whole year in a dry goods store at Worcester, Mass., but he had given up that business as too confining. He had also taught the district school one winter, but was thought deficient in discipline, and was not asked to teach a second time. While nothing could be said against him, the older people rated him much below Backus in prospective usefulness and position. The girls considered him as "just too nice for anything," but thought, and some of them said, that Henry Backus was "an old cross-patch." They unanimously predicted that James Atwell would have a "walk-over" in the contest for supremacy in Mabel's affections. But this prediction did not have any speedy fulfilment, as both the young men were equally well received at the Hancock mansion, and so a whole year wore away without any material change in the relation of these young people to one another, but close observers saw that Backus was wonderfully smitten with Mabel, a fact which he did not try to conceal. Yet it gave his mother considerable concern, for she well knew the intensity of his nature, and how restless he became under even slight disappointments.

A change, however, was soon to come. While returning from a dancing party in the winter of 1838, Henry proposed, and was at least partially accepted by Mabel as her future husband. At her request the partial agreement was to be kept a secret, much against Henry's wish, but he loved the girl too much to deny her anything. While this understanding was being faithfully observed between them, invitations came for the grand winter wind-up dancing party, to be held at the county town, and Henry was duly accepted as Mabel's escort thither. When the evening of the party drew on, he started in his sleigh for his companion, but the snow was deep, and in trying to turn out for a loaded team his cutter was upset, himself thrown out, and the horse ran away. It took fully two hours to recover the horse and reach the Hancock mansion, and then only to find that Mabel had become tired of the delay, and, in a moment of pique, had accepted James Atwell's proffered escort and gone to the dance with him. Backus was thunderstruck, and finally burst into a passion of tears, due as much, probably, to the excitement he had just passed through, as to the unexpected departure of Mabel with his rival. His jealousy was terribly aroused, and he at once reached the conclusion that his delay had been gladly taken advantage of by her in order to accept the company of one whom she loved more than himself. He did not go to the dance, nor would he make much reply to Mrs. Hancock's trembling efforts to put Mable's action in a favorable light, but went straight home and made such explanations as he could to his tearful mother. Talk as she might, she could not move him from a sullen fit of depression, which the night did not wear away, and in the morning he harnessed his horse and drove away, with a determination to have a final understanding with Mabel. He demanded that their betrothment should be made public, and be sanctioned by her parents. That young lady bore herself during the interview with considerable independence, declaring herself as satisfied with what she had done, and captiously declined to ask her parents to ratify their engagement, which she declared was not considered as final, but rather as a matter subject to further contingencies, in all of which she developed a feminine spirit of contention so characteristic of that sex. After much talk and expostulation they parted in anger, utterly estranged — she most likely believing that it would result in a lover's reconciliation, and never dreaming that she would not soon see Henry Backus again. But with him the case was closed. He felt that he had loved and lost, and that, in the eyes of his acquaintances, he had been made a fool of by a heartless woman. His fine sleigh was not used again that winter. The social parties missed him, and as the trouble between the lovers gradually came out (but though never a word from him), the country people took two sides in discussing the matter, nearly all the women upholding Henry; and the men, more gallant, taking the part of Mabel. But she, too, went no more abroad, refusing even to see James Atwell, though he both called and wrote. Doubtless, like many another, she felt a secret desire to repossess what she had recklessly thrown away, and felt too proud to make any effort towards a reconciliation.

Try as he would, young Backus failed to take his former interest in life. His mother's tearful face would at times force him to active exertion on their farm, but it was plain to be seen that his spirit was broken, and that a sullen despondency had taken possession of his mind. Having struggled along through the summer's work and the harvesting, he besought his mother to let him hire a steady young man to do the farm work, and then be allowed to go away for a while. His mother, thinking a change of scene would help her son, reluctantly gave her consent, and late in November, Henry left his home to become a wanderer. But travel as long and as far as he could, he found it impossible to get rid of himself. His burden would not be cast off. For a month he remained at Albany, and then went north to Watertown, Prescott and Ogdensburg, N. Y., and finally to Ottawa, in Canada. The Indian strain of blood, which it was said he had inherited, began definitely to assert itself, more vigorously, perhaps, at the sight of the adjacent forests, and he resolved to leave civilization behind him and forget that busy world where he had been so sadly deceived, and with which he now had so little affiliation.

Those who have visited Ottawa will remember the dense forest which environs that delightful city beyond the rapid river towards the north. Within a few miles of this Canadian capital you can readily lose yourself in the dense growth of trees; and into this then almost unbroken wilderness Henry Backus launched himself, fully resolved never again to live among civilized men. Farther and farther he journeyed, until the stage route dwindled to mere "buckboard" travel, then to solitary paths marked by blazed trees, until Alexis-le-Beau, upon the Upper Gatineau, was reached, and then up that rapid stream he pressed a hundred miles to Desert, which was a mere fringe of clearing in that almost unbroken primeval forest. There Backus passed the late spring and summer. Gradually the need of employment for his mind and strength asserted itself, and he built a small log cabin with store-room in front, and began to trade with the Indians for their furs. When winter came on he made a journey out from the woods to Ottawa, where he perfected an arrangement for the annual sale of his peltry and for a regular consignment to him of such goods as his trade at Desert demanded. He was gone a month, and on his return took up his daily life as before, a solitary, independent, silent man. I leave the imagination of the reader to depict his feelings, his yearnings for his mother, his moments of frantic love for Mabel Hancock, his resolve to break the spell that was upon him and return to his old home and friends, and for the reader to comprehend the depth of a nature that could endure in silence a disappointment so bitter.

For a long time Mrs. Backus expected to see Henry walk into the house almost any day. She managed her farm much better than she had expected, saving something every year. After five years had passed, she lost faith in Henry's return, and almost gave him up as dead. She fell sick, and was in bed for a long time; then it was that Mabel Hancock developed the good that was in her. Humbly she went to the sick woman's bedside, confessed her undying love for Henry, took all the blame upon herself for his departure and long absence, and volunteered to nurse Mrs. Backus through her sickness. At first she was not at all drawn towards the girl, but her remorse and self-condemnation so plainly attested her sincerity that she was permitted to remain. She soon became a permanent fixture at Henry's old home, and so won the mother's heart that they never separated. Jointly they managed the farm, and became so knit together by mutual regard that strangers looked upon them as mother and daughter. James Atwell had married Harriet and they had moved away, but Mabel did not attend her sister's wedding. Womanlike, she cast upon Atwell most of the blame for the unfortunate separation from her lover, when, in fact, she was the one mainly at fault, though there were those who thought Henry Backus himself not without grave responsibility for the turn affairs had taken. And so the years wore on until Mabel was nearly 40 years of age — comely in figure, but with a sad face, seldom lit by a smile. Her constant prayer was that she might be able to pay back to Henry's mother that fealty and support which had been lost when an unwise and needless quarrel had driven away her son.

———

The coming of the balloon men made an abiding impression upon Backus. He felt a return of that longing for home which he thought he had entirely conquered. He even found himself full of self-accusation, because he had not volunteered to personally accompany them to Ottawa, for from there he could have telegraphed or written to his mother. He found it difficult to put aside the influence these two eager, pushing men had exerted upon him. They were resolutely bent upon returning to that civilization he had been so willing to leave, and he began to feel a conviction that they were right in their course and that he had been wrong in his. For three weeks this struggle went on in his heart until he began to realize the selfishness and folly of his course. He felt like loathing his surroundings as wholly unworthy one who had in his youth given such ample promise of usefulness and honor. Hard as was the struggle, however, and much as he felt the value of what he had too ruthlessly cast away 20 years before, it might have been doubtful what course he would ultimately have taken had not Providence unmistakably warned him that he was trifling with his own best interests, to say nothing of his disregard of filial duty.

About the middle of October, 1859, a party of river men, on their way up from Alexis-le-Beau, the nearest postoffice, brought him a letter, which may have read as follows:

AT HOME, *October* 10, 1859.

MY DEAR SON, if indeed you are my son: I read last week in the Springfield *Republican* an account of the adventures of the lost balloon men, who gave credit to one Henry Backus, a trader at Desert, on the Gatineau river, in Canada, for having aided them in their efforts to return to their homes. My heart prompted me to write to Mr. Haddock, at Watertown, N. Y., for a description of this Henry Backus, and Mr. H. immediately answered my letter. Making full allowance for the changes 20 years may have made, I feel quite hopeful that you are my long lost and deeply mourned son. If so, do not delay an hour, but come home before it is too late to see your poor mother, now past her 60th year, but whose prayer has ever been for her absent son.

Mabel Hancock has lived with me for the past 18 years. She is my stay and greatest comfort, and she desires me to enclose a word from her, for we are more and more convinced that you are my lost son. My heart is too full to write more, but if you are my son hasten to my arms, for a fresh disappointment or long delay may prove too much for my poor strength. Affectionately, your mother,

RACHEL BACKUS.

The note enclosed was from Mabel; it read:

DEAREST FRIEND — If you are that Henry Backus to whom I was once betrothed in marriage, I feel that I owe much in the way of apology for the treatment you received at my hands when I was a young and inexperienced girl. My past life I offer as an evidence of my feelings towards you then and now; yet that life for many years has been a burden, which I could only have borne for your dear mother's sake. If you are the lost one you cannot be too quick in hastening to your true home, for your mother is not long for this world.

Your attached friend,

MABEL HANCOCK.

If Backus had been tardy in carrying out the plans which the coming of the lost balloon men appeared to prompt, he was on fire now with impatience, and counted every hour as lost that kept him from the telegraph. Placing a trusted clerk in charge of his business, he packed up his important papers, and, on the morning of the fourth day, was in Ottawa, sending a message to distant Berkshire that he was indeed the lost son, who had come to himself and would soon be there.

Having thus far dealt in facts, I will invite the reader himself to imagine that meeting, when Backus found under the same roof his beloved mother and that Mabel Hancock who was thenceforth to reign as the undisputed idol of his heart. The natural inclination of a newspaper editor to follow out any incident of more than passing interest with which he had become interested, impelled me to make inquiry of Backus' subsequent career, as well as of all that might shed any light upon his history before we met him at Desert. On the 1st of January following his return, he and Mabel Hancock were married, and the whole neighborhood shared in the merry-making. He soon sold his possession at Desert, and settled down in a prosperous career, becoming a leading citizen of his native county. Himself and wife were noted for their hospitality and open-handed charity, and it was especially remarked that they were exceedingly lenient in their treatment of any one who had lapsed from duty or against whom society held its doors askance. The poor and the outcast found ready sympathy with them, and no hungry wayfarer was ever sent away unfilled.

The casual reader may not be much impressed with the extraordinary means through which Henry Backus came to be thus "awakened" to his true condition, but those who take a broader view of these incidents can, perhaps, discover in them the workings of that Supreme Omniscience which notes even the fall of a sparrow.

THE WAR OF 1755.

WITH AN ALLUSION TO THE "LOST CHANNEL."

THE most formidable military display which ever swept over the waters of the St. Lawrence, was that of 1760, commanded by Gen. Jeffrey Lord Amherst. It consisted, according to Knox, of the 1st and 2d battalions of the Royal Highlanders, the 44th, 46th, and 55th regiments of the line, the 4th battalion of the 60th, eight companies of the 77th, five companies of the 80th, 579 Grenadiers, 597 Light Infantry, three battalions of the New York regiment, four battalions of the Connecticut regiment, a regiment from New Jersey, 146 Rangers, 157 of the Royal Artillery, and a force of Indians under Sir William Johnson, the whole amounting to an effective force of 10,142 men. The transportation for this army, consisted of two armed vessels, the Onondaga and the Mohawk; the first, under the immediate command of Capt. John Loring, who was also admiral of the fleet, was armed with four nine-pounders, and fourteen sixes, with a crew of 100 men. The second carried sixteen sixes, and a crew of ninety men; and in addition to these, there were seventy-two whaleboats, and 177 batteaux. Several of the whaleboats were armed with a gun each, and some of the batteaux carried howitzers. Besides these, there were staff, hospital and sutler's boats, the whole to quote from a writer of that time, who was an eye witness, "making a most imposing array."

The primary object of the expedition, was the capture of Montreal, it being one of three set on foot for that purpose; but its immediate destination was Fort Levis, a strong French fortification the ruins of which are yet to be seen, on what is now called "Chimney Island," in the St. Lawrence river, a few miles below Ogdensburg, which was known to the French as "La Presentation." At that time, Fort Levis, was the only French stronghold above Montreal, and its reduction was a military necessity. The fort, according to the historian Manté, was begun early in 1759, by Chevalier de Levis, who was afterward a Marshal of France, and completed by Captain Pouchot, by whom it was so ably defended. This officer arrived at the fort in March, and proceeded to put it in as complete a condition for defense as was possible with the means at hand. On taking command, he found it garrisoned by 150 militia, six Canadian officers, some colonial cadets, and M'Bertrand an officer of artillery. A reinforcement of 100 men was sent him from below, but of these, twenty soon deserted, carrying away with them the batteaux belonging to the fort. One of these deserters was a lad named Pierre Rigand. A few days later his father brought him back, feeling deeply the disgrace consequent upon having a son who was a deserter.

It would be a pleasure to find that Capt. Pouchot's Memoirs, in which this incident is related, has been able to add that the young man fought bravely, wiped out the disgrace of desertion and returned to the arms of his father, who not only forgave him but received him with open arms and affectionate pride; but they do not. They only state that: "In the battle which followed, Pierre Rigand was killed."

As it is no part of our intention to enter into a minute description of the investment and capture of the fort, we shall content ourselves with a description of the expedition as related by its historian, in its progress down the St. Lawrence river. On the 7th of August, 1760, Capt. Loring with his two vessels sailed from Oswego for Grenadier Island, at the foot of Lake Ontario. Following in boats were the Royal Highlanders and Grenadiers, commanded by Lieut. Col. Massey; the light infantry under Lieut. Col. Amherst, with two companies of Rangers, the whole under the command of Colonel Haldimand, who afterward succeeded Sir Guy Carleton, as Governor-General and Commander-in-Chief in Canada. On the 10th, Gen. Amherst himself embarked with the remainder of the troops, being joined the next day by Gen. Gage with the Provincial troops, among which was a Connecticut regiment under the command of Lieut.-Col., afterward Brigadier-Gen. Israel Putnam. On the 13th of August, 1760, the whole army was encamped on Grenadier Island, and their boats safely moored in Basin Harbor.

By noon of the 14th, everything was in readiness to move, and the troops were ordered to get their dinners and then embark at once. At two o'clock they were sweeping down the south channel of the St. Lawrence in two lines of boats which reached almost from shore to shore. It was an inspiring sight. The long lines of boats, decorated with flags and streamers and guidons, the rowers keeping time with their oars to the music of the military bands, relieved at times by the bugles of the Grenadiers and the pipes of the Scotch Highlanders, while the two vessels, the Onondaga and Mohawk, led the advance.

But the French were not asleep. For some time a squad of soldiers, under the command of a lieutenant, had been stationed on Isle aux Chevreuils, now Carlton Island, from the high grounds of which a splendid view of the lake is to be had, as a corps of observation. With this squad was a small body of Indian scouts, one or two of whom, in swift canoes, were detached at intervals to the fort below to warn its commander of the approach of the English army. Waiting until the entire fleet had entered the river, so that there was no longer any doubt as to its destination, the lieutenant and his men went on board a batteau, and rowed away down the river. It was this batteau which led Capt. Loring of the Onondaga into trouble. But we will let an extract from the journal, kept by the gallant captain, tell the tale:

"Aug. 14th.—This afternoon the entire fleet set sail, and at three of the clock was well within the south channel of the St. Lawrence river, near the island called, by the French, Isle aux Chevreuil, and by us Buck Island, from the foot of which the lookout at the masthead discovered a batteau loaded with French soldiers put off, when I knew at once that the enemy had knowledge of the expedition, and though the wind was light, I signalled the Mohawk and gave chase, hoping to get the batteau within range of my bow guns, but which I failed to do. The Onondaga was now nearly a league ahead of the Mohawk, and the flotilla was yet another league in the rear, the entire fleet being fully eight leagues from where it set sail. At a point where three hills project into the river, the batteau veered away and ran down through a long narrow channel between what seemed to be a large island and some smaller ones, and out into a large bay, beyond which stretched another broad channel, easily seen from the masthead. Having sounded and found deep water, I decided to follow; but owing to light winds our progress was slow, though in running through the narrow channel we gained somewhat on the batteau, which we soon lost sight of among the islands in the north channel, which are very numerous, with narrow swift channels in every direction between them, very difficult to sail among unless favored with a strong breeze, which, unfortunately for us, was now very light, and to add to our difficulties, night was at hand. Had we not been able to distinguish the islands from the lookout at the masthead, we might have thought that the main land lay ahead of us, but with what we could see from that point, and finding that the current set strongly in that direction, and knowing from some previous experience among the islands above that the channels between the islands were likely to be deep, I determined to hold on to our course, not doubting that we should run safely through the archipelago, if it be proper to so call a cluster of islands that are not in the sea. So the Fates would have it, however, we were no sooner fairly within what seemed to be the largest channel than the vessel was attacked on every side from the summits of the islands, which were covered with trees and thickets, and our deck was fairly swept with arrows and musketry, while at the same time we seemed about to strike 'bows on' to a precipice directly ahead. I immediately ordered Coxswain Terry and his crew to lower away one of the quarter boats, with a message to the Mohawk to turn back to the other channel. and then sent the men to the guns quickly, driving the enemy from the summits of the islands and into their canoes, when they soon escaped into the numerous channels on either hand.

Ordering another boat lowered, a suitable channel was soon found, through which we passed safely, and anchored about a league below the thickest of the group of islands, and waited for Coxswain Terry and his crew to return. After some time, I ordered Ensign Barry to take the cutter and search for the coxswain and his crew. After some hours Ensign Barry returned. He had been bewildered among the numerous channels, not being able to even distinguish the channels through which the vessel had come, nor the one by which she entered the group of islands, nor had he discovered the first boat lowered. Ensign Barry called it "The River of the Lost Channel," and in that way was it ever after spoken of among the men. Thinking that Coxswain Terry and his crew had boarded the Mohawk, and that they would return to us when we joined the fleet, I determined to sail as soon as the wind freshened.

"Aug. 15th. All this day there was a strong head wind, and after sounding and finding shallow water in several places, I did not think it best to tack for fear of running aground."

"Aug. 16th. The lookout discovered a vessel this morning at a distance of about four leagues coming up the river, but we could not make her out. Presuming that it was a French vessel, as we knew that they had an armed brig below, we got springs on our cables in order to veer if attacked, but she did not come nearer to us than three leagues."

"Aug. 17th Wind still contrary. There has been heavy cannonading down the river to-day about four leagues distant but hid from us by islands. It cannot be at the French Fort, which cannot be less than fifteen leagues distant."

"Aug. 18th. Got under weigh this afternoon, and will soon be with the army."

"Aug. 19th. Reached the army to-day, and reported to Gen. Amherst. Coxswain Terry and his crew are undoubtedly lost, as they did not board the Mohawk, but started to return to the Onondaga. The firing on the day before yesterday, was the attack on the French brig by our armed gallies under the command of Col. Williamson, who captured her after a severe engagement lasting four hours. It was a most gallant affair. The brig has been named the Williamson, after the gallant colonel. The fort is to be invested to-morrow."

In speaking of this very affair the historian Manté says:

"All this while, one of the enemy's vessels kept hovering about the army, and as Captain Loring had not yet got into the right channel, it became necessary for the safety of the army, either to compel this vessel to retire or to take her. The general was therefore obliged to order Colonel Williamson with the row gallies well manned, to do one or the other."

Then follows an account of the battle and of the ill luck which seemed to have followed Captain Loring during the attack on the fort, at which time his vessel ran aground and was very nearly taken possession of by the enemy. But as any further description of the capture of Fort Levis is not germane to our history, because it took place beyond the limits of the Thousand Islands, we bring the article to a close, having shown the reader that the name "Lost Channel" is by no means a modern invention.

FRANK H. TAYLOR.

FRANK H. TAYLOR, THE ARTIST.

AMONG the favored residents at the pleasant summer colony of Round Island there are none better known or more enthusiastic regarding the charms of the Thousand Islands than Mr. FRANK H. TAYLOR, one of the few Philadelphians who spend their summer in this region. After much and varied travel as an illustrator and writer, Mr. Taylor came to the St. Lawrence upon a mission for Harper's Weekly in 1881, and at once recognizing the certainty of its supremacy as a summer resort, he built the pretty cottage at the foot of Round Island, which he calls "Shady Ledge." Mr. Taylor, with his wife and only son, who is also an artist, return here each season with great regularity in June, and devote the summer to the congenial work of the water colorist. Mr. Taylor's illustrations of island life, accompanied by vivid descriptions, have appeared in many publications, and have done much to popularize these beautiful islands throughout the country. The writer is indebted for several picturesque chapters in this work to Mr. Taylor's facile pen. He has done more to popularize the St. Lawrence Archipelago than any other man. This he has been enabled to do from the fact that he is not only a fine writer, but an artist as well, and can both describe and delineate anything he desires to present. This is a most happy combination of talent, as valuable as it is rare. Mr. Taylor's delineations have been delicate but most expressive. He is one who brings the love of nature into his work, fully believing that honest delineation of scenery is very much above any attempt to introduce fancy effects.

The regular visitors to Round Island and other points upon the river always welcome Mr. Taylor and his family as desirable people to know. Grand Army men, in particular, have experienced great pleasure at the campfires held on the lawn in front of Comrade Taylor's fine residence upon the east side of the island. There has never occurred one of these unique entertainments that has not been marked by good speaking and singing. Comrade Taylor gets true enjoyment by contributing to the enjoyment of others, and that is a great thing to find out and to really believe in — it may indeed be almost like finding the real philosopher's stone, which is said to turn all things it touches into gold.

THE CASTORLAND COLONY.

TO the excellent article by Hon. Mr. Ingalls, upon the "Waterways of Jefferson County" (see pages 9-12 of Haddock's History), we wish to add a few general remarks. It is a peculiar characteristic, marking all the rivers that flow in and around Northern New York, that, excepting only the Mohawk, all of them flow from and through larger or smaller chains of lakes. The noble St. Lawrence itself, which forms the natural and intensely picturesque northwestern boundary of Jefferson county, seems to be the vast prototype and pattern for all the others, as it flows from its own great continental system of lakes. The Hudson, flowing eastward like the Mohawk, is fed by a system of forest branches which spread over the entire mountain belt of the Adirondack wilderness, the head waters of some of its tributaries being over 5,000 feet above the level of the sea. But, however interesting it may be to follow out this train of thought, our space constrains us to confine our remarks to the streams which flow into and through Jefferson county, or relate to waterways touching that county. Their influence upon the early settlements of the northern wilderness of 1793, in drawing to the Black River country those in pursuit of water power to drive factories, can never be prized too highly, nor too patiently described. These waters attracted to this locality those whose minds were profoundly stirred by that intense activity which always precedes great discoveries and great movements of populations.

The Black River bounds the Great Wilderness plateau of Laurentian rocks on the west, and its valley bounds the Lesser Wildnerness on the east. The principal confluents that enter the Black River from the Great Wilderness, are the Moose, Otter Creek, the Independence, and the Beaver.

The Moose River rises near the Raquette Lake in the center of the wilderness, and winds through and forms the celebrated Eight Lakes of the Fulton chain. The Moose passes in its course the hunting station known to all frequenters of the woods as Arnold's, or the Old Forge, on Brown's Tract. This secluded spot has long been famous in forest story as the scene of John Brown's[*] fruitless attempt at settlement, of the failure and tragic death of his son-in-law Herreshoff, of the exploits of the hunter Foster and his victim, the Indian Drid, and of the life-long home of Otis Arnold, the hunter and guide.

The Independence River rises near the Eight Lakes of the Fulton chain and runs into Black River in the town of Watson, Lewis county, between the Moose River and the Beaver River. In its course, this river crosses the tract of wild land known to land speculators as Watson's West Triangle. The Independence River was so named in honor of our national holiday by Pierre Pharoux, the engineer and surveyor of Castorland. Near the south bank of the Independence, not far from the old Watson house, is Chase's lake. This lake has long been a favorite resort, and is one of the most accessible in the Wilderness for the invalid or pleasure seeker. The Beaver River rises in the heart of the Wilderness to the north of Raquette Lake, and running in its course through Smith's Lake, Albany Lake, and Beaver Lake, waters the territory of ancient

[*] Not the John Brown, of Harper's-Ferry fame, "whose body lies a mouldering in the ground, but whose soul is marching on."

Castorland, the seat of French influence on the Black River. Beaver Lake, an expansion of this river at Number Four, a famous summer resort, is one of the most charming lakes in the wilderness.

Among the problematical places of the olden times in Northern New York, whose names were once familar in European circles but are seldom heard in modern story, no one was once more famous than La Famine.

Two hundred years ago, La Famine was a well-known stopping-place upon the eastern shore of Lake Ontario for the weary hunter and the bold explorer, and the spot where even armies encamped, and the ambassadors of hostile nations met in solemn council.

of the Lesser Wilderness from the west was the Salmon River. On their way to the hunting ground through Lake Ontario, the western Indians landed at the mouth of this river, and their trail then led up its banks.

La Famine then was the ancient seaport of this famous hunting ground of the Lesser Wilderness, and was situated near what is now the village of Mexico, Oswego county. Hence we find on a map of New France, published by Marco Vincenzo Coronelli, in 1688, this place put down at the mouth of what is now known as the Salmon River, but in his map it is called La Famine River. It bears the following inscription: "La Famine, lieu ou la plus part des Iroquois des barquet pour

MEDAL ISSUED BY THE CHASSNAIS FRANCO-AMERICAN LAND COMPANY.
[Enlarged one-half, from an original in possession of the Jefferson County Historical Society.]

To-day its name can only be found on the historic page and in the old maps and musty records, while its locality is often a matter of controversy. The ancient Indian landing-place and camping-ground known to the French as La Famine, was situated on the shore of Famine Bay, now called Mexico Bay, in the southeast corner of Lake Ontario, at the mouth of La Famine River, now known as Salmon River.

The Salmon River, the ancient French La Famine, rises in the central part of the plateau of the Lesser Wilderness in the southwest corner of Lewis county, and runs westerly through the northern part of Oswego county into Lake Ontario. The Lesser Wilderness was one of the beaver-hunting countries of the Iroquois. The key to this hunting ground

aller in traitte du Castor," which may be translated thus: "La Famine, the place where the greater part of the Iroquois embarked to go upon the trail of the beaver."

The Lesser Wilderness of Northern New York is situated upon the long narrow plateau which stretches first westerly and then northerly from the Upper Mohawk valley and the Oneida Lake almost to the village of Carthage. The rocky ground-work of this plateau is composed of level strata of limestone and slate, which rise in a series of terraces of a mile or two in width from its borders into a high level table land, which has an elevation of nearly 2,000 feet above the level of the sea. Upon the central part of this table land are situated the forests, swamps, marshes and wild meadows of the Lesser Wilderness.

Down the more regular terraces of its western slope, locally called Tug Hill, the streams which rise in the swamps of the Lesser Wilderness hurry in a series of falls and cascades into the Black River, wearing deep chasms in the yielding rocks along their courses. Among these streams are the Deer River, the Silvermine, the Martin, the Whetstone and other creeks.

This Lesser Wilderness was one of the most famous hunting grounds of the Indian. Its woods were literally filled with game, and its streams with fish. La Hontan says that there were so many salmon in La Famine River that they often brought up a hundred at one cast of the net.

CASTORLAND.

The summer tourist, on his way from Trenton Falls to the Thousand Islands, may pass through the beautiful and flourishing valley of the Black River, over the Utica and Black River Railroad. As the train draws near to the first station north of the village of Lowville, he will hear the sharp voice of the brakeman crying out "Cas-tor-land." He will look out of the car window and see a wide level clearing of pasture-land and meadow, skirted by forests, one side of which is bounded by the river. In the middle of this clearing he will see only the small station house, and three or four scattered buildings surrounding it, and will doubtless wonder whence comes the high-sounding name for such meagre surroundings.

The story of Castorland is the often repeated tale of frustrated settlements in the old wilderness—the story of an attempt of the exiled nobility and clergy of the old régime in France to found a settlement in the wilds of the New World, where they could find a secure retreat from the horrors of the Revolution in the Old.

This attempt was made at the close of the last century in the valley of the Black River, on the western slope of the Great Wilderness. But, like the settlement of the first Catholics on the Patuxent, the Jacobites with Flora McDonald at Cape Fear, the Huguenots with Jean Ribault at Port Royal; like New Amsterdam on the Hudson, New Sweden on the Delaware; like Acadie in Nova Scotia,—Castorland on the Black River lives now only in poetry and history. Its story is one of brilliant promises all unfulfilled, of hopes deferred, of man's tireless but fruitless endeavor, of woman's tears.

To rescue this name so fraught with historical associations from oblivion, it was applied to the railroad station which is nearest to the site of the largest projected city of ancient Castorland. That city was laid out on the Beaver River, which flows into the Black River from the wilderness nearly opposite this station.

For the purpose of effecting the settlement of Castorland a company was formed in Paris, under the laws of France, in the month of August, 1792, and styled La Compagnie de New York. On the 31st day of the same month the company, by its agent, Pierre Chassanis, bought a large tract of land lying in the valley of the Black River, of William Constable, who was the owner of Macomb's Purchase. This tract lay along both sides of the Black River below the High Falls, and extended westerly through the counties of Lewis and Jefferson to Lake Ontario, and easterly into the heart of the Great Wilderness. The Castorland purchase at first comprised the whole of great lot No. 5 of Macomb's purchase, and contained 610,000 acres. But subsequently all south and west of the Black River, being the part which now constitutes the richest towns of Lewis and Jefferson counties, was given up, and only that lying to the north and east of the river retained. The portion so retained contained only 210,000 acres. This was the Castorland of the olden times.

The name Castorland, that is to say, the Land of Beavers, is doubtless a literal translation of the old Indian word, which means the "Beaver Hunting Country," Castorland being taken out of the western half of this old Indian hunting ground.

During the negotiations between Constable and Chassanis for this tract, the French Revolution, that had been so long smouldering, burst forth in all its savage fury, and the streets of Paris were slippery with human gore. Constable locked the door of the apartment in which they met, with the remark that "if they parted before the purchase was completed they might never meet again." The palace of the Tuilleries was already surrounded by the bloodthirsty mob. The attendants of the royal family were butchered, and the feeble king cast into a dungeon. In comparison with such awful scenes as these in the very heart of the highest civilization the world had ever seen, the savage wilderness of the old American forests was a scene of peaceful rest. To the fugitive noblesse of France, the former possessors of great titles, rank, wealth and culture, the quiet shades of Castorland afforded a secure asylum from the horrors of the Reign of Terror.

SCHEME OF SETTLEMENT.

A romantic scheme was at once conceived and perfected by the company in Paris for the settlement of Castorland. In pursuance of this scheme a pamphlet was printed in Paris and issued by the Company, containing a programme of colonization under its auspices. This pamphlet was entitled "Association for the purchase and settlement of 600,000 acres of land, granted by the State of New York, and situated within that State, between the 43d and 44th degrees of latitude, upon Lake Ontario, and thirty-five leagues from the city and port of Albany, where vessels land from Europe." It set forth, among other things, in glowing colors, the wealth of agriculture presented by its fertile soil, the fine distribution of its waters, its facilities for an extended commerce on account of its location in the vicinity of a dense population, and above all the security afforded to its inhabitants by the laws of a people who were independent and rich with their own capital, thus extending to the immigrant all the benefits of liberty with none of its drawbacks. It was stated that the object of the proprietors was to form of the colony a sort of family, in some way united by common interests and common wants, and that to maintain this union of interests a plan had been devised that rendered each member directly interested in the whole property. It was to be done by and in the name of Sieur Chassanis, in whose name they had purchased the estate, and who alone had power to issue certificates of ownership.

There were 6,000 certificates to be issued, each entitling the holder thereof to ownership in manner following: The whole tract at that time consisted of 630,000 acres. Of this 600,000 were divided into 12,000 lots of fifty acres each, and the price of each share fixed at 800 livres ($152.38). In the beginning, 6,000 lots were set apart for individual properties, and the other 6,000 lots were to belong to a common stock which was to be divided at some future time, after improvements had been made thereon by the company. Each holder of a certificate was to receive at once a deed for a separate lot of fifty acres, to be drawn by lot, and also a lot of fifty acres in the common undivided stock.

Of the 30,000 remaining acres, 2,000 were set apart for a city to be formed on the great river in the interior, and 2,000 more for another city on Lake Ontario, at the mouth of the Black River, which was to form a port and entrepôt of commerce. Among artisans 6,000 acres were to be divided and rented to them at twelve sous per acre. The proceeds of the 20,000 acres remaining were to be expended by the Company in the construction of roads, bridges and other improvements.

The two cities were divided into 14,000 lots each. Of these lots, 2,000 were set apart for churches, schools, markets, etc. The remaining 12,000 lots were to be divided among the 6,000 holders of certificates in the same manner as the large tract,— each holding one separate lot and one in common.

The affairs of the company were to be managed by five trustees, three to remain in Paris and two upon the tract.

Such was the scheme matured in the salons of Paris for the settlement of Castorland. Beautiful and promising beyond measure upon aper, as an ideal, but utterly impracticable and bitterly disappointing as a reality. Yet many shares were eagerly taken.

ORGANIZATION.

On the 28th of June, 1793, it being the second year of the French Republic, the actual holders of certificates convertible into shares of La Compagnie de New York met in the rooms of Citizen Chassanis, in Paris, to organize their society upon the basis already established, and to regulate the division, survey and settlement of their lands. There were present at that meeting forty-one shareholders in all, who represented 1,880 shares. They perfected and completed their organization; they adopted a long and elaborate constitution; they chose a seal for their corporation, and appointed five commissaries to manage its affairs, three for Paris and two for Castorland. In the meantime the tract had been re-conveyed, and the large part lying west and south of the Black River given up, the part retained being that lying east and north of the river, and containing only 210,000 acres. To accord with this fact the number of shares was reduced from 6,000 to 2,000. It was at this meeting that a silver piece was ordered to be struck, termed a "Jetton de presence," one of which was to be given at every meeting to each commissary as an attendance fee.* [See engraving, p. 170.]

---

* These pieces occur in coin cabinets, and have been erroneously called "Castorland half-dollars." A jetton is a piece of metal struck with a device, and distributed to be kept in commemoration of some event, or to be used as a counter in games of chance. The one here noticed was termed a "jetton de presence," or piece "given in certain societies or companies to each of the members at a session or meeting." It was engraved by one of the Duvivier brothers, eminent coin and metal artists of Paris. The design represents on the obverse the head of Cybele, who personified the earth as inhabited or cultivated, while on the reverse Ceres has just tapped a maple tree, in which will be observed a spout provided with a stop to withhold the sweet sap when it flowed too fast.[1]

The Latin legend on the reverse is a quotation from Virgil, which, with its context, reads:

"*Salva magna parens frugum, Saturnia tellus magna virum.*"

The commissaries appointed for America were Simon Desjardines and Pierre Pharoux, who lost no time in proceeding to America to execute their important trust. Desjardines had been a Chamberlain of Louis XVI. He was of middle age, an accomplished scholar and gentleman, but knew not a word of English when he arrived. He had with him his wife and three children, and his younger brother, Geoffry Desjardines, who shared his labors and trials. He also brought with him his library of 2,000 volumes. Pierre Pharoux, the surveyor, who was afterwards drowned, was a distinguished young architect and engineer of Paris, of high scientific attainments and marked ability. He was earnestly and faithfully devoted to his duties; and his love of science, his honesty, his good sense, and genial and ardent friendship were manifested in all his doings. He left behind him in France an aged father to mourn his untimely death.

They sailed from Havre on the 4th day of July, 1793, in the American ship Liberty, but did not arrive in New York until the 7th of September following. There came over in the same vessel with them a young French refugee named Mark Isambart Brunel, who afterward filled the world with his fame as an engineer in England. Brunel had been in the French navy, and was driven from home on account of his royalistic proclivities. He went with them in all their journeys through the wilderness, and shared in all their hardships during the first year, but does not seem to have been employed by them in Castorland.

THEIR FIRST EXPLORATION.

Soon after their arrival in this country, Desjardines and Pharoux, with their friend Brunel, set out on a voyage of exploration to their "promised land" in the wild valley of the Black River. To realize the difficulties of the undertaking, the reader must bear in mind that the country they were in quest of lay far from Albany in the depths of a howling wilderness, which had then never been visited by white men, except around its border, or when carried across it as prisoners in savage hands; that the only route to it was up the Mohawk, in batteaux, to Fort Stanwix, now the city of Rome; thence by the way of Wood creek, the Oneida lake, and the Oswego river to Lake Ontario, and from Lake Ontario up the unexplored route of the Black River. It was over the old Indian trail, the savage warpath of the French and Indian and of the Revolutionary wars, and even then there was threatened a general Indian war by all the tribes around our borders. But in the face of all these difficulties our explorers, in the autumn of 1793, set out for Castorland.

In describing their passage over the carrying place from Fort Stanwix to Wood creek, of these trunks, presenting at once the images of life and death."

The fort at Oswego was still held by a British garrison. Jealous of Frenchmen, the commander at first refused to allow them to pass into Lake Ontario, but it was finally arranged that Brunel should remain as a hostage for the good conduct and safe return of the others. Brunel, however, was refused access to the fort, and was ordered to encamp alone in the woods on the opposite side of the river. Considering that such treatment invalidated his parole, he escaped from Oswego disguised as a common sailor, and proceeded with his friends on their expedition. They

near where the four busy tracks of the New York Central Railroad now run, they wrote in their journal, under date of October 10th: "Upon taking a walk into the woods a short distance we saw on every hand it was a fearful solitude. You are stopped sometimes by impassable swamps, and at other times by heaps of trees that have fallen from age or have been overthrown by storms, and among which an infinite number of insects and many squirrels find a retreat. On every hand we see the skeletons of trees overgrown with moss and in every stage of decay. The capillaire and other plants and shrubs spring out proceeded cautiously along the shore of the lake over the route that had become historic by the presence of M. de la Barre and his army in their visit to La Famine in 1684, and of Father Charlevoix in 1720, and which had so often been traversed by their countrymen in the palmy days of the old French occupancy, until their arrival at Niaoure bay, now called Black River bay. Here after a long search they discovered the mouth of the Black River, the great river that watered Castorland. But it was already so late in the season that they only explored the river up to the point some five or six miles above the falls at Watertown, and then returned to Albany to complete their preparations for the next year's journey.

In the autumn of 1855, the Hon. Amelia M. Murray, maid of honor to Queen Victoria, made a tour of the United States and Canada, through the lake belt of the Wilderness, over the route now so much travelled. Her companions were Gov. Horatio Seymour, the Governor's niece and other friends. On their way they stopped, of course, at Arnold's. But I will let the Lady Amelia tell the story in her own words, as written in her diary, under date of September 20, 1855: "Mr. Seymour remained to make arrangements with the guides, while his niece and I walked on to Arnold's farm. There we found Mrs. Arnold and six daughters. These girls, aged from twelve to twenty, were placed in a row against one wall of the shanty, with looks so expressive of astonishment, that I felt puzzled to account for their manner, till their mother informed us they had never before seen any other woman than herself! I could not elicit a word from them, but, at last, when I begged for a little milk, the eldest went and brought me a glass (tin cup). Then I remembered that we had met a single hunter rowing himself on the Moose River, who called out, 'Where on 'arth do them women come from?' And our after experience fully explained why ladies are such rare birds in that locality."

THE SETTLEMENT OF CASTORLAND.

The next spring, being in the year 1794, the Desjardines Brothers and Pharoux, with a large company of men, with their surveyors and assistants, took up their toilsome journey from Schenectady to their forest possessions, being this time fully equipped to begin their settlement. Their route this year was up the Mohawk in batteaux to Fort Schuyler, now Utica, thence overland across the Deerfield hills sixteen miles, to the log house of Baron Steuben, who had then just commenced his improvements upon his tract of 16,000 acres granted him by the State. From Steuben's it was twenty-four miles further through the trackless forest to the High Falls on the Black River in Castorland.

The difficulties of the journey then still before them can scarcely be imagined by the reader of to-day. At length they reached

38½ MUSKALLONGE.

their tract on the welcome banks of the Black River, and began their labors. But there is no space in these pages to follow them in their operations, in their sore trials and their bitter disappointments, their final discomfiture and utter failure.

Suffice it to say that they began a little settlement on the banks of the Black River, at the place now called Lyon's Falls. That they surveyed their lands and laid out one of their cities, Castorville, on the Beaver river, at a place now called Beaverton, opposite the little station now called Castorland, in memory of their enterprise. That they laid out their other city, the lake port, which they named "City of Basle," at what is now Dexter, below Watertown, and in 1795 they founded the present village of Carthage. That Pharoux was accidentally drowned in the river at Watertown in the fall of 1795. That Desjardines gave up the agency in despair in 1797 and was succeeded by Rudolphe Tillier, "Member of the Sovereign Council of Berne," who in turn gave place to Gouverneur Morris in 1800, and that the lands finally became the property of James Donatien Le Ray de Chaumont, his associates and grantees.

"After toil and many troubles, self-exiled for many years,
Long delays and sad misfortunes, man's regrets and woman's tears;
Unfulfilled the brilliant outset, broken as a chain of sand,
Were the golden expectations by Grande Rapides' promised land."

DEATH OF PIERRE PHAROUX.

One of the saddest incidents in the story of Castorland is the death of Pharoux, at the falls of Watertown, in 1795. In September of that year, after the river had been swollen by heavy rains, Pharoux set out with Brodhead, Tassart and others, all surveyors, on a journey to Kingston. In passing down the river on a raft, they were drawn over the falls. Mr. Brodhead and three men were saved, but Pharoux was drowned. The survivors made unremitting search for Pharoux's body, but it was not found until the following spring. It was washed ashore upon an island at the mouth of Black River, where it was found by Benjamin Wright, the surveyor, and by him decently buried there. M. LeRay de Chaumont many years afterwards caused a marble tablet to be set in the rock near his grave, bearing this inscription:

TO THE MEMORY OF
PIERRE PHAROUX,
THIS ISLAND IS CONSECRATED.

The reader will remember that the year before his death, Pharoux had discovered and named the river Independence, in Castorland, and had selected a beautiful spot at its mouth on the Black River, near a large flat granite rock, for his residence. This spot, called by the Desjardines Brothers Independence Rock, was ever afterwards regarded by them with melancholy interest. They could not pass it without shedding tears to the memory of their long-tried and trusted friend. Under date of May 28, 1796, Simon Desjardines, the elder brother, recorded in his journal: "Landed at half-past two at Independence Rock, and visited once more this charming spot which had been so beautifully chosen by our friend Pharoux as the site for his house. The azaleas in full bloom loaded the air with their perfume, and the wild birds sang sweetly around their nests, but nature has no longer any pleasant sights, nor fragrance, nor music, for me."

CASTORLAND, ADIEU!

And now ancient Castorland may be added to the long list of names once famous in the cities of Europe, and long celebrated in the forest annals of Northern New York, but now forgotten, and found only in history and song — feebly commemorated by the name of an insignificant railway station.

ART OF THE ANGLER.

As fish have grown more knowing, man has grown more cunning, and has devised new schemes to outwit his prey. Now, instead of fishing downstream, he fishes upstream, that he may be below and behind the fish, and, therefore, less in sight; for fish, it must be borne in mind, always lie with their heads upstream. Moreover, where he used to stand, he now kneels or crawls. That his rod may not be seen he moves horizontally—not vertically, as of old—and he never, if he can help it, allows the point to extend over the water. That his line may be seen as little as possible, he no longer searches the water at haphazard but reserves his cast until he has found and noted the exact position of a rising fish, or, at any rate, of a fish lying so near the surface as to suggest the strong probability that it is on the watch for flies. Then, instead of using two or three flies, he selects one, imitating, as closely as may be, in color and size, the natural flies he has observed on the water.

This he deftly casts, so that it shall fall on the water as lightly as a flake of snow, some 18 inches or so above the fish, and floats with its wings erect— "apeak," as they say of a cutter's foresail — and he allows it, without check or suspicious movement, to be carried by the stream over the nose of the trout. At the same moment, if fortune smiles, he sees a bubble rise, hears a faint sound like a baby's kiss, and the tug of war begins. If the trout refuses, or if the cast was not quite accurately made, he lets the drift float on, far below the fish, so that the ripple may not disturb the trout, and proceeds, *verberare nebulas*, to dry his fly by whipping it backward and forward through the air until it is once more buoyant. He then tries it again. Should the trout refuse at the second time of asking, the angler, if wise, will change his fly; if very wise, will change his fish, making a mental note to call again. This slight sketch will enable the reader to see the importance of closely imitating the flies on the water, and the skill required in presenting the counterfeit to the fish.

HISTORY OF THE LOST CHANNEL.

DURING the French and English war, which began in 1755 and ended in 1760, an expedition was fitted out at Oswego, in August of the latter year, for the final subjugation of the Canadas. The only remaining strongholds of the French were Montreal, and a strong fort on an island in the St. Lawrence river, about three miles below the present city of Ogdensburg, known as Fort Levis, commanded by a distinguished French officer—Capt. Pouchot. The expedition consisted of 10,142 British regulars and Colonial troops from Massachusetts, Connecticut, New York and New Jersey. Among the Massachusetts troops was Israel Putnam, of Revolutionary fame, then a lieutenant-colonel. In addition to these troops, there was a force of about 1,000 Indians, under the command of Sir William Johnson. The commander of the expedition was Gen. Jeffrey Amherst, the second in command being Gen. Gage, of Boston fame. At that time the English had two armed vessels on Lake Ontario, the "Onondaga" and the "Mohawk," commanded by Capt. John Loring, as admiral of the fleet, which consisted of the two vessels, 177 batteaux and 72 whale boats, besides staff boats, hospital boats, and boats for sutler's use. The first detachment of troops sailed in the two vessels on the 7th of August, for the rendezvous at "Basin Harbor," Grenadier Island, at the head of the St. Lawrence river. On the 13th, the entire army were assembled on the island, and early on the morning of the 14th the entire expedition set forth. Capt. Loring, with the two vessels, had gone ahead, and instead of keeping straight down the South channel, he crossed just below the foot of Wolfe Island into the Canadian channel. The French had been expecting an attack from this direction for a whole year; and, in consequence, had kept a lookout on Carleton Island, from which point they could readily see when the British forces entered the river; and with swift war canoes they could easily convey the intelligence to the fort below. When Capt. Loring had fairly entered the Navy group, he was assailed on every hand. The islands seemed to swarm with French and Indians, who were raking his deck with musketry. To add to his discomfiture, he knew nothing of the river nor of the labyrinth of islands in which he found himself; but, lowering away a boat and crew, he sent them back to prevent the "Mohawk" from entering the island group; and manning his guns, he swept the islands around him with grape and cannister, as he drifted with the current, he knew not whither. Fortunately, he got safely clear of the islands, when, coming to an anchor, he sent two other boats to find the first one sent out, but they returned unsuccessful; nor could they even distinguish which of the channels was the one in which the first boat was lowered. They never saw boat nor crew again; and ever afterward, in speaking of it, they called it the "Place of the Lost Channel." Two or three years later, the crew of a batteau found a broken yawl boat bearing the name "Onondaga," at the head of one of the channels, which, since that time, has been known as the "Lost Channel," and which Cap. Visger so happily renamed. The probability is that the crew of the yawl boat were killed and scalped by the Indians, and their boat stove and sunk; and, after all, we have no absolute certainty that this, more than any other of the numerous channels on every hand, was the one in which Capt. Loring first lowered his yawl boat. All that Capt. Loring's journal says about that part of it is the simple statement that they "called it the place of the lost channel."

WHAT CAUSED THE GREAT ST. LAWRENCE RIVER, AND WHY DOES IT FLOW WHERE IT DOES?

PREPARED BY F. A. HINDS, C. E., OF WATERTOWN.

THESE are questions that will ever present themselves as the majesty and immensity of this noble river impress themselves upon us.

Prof. James D. Dana, of Yale College, in his Manual of Geology, declares it is not by chance, or a haphazard circumstance, that there is a great water-course flowing through a valley to the eastward in the middle of the North American continent; but that it is "a law of the system of surface-forms of continents." In his chapter on Physiographic Geology he says:

"First. The continents have in general elevated mountain-borders and a low or basin-like interior.

"Secondly. The highest border faces the larger ocean.

"A survey of the continents in succession with reference to this law will exhibit both the unity of system among them and the peculiarities of each, dependent on their different relations to the oceans.

"The two Americas are alike in lying between the Atlantic and the Pacific; moreover, South America is set so far to the east of North America (being east of the meridian of Niagara Falls), that each has an almost entire ocean-contour. Moreover, each is triangular in outline, with the widest part, or head, to the north.

"North America, in accordance with the law, has on the Pacific side — the side of the great ocean — the Rocky Mountains, on the Atlantic side the low Appalachians, and

FRONTENAC HOTEL, ROUND ISLAND.

between the two there is the great plain of the interior.

"To the north of North America lies the small Arctic ocean, much encumbered with land; and, correspondingly, there is no distinct mountain-chain facing the ocean.

"The characteristics of the interior plain of the continent are well displayed in its river systems: the great Mississippi system turned to the south, and making its exit into the Gulf of Mexico between the approaching extremities of the eastern and western mountain range; the St. Lawrence sloping off northeastward; the Mackenzie, to the northward; the central area of the plain dividing the three systems being only about 1,700 feet above the ocean, a less elevation than about the headwaters of the Ohio in the State of New York.

"South America, like North America, has its great western range of mountains, and its smaller eastern; and the Brazilian line is closely parallel to that of the Appalachians. As the Andes face the South Pacific, a wider and probably much deeper ocean than the North Pacific, so they are more than twice the height of the Rocky Mountains, and, moreover, they rise more abruptly from the ocean, with narrow shore plains.

"Unlike North America, South America has a broad ocean on the north—the North Atlantic, in its longest diameter; and, accordingly, this northern coast has its mountain chain reaching along through Venezuela and Guiana.

"The drainage of South America, as observed by Professor Guyot, is closely parallel with that of North America. There are first, a southern—the La Plata—reaching the Atlantic towards the south, between the converging east and west chains, like the Mississippi; second, an eastern system—that of the Amazon—corresponding to the St. Lawrence, reaching the same ocean just north of the eastern mountain border; and, third, a northern system—that of the Orinoco—draining the slopes or mountains north of the Amazon system. The two Americas are thus singularly alike in system of structure; they are built on one model."

Thus one of the most noted and most credited geologists of our time, declares it to be as it were a fixed law, in the forming of continents, that there should be a great river system flowing from the middle portion of each continent eastward, or toward the lesser ocean.

Whatever may have been the conditions of this locality in the earlier ages of the world, with regard to subsidences and elevations of the earth's crust, it is quite probable that the relation between the river valley and the adjoining hills and mountains has remained approximately the same; that is, it was always a valley.

There is evidence, however, that there was an age when even this mighty river was turned back upon itself, and the waters were refused an outlet to the sea. This evidence is found in the elevated lake borders and gravel or pebble ridges that are to be seen along the adjoining highlands in New York State and Ohio.

Prof. G. Frederick Wright, of Oberlin College, in his book, "The Ice Age in North America," after discussing the present topography of Ohio, and the evidence that glacial action has changed the course of many ancient streams, says:

"On coming to the region of the Great Lakes, the influence of ice-barriers in maintaining vast bodies of water at a high level is very conspicuous. Around the south shore of Lake Erie there is an ascending series of what are called lake ridges. These are composed of sand and gravel, and consist largely of local material, and seem to maintain throughout their entire length a definite level with reference to the lake, though accurate measurements have not been made over the whole field. The approximation, however, is sufficiently perfect to permit us to speak of them as maintaining a uniform level. These ridges can be traced for scores of miles in a continuous line, and in the early settlement of the country were largely utilized for roads. In Loraine county, Ohio, an ascending series of four ridges can be distinguished at different levels above the lake. The highest is from 200 to 220 feet above it; the next is approximately 150 to 160 feet; the next lower is from 100 to 118 feet, and the next lower less than 100 feet, while some appear on the islands near Sandusky, which are not over 70 feet above the water level. Eastward from Buffalo portions of this series have been traced, according to Gilbert, until they disappear against the highlands, near Alden, on the Erie railroad.

That the ridges on Lake Erie mark temporary shore-lines of the lakes cannot well be doubted, for they are not related to any great natural lines of drainage, but follow the windings of a definite level, receding from the lake wherever there is a transverse valley, and forming in some cases parallel embankments on either side of such valley, running inland as far as to the general level of the series, and then returning on itself upon the other side, to strike off again parallel with the shore at the same level. Their relation to the lake is also shown by the local character of the material. It is usually such as would wash up on the shore out of the rock in place. In the sandstone region the ridges are largely made up of sand, mingled with fragments from the general glacial deposit. Over the regions of out-cropping shales, the ridges are composed largely of the harder nodules which have successfully resisted the attrition of the waves. Other evidences that they are shore-deposits are their stratification, the relative steepness of their sides toward the lake and the frequent occurrence of the fragments of wood buried at greater or less depths on their outer margin.

It need not be said that there has been much speculation concerning the cause which maintained the waters of the lakes at the levels indicated by these ridges, and permitted them to fall from the level of one to that of another in successive stages, so suddenly as they seem to have done; for, from the absence of intermediate deposits, it is evident that the formation of one ridge had no sooner been completed than the one at the next lower level began to form. In the earlier stages of glacial investigation, before the full power and flexibility of glacial ice were appreciated, and before the exact course of the southern boundary of the ice-sheet was known, the elevation of the water to produce these ridges was supposed to have resulted either from a general subsidence of the whole region to the ocean level, or from the elevation of a rocky barrier across the outlet. Both these theories were attended with insuperable difficulties. In the first place, there is no such amount of collateral evidence to support the theory of general subsidence as there should be if it really had occurred. The subsidence of the lake region to such an extent would have left countless other marks over a wide extent of country; but such marks are not to be found. Especially is there an absence of evidences of marine life. The cause was evidently more local than that of a general subsidence. The theory of the elevation of a rocky barrier would also seem to be ruled out of the field by the fact that no other direct evidence can be found of such recent local disturbances. Such facts as we have point to a subsidence at the east rather than to an elevation.

But a glance at the course of the terminal moraine, and at the relation of the outlets of these lakes to the great ice movements of the glacial period, brings to view a most likely cause for this former enlargement and increase in height of the surface of the lower lakes. It will be noticed that the glacial front near New York city was about 100 miles further south than it was in the vicinity of Buffalo. Hence the natural outlet to the great lakes through the Mohawk Valley would not have been opened until the ice-front over New England and Eastern New York had retreated to the north well-nigh 150 miles. A similar amount of retreat of the ice-front from its farthest extension in Cattaraugus county, in New York, would have carried it back thirty miles to the north of Lake Ontario, while a similar amount of retreat from eastern Ohio would have left nearly all the present bed of Lake Erie free from glacial ice. With little doubt, therefore, we have, in the lake ridges of Upper Canada, New York and Ohio, evidence of the existence of an ice barrier which continued to fill the valley of the Mohawk, and choke up the outlet through the St. Lawrence, long after the glacial front farther to the west had withdrawn itself to Canada soil. A study of these ridges may yet shed important light upon the length of time during which this ice barrier continued across the valley of the Mohawk.

By the work of our local civil engineers in and about Jefferson county, it has been found that the gravel deposits and beds of waterworn pebbles found along the first escarpment of the Rutland Hills and the Dry Hills, so called, of Jefferson county, correspond in actual elevation with about 100 feet above the level of Lake Erie, and, therefore, quite probably mark a shore-line of the same lake referred to by Professor Wright, as marked by gravel ridges along the south shore of Lake Erie and as 100 feet above its level, and being caused by the damming up of both the St. Lawrence and the Mohawk River valleys. In this way we can also find a plausible theory for the formation of our own lower gravel ridges, in the fact that after the glacier front had receded farther, and the Mohawk Valley was opened as an outlet, the great inland lake was drawn down to a correspondingly lower level, and its waves and surface motion lashed a new shore-line, and gave us a new line of ridges and water-worn pebbles.

The grooves and lines, and the polishing of the rocks in Jefferson county, show plainly that the general direction of the moving ice of this locality was in parallel lines with the general direction of the St. Lawrence River, only the ice was moving up-stream or to the southeast. The streams and valleys of Jefferson and St. Lawrence counties also in general follow the same trend. The Oswegatchie and the Indian Rivers flow first southwesterly and then, making a sharp turn, each flows back almost parallel with their former course and with the guiding trend of the St. Lawrence. Even the Grass and Raquette Rivers, further east, find themselves swung around into this general course. The same course is followed in the deep valley known as Rutland Hollow, about three miles east of the city of Watertown, and the Sandy Creek and Stony Brook in the southerly part of Jefferson county follow the same general course. The Black River itself, from the Great Bend to Watertown, takes the same course, and a valley now occupied by low, swampy land continues the same direction to the lake, though the river itself, from Watertown city, takes a lower and shorter direction through rocky gorges to its present mouth at Dexter.

During the period of this higher glacial lake the mouth of the Black River must have been near Carthage, and the great sand deposits in the towns of LeRay and Wilna, known as the Pine Plains, were probably the shoal water or sand-bar formation, such as usually occurs at the mouth of a stream where it enters a lake or sea. There was also, probably, a glacier coming down the Black River Valley and joining in, and following along with, the greater St. Lawrence Valley glacier, heretofore described, as moving to the south-west. The above fact is proven by the well-defined medial moraine, extending from near Carthage through near Tylerville and the towns of Rodman and Ellisburg, to the lake just south of Ellis village. This moraine is almost entirely of granitic stones and bowlders, the characteristic rock of the right bank of the Black River Valley, and the moraine itself from Carthage to the lake is exactly parallel with the St. Lawrence river.

A glance at the map of the Thousand Islands shows the general outline of the islands to be long and narrow, and laid lengthwise of the river. An inspection of the rocks and ledges, and hills and valleys of the adjoining shores, and the surface of the islands themselves, develop the fact that all have followed the same law of direction.

The ice age no doubt has wrought great changes in the present surface forms, and to its influence we may properly ascribe the rounded and smoothed surfaces of the hard rocks and ledges, but it is also probable that there was a general direction given when the Azoic and Laurentian rocks were cooled off from the great molten mass, and that the St. Lawrence Valley, with its adjacent uplands, was an early and original form of the surface, and that the direction of the glacier movement here was due to this original configuration.

The parallelism, however, of the streams and valleys of the adjoining country, and the grooving and wearing off of the rocky projections, and the filling up of old channels, and the depositing of long lines of stones and bowlders, foreign to the locality where they are found, and the depositing of large areas of sand-beds — all these, and many other features, are, beyond doubt, the work of a glacial age.

THE TECHNIQUE OF FISHING.

IN GOVERNOR ALVORD's most interesting and instructive articles upon the Great River, he has much to say about the "men he has met," and he speaks of all of them more as beloved comrades than as mere acquaintances or as the passing visitors of an hour; but he does not say much about the technique, the appliances, the methods of fishing. Ourself an amateur, we have not failed to seek information upon the points indicated; and, like all amateurs, we try to believe that there is some "royal road to learning," by pursuing which we may exceptionally "get there" without the labor and inconveniences of learning by experience. From the great IZAAK WALTON himself down to our own day, and taking our distinguished GOVERNOR ALVORD as one of the brightest teachers of modern times in all arts piscatorial, the methods, the little incidentals by which the agile water-denizens are lured into the voracious frying-pan, have been much disputed — this grand "faculty" of becoming an expert fisherman being as elusive, various, and sometimes as intricate as wooing one of the fair sex, whose moods are often as contradictory as are those of the most artful muscalonge or bass, and yet, when captured, are almost "too sweet for anything." From the crookedest tree-limb, with a piece of twine at its end, to the jointed and polished rod, with silken line and silver reel, the margin is wide and expensive. The poorest and the best of these appliances have each won great renown, but generally in the hands of those who know how to use them, the fish being largely democratic, and as willing to take a wriggling worm from a pin-hook as from one of Skinner's best treble-arranged, feather-decorated devices. As in all good things, in fishing there are many methods; but in all fishing, good bait is an indispensable adjunct. With it you feel as a soldier feels with a good gun in his hand; it is his guaranty of probable success.

The improvements in fishing tackle have been immense during the past forty years. In 1849, the writer saw the elder Walton, long since dead, at work upon spoons that could not now be given away — yet of those rude attempts he could dispose readily of as many as he could put together. Chapman, at Theresa and Rochester, had made many beautiful and successful fishing appliances. But the most successful man in the business for very many years has been Mr. G. M. Skinner, of Clayton, whose goods are now known all over the United States and Canada. He began to study the art piscatorial upon the Great River itself, having been long a resident of Gananoque, Ontario, in his early youth. He finally located at Clayton, a place possessing some advantages not apparent to the superficial observer, among them being a prominent angling resort and the principal gateway for tourists coming to the river over the only avenue on the American side, viz.: the N. Y. C. System, comprising the R., W. & O., and U. & B. R. R. R. It is the distributing point for those desiring to reach, by water, the numerous islands and parks in its immediate vicinity, and, also, the fashionable resort, twelve miles down the river, of Alexandria Bay.

In this romantic and favored vicinity he served his apprenticeship in fishing and experimenting with all sorts, sizes and shapes of artificial baits obtainable. He was not content, but strove to construct a spoon for his own use, which should have decided advantages over any used. As a result of such effort, two corrugated or fluted spoons were made; one being given to a fishing companion, the other he retained for his own use. In numerous practical trials, these two spoons gave satisfactory evidence of having uncommon merit, notably in the capture, by his wife and self, of a muscalonge, measuring four feet eleven inches in length and weighing forty pounds.

Mr. Skinner himself says: "I have been frequently asked, what I considered a spoon to represent, as revolving while fishing, and why are fish attracted by them to such an extent that they will seize them, even when unprovided with any other attraction save the glint of the cold metal. In reply, I offer those of an inquisitive turn my humble opinion that the motion or action of a revolving lure, unquestionably simulates or means, life — prey, to fish, and as a natural sequence, life means food — sustenance."

Mr. Skinner also relates the following: "A party from Clayton went to Hay Bay, Bay of Quinte, to fish for muscalonge. The water in Hay Bay is not very deep where the fish are caught and the weeds come very near the surface. To prevent the trolling-spoon fouling, a gang of naked hooks is attached to the line some distance ahead of the spoon, which breaks off or pulls up the weeds and allows the spoon to go free. Messrs. D. Pratt and Edwin Seymour, of Syracuse, were fishing in one boat. Mr. Seymour, in letting out line, felt a tug when the line was out but a few yards. Turning he saw the water break where the naked hook was and commenced to haul in, finding he had caught a muscalonge upon the naked or weed-guard hook.

"One of the party trolling with two hand lines caught a large pike under somewhat unusual circumstances. The voracious fish had captured one troll and made a race for and secured the other, having both of them securely hooked in his mouth when hauled in.

"A most unusual occurrence I would like to place on record. In August, 1883, Miss Annie Lee, at that time eleven years of age, while trolling near Clayton for bass, with a No. 3 gold fluted spoon, which size is fitted with a No. 2 hook, struck and successfully brought to boat a muscalonge weighing thirty-six pounds, measuring four feet six inches in length. In the effort to secure this large fish the guide's gaff was broken, showing the enormous strength of the fish, yet it was finally secured, brought in and exhibited with those slight hooks still fast in its capacious mouth — an evidence not only of good tackle, but of skillful handling."

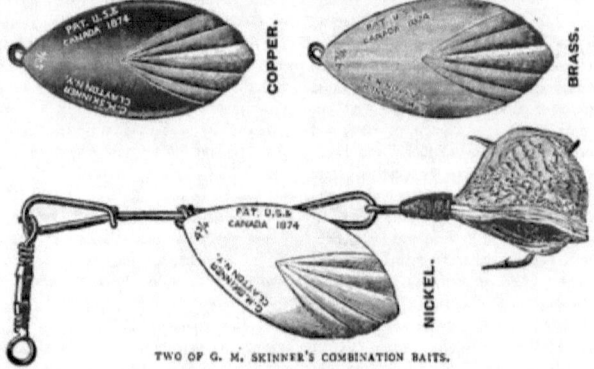

TWO OF G. M. SKINNER'S COMBINATION BAITS.

GANANOQUE—PAST AND PRESENT.

THE pleasant village of Gananoque, with a population of about four thousand souls, situated on the north shore of the St. Lawrence, opposite Clayton, and at the outlet of Gananoque River, is a place of no small importance as a manufacturing center. It has an excellent water power, aggregating many hundreds of horse-power, much more of which might be utilized for manufacturing purposes.

As a place of summer resort, it possesses exceptional advantages in the way of locality. Its position at the foot of the "Admiralty Group" of islands, in which is "Bostwick Channel," the finest in many respects of any of the island channels in the river (the entire group being made up of islands in themselves exceedingly picturesque), is, in its entirety, one of great beauty and attractiveness. Already cottages are erected on many of the islands, and as the great desirableness of the locality becomes better known, the number of these cannot fail to increase; and still more so, if the present very unjust and inconsistent policy of the Ottawa government should be modified, as, indeed, it should be for the benefit of the village of Gananoque itself.

The name "Gananoque" is evidently of Indian origin; but which of two Indian names as first applied to the locality is to be considered as having given rise to the present name, is a matter of some doubt. The original orthography of the word was "Cadanoryhqua," meaning the "Place of Health," or what was evidently a synonymous phrase "Rocks-Seen-Under-Running-Water," both of which are descriptive of the locality, so far as physical conditions and a natural fact are concerned. On the other hand, the Hurons called the place "Gananoqui," which means "The Place of the Deer." Another tribe translates their term to mean "A meadow rising out of the waters," so that the real source from which the present name is derived is a matter of some doubt. Be that as it may, the Mississauga name "Cadanoryhqua" was for several years retained in official documents, and it was not until after the year 1800 that the name "Gananoque" came into use. At the time of the survey of Leeds, the name of the Gananoque River was changed to "The Thames," but it never was generally used; in fact it only appears in a proclamation of Lord Dorchester (Sir Guy Carlton) while for the second time Governor-General of Canada, in 1788.

From the variety and extent of its manufacturing interests, Gananoque has been, not inaptly, named the Birmingham of Canada, and as a settlement has now entered upon the second century of its existence. A brief sketch of its early settlement may be of some interest to the general reader, and is therefore subjoined. Two men, Sir John Johnson, an officer of the British army during the War of the Revolution, at which time he commanded an organization of loyalists popularly known as "Johnson's Royal Greens," and Colonel Joel Stone, were the first to receive grants of land which covered the entire limits of the village, and more, as it now stands. Of these two, Col. Stone was the first settler, coming up the river from Cornwall in the summer of 1792, taking passage in a batteau which was bound to Kingston. These grants of land were made in 1792, and the patent to Col. Stone was issued December 31, 1798, and covers "A certain triangular tract upon the River Cadanoryhqua," etc., which was located on the west side of the river. Sir John Johnson's tract was located on the east side of the river, but his patent was not issued until May 17, 1802. Each grant extended to the center of the Gananoque River, then known by its Indian name as above.

Col. Stone's patent was computed to contain 700 acres of land, to which were added, later, two additional patents of 200 acres each, making in all 1,100 acres; while Col. Johnson's grant covered 1,534 acres. At the time of Col. Stone's arrival, a Frenchman, named Carey, lived on Tidd's Island, now Fremont Park, with whom he formed a temporary partnership, erecting a shanty on the mainland, on the point now occupied by a lumber yard. Having secured a couple of cows, their shanty was opened as a house of entertainment, being the first tavern for many miles along the Canadian shore of the St. Lawrence. During the absence of the proprietors one day, the hotel burned and the partnership ended, each of them entering into business for himself. Mr. Stone proceeded to clear a plot of land on what is know King street, on which he erected a log-house, it being, with the exception of the shanty above spoken of, the first house erected in Gananoque. His next enterprise was the building of a schooner of forty tons measurement, called the "Leeds Trader," which ran on the lake and river for many years. Then he built a saw-mill, which stood on the site of the present Electric Light Company's building; following that with a frame house of two stories in height, fastened with wrought nails brought from England. It was erected in 1796, and for half a century it was known as the "Red House," having been painted that color. This was built on the point near where the upper end of the lumber yard wharf is now. Where the steel and wire shop now is, Mr. Stone built another frame house, known as the "Yellow House," and which became his residence, after his marriage to Mrs. Dayton. Later, he built a long, low frame house with a veranda along its entire front, just west of the "West End Store," which he made his residence as long as he lived. The building was burned only thirteen years ago, and the lot where it stood is yet vacant. In 1852, the late John Bulger tore down the "Red House," and the frame was re-erected on Garden street. It is the house now occupied by Mr. James Beatty. The "Yellow House" was burned in 1850.

Col. Stone was evidently a man of great energy, and was unceasing in his efforts to improve his holdings, keeping all the time an eye to the "main chance," as did his ancestors, and as he himself had been trained to do in the school of actual business. His procedure was in direct contrast with that of Sir

COL. STONE.
(Kindly loaned us by Mr. Britton, editor "Recorder.")

John Johnson, who paid no attention whatever to his estate, only through an agent; in fact, it is a question whether he ever visited his possessions in person, so that to Col. Stone belongs all the honors of a first settler; and hence a brief biographical sketch may prove interesting. .

Joel Stone was born in Guilford, Connecticut, August 7, 1749. Before he was two years of age, his father removed to Litchfield, where, "by indefatigable labor and industry, he improved a competency of land of which he was proprietor." During his minority, Joel labored on the "competency," but when he became of age, he adopted a more active mode of life, and became a travelling merchant; or, in the vernacular of those days a "Yankee peddler." Within three years he travelled over very nearly the whole of the then settled portions of the country, returning with a large amount of property. In 1774, he entered into a mercantile partnership with Jabez Bacon, of Woodbury, Conn., their articles of copartnership binding them for six years as copartners in "Merchandizing and all things thereto belonging; and in buying, selling, vending and retailing all sorts of goods, wares and commodities whatsoever." These articles of copartnership are yet in existence. This partnership flourished, and the partners became wealthy; but the breaking out of the Revolutionary War ended the partnership and one of them assumed the hazards and glories of a military life.

Mr. Stone attempted for a time to remain neutral and trade with both parties, though his sympathy was with the Royalists. But he was soon obliged to declare himself for one side or the other. To remain neutral, was to be suspected by both, and in 1776 he was peremptorily ordered by the officials of Congress to declare immediately whether he would take up arms against the British government, or furnish a substitute. He refused to do either; and being warned that he would be called to a strict account, he fled hurriedly to New York, which was then held by the British forces, and which he reached in safety; and on the 20th of June, 1777, he was enrolled in Governor Wentworth's command, by a commission dated April 16, 1778. He recruited fifty-four men or more for two years' service, under command of Sir William Howe. He went on this mission to Huntington, Long Island, where he was surprised while asleep and taken prisoner, May 12, 1778, by a company of whaleboat men, and conveyed to Fairfield, Connecticut. He was held in close custody and charged with high treason. But he managed to escape on the 23d of July, and a week later was back on Long Island.

In the meantime, the selectmen, the constables, bailiffs, and the courts of Connecticut had been attending to the property left there by Mr. Stone when he fled to New York. By due process of law, as it then obtained, his real and personal estate was confiscated, and the proceeds, after deducting costs, were rendered for benefit of the State. Not only did the magistrates and County Court adjudicate in the matter and issue executions, but the Probate Court was also called into operation, as dealing with the effects of one who was described in the inventory as "politically dead." The personal property thus escheated appears by the returns to have amounted to £491: 6: 9, "at the rate of twenty-eight shillings for an English guinea, or six shillings for a Spanish milled dollar." The real estate was appraised under oath at £354: 13: 0. One piece of land, in which Mr. Stone had a one-half interest, in the township of Winchester, was not included, for the reason, probably, that his pursuers had no knowledge of it. According to Mr. Stone's own statement, the firm of Bacon & Stone had a capital of £12,000 sterling in stock; and that in addition to his share of that, his books, bonds and all his personal effects were confiscated.

During his residence in New York, Mr. Stone formed an acquaintance with the family of William Moore, a sea captain, and on the 23d of March, 1780, he was married to Leah Moore, the captain's daughter. The marriage ceremony was celebrated by Rev. Charles Inglis, who was then rector of Trinity church, New York.

In addition to his pension, Mr. Stone, in common with all who had served the King in the Revolutionary War, was entitled to a grant of land. And after his arrival at Quebec, he endeavored by inquiries and personal investigation to ascertain what would be the most suitable locality.

Mr. Stone settled in Cornwall with his family, then consisting of his wife, his son, William Moore Stone, and his daughter, Mary. He purchased some land at Cornwall, and expected to draw 800 or 1,000 acres besides. He erected a dwelling and still house, and otherwise endeavored to provide a permanent home. But he was unable to secure as much land as he wanted. Most of it had been pre-empted before he arrived, and he was, therefore, compelled to come further towards the west in search of unclaimed territory. He went to Quebec and spent some time in an effort to secure all the land along the Gananoque River. But Sir John Johnson brought sufficient influence to bear upon the government to cause a compromise of claims. It was decided that Sir John should be awarded all the land on the east side of the Gananoque River, and Mr. Stone all on the west side, the boundary of each to be the center of the river. Just when this decision was arrived at is not set down. But Mr. Stone took possession of his portion in 1792, and the patent was issued six years later.

In 1791, Col. Stone went to Connecticut with his two children, William and Mary, whom he placed at school in Hartford, having previously placed a son at school in Montreal. Leah, his wife, died at Cornwall, about 1793, but the exact date is not known. In 1798, Mr. Stone, who had then been five years a widower, and had established himself at Gananoque, decided to marry a second time, and made formal proposal to Mrs. Abigail Dayton, widow, who lived in the township of Burford, in Upper Canada.

Suffice it to say, that the wooer prosecuted his suit with vigor, and in time, the fair object of his affections surrendered at discretion, but not in haste. They were married in the summer of 1799, removing to the residence of Col. Stone, at Gananoque.

From that time on, the particulars of Mr. Stone's life are so much a part of the progress and growth of Gananoque as to belong more properly to the history of the town. He filled numerous offices both under the government and by local appointment. He was the first Collector of Customs; a Commissioner, or Justice of the Peace; Chairman of the Court of General Sessions of the Peace for the Johnstown District; Commissioner for administering the oath to half-pay officers; Returning Officer at County election of Member of Parliament in 1812; a member of the Land Board for District of Johnston, established in 1819 for locating settlers; and Road Overseer for the Township of Leeds.

By a commission dated 3d January, 1809, under the hand and seal of Francis Gore, Lieut.-Governor of Upper Canada, he was appointed colonel in the 2d Regiment of Militia for the County of Leeds, and was thereafter known as Colonel Stone. This office he resigned in January, 1822.

Three children were born to Mr. Stone during the life of his first wife. His eldest son William, who is referred to as "Billy" in Mr. Stone's letters, grew to maturity at Gananoque, assisting in the general affairs of his father, and for a time holding the position of Deputy Collector of Customs. He died in 1809, aged twenty-eight years.

In the fall of 1833, the Colonel caught a severe cold, and died on the 20th November, in the eighty-fifth year of his age. Mrs. Stone survived him by nearly ten years, and died August 4, 1843, in her ninety-third year.

The events of his settlement in Gananoque have already been alluded to, but we will add one brief letter, which sets forth the energy and thrift of Col. Stone, better by far than any description could:

MONTREAL, 16th July, 1801.

MY DEAR:—I received your letter dated the next day after I left home, 7th June, about three days past by mere accident. I mark well the contents thereof, approve of what you have done, and must with pleasure submit to your own wisdom to do as you think best until I can get home, which I do not intend shall be long, but I have not yet been able to deliver any of my boards and plank. Andrew, William and David will sett off to-morrow morning with the boat loaded with the following packages and articles agreeable to the enclosed bills: One large cask wine, two trunks, one small trunk, the box or chest, two barrells, two kegs (one best Madeira wine, one cider vinegar), one cask nails, two small bales, one shovel, one spade. Enclosed I send you four keys, one to each of the trunks, and one to the chest. Please to be careful in unpacking the pork barrel. It has a bottle of castor oil and a phial of pickery roped up in the blankets.

In the barrels, and in your chest, you will find a number of articles we had on board the raft, two or three axes, &c., and you will find tobacco and snuff (viz.), 2 lbs. snuff only; also Bohea tea in one of the casks, and Hyson tea in one of the large trunks. The Bohea tea is 6s. per lb. in case you sell any, and the tobacco 3s. Please to put the tobacco in some moist place.

The other articles I have marked the price to sell at in the bills in my own hand writing. I need not caution you to sell for cash only, except where we owe and to pay for what we must buy. The large cask of wine may be very good to drink as wine and water, and you may sell it at 5s per gallon if you can, but I bought it with a view of making vinegar only. I gave 1s per gallon for it. The articles in the large trunk where the Hyson tea is are not marked, nor is the bill sent. You will find Turlington's drops in the trunk where the Hyson tea is, which you may sell at 5s per bottle, but those in the pork barrel, large phials keep for your own use. You will set the people at work as you find most necessary until I get home. I must, if possible, bring down another raft this season. Old Mr. Chaple will be up again as soon as he has done visiting his friends.

I am my dear in great haste, with a very bad pen and ink and my best exertions,

Your most affectionate,
JOEL STONE.

For much of the matter relating to Col. Stone, we are indebted to FREEMAN BRITTON, Esq., editor of the "Gananoque Reporter."

So far as the improvement of his water-power was concerned, Col. Stone did but little towards it, leasing it finally to his son-in-law, Charles McDonald, who, in 1812, began to carry on an extensive business. He built a saw-mill, and a small grist-mill, and engaged largely in the lumber trade, shipping large quantities to Quebec, and also supplying the government with ship timber, several war vessels being on the stocks at Kingston, at that time. In 1817, Chas. McDonald was joined by his brother John, and later by another brother Collin; and in 1826, the firm of "C. & J. McDonald and Brother" erected the largest flouring mill in the Province. To supply this mill, grain was brought in schooners from the West; and owing to its capacity of 250 barrels per day, was for many years enabled to supply one-quarter of all the flour received at Montreal. The flour was sent down in batteaux and Durham boats, a batteau load being from ·150 to 200 barrels, while a Durham boat carried 450 barrels. The forwarding business at that time was in the hands of H. & S. Jones. The block houses built at Gananoque, and on Chimney Island, were built for the government by Charles McDonald.

The first store in Gananoque was opened in 1812 by Chas. McDonald, and the McDonalds also built the first church in the place. It was free for all denominations, and was erected in 1832. Some four or five years later, the Methodists erected a small wooden building on the site of the present church. This denomination furnished the first regular services in the village. The first resident minister was Rev. William Carson. Among the first settlers of the village was Ephraim Webster, who was afterward collector of customs at Brockville. In 1831, the steamer William IV was built at Gananoque by a joint stock company. This was the steamer that the noted Bill Johnston and his followers attempted to capture during the so-called Patriot war, by stretching a chain across a narrow channel between two islands. The attempt failed, but was successful as to the Sir Robert Peel, related elsewhere.

The writer's acknowledgments are due to his honor the mayor and several aldermen for many favors in the way of information afforded, but especially to the Hon. C. E. BRITTON, whose interest in the welfare of his town is strong and abiding.

In concluding this brief sketch of the early history of Gananoque, the writer desires to add, that steps are now being taken to build an electric railway from that village to the city of Kingston. In fact there is at this writing a bill before Parliament asking for an act of incorporation, which will no doubt be granted. Its situation, its water power, its commercial opportunities, its manufacturing privileges, entitle Gananoque to a population of fully 15,000 souls; and this it cannot fail to realize, unless its leading citizens, by injudicious acts, shall retard the onward march of improvement, and paralyze progress. A great number of lakes in its rear not only guarantee the perpetuity of its water power, but make the village the gateway to the finest fishing and hunting grounds in America. That Gananoque is destined to become one of the thriving cities of the St. Lawrence region admits of but slight doubt.

BROCKVILLE.

THE GATE-CITY TO THE THOUSAND ISLANDS.

JUST at the foot of the Thousand Islands, 126 miles west of Montreal, and fifty miles east of Kingston, stands the beautiful town of Brockville. Its history is one of interest, as being one of the oldest towns in Ontario, and as one which has not stood still, but has made a steady progress, a solid substantial growth, in step and cadence with modern improvement. The modern "booms," with their consequent reaction, have never been inflicted upon Brockville, and in consequence it has felt none of the enervating influences sequent upon periods of undue inflation.

In 1784, one hundred and eleven years ago, Adam Cole, having left the United States, and being still desirous of remaining under the protection of the British flag, to which he deemed his allegiance due, sailed up the St. Lawrence, and landed on the site of the present city of Brockville; but from the fact that to him the land seemed rough and uninviting, he pushed on to a point six miles above, and finally settled at what is now known as Cole's Ferry. In the following year, another enthusiastic U. E. Loyalist, William Buell, located on the lot where a large part of the western portion of the city now stands. Shortly afterward, Charles Jones, following in the footsteps of his predecessor, took up the adjoining lot on the east. These first settlers were of course subjected to all the inconveniences incident to pioneer life; but in a short time the little settlement became a distributing point for government stores, which were supplied to settlers in the shape of provisions and implements, and quite soon it sprang into some prominence, and began to grow.

The surrounding township was named Elizabethtown, and for a number of years the village was known by that name, and also by the name of Buell's Bay. Finally, the residents began to favor a more dignified title, and then no little difference of opinion arose concerning the name of the place, which, as is almost always the case, resulted in a patronymic bestowed by outsiders, which was far more expressive as to fact, than conducive to dignity. Mr. Buell and his friends were extremely desirous of naming it "Williamstown," in honor of William Buell, the first settler. On the other hand, Mr. Jones and his adherents, insisted that "Charlestown" should be the name, after Mr. Charles Jones; and between the factions such a strife was engendered, and so bitter was this miniature war of the rival roses, that the outlying residents becoming disgusted with the endless bickerings, incontinently bestowed the nickname of "Snarleytown" upon the place, which adhered to it for a long time.

In 1811, however, a new system of grand tactics was introduced into the local war, and Mr. Buell demonstrated his ability as a tactician by having his property surveyed and laid out into town lots, setting aside grounds for a public square, court-house, etc., of which he had a map published on which was duly set forth desirable properties for sale, thus inaugurating for that day and age a veritable approach to the modern "boom," or, at all events, as near to one as Brockville has ever experienced. Desirous of becoming a large landed proprietor, Mr. Jones was averse to disposing of his property in like manner, and therefore practically acknowledged that he was out-generaled, but he was by no means defeated. The factions grew and multiplied in numbers, and the feud in intensity, for a decade, until it seemed a foregone conclusion that "Snarleytown" was likely to become the permanent designation of the locality. Finally, in 1821, Governor-General Sir Isaac Brock, being in the place, the dispute was referred to him, and he immediately settled the difficulty by bestowing his own name upon the place. It was a happy thought, and like schooner Julia, and two British vessels, the Earl of Moira and the Duke of Gloucester, had an engagement opposite the town, which lasted for three hours, ceasing by mutual consent when darkness came on, neither party having suffered any material damages;— an emphatic and significant comment upon the skill of both parties in the use of artillery. On the night of the 6th of February, 1813, Capt. Forsyth, of the Rifles, then commandant at Ogdensburg, marched up the river to Morristown, and, crossing on the ice, took posses-

LOOKING EAST FROM ARCADE, WATERTOWN, N. Y., SHOWING SNOW OF WINTER 1894-95.

pouring oil upon troubled waters, it calmed the storm by satisfying the contending factions, who merged their differences into "Brockville," a name ever since retained, and one to be proud of. As an old resident of the city remarked to the writer: "It was a shrewd exemplification of the fable of the monkey, the cats and the cheese — but it worked well and satisfied all parties."

During the war of 1812-15, Brockville was often the scene of lively operations. On the 29th of July, 1812, the United States armed sion of the town, capturing several of its prominent citizens, and releasing several prisoners from the jail, most of whom were Americans who had been taken prisoners and confined there. It is related that Capt. Forsyth refused to release a prisoner who was incarcerated on a charge of murder; but in his defense his counsel sought to win a point in his favor by establishing the fact that, while he might have escaped, he would not, thus creating a strong inference of his innocence. He was, nevertheless, convicted and hanged.

Fifty-two prisoners, with a large amount of stores and ammunition, was the result of the capture of Brockville, and an equal number of American prisoners was the result of a reprisal which immediately followed, in which Capt. Forsyth was badly beaten at Ogdensburg by the Canadian volunteers under Capt. McDonnell, who, in addition to the prisoners, captured a large amount of military stores, several pieces of artillery, some small arms, besides destroying the barracks. The Americans lost twenty-three in killed and wounded, and were forced to retreat to Black Lake. Since the senseless and uncalled for disturbance of 1837, which culminated in the surrender of the rebels at the Windmill, and the ripple caused by the Fenian Raid, Brockville has enjoyed uninterrupted peace, and has steadily thriven, pursuing the even tenor of its way, until now we have

THE BROCKVILLE OF TO-DAY.

With a population of very nearly, if not quite 10,000, Brockville is fairly on the road toward the dignity and importance of a city. The old methods of navigation on the St. Lawrence, batteaux and Durham boats, have given way to elegant steamers, which have reduced the time from Montreal from weeks to hours. Railways have replaced the uncertain stage coach, and now few towns are more favorably situated than is Brockville, as regards connections both by water and by rail. The main line of the Grand Trunk Railway runs through the town, and has been an important factor in its development. Direct communication with Ottawa, the capital of the Dominion, only seventy-four miles distant, is afforded by the Canadian Pacific Railway, which absorbed into its gigantic system the old Brockville and Ottawa Railway. Already the Brockville, Westport and Sault St. Marie Railway has been completed to Westport, and in addition to making a large section of country tributary to Brockville, when completed to the "Soo," and connecting there with the American railways, this will become one of the great trunk lines, connecting the Atlantic

THE SNOW IN STREETS OF WATERTOWN, WINTER OF 1894-95.

seaboard with the Great West. Besides, there is now projected an electric railway to run between Brockville and Ottawa, which will open the Rideau country, and be of great benefit to that entire section. By steam-ferry to Morristown, connection is had with the Rome, Watertown and Ogdensburg Railway, which forms a part of the great Central system of New York; the largest on the American continent — and now it is proposed to build a bridge across the St. Lawrence at this point, to connect the Canadian and American systems, the preliminary steps to which have already been taken, charters secured in both countries, and it is confidently expected that active steps in the way of construction will be taken within a few months at the farthest.

During the season of navigation, the steamer service is excellent. The steamers of the Richelieu and Ontario Navigation Company call daily on their trips between Toronto and Montreal and various American ports among the Thousand Islands. Besides these, the Ocean, Alexandria, Cuba, etc., do a large freight and passenger business, so that water facilities are of the best quality, and readily available at the minimum of delay. The steamer service to the Thousand Islands has of late years been supplied by the John Haggart, a commodious vessel, well adapted to the purpose.

As a summer resort, Brockville offers exceptional advantages. The great American resorts among the islands are within easy reach, being only from twenty-five to thirty miles away, and easily reached by any one of the daily line of steamers which ply during the watering season. Besides these, the Empire State, America and St. Lawrence, all splendid steamers, make almost daily excursions. These steamers belong to the Thousand Island Steamboat Company line, a company that is sparing no pains nor expense to furnish a river service on the St. Lawrence which cannot be excelled. During the past decade some elegant resorts have sprung up on the Canadian side of the river; among which are Fernbank, Hill Crest, and Union Park, while between these nearly every favored spot is taken up, and every year sees new and beautiful summer homes spring into view. Residents of New York, Ottawa and Montreal, recognizing the beauties of these locations, have already erected fine summer residences, or are prepared to do so in the near future.

Between Brockville and Union Park, seven miles above, a steamer makes four round trips daily, so that business men can attend to their duties during the day, returning to their cottage homes in the evening. In addition to its river attractions, Brockville has some beautiful drives, prominent among which, for beauty and picturesqueness, is the drive to Fernbank Park and the village of Lynn, five miles away. The best known and patronized, however, is that to Prescott, a distance of twelve miles along the bank of the river. Brockville is supplied with water through the celebrated "Holly" system, and it has an excellent system of sewerage, so that as a place of excellent sanitation it is unexcelled. The streets are well lighted with both gas and electricity, or rather a combination of the two. They intersect at right angles, and for the most part are beautifully shaded, so that one might aptly name Brockville the "Forest City," and not go far astray.

In religious and educational matters, Brockville stands deservedly high. Some of the church edifices are magnificent and costly triumphs of architectural skill. There are three congregations of the Church of England, two Presbyterian, two Methodist, one Baptist, and one Roman Catholic, besides some smaller sects. Their pastors are men of marked ability. The schools of Brockville are of a high order. The public schools consist of a central High school, known as the Victoria School, and four Ward Schools. The Separate School is a large and commodious structure, provided with all the modern appliances. The Convent de Notre Dame is a superior ladies' school. There is also an excellent Kindergarten in successful operation, together with some first-class private schools. The Collegiate Institute is one of the best higher educational institutions in the Province. Students are here prepared for matriculation in the various colleges, and for entering upon any of the professions. Brockville has also a Business College equal to any in the country in its methods and in the thoroughness of its work. Last, but by no means least among the educational institutions of the town, is the Art School. This has attained a provincial reputation from the excellence of the work exhibited by its pupils in competition with other Art schools in Ontario. The Mechanics' Institute, with its library of many thousand volumes, its ample and well-supplied reading-room, filled with all the current reading matter of the day, is surely an educator whose influence upon the masses can hardly be over-estimated. In this respect, Brockville is but another demonstration of the well-known fact that, given a good, well-selected library, and a reading-room abundantly supplied with the literature of the day, a community will stand infinitely higher, morally and intellectually, than will one deprived of those privileges. Brockville has two excellent newspapers, the Times and Recorder, both of which are live sheets and fully up to date, not only as regards the news in general, but also fully alive to the interests of their town. There are many enterprising manufacturing firms, but lack of space prevents the insertion of a list.

For the care of the sick and afflicted, Brockville has two excellent hospitals, the Brockville General Hospital and the St. Vincent de Paul Hospital, both being fully equipped and well managed. The crowning institution, however, is the newly erected

BROCKVILLE INSANE ASYLUM.

This is an elegant structure, standing on a commanding site on what was known as the Pickens Point property, at the left of the Prescott road. From it, the view across and down the St. Lawrence is magnificent. The premises contain 207 acres. The main building stands about 350 yards north of the Prescott road. It is built in the form of a cross, being three stories high in the center and two stories in the wings, having a frontage of 400 feet. The front of the central part is surmounted by a tower 128 feet in height. The central part of the main building projects to the rear 200 feet. There are ample basements, storage rooms, coal vaults, laundries, sewing rooms, offices, dining rooms, kitchens, patients' rooms, bath rooms, linen rooms, with ample accommodations in the main building for 240 patients. In short, the building is provided with every appliance that science, skill and experience could suggest as being beneficial in an institution of the kind. Six cottages, each forty by sixty feet, two stories high, with all the appliances to accommodate sixty patients each, are also a part of this institution. Although interesting, space forbids an extended description of this fine public institution, so likely to prove one of the attractions of Brockville.

The Canadian shore of the St. Lawrence river, it will be noticed, is, in the main, bluff and rocky, and in many places exceedingly precipitous, with here and there occasional breaks, where the land slopes gently to the water's edge. It is in one of these breaks that Brockville is situated, with high bluffs above and below and high ground to the rear. From the river the place presents a very fine appearance. The bluff at the east end of the town rises to a height of fully fifty feet, and is commonly known as "High Rocks," which, with its overhanging shelves, clinging vines and wild honeysuckles draped over the entrances many small caves, presents a charming bit of scenery to the eye of the river tourist, but which is scarcely appreciated by the citizens themselves. This beautiful spot is the home of a legend or tale which may be too true in fact, to relegate to the regions of romance or legend. Be that as it may, it is here "set down," the reader to be the judge.

THE LEGEND OF THE CLIFF.

At a point where the face of the cliff is comparatively smooth, may be seen traces of a painting which is now nearly obliterated, but which, until within a few years past, was visited every spring by a band of Indians, who, with weired ceremonies and incantations, brightened the picture with fresh paint and departed. The picture was a rough representation of a canoe, propelled by several Indians, out of which two white men were falling. The legend relates that in the early days of the French occupation of Canada by Count Frontenac, there was a continual struggle between the New France and the New England, as to which should secure the alliance of the Indian tribes; and although nominally France and England were at peace, there is no doubt that English officers stationed in the colonies, did all in their power to forward this much-to-be-desired consummation. The French had succeeded in securing the alliance of the Algonquins and Hurons, but the great confederacy of the Iroquois held aloof from any entangling alliances, the more, it is presumed, because they were deadly foes to both Hurons and Algonquins, the former of which were settled around lakes Huron and Superior, while the Algonquins were the tribes of the east. The Hurons, to reach the great fur markets of Montreal and Quebec, were obliged to pass through the country of the Iroquois, which that confederacy promptly opposed, and so great was the terror inspired by the Iroquois, that Count Frontenac, then Governor of the New France, decided to protect his allies, and administer such a rebuke to their foes that they would long remember it. The Count's expedition, however, was not an unqualified success; and though he brought off many prisoners, he returned with his army badly crippled, a fact of which the Iroquois were well aware.

At all events, among the prisoners captured by the French were a couple of English officers, who belonged, so history informs us, to the garrison at Oswego; for up to this point, dear reader, our relation is but a veritable historical fact, or facts, if you so choose. These officers were placed in care of a party of Indians, who were to take them to Montreal. Embarking in a canoe, they proceeded down the St. Lawrence, and, when at a point just above Brockville, they were struck by a terrible storm, and being heavily loaded they tossed the British officers overboard, not only to lighten the canoe, but to appease the storm-god by a human sacrifice. But the storm-god was not appeased. The gale increased in intensity, and the storm king howled and shrieked in the ears of the now dismayed Indians, who began to regard their actions in throwing the two men overboard as cowardly. They felt that the Great Spirit would punish them for the act, and so the wail of their death songs, mingled with the shrieks of the tempest, and when opposite the High Rocks the canoe went down with all its human freight, among whom was a distinguished chief. The judgment was well deserved. Of course, those savages did not intend to release their prisoners, but just to torture them at the stake. Had they not been so cowardly as to throw them overboard to drown, how much pleasure they might have afforded the whole tribe, and what horrible tortures, so dear to the savage heart, they might have subjected them to. But they drowned their prisoners instead, and were themselves drowned. Served them right. For more than a hundred years a band of Indians has repainted the picture each spring, at the same time performing incantations to the Great Spirit, whose anger, because they drowned the officers instead of burning them at the stake, must be appeased. As it has now been several years since the picture has been renewed, let us hope that the Indian deity is satisfied.

For much information concerning Brockville, the writer is indebted to Mr. R. LAIDLAW, of the Brockville Times, and to Mr. GEO. P. GRAHAM, of the Recorder, genial gentlemen both, and fully alive to the interests of their town.

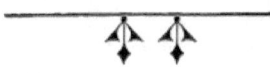

THE SPORTSMAN'S SONG.

BY MAURICE THOMPSON.

Ho! for the marshes, green with Spring,
  Where the bitterns croak and the plovers pipe,
Where the gaunt old heron spreads his wing
  Above the haunt of the rail and snipe;
For my gun is clean and my rod's in trim,
  And the old, wild longing is roused in me;
Ho! for the bass pools cool and dim—
  Ho! for the swales of the Kankakee!

Is there other joy like the joy of man
  Free for a season with rod and gun,
With the sun to tan and the winds to fan,
  And the waters to lull, and never a one
Of the cares of life to follow him,
  Or to shadow his mind while he wanders free?
Ho! for the currents slow and dim!
  Ho! for the fens of the Kankakee!

A hut by the river, a light canoe,
  My rod and my gun, and a sennight fair—
A wind from the south and the wild fowl due—
  Be mine! All's well! Comes never a care!
A strain of the savage fires my blood,
  And the zest of freedom is keen in me;
Ho! for the marsh and the lilied flood!
  Ho! for the tarns of the Kankakee!

Give me to stand where the swift currents rush,
  With my rod all astrain and a bass coming in,
Or give me the marsh, with the brown snipe aflush,
  And my gun's sudden flashes and resonant din;
For I'm tired of the desk and tired of the town,
  And I long to be out, and I long to be free,
Ho! for the marsh with the birds whirling down!
  Ho! for the pools of the Kankakee!

THE ORIGIN OF PRINTING ON THE SHORES OF THE ST. LAWRENCE.

BY J. L. HUBERT NEILSON, M. D., R. C. A., DEPUTY SURGEON-GENERAL.

IN the year 1749 a learned Swede, Peter Kalm, professor in a Swedish University, a disciple of the great Linnaeus, visited the United States and Canada. He informs us, in the interesting volumes of travel which he subsequently published, that there was then no printing press in Canada. He was told, though, that at one time there had been one. This bit of information appears, however, to have been not in accord with fact. Kalm adds: "All books are brought from France, and all the orders made in the country are written, which extends even to the paper currency. They pretend that the press is not yet introduced here, lest it should be the means of propagating libels against the government and religion. But the true reason seems to be in the poorness of the country, as no printer could put off a sufficient number of books for his subsistence; and another reason may be that France may have the profit arising from the exportation of books hither."

Whatever the cause may have been, and all seems to indicate that reasons of state policy were the true cause, a public press was an absolutely unknown quantity in Canada from the foundation of Quebec, in 1609, until after the conquest by the British arms and final cession in 1763. It had been very different over the border in the New England provinces. Within twenty years of the landing of the Pilgrim Fathers a press had been established at Cambridge in 1638, by Steven Daye. At first, and for many years, small works of a

Godly character were its only output. Gradually matters of a more worldly nature were served by it. But it was not until 1704 that such a secular object as a newspaper made its appearance, and met with sufficient public support and appreciation. It is believed that as early as 1545 a printing press was operated in the city of Mexico.

Well, in the year 1763 — it being made known to the world that Canada was to be irrevocably attached to the British Crown — it occurred to one William Brown, a young printer in Philadelphia, that Canada might be a new field worth trying. Canada was still under military rule. After a short correspondence with the then Governor General, James Murray, for the double purpose of making sure that his scheme would not only be permitted but favored by the authorities, he did not hesitate to put his small savings into the venture.

William Brown, like so many other leaders among men, pioneers and benefactors of their race, was a native of Scotland. He was born in Kirkcudbrightshire, province of Galloway, in 1737. His father, John Brown, was laird of Nunton, in the parish of Twynholm, and of Langlands, in Borgue. William, being a younger son, was sent to paternal relatives in Virginia, to make his fortune as best he could. In 1851-2-3 we find him studying the classics and mathematics at William and Mary College, in Williamsburgh. The year following he had entered a counting house as clerk, but soon there came the seven-years' war; the defeat of Braddock at Monongahela was followed by commercial dislocation and a financial crash which brought an end to Brown's incipient career as a bank clerk.

Unemployed, stranded, and with but slender means in hand, young Brown bethought himself of a trade, which possessed greater elements of stability than banking in those tempestuous times. The printing business, moreover, seemed to him congenial. He accordingly directed his steps towards Philadelphia, with a view of there acquiring the art of printing. He first served as apprentice in the celebrated establishment of William Bradford, which then existed at the corner of Black Horse alley. It is traditional, however, that he finished his time with Franklin & Hall, then publishers of the Pennsylvania Gazette.

In 1758 he had transferred his services to William Dunlap, a printer who was also largely interested in bookselling. Dunlap had married a relative of Benjamin Franklin's wife, and through this family connection had recently been appointed postmaster of Philadelphia. In 1760 he was for a short time partner to James Rivington in the book-selling business in New York. Their book store was at the lower end of Wall street. Brown soon withdrew, returned to Philadelphia, and together with a nephew, John Dunlap, became business managers of the elder Dunlap's concern. In that capacity we find him next residing for two years in Bridgetown, Barbadoes, winding up a bookselling and printing enterprise which Dunlap had there. It was on his return from Barbadoes, in 1763, that he formed the project of trying his fortune in Canada. He selected as partner one Thomas Gilmore, a native of the north of Ireland, a relative of Dunlap's, who generously bolstered up the venture of his two young friends to the extent of £450.

On the 6th of August he left Philadelphia for Boston. He informs us, in his "diary," that he met with disappointment in not finding there a vessel bound for Quebec. He had no choice left but to purchase a horse and make his way as best he could towards Quebec, via Albany, Lake Champlain. Montreal and down the St. Lawrence to Quebec. Brown's diary is replete with details of this journey, now of great interest, but space prohibits quotations. While Brown was proceeding overland, Gilmore was sent to London to purchase the press, type and paper for the new Quebec printing office, the whole to be brought out by the first vessel the following spring.

Brown, after adventures which would be well worth repeating, finally reached Quebec on the 30th of September, 1763. The ensuing autumn and winter months he devoted to perfecting himself in the knowledge of French, canvassing for subscribers, distributing his prospectus, and making things ready for the installation of the press. He had secured a small house "in Parlour street, in the Upper Town, a little above the Bishop's Palace." Gilmore arrived early in June, with a brand-new hand press and excellent type, which he had secured from Kenrick Peck, of London. He was also provided with a sufficient supply of paper, ink and other necessaries. On the 21st of June, 1764, the first number of the Quebec Gazette was offered to the public.

It will thus be seen that to these citizens of old Philadelphia is due the honor and glory of having planted the first press in its sister colony on the shores of the St. Lawrence, in the now vast and prosperous Dominion of Canada. A word of the worthy William Dunlap, Franklin's relative, who was in a way the sponsor and financial backer of Brown and Gilmore's venture, may not be out of place. By trade he had been a job printer, bookseller and paper manufacturer, and, in 1758, successor to William Franklin as postmaster of Philadelphia. Dunlap had also a printing and bookselling establishment in Barbadoes. He was also interested in the Barbadoes Mercury. His agent there was George Esmond, who so neglected his patron's interest that, in 1765, Dunlap had to go there himself, and there he spent two years in vain attempts to obtain a settlement of his affairs. While in Bridgetown, although advanced in years, he decided to devote himself to the ministry of the Church of England, commenced his theological studies, and, in 1767, went to London to be ordained. He then returned to Philadelphia, his wife having, meanwhile, become insane. John Dunlap, his nephew, took charge of the interests which he still retained in the Philadelphia printing and bookselling establishment. This firm continued to furnish supplies of printing paper, stationery, etc., to Brown and Gilmore in Quebec until the outbreak of the Revolutionary war. These goods were usually forwarded to them by sailing vessels via the Gulf of the St. Lawrence. But they looked for more than inert supplies from Philadelphia. I quote from a long half-business, half-affectionate letter written by Brown to the Rev. William Dunlap, on April 29, 1768:

"* * * Having been long embarrassed with Canadian Boysas menial servants about the Printing Office, who will not engage for any considerable time and as soon as they find themselves useful augment their wages and become intolerably insolent, we are at last come to a Resolution of trying to get a Negro Boy, wherefore we beg you will endeavour to purchase one for us, between 15 and 20 years of age fit to put to Press, who has had the Small Pox, is country born and can be recommended for his Honesty; we would not begrudge a pretty good Price for such a likely Negro; or if you should be inclined to part with your Boy Priamus we would be glad to have him and would be glad to give what would be judged a reasonable price for him. We pray you may try and procure us one so that he may reach us here in the fall; and as soon as you shall be certain of him or determined to part with your own we beg you may loose no Time in acquainting us of the Price, which we will immediately remit to you on a Bill on York (sic) as we shall keep the cash ready till we hear from you. Should it be too late for an opportunity from Philadelphia there has always been vessels from York in August and Sepbr, and we doubt not that there will be this Year. * * *" In a P. S he adds: "If you are so lucky as to get us a Negro, before you embark him we beg he may be *insured*."

William Dunlap evidently took the most kindly, even fatherly, interest in his two protégés in Quebec, judging from the many letters he wrote them, several of which are in my possession. A son named Tomy appears to have been at this period with the printers in Quebec, for he more than once refers to him. He always subscribed himself, "I am, dear gentlemen, Your affectionate W. Dunlap." His confidence in them was not misplaced, for that very year they repaid him in full his advance of £450, with interest at six per cent. There being none or few regular banks in existence in the North American provinces, remitting money was both a difficult and costly matter. Opportunities of purchasing a bill of exchange on a good, solvent firm or individual were few and far between. About this time, 1768, W. Dunlap severed his connection with business to become rector of the parish of Stratton in King and Queen's county, Virginia, where, I presume, he ended his varied earthly career.

Brown & Gilmore had calculated on a subscription list of at least 150; when the first number appeared, only 110 had given in their names. General Murray subscribed for ten copies and two other officials five each. Among these 110 names not more than a dozen French names can be found, most of these were priests. The paper was printed on a folio sheet, with four double-column pages, one column being English, the opposite one a translation into French. A cut of the Royal Arms headed the paper, to one side of which was the title, "The Quebec Gazette," while on the other was the French title, "La Gazette de Quebec." At the foot of the fourth page was the colophon, "Quebec, printed by Brown & Gilmore, at the printing office in Parlour street, in the Upper Town, a little above the Bishop's palace, where subscriptions for this paper are taken in; advertisements of a moderate length (in one language) inserted for five shillings Halifax, the first week and one shilling each week after; if in both languages seven shillings and six pence Halifax, the first week and half a dollar each week after; and all kinds of printing done in the neatest manner, with care and expedition." It appeared once a week, on Thursdays.

The two first pages contained foreign European news, seldom less than six weeks or two months old; occasional items relating to the neighboring Provinces and extracts from their newspapers; then followed scanty allusions to matters of local interest; the third and fourth pages were filled with official proclamations, government and private advertisements, many of which convey curious and important information. Brown appears to have been the business head — editor and manager — of the concern; he and Gilmore had evidently been trained at an excellent school; witness the correctness and neatness of their work. Brown was the essence of regularity and precision in all his work; his diary, his letters, his office books, dating from his arrival in Canada until his death, detailing every business transactions of the printing office and every item of his own personal expenses from 1763 to 1789, are written most carefully in rounded hand; they are all preserved among the collections of the writer of this sketch.

Broadsides, pamphlets and small volumes soon followed the appearance of the "Quebec Gazette;" the first was the "Presentment" of the first Canadian grand jury, a small quarto of forty-two pages, an important and unique document; but one copy is known to exist, and that is to be found in the writer's collection. The second volume was "Le Catechisme du Diocese de Sens in 1765;" a unique copy is in the possession of the Honorable Judge Baby of Montreal.

A curious and now excessively rare book, printed by Brown & Gilmore in 1767, is the "Nehiro-Irinui," a small 8vo. of 96 pages, printed with great neatness and fine type, but entirely in the Montagnais language. It is a prayer book, catechism, etc., composed for the Indians of the Saguenay Valley by their celebrated and saintly missionary, Father La Brosse, a Jesuit, whose life-work and death are the subject of more than one legend, repeated with reverence to this day among the Indians and peasants of the lower St. Lawrence. Miss Machar of Kingston and Gananoque, familiar to many readers under the "nom de plume" Fidelis, has recently rendered one of these La Brosse legends in charming verse. J. C. Pilling in his "Bibliography of the Algonquian Languages," published by the Smithsonian Institution in 1891, gives a good description of Father La Brosse's writings and works. The labor of composing and revising the proofs of such a book must have taxed the patience and time of the printer to their very utmost, yet he charged but £45 for 2,000 copies of 6 sheets, 8vo.

Enough of the early issues of the Quebec press — more would cease to interest the general reader. Brown & Gilmore remained in partnership for nearly ten years when, in 1773, Thomas Gilmore died. During the two or three years preceding his death he had been unable to withstand the temptations attending prosperity, he had fallen into loose habits, neglected his work, overdrawn his account — in fact, had become a thorn in Brown's side.

Brown continued the business alone, but in a very careful and conservative manner. At this time much sympathy was felt throughout Canada for the victims of the Boston massacre and their families; subscriptions were collected for the latter. Brown contributed £50 to this fund, a very handsome sum in those days.

Then came the time when the old French province was invaded by the Congressional army, when the citadel city of Quebec remained the last foothold of England in Canada. Brown's sentiments of loyalty to the British crown and institutions were too deep rooted to permit him to sympathise with men whom he considered to be rebels. He shouldered his musket and served devotedly as a militiaman, on the walls of the city, at the battle of the 31st of December, 1775, when Montgomery was killed, and until the end of the siege in May following, when the retreat of the besiegers under General Wooster became a rout. After the beginning of the siege in December, 1775, all affairs were at a stand-still and the "Quebec Gazette" ceased to appear until the August following, when the country had recovered, to some extent, its normal condition.

It was at this time that a second press made its appearance in Canada. The printers were Fleury Mesplet and Charles Berger, both printers originally from old France. They had settled in Philadelphia; there they had been picked up by Franklin who, together with Samuel Chase and John and Charles Carroll of Carrollton, had been deputed to Canada as Commissioners of Congress, for the purpose of inducing the French Canadians to espouse the Revolutionary cause. It was deemed that French printers would be important factors in disseminating the offers and blandishments of Congress, and with that object in view these two men and a press followed on the heels of the Commission. The Commissioners perceiving their mission a failure, wisely recrossed the borders, but left behind their printers, press and materials. These two worthies first opened an office in Quebec, and their first output was a volume of French hymns. Soon after they returned to Montreal, where they printed several small works of a religious character. Meanwhile, Charles Berger disappears from the scene, leaving Fleury Mesplet alone to prosecute his trade. He signalized himself, in 1778, by publishing the first French newspaper in Canada, "La Gazette Littéraire," also a small almanac for 1778 and 1779, both of extreme rarity. At this time his labors were violently interrupted; he was accused of republican sympathies, sedition, etc., and thrown into prison in Quebec. There he remained incarcerated in the Recollet convent until the peace of 1783, when the mother country and her daughter agreed to live apart. Mesplet, set free, lost no time in recriminations, but founded the "Montreal Gazette," which, although still extant, had at first a very fitful and uncertain existence in the hands of several masters, viz.: Mesplet, L. & J. Roy, Edward Edwards, James Brown a nephew of William Brown, and others.

Meanwhile our friend William Brown and his Quebec Gazette continued the even tenor of their ways. The large number of troops stationed in or coming through Canada during the war, and when peace came, the renewal of commercial activity brought subscribers, printing orders, and gold into his strong box. Previous to 1779 annual sheet calendars had been found amply sufficient for the needs of the country. Brown now judged that almanacs would be appreciated by the public, and that year was issued the Quebec Almanack for 1780, the first of that most important series of almanacs which continued to appear year after year until 1841. The older numbers are now exceedingly scarce — they are valued by collectors at from fifteen to twenty dollars apiece — all are rare and much sought after on account of the curious and important records they contain.

William Brown died suddenly on the 22d of March, 1789, aged about fifty-three. He was buried in St. Matthew's Cemetery, John street, Quebec. He had never married. Four years before his death he had prevailed on his widowed sister in Scotland, Mrs. Isabel Brown Neilson, to confide to him the future of her son Samuel. Subsequently John followed his brother. Although but mere boys at the time of their uncle's death, they continued to manage his printing business, the Gazette, his government contracts, in a word, his large estate, in their own behalf and also for the benefit of other heirs in Scotland, for Brown had died intestate. Samuel survived his uncle but four years. He died in January, 1793. His death was a distinct loss to the Province, for few men are endowed with more practical and brilliant qualities than he had. He was a particular favorite at the Chateau Saint Louis and in social circles. H. R. H. Prince Edward (Duke of Kent, father of Queen Victoria) honored him with his friendship — he was then colonel of the 7th Fusileers in garrison at Quebec. It is said that Samuel Neilson contracted the cold which caused his death while enjoying a tandem sleigh drive with the prince. André Michaud, the botanist, mentions him in his memoirs as being a man of surprising scientific attainments.

The young Neilsons showed enterprise and push enough, first, to found the "Quebec Magazine," in 1791, a monthly issue (some numbers illustrated); it died for want of support after its third volume, shortly after the death of Samuel; second, to buy out the stock in trade, press, etc., of a small rival sheet which had been in existence a few years in Quebec. They sent this material and one of their foremen, named Louis Roy, to found a printing office and newspaper at New Ark, on the Niagara River, the new capital of the new province of Upper Canada, in 1793. The "Upper Canada Gazette or American Oracle," April 18, 1793, was the result of their enterprise, the pioneer press of the west. Louis Roy, however, left alone to himself, disappointed his patrons, abandoned his post, and returned to Montreal the year following. G. Tiffany picked up the work where Roy had dropped it, and continued the publication of the U. C. Gazette until its transfer to York (now Toronto) in 1799, where it was printed by W. Waters and T. G. Simons. These printers proved unequal to the task. This gave John Neilson, of the Quebec Gazette, a second opportunity of opening a branch printing establishment in Upper Canada. He selected for that purpose his trusted foreman, John Bennett, and supplied him with a fair equipment from his office. Bennett started from Quebec in June, 1801. It took him one month and three days to reach York. On the 20th of August he wrote to John Neilson: "* * * I waited on the Governor (Sir Peter Hunter, nick-named Blue Peter), when His Excellency appointed me "King's Printer for Upper Canada," and Sheriff MacDonell sent with me to demand the types from my predecessors, who had not the least wind of the business. Mr. Simons is a young man of some abilities, and much believes in York's future, but it appears his sentiments were rather inimical to government. Waters, whom I have now to assist me, is as honest, good-natured a fellow as I would wish to see, only he likes to take a hearty twist at the bottle, etc. * * * Simons has acquired a genteel property since he has been in government employ, and Waters is also possessed of some."

Bennett took over the publication of the Upper Canada Gazette, and set immediately about printing the first volume of the "Journals of the House of Assembly of Upper Canada," in 1801, a quarto of 74 pages. The "Statutes" followed in 1802; a beautifully printed "Almanack" for 1803, etc., etc.; all which are of exceeding scarcity. Bennett, unfortunately by contamination, or natural inclination, drifted into habits similar to those of his assistant, Waters. He neglected his business; he became involved in all sorts of trouble; finally, John Neilson, in 1807-8, had to come to York to close in disgust his connection with the printing business in Upper Canada.

At the end of last century, G. and Sylvester Tiffany continued printing at Niagara. Their paper was known as the "Constellation." They issued an almanac in 1802. The other pioneers of the press, on the banks of the St. Lawrence, were: S. Miles, who founded the "Kingston Gazette" in 1810, at Kingston, now represented by the "Daily News." The same printer started the "Prescott Telegraph" in 1823. The "Brockville Recorder" was originated in 1820.

The population of both Canadas now increased with rapid strides, and with it innumerable presses and periodicals of all sorts—some possessed of vitality; others of the mushroom tribe, and ephemeral in nature, arose, lived and vanished in every new village.

To return to the old Quebec press. After the death of his brother Samuel, in 1793, John Neilson continued the publication of the Quebec Gazette. Under his editorship and management it gained in influence and importance; addressing itself in its French and English columns to both nationalities, with no serious rival in sight, it became a power in the land, while, at the same time, it was the vehicle of government proclamations and mandates. John Neilson was elected to the legislature in 1817, and he occupied a seat in the councils of the nation until his death. His great abilities, his integrity, his devotion to the public weal, his eloquence, his powerful editorials in his paper, soon brought him to the front rank among the public men of his day. Thrice he was deputed to London by his fellow citizens to watch over their interests, and on one occasion to present petitions for redress at the foot of the throne. He died in 1848, aged 73, regretted, loved and revered by all.

The Quebec Gazette celebrated its centennial sixteen years after his death, in 1864. Thirty-one years have since then elapsed, and the Quebec Gazette continues to appear. Its last number, now before me, is dated Wednesday, May 1, 1895, No. 12,371, vol. cxxiv. For some years past it has been practically the weekly edition of the Quebec Chronicle, and owned by the same proprietor. It is twenty-three years older than the London Times, and now one of the oldest newspapers in the world. It may be of interest to the readers of this historical sketch to know that its writer has in his collection a complete file of the Quebec Gazette, from its prospectus and first number, on June 21, 1764, up to 1830, the subsequent years are unfortunately not quite so complete. Such as it is, this long series of files of the same newspaper, covering nearly a century and a half of time, is believed to be unique.

It is safe to state that the preceding pages embody more facts relating to the origin of printing in Canada than has yet been given to the public by any other writer on this subject.

BIOGRAPHICAL SKETCH OF J. L. H. NEILSON,

M. D., R. C. A., DEPUTY SURGEON-GENERAL.

Few, if any, officers at present in the military service of Canada, have experienced such varied war service as the subject of this sketch. Shortly after graduating as M. D., he was appointed assistant surgeon to the Royal Artillery in Canada, in October, 1869. In April, 1870, he was selected to form part of the medical staff of the small army sent under colonel (now Lord Wolseley), to suppress the first Red River rebellion. This proved to be one of the most difficult and arduous expeditions ever undertaken by British troops, but attended with complete success. He remained eighteen months attached to the military service in the north-west, volunteering meanwhile to attend the victims of a frightful small-pox epidemic which raged among the Indians on the plains. In the autumn of 1871, he was recalled to Canada to assist in the organization of A and B Batteries of regular Canadian Artillery, and since that time has remained connected with the artillery service. He accompanied his corps in several bloody encounters with the mobs of the ancient capital during the labor riots from 1872-7. At this time he was attached to the Army Medical School at Netley, in England. During the Russo-Turkish campaign in the Balkans, he volunteered in the Red Cross ambulances. At the close of the campaign he returned to his former duties in Canada. During the winter of 1879-80, he spent some weeks in Washington, studying the admirable medical organization of the United States Army, then under the able administration of those war veterans, Generals Barnes and Crane.

In 1884, when it was decided to select the Nile route for the Gordon relief expedition, organizing, equipping, disciplining and conducting to the land of the Pharaohs these rough, half-wild backwoodsmen and Indians, previously unaccustomed to restraint or control of any sort; yet, within six weeks of the issue of the first cable order, 480 voyageurs were landed in Alexandria, and ten days later

J. L. HUBERT NEILSON, ESQ., M. D., R. C. A., DEPUTY SURGEON-GENERAL

Lord Wolseley called to his aid the hardy Canadian voyageurs to assist the troops in overcoming the cataracts and rapids of the Nile. Lord Wolseley specially selected Col. Denison and Dr. Neilson, whom he remembered favorably during the Red River expedition of 1870–71, for the purpose of recruiting, they were at work in the Soudan. After his arrival in Egypt, Dr. Neilson was attached to the first field hospital. He followed the troops in their arduous march across the Bayuda desert, was present at Abu Klea, etc. Then later he was sent to Suakim, on the Red Sea coast. For these services in Egypt, he was specially mentioned in Lord Wolesley's despatches, as published in the London Official Gazette of August 25, 1885. He was rewarded with the Egyptian war medal with two clasps, the Khèdivial bronze star and made Knight of the Royal Order of Milusine, for special services gratuitously given to Christian refugees, who had fled from Khartoum before the siege commenced.

Since that date, Dr. Neilson has served in peace, chiefly as medical officer of the Royal Military College of Kingston, Canada (see page 28 of this volume), and of the garrison of Kingston as Chairman of the Board on Militia Medical Organization, etc., etc.

He has found time between his many professional callings to follow his natural bent towards historical research. His library of books, MSS., maps, portraits and reviews—relating to the history of America, and of Canada in particular—is one of if not the largest possessed by any private individual; in fact, it is quite unique. This famous library was commenced in 1801, when his grandfather, the late Honorable John Neilson, of the Quebec Gazette, purchased the greater part of the rare books and MSS. belonging to the old Jesuit College in Quebec when it was sold by order of the Government. To these beginnings have been added the collections of three lives. We might enumerate a few of the MSS.: One was written by Père Marquette in 1671, the discoverer of the Mississippi, entitled "Præces Illinicae," written in the dialect of the Illinois Indians; it is thought to be all that remains extant of this language. The Père Sylvie MS. of about 1680, is a dictionary of the Montagnais language, and philologically important, as well as four other old Jesuit MSS. All the Wm. Brown correspondence with Philadelphia, relating to the origin of printing in Canada, his diary, and all his account books from 1764-89, and the office books of the Neilsons and their correspondence until 1850, containing all their printing transactions; an enormous number of correspondence and letters of public men, from the beginning to the middle of the present century, etc., etc., form part of its riches. Among the printed, books are a complete file of the Quebec Gazette from June, 1764, to the present day; fifty-five years of the Quebec Almanacks from 1781 to 1841—by far the most complete series known; the presentment of the grand jury, Quebec, 1765 ; the Stamp Act, Quebec, 1765; Labrasse's Nehiro-Irenui, 1767; Cugnet's Laws, Quebec, 1775; the Traité des Messieurs, Quebec, 1772; the Mohawk Prayer Book, Quebec, 1780; Réglement de la Confrérie Mesplet, Montreal, 1776 (first book printed in Montreal) ; the Upper Canada Almanack, York, 1802, together with all of Bennett's and Louis Roy's correspondence relating to the early Upper Canada press; the Quebec Directory, 1790; the Quebec Magazine, three volumes, 1791-2; the British-American Register, Quebec, 1805; the Canadian, 1807-10, etc., etc.; the original Jesuit relations, Champlain, 1619; Léscarbot, 1611; Sagard, 1630; DeLact, 1640, are represented by choice examples. To these value is added by the binder's best efforts. This collection is also exceptionally rich in early Canadian pamphlets.

Dr. Neilson has supplied the press and magazines with many articles embodying his researches: "The Royal Canadian Volunteers, 1794-1802;" "The Diary of a French Canadian Officer during the war of 1812;" "The Last Days of Fort Frontenac under the Fleur de Lis," are historical sketches of real merit. The article on the "Origin of Printing on the Shores of the St. Lawrence," in this volume, is from his pen. Dr. Neilson has, for years, given much attention and labor to the collection of material for a history of the origin of the press in Canada, and a bibliography of the early Canadia printers up to 1820, and we have reason to believe that his volume may appear before many months.

Dr. Neilson is one of the founders and first vice-president of the Kingston Historical Society, and for the second time president of the Mechanics' Institute; he is honorary member of the Numismatic and Historical Society of Montreal; of the Societa Araldicae Historica of Rome; of the Institut de Psychologie of Paris, etc., etc. He is hereditary Seigneur of the

Seigniory of Hubert, in the province of Quebec. His private residence is Glendornal, Neilsonville, P. Q.

His medical sphere of action is strictly limited to the military under his immediate charge. Professional reading engrosses much of his time, being favored with an open, liberal and independent mind — unhampered by the dogmatic teachings of schools — new ideas and new methods enlist his sympathy, and if possessed of merit are adopted by him; he has thus become an adept of the system of medicine known as Burgrasvian or Dosimetric — he has for years investigated the application of Hypnotism to the treatment of certain forms of disease. Under this head he has contributed articles to the "Revue de l'Hypnotism," published in Paris, which have attracted attention abroad.

Dr. Neilson is unassuming, easily approached, a man of many admirable traits of character. As a bibliographer he is probably not excelled in the country. From his library have come the excellent pictures of Count Frontenac and the Chevalier La Salle, which are reproduced in this volume; two pictures that would be difficult to duplicate in Canada. Deputy Surgeon-General Neilson's services in the field have won for him merited promotion, but his real worth is best appreciated by those with whom he has served, and by those who know him best.

MELZAR FOWLER.

MELZAR FOWLER, now only dimly remembered by the older people of Jefferson county, N. Y., was born in Edinburgh, Saratoga county, N. Y., in 1803, and came to Depauville in the early twenties with his parents, Anson Fowler and Maria Esselstyn Fowler. His sister Jane also accompanied them (she subsequently marrying Eldridge G. Merick), and her brother John. The father commenced a mercantile business in Depauville, a new settlement which had just begun to develop its lumbering interest. This settlement was on the rapids of Catfish Creek, which at that time was a stream of fair size, with sufficient water to float timber down to its mouth at Lake Ontario — not at all resembling the greatly diminished stream it now appears, after having its banks, along its whole course, denuded of timber. The care of this business early fell upon Melzar, the eldest son, and when he was about twenty years of age he bore the responsibility of his father's mercantile affairs.

After some years, wishing to extend his operations, Melzar established a store at Brownville, and went there to live, still maintaining the supervision of the store at Depauville. His younger brother, John, also came to Brownville as a clerk, and was given an interest in the business.

At that time one branch of Mr. Fowler's mercantile business was the manufacture of pearl ash from wood ashes. The forests of Jefferson county furnished the only fuel in those days, and the people of the country saved their ashes and sold them to him, and, in a building for the purpose, he converted these ashes into pearl ash, which was an important article of commerce, and found steady market in New York.

Shortly after establishing himself at Brownville, Melzar married Miss Clarissa Spicer, a sister of Mr. Silas Spicer, of Perch River, and during their residence there their two children, Eldridge and Nettie, were born. During these years Melzar enlarged his field of operations at Depauville by engaging with Mr. Merick in the business of getting out oak timber and rafting it to the Quebec market. In the spring of 1835 he moved his family to Depauville, giving up the business in Brownville, in order that he might give his entire attention to the Depauville operations, and be with his aged parents, while John went to Clayton in the interest of Smith & Merick.

At that early day, Watertown was, as it is

now, the business center for the surrounding country, the only method of travel being by private conveyance. It was while going there on business in August, 1835, soon after the family moved to Depauville, that Mr. Fowler had the great misfortune to have a pair of horses, one of which was vicious and unreliable.

He stopped at a hotel, and when it came time to feed the animal the hostler was afraid to enter the stall, and called Mr. Fowler from the hotel, who at once took the feed-measure in his hand and entered the stall. The vicious horse, not recognizing his master, dealt him a blow with one of his forefeet, which proved fatal in three days. Everything was done for Mr. Fowler that could be known, but the blow had produced an internal rupture.

Thus died, in the flower of his youth, and in the midst of his usefulness, one who had the warm regard of all his business associates, and whose morning of life was full of promise.

It is remembered of Mr. Fowler that many farmers brought their sons to him to educate in mercantile pursuits, so great was their confidence in his possessing all the traits that would bring such youths into an earnest and successful manhood.

His death, so sudden, so tragical, elicited universal regret and sympathy. His wife and her two children remained at Depauville, but the faithful mother never was herself again. A woman of superior mental ability and personal beauty, and with a natural refinement much beyond most of those by whom she was surrounded, her loss wore upon her energies, and she survived her husband only seven years.

The two children, Eldridge and Nettie, thus left orphans at the age of nine and seven years, respectively, were tenderly cared for by their grandmother Fowler and their uncle, Hon. E. G. Merick.

Eldridge went later to live in the family of Mr. Hugh Smith, of Perch River, and afterwards with his uncle John Fowler until coming of age, when he went West, where he has since lived and become indentified with large lumber and land interests in Michigan, Minnesota and Canada.

The daughter grew to womanhood in the home of her grandparents and her uncle and aunt Merick, receiving at their hands the best educational advantages. She married Cyrus H. McCormick, of reaper fame. Both as the right-hand helper of her husband during his life-time, and later in the administration of his estate (with her son Cyrus), she has been called to bear some of the heavier responsibilities of life.

JOHN N. FOWLER.

THE writer of this sketch never had any personal acquaintance with the subject of it. For the facts stated herein he is indebted to several old residents of Clayton, chiefly the following, viz.: Thomas Rees, a partner of Mr. Fowler in some of his business enterprises, who made a written statement of facts; Messrs. D. C. Porter and Perry Caswell, members of the M. E. Church with Mr. Fowler, who was a faithful and substantial member of that church; A. F. Barker, John Johnston and Capt. William Rees.

The father of Mr. Fowler came from the eastern part of this State and settled in Depauville in the early part of this century. There he engaged in mercantile business and reared his family. In time, one of his daughters became the wife of Hon. E. G. Merick, subject of a biographical sketch elsewhere in this volume. One of his sons, Melzar, was father of Nettie Fowler, afterwards the wife, and now the widow of Cyrus H. McCormick, of Chicago. A lady of great wealth, and whose generous heart and bountiful hand have justly earned her a reputation, of which it is no exaggeration to say it is national.

John N. Fowler left Depauville in 1835, and came to Clayton. He purchased the interest of a Mr. Moreton in the old store of Smith & Merick, standing on the bank of the river, where Simon Breslow's store is now located. Stephen Hale, a clerk for Mr. Fowler for a few years, afterwards became his partner in the store. But Mr. Fowler could not confine himself to mere storekeeping. The country was new and rich in both soil and timber. In 1836 or 1837 he purchased several hundred acres of land lying about two miles south of Clayton. In a few years this wild land was converted into a farm, so well improved that the County Agricultural Society bestowed on its owner a first prize for his improvements.

In 1844, Mr. Fowler formed a partnership with Henry Esselstyn under the name of Fowler & Esselstyn. The latter had for years been bookkeeper in the large lumbering business of E. G. Merick, and the business of Fowler & Esselstyn was carried on in conjunction with his. It consisted of rafting and forwarding to the Quebec market a vast amount of timber and staves, brought to Clayton in vessels from the shores of the upper lakes, and in ship building. For many years they built one to four steamers and sailing vessels every year. All the following named, and many more, were built at their yard in Clayton, viz.: Bay State, Cataract and New York. The British Queen and British Empire, designed for use down the river, were built by them at Port Metcalf in Canada.

During much of the time Mr. Fowler was so engaged with Mr. Merick, he dealt largely in real estate on his own separate account. He bought a large tract lying contiguous to Clayton, known as the Lawrence Lands. He disposed of the property to actual settlers, and invested the proceeds in timber-lands in the West; and, as coincidently, the lumbering business of the firm was, year after year, extending farther and farther westward, there was a constantly growing necessity to move the place of business in that direction. At first a branch office was opened in Detroit. But with Clayton as a base of operations, Detroit was found to be an inconvenient outpost with the means of communication then in vogue. And, more than this, Detroit had become a city, rapid in growth, brilliant in prospects, and already taking a prominent position in shipbuilding for the upper lakes. Cut off from that region by the small proportions of the Welland canal, and at great disadvantage in the matter of timber, not to speak of other important items in shipbuilding, little Clayton could no longer hold this great and enterprising firm. In 1856 their Clayton property and business was disposed of to Thomas Rees, and they moved to Detroit. There they opened an immense drydock and ship-yard, and continued lumbering operations in the West, under the firm name of Merick, Fowler & Esselstyn.

The old acquaintances of Mr. Fowler still living in Clayton, speak of him as a man of great energy and wonderful endurance, a strict church member, a public spirited citizen, an honorable man and one highly exact in his requirements of others, while holding himself bound by the same rule of conduct. To him may be applied this grand and safe rule of excellence and ability — in every station where he was known, boy or man, and in whatever he undertook, he measured fully up to the requirements of the occasion. That is a test which can be applied to but few men.

G. H. S.

THE SPICER FAMILY.

STANDING well up from the river's edge, on Hemlock Island, one mile west of Thousand Island Park, is the cottage shown above, built in the winter of 1875-6, being one of the earliest upon the river. It is the summer home of Hon. Henry Spicer, for nearly his whole lifetime a resident of Perch River, N. Y.

The Spicer family was one of the early arrivals in Jefferson county, and trace their lineage in an unbroken descent from three brothers, natives of Normandy, who came into

England as "gentlemen volunteers" with William the Conquerer. These brothers settled respectively in Devonshire, Warwick and Kent, England. The two who settled in Devonshire and Warwick still have descendants residing there. In the 36th year of Queen Elizabeth's reign (1594) an account is given of this family, from their first "being officers and magistrates of the honorable city of Exeter, beginning with the first year of England's first Edward (1273) and continuing to the 7th year of Queen Anne (1708); and honorable a city, continuing for so long a course of years, their estate being also equivalent to their antiquity—they having also bestowed a considerable one on the chamber of Exeter, to uphold its guardian." In 1357 it is further related that " the Black Prince (son of Edward III) came out of France bringing with him prisoner, King John of France, whom he had taken a little time before at Poictiers. He landed at Plymouth, and came to Exeter, where John Spicer was mayor, who received the prince and his prisoner with much

"GLEN-COVE" COTTAGE, HEMLOCK ISLAND.

during the whole of these 435 years some one of the Spicer family was mayor of Exeter. Of this illustrious line " John Spicer " was mayor from 1252 to 1359—107 years, though, of course, there were several individual " Johns."

In an accurate account of the ancient family of Spicers, taken from an original manuscript extracted from a description of the County of Devon, A. D., 1714, we learn that "but few families in England can show such a precedent of the office of mayor of so ancient and display." It is further related that the "family of Spicers in the times of the three Edwards were principal officers and magistrates of Exeter, and were then considered for their many and gentlemanly qualities and virtues ; for in those days such men for their virtues and not for their wealth, were magistrates and governors, and in all places of trust."

Members of this distinguished family were in Jamestown, Va., in 1618, and in Rhode Island in 1660. They were also settled in the vicinity of Stonington, Conn., until after the Revolutionary War. They were both officers and privates in the Continental Army, and fought from Bunker Hill to Saratoga. They came into New York in 1792, and into Jefferson county in 1812.

The Esselstyns.

The author of this volume has had access to papers, well authenticated, which show that the Esselstyn family (commencing with King Clovis in 500 A. D.) were of the same stock as those of that name who came to America, but the date of their arrival in this country is yet uncertain.

The Chittendens.

Another fact he has discovered, that the Chittenden family are related to the Esselstyns and the Fowlers. Thomas Chittenden, a linen weaver, came with his son Isaac into America in 1635 from Wapping, in Kent, England, settling in Plymouth county. Mass., and his descendants are still found there. William Chittenden was one of the company of twenty-five, gathered chiefly from Kent, Surrey and Sussex in the South of England, who determined to leave their native country and seek a new home in the wilderness of America. Their first recorded acts as a separate community was a covenant which they signed on ship-board, while on the passage, binding each other to plant themselves in New England, near Quinnipiack, if possible, and to be helpful to each other in every common work, according to every man's ability, and as need should require. Besides William Chittenden there were twenty-four other signers to this agreement, and, so far as history has been able to indicate, it was solemnly kept.

This William Chittenden had several children born to him in England. His wife was Joanna Sheaffe, whose sister Dorothy was the wife of Rev Henry Whitfield, the first minister and a leading member of the Guilford Colony. The date of William Chittenden's sixth child's birth is upon the Guilford record, as of November 15, 1649. February 1, 1660, he died. He was undoubtedly the progenitor of the older families of his name in the United States, and the Chittendens of Oneida and Jefferson county undoubtedly sprang from this stock.

Joseph Chittenden, son of Joseph, who was descended in a direct line from the original William, was aged 92 when he died, April 7, 1794. Lucy, his daughter, born at Guilford October 8, 1736, married Melzar Fowler, March 10, 1768. He was the progenitor of the Fowler family in Jefferson county, known so well at Clayton, and represented in this history by the biographical sketch of John Fowler and his brother Melzar, this latter being the father of Mrs. Nettie F. McCormick. This family and the Esselstyns are related through the fact that Anson Chittenden, born December 18, 1768 (son of the above-named Lucy Fowler), married Maria Esselstyn, and in that way the Fowlers, Esselstyns and Chittenden families of Jefferson county are related to one another by marriage.

LA SALLE.

In 1643, at Rouen, in France, was born Robert Cavalier, better known by the designation of La Salle. His name in full was Réné-Robert Cavalier, Sieur de la Salle — the latter affix being the name of an estate near Rouen, belonging to the Cavaliers. His education was liberal, and he early manifested the traits which afterwards made him so illustrious.

He was a Catholic in faith, and a member of the order of Jesuits. He had an elder brother in Canada, and this fact doubtless shaped his destinies, for in the spring of 1666, in his 23d year, we find him in Canada, where the Seminary of St. Sulpice, a corporation of French priests, had already made a settlement under ern New York, who had already, notwithstanding their other vast possessions in America, began to feel a desire to possess Canada, and thus extend their sway—as it is seen to day—from Newfoundland to the Northern Pacific and Arctic Oceans. In La Salle they perceived a young man of fine appearance, eager

THE CHEVALIER LA SALLE.

very extensive landed and proprietary grants from the French king. These priests were in great terror continually from the Iroquois Indians, who had lately been severely chastised by Coursell, the Governor of Canada, and their hate was unbounded against the French, stimulated, doubtless, by the English in East- for just such an engagement as these priests desired to make, which was to procure a man of energy and military capacity who would lead any body of armed men they could raise to defend Montreal, and the settlements thereabouts, from the dreaded Iroquois. They gave La Salle a large tract of land nine miles above Montreal, their actual outpost of civilization, which is now known as La Chine, above the great rapids of that name. La Salle entered upon the improvement of his large domain, and began to sell his acres to such as he could induce to join him.

That this young man had come to Canada with a settled purpose in view, now began to be apparent. He began to study the Indian dialects. Hemmed in as he was by the great and apparently interminable forests which surrounded the palisade he had erected for defense against an Indian attack, his fertile mind went beyond his narrow environment, beyond even the great river which roared and fretted upon one side of his domain, and soared westward and southward towards an easier way to China and Japan than had as yet been attained. So imperfect at that time were even educated people's ideas as of the earth's geography, that La Salle did not understand that the countries his enterprising mind would reach were upon the other side of the globe, thousands of miles away. On one occasion he was visited by a band of the Seneca Iroquois, who told him of a river called the Ohio, rising in their country, which flowed southward into the sea. La Salle at once conceived the idea that this great river must needs flow into the Gulf of California, and thus he could find what his soul was on fire to obtain—a western passage to China. His resolution was soon formed. Obtaining, first, the consent of the governors of the seminary to the enterprise he had in hand, he sold to them his lands near La Chine, in order to raise needed money for his enterprise, the whole expense of which was to be borne by himself. He purchased four large canoes, and engaged fourteen men. On the 6th of July, 1670, he set out upon his double expedition for exploration and the purchase of furs from the Indians. We cannot follow his footsteps with the pertinacity of Parkman, whose excellent history is before us, and can, at the best, only generalize the subsequent career of this great explorer.

Thirty-five days after leaving La Chine, they reached Irondequoit Bay, on the south side of Lake Ontario. Here they remained a month or more, and on the 24th of September were at an Indian village only a few miles north of the present city of Hamilton. These Indians proved more friendly than those upon the south shore of the lake, and promised to show La Salle a more direct road to the Ohio. It was here he met Louis Joliet, a young man of about his own age, and also an explorer. He had come from the southwest, the very region La Salle was striving to reach. Palon had sent Joliet to explore the copper mines of Lake Superior. This meeting caused a change of La Salle's plans, for Joliet showed him a map of the region he himself had traversed, including Lake Superior and the Grand River. Step by step La Salle moved westward, spending much time with the Indians, and in 1670–71 he had embarked on Lake Erie, descended the Detroit to Lake Huron, coasted the shores of Lake Michigan, passed the straits of Mackinaw, afterwards reaching a river with a southwestern flow (the Illinois), which took him into the Mississippi, and he may be said to have been the first white man upon that mighty affluent in its upper region. It is claimed by some that he also discovered the Ohio; but if so, he never descended it as far as its junction with the Mississippi. He undoubtedly preceded Joliet, but both La Salle and Frontenac, his ardent supporter, believed, as late as 1672, that the Mississippi flowed directly south into the Gulf of California, and that it thus afforded in reality a direct connecting link to the Pacific Ocean, across which they well knew were China and Japan.

Circumscribed as our limits are, we are unable to follow La Salle much further. Parkman represents him as a man of extraordinary determination, full of virile vigor, with a stalwart frame, and with so enlarged an intelligence that the Jesuit Fathers were afraid of him. They called him visionary, and unstable, and such they have always designated those who were not loyal to their teachings or brought fully under their influence.

In Frontenac, however, the Cavalier de la Salle had an uncompromising and devoted friend. Thus far his dream had been of a short route to China; but when he saw the grand possibilities of the great valley of the Mississippi, with the illimitable prairies which we now see mapped out into Illinois, Wisconsin and Iowa, with the immense forests that line both sides of the river below Cairo, where the Ohio joins the Mississippi, he relinquished as somewhat chimerical, or perhaps postponed for a time, his idea of a short route to China. Then it was that he resolved to leave frozen Canada behind him forever, and lead a French civilization into the great country he had discovered. It was for him to call into light the latent riches of the great West. Frontenac, with whom he kept himself well allied, favored him in all his efforts. They were both great men, and both deserve the highest commendation in history. They were both faithful to their king and France, and their discoveries were of such a character as to make every human being in America their debtor.

In April, 1682, after many adventures and much opposition from the Jesuit Fathers, much struggling with Indian tribes and passing through great dangers and heavy toil, at the mouth of the Mississippi, he had at last the satisfaction of proclaiming "Louis Le Grand," king of all that country we now call Louisiana, and which the English never conquered, but came peaceably into the possession of the United States by friendly negotiation and purchase.

In 1683, somewhat broken in health, he descended to Quebec and sailed for France. Arrived at court, this student and recluse in his youth, but backwoodsman in his matured manhood, had to encounter the risks of a presentation to Royalty and to make headway against the intrigues and jealousies which always surround a king. Louis XIV, however, appreciated him, but the best that could be done for him was to give him a divided command in America, which he was to share with Beaujen, the jealous and incompetent. On July 18th, 1684, he wrote to "his most honored mother" that he was about to sail with four vessels and four hundred men. This voyage to America was principally passed in disputations with Beaujen, and when they landed at St. Domingo, more than half of the people on the vessel were prostrated with fever, among them being La Salle. He soon recovered, however. Proceeding upon their journey they disembarked at Matagorda Bay, thinking it one of the mouths of the Mississippi. Here the Amaible, the ship which contained nearly all their provisions, was wrecked. As we have only imperfectly followed him thus far, and have only but slightly sketched the character of this great man, we must make short work of the matters that led up to his death. While upon a journey of exploration, anxiously desiring to better the condition of the party whom he was trying to lead out of trouble, as Parkman graphically expresses it, "a shot was fired from the grass instantly followed by another, which pierced through his brain, and La Salle dropped dead." Doubtless he was killed by a wretch who had become disobedient and insolent, and whom La Salle had been compelled to rebuke. Thus died at the early age of forty-three, Robert Cavelier de la Salle, one of the greatest men of his age, and one of the most remarkable of the explorers whose names live in history.

His firmness and his courage would have left a more marked impression upon his time, and he would have been better able to completely carry out his grand plans of creating in America a New France, had he been less imperious and haughty in his manner, and less harsh to those under his command, which at last drew upon him an implacable hatred, and caused his death. J. A. H.

COUNT FRONTENAC

WAS perhaps the most remarkable man ever representing the court of France in the new world. From very unpromising beginnings. he rose equal to every emergency that confronted him. His whole career was one of conflict, sometimes petty and personal, sometimes involving the greatest consequences. Under Frontenac occurred the first serious collision between England and France in America, which may be said to have been the opening of a grand scheme of military occupation, designed to hold in check the industrial efforts of the English colonies. All his later energies were directed to making that scheme possible. The contemporaneous history of those times, so ably prepared by Parkman, shows how valiantly New France battled against a fate which her own lack of organizing capacity made inevitable. The drama was a great and significant one, enacted amidst untamed forests, largely by men who had been reared in France, and some of them favorite courtiers of the French king. The wife of Count Frontenac was Anne de la Grange-Trianon. She was born at Versailles, and grew up a favorite companion of Mademoiselle de Montpensier, the favorite granddaughter of Henry IV. She was married to Frontenac in 1648. The happiness of the newly-wedded pair was short. The wife's love soon changed to aversion, which continued even after the birth of her son.

Count Frontenac came of an ancient and noble race, said to have been of Basque origin. At the age of fifteen the young Louis showed a decided passion for the life of a soldier. He served in Holland under the Prince of Orange. He was at the siege of Hesdin. He was at Arras and at Aire, as well as at Callioure and Perpignan. At twenty-three he

COUNT FRONTENAC.

was Colonel of the Normandy regiment, and commanded it in the Italian campaign.

In 1673 he received the appointment of Governor and Lieutenant-General for the king in all New France. Notwithstanding all his ability as a soldier, it was court gossip that he was sent to America to relieve him from the unhappy relations he was known to maintain with his wife, whose temper was outrageous, carrying herself with such a high head that her best friend, Mademoiselle de Montpensier, was obliged to dispense with her services as one of her maids of honor. Madam Frontenac declined to accompany her husband across the sea.

Frontenac was fifty-two years of age when he landed at Quebec. Parkman says that "had nature disposed him to melancholy, there was much in his position to awaken it. A man of courts and camps, he was banished to the ends of the earth, among savage hordes and half-reclaimed forests. He exchanged the splendors of St. Jermain and Versailles for a stern gray rock, haunted by somber priests, rugged merchants and traders, blanketed Indians and wild bush-rangers." It was his to see that Quebec should be made the capital of a great empire, which should be tributary to distant France. He took an active interest in all the duties of his new position. It was a strange freak of his that he should administer the oath of allegiance to every person in Quebec. On the 23d of October, 1672, what was known as the "Three Estates of Canada" were convoked with considerable pomp. To these he administered the oath, and then the assembly was dissolved. This very act, is, in brief, a striking illustration of the French colonial rule in Canada. It was a government of excellent intentions, but of the most arbitrary methods. Frontenac unwisely set himself against the prevailing democratic current. The arbitrary government of a land like France, where the Bourbons who "learned nothing and forgot nothing" had held sway so long, was not adapted to a new country where people from all sections had come to accumulate wealth, and (as in all new countries) were possessed of very radical ideas of personal freedom.

The name of Frontenac is one of the most interesting in connection with our own Great River. Courselle, his predecessor in the Governorship of Canada, had begun at what we now call Kingston, a fortification large enough to receive into its stockade such refugees as might desire to fly to a place of comparative safety in the event of any Iroquois invasion, which had then but lately devastated Quebec, and caused the loss of hundreds of innocent lives. Frontenac's attention was soon directed to this beginning of a fort, and he was fortunate in making the acquaintance of a young man who had been in the employ of the French priests at Quebec, and had reached Kingston on his way westward to trade in furs and make the explorations which were yet to make him famous. By direction of Frontenac, La Salle had previously gone to Onondaga, the political center of the Iroquois, and invited the great men of that nation to a council on the Bay of Quinte. Before setting out, La Salle had sent the new Governor a map recommending as a site for the proposed fort the point at the mouth of the Cataraqui, now occupied by the present grand old historic city of Kingston. Frontenac ascended the St. Lawrence quite leisurely, with one hundred and twenty canoes and four hundred men. Parkman says: "Soon they reached the Thousand Islands, and their light flotilla glided in long line among those watery labyrinths, by rocky islets, where perhaps some lonely pine towered like a mast against the sky; by sun-scorched crags, where the brown lichens crisped in the parching glare; by deep dells, shady and cool, rich in rank ferns, and sponges, dark green mosses; by still cove, where the water-lilies lay like snowflakes on their broad, flat leaves, till at length they neared their goal, and the glistening bosom of Lake Ontario opened on their sight."

This grand flotilla, piloted by Indians in their birch canoes, entered the broad water, passing along the shores so familiar now as the site of Port Henry on one side, and the "West Point of Canada," upon the other, reaching at last the point of land where the artillery barracks now stand, at the western end of Cataraqui bridge. Here they all disembarked, and here were subsequently laid, broad and massive, the foundation of what was subsequently named Fort Frontenac — not so named by the Governor himself, but by the engineer in charge of the work. [See pp. 35, 211.]

It is at this point that La Salle comes prominently into public notice, especially as the friend of Frontenac, whose cause he had espoused at Quebec during the famous quarrels between the new Governor and the priests, whom we describe elsewhere as meddlesome and querulous.

It is a curious historical fact that the old stone fort Frontenac was built by La Salle with his own money, he having been sent to France by Frontenac with letters of the highest recommendation, and the King had made to him a grant of the then fort (a mere stockade) a tract of land of four leagues in front and half a league in depth, including the neighboring islands. In consideration of this rich grant, La Salle completed the fort, armed it at his own expense, and maintained it until near the time of his death, when it reverted to the King, as did all his great tract of land, if we are correctly informed.

Count Frontenac was too independent and able a man to submit quietly to the opposition of the priests, who claimed by both their rights of seigneurage and of their holy office, to interfere with his authority. The most violent of these he arrested and confined in prison, and was in the end sustained by his King, the quarrel having been referred to France for final settlement. Our space, as in the case of La Salle, does not permit us to more than glance at some of the more leading traits and performances of Frontenac, whose abilities were marked and actively developed in the new field he had entered upon. But there was jealousy between Quebec and Montreal, promoted by rival fur dealers and shared in more or less by the meddling priests, whose fingers were in everybody's pie, and the result was that in the end Frontenac was recalled by his king. For seven years he was idling around the French court. But he had powerful friends, and his wife, who seems to have been more affectionate when he was under a cloud than when his word was law and his success apparently assured, became his most powerful intrigante at the French court.

At last the King perceived that he had made a mistake in recalling Frontenac, matters in Canada having gone from bad to worse, until at last his patience was exhausted, and he asked Frontenac to again accept the governorship. The Count was then seventy years of age, but he was tired of inaction and of the petty jealousies of the court of France, and finally accepted the appointment.

We have not space to follow him further in his adventurous career. He returned to Quebec, but Louis XIV had already entered upon his decline from being the first monarch of Europe. William of Orange was coming to the front in England, and before his judicious plans and energetic management, France was soon to be relegated to an inferior position, to lose her possessions in Canada, and, save her ever-faithful Louisiana, to give up, one by one, all she held in America. But the contest was not an uneventful one, though the end was inevitable from the first.

In November, 1698, Frontenac, worn down by many arduous labors, and in his seventy-eighth year, was taken violently ill. On the 28th of that month he died, in full possession of all his faculties.

As will be seen, the portrait of this distinguished man, whose name must forever be inseparably connected with our Great River, was copied from a drawing made as he lay in his coffin. It is undoubtedly a faithful portraiture, and we are indebted for it, as well as for that of La Salle, to Dr. Neilson, Deputy Surgeon-General of Canada, a ripe scholar, a gallant officer, an accomplished historian and archæologist, and a true gentleman. [See his biographical sketch, p. 201.]   J. A. H.

POETIC ASSOCIATIONS OF THE THOUSAND ISLANDS.

CANADIAN BOAT SONGS.

MOST early travellers speak of the songs with which the Canadian voyageurs were accustomed to beguile their labors at the oar, and of the impressions they left upon the memory. These are now entirely unknown upon this part of the St. Lawrence, but are still heard upon the upper waters of the Ottawa, and in the regions not yet invaded by the power of steam.

These souvenirs of travel belong to a period in society that appears to be passing away, and like the popular songs of all countries, that perpetuate their historical legends and the traditions of ancestors, they are unknown in cities, and are found only in rural life. In this instance, they may be often traced back to an European origin, and are of the kind that tend to keep alive the poetic associations of a gay and happy peasantry, rather than the historical memories of a great and powerful people. In fact there appear to be very little sense, much less a connection of narrative, in any of these popular songs of these people, and the most that can be said of many of them is, that they were a jolly string of words without rhyme or sense, with frequent repetitions, and a joyous refrain.

In their incoherent stanzas and their repetitions, they resembled in some respects the slave-songs of the south before the late war, although wholly devoid of that religious sentiment which formed a feature in many of the social songs of the slaves.

Some years since, Mr. Ernst Gagnon, of Quebec, prepared a collection of these Canadian songs. It contains only those most commonly known, for according to this author, "ten large volumes would scarcely contain them." He further remarks, that as a general thing there is nothing indelicate or wanton in these popular melodies, and that even in some of this description that can be traced back to French origin, the objectionable features have been dropped. In other cases, the change in these airs has been so great that their origin can scarcely be traced back beyond the period of emigration, and in others they are unmistakably and entirely Canadian.

We will limit our notice of these songs to two or three of the most popular and well-known, and of these the one first given is altogether the most important :

"A LA CLAIRE FONTAINE."

Says Mr. Gagnon:—" From the little seven-year-old child to the gray-haired old man, every body in Canada knows this song. There is no French Canadian song that in this respect will compare with it, although the melody is very primitive, and it has little to interest the musician, beyond its great popularity."

It is often sung to a dancing tune, and is even brought into the fantasies of a concert. It is known in France, and is said to be of Norman origin, although M. Marmier thinks it came from La Franche Comtè. and M. Rathery thinks it was brought from Bretagne, under the reign of Louis XIV. In France it has nearly the same words, but with this difference — that the French song expresses the sorrow of a young girl at the loss of her friend Pierre, while the Canadian lad wastes his regrets upon the rose that his mistress rejected. The air as sung in France is altogether different. Some years since this song in its Canadian dress was brought out in all the principal theatres of Paris with immense success. This led to a distressing burlesque of "La Claire Fontaine, as they sing it in Paris."

On the occasion of the visit of the Prince of Wales to America in 1860, a little incident occurred on board the "Hero," on the last evening before the landing at Quebec, that brought this song and its air into notice upon a much wider field than before. Several prominent Canadians had come on board, and as the evening wore away, Mr. Cartier, a high official in the Colonial government, stepped forward, and began to sing this song in a clear and melodious voice.

The chorus was easily picked up by the listners, and after once hearing it, a few voices joined in — at first in subdued and gentle murmur, but at each return more clear and strong, until at the end, the whole party were in full accord, and singing with enthusiasm the oft-repeated declaration —

"Il ya longtepas que je t'aime,
Jamais je ne t' oublerai."

From this time onward till the end of his journey in America, this simple melody became the favorite piece, or was brought in as an accompaniment to other music, at receptions and parties, and in short, upon all occasions wherever music was in order. and for this reason it is now better known outside of Canada than all the rest of French-Canadian songs put together.

The following not-very-literal English translation of this chanson, has in one sense more poetic merit than the original, inasmuch as it has a rhyme, to which the French does not pretend.

As by the crystal fount I strayed,
On which the dancing moonbeams played,
The water seemed so clear and bright,
I bathed myself in its delight:
 I loved thee from the hour we met,
 And never can that love forget.

The water seemed so clear and bright,
I bathed myself in its delight;
The nightingale above my head,
As sweet a stream of music shed,
 I loved thee. etc.

The nightingale above my head,
As sweet a stream of music shed,
Sing, nightingale, thy heart is glad,
But I could weep, for mine is sad !
 I loved thee, etc.

Sing, nightingale, thy heart is glad,
But I could weep, for mine is sad !
For I have lost my lady fair,
And she has left me to despair !
 I loved thee, etc.

For I have lost my lady fair,
And she has left me to despair,
For that I gave not, when she spoke,
The rose that from its tree I broke.
 I loved thee, etc.

For that I gave not, when she spoke,
The rose that from its tree I broke,
I wish the rose were on its tree.
And my beloved again with me.
 I loved thee, etc.

I wish the rose were on its tree,
And my beloved again with me,
Or that the tree itself were cast
Into the sea, before this passed.
 I loved thee, etc

Of the above chanson, Marmier observes. "As you notice, there is neither verse nor rhyme, nor anything else besides an outlandish measure of syllables ; * * * * Yet these rude couplets, sung in the rudest of melodies, have in them an indescribable melancholy that penetrates the soul."

An English writer who published his observations in 1864, gives one of these songs, prefaced with the following descriptive account of its execution:

"The French Canadian boatmen seem to be a happy devil-may care sort of fellows, who did not allow the thought for to-morrow to interfere in any way with the enjoyment of to-day. They sing in concert very plaintively; and some of their favorite ballads are highly pathetic. One day I was prevailed upon by a friend to take an excursion in a canoe, manned by half a dozen of these thoughtless people. Upon sailing up the St. Lawrence, as they warmed to their work, they commenced singing the following chanson, and so prettily was it executed, that the effect was most extraordinary:

The following rather free translation has
been furnished us:

    With hearts as wild
    As joyous child,
Lived Rhoda of the mountain ;
    Her only wish
    To seek the fish
In the waters of the fountain.
    Oh, the violet, white and blue !

    The stream is deep,
    The banks are steep,
Down in the flood fell she,
    When there rode by
    Right gallantly,
Three barons of high degree.
    Oh, the violets, white and blue !

    "Oh, tell us, fair maid,"
    They each one said,
" Your reward to the venturing knight
    Who shall save your life
    From the water's strife
By his arm's unflinching might."
    Oh, the violet, white and blue !

    "Oh ! haste to my side,"
    The maiden replied,
" Nor ask of a recompense now !
    When safe on land
    Again we stand
For such matters is time enow."
    Oh, the violet, white and blue !

    But when all free
    Upon the lea
She found herself once more,
    She would not stay,
    And sped away
Till she reached her cottage door.
    Oh, the violets, white and blue !

    Her casement by,
    That maiden shy
Began so sweet to sing ;
    Her lute and voice,
    Did e'en rejoice,
The early flowers of spring.
    Oh, the violet, white and blue !

    But the barons proud
    Then spoke aloud :
" This is not the boon we desire ;
    Your heart and love,
    My pretty dove,
Is the free gift we require."
    Oh, the violets, white and blue !

    "Oh, my heart so true,
    Is not for you,
Nor for any of high degree ;
    I have pledged my truth
    To an honest youth,
With a beard so comely to see."
    Oh, the violet, white and blue !

TOM MOORE'S BOAT SONG.—(1804).

In the years 1803-4, the social favorite and graceful writer, Thomas Moore, made a hasty tour through the Middle and Northern States and Canada. It would appear from his writings, and it has been strongly intimated, that this visit to America was designed to afford capital for satire and song in the interest of British prejudice, and under the political agitations of the day there can be no doubt but that this result was in some degree realized.

But whatever may have been the animus or the effect of his writings, we may well afford, after this lapse of time, to forgive him, since he has left us some verses that throw a charm over the places he described, and impart an interest, due to the smoothness of their measure and the poetic sentiments which they embody. His lyrics, entitled " The Lake of the Dismal Swamp," and " The Canadian Boat Song," are of this number. Moore was born in 1779, and when he passed this way, in 1804, was therefore about twenty-five years of age. He had already gained popular notoriety by his writings ; and the extraordinary attentions paid to him, especially among English officials in Canada and elsewhere. gave a prominence to his presence wherever he travelled. In a letter to his mother, written soon after his passage down the St. Lawrence from Niagara in a sailing vessel, in August, 1804, he shows how exceedingly flattering to his vanity these attentions were, making him at once satisfied with himself and with all the rest of mankind. He says :

" In my passage across Lake Ontario, I met with the same politeness which has been so gratifying, and, indeed, convenient to me, all along my route. The captain refused to take what I know is always given, and begged me to consider all my friends as included in the compliment, which a line from me would at any time entitle them to. Even a poor watch-maker at Niagara, who did a very necessary and difficult job for me, insisted I should not think of paying him, but accept it as the only mark of respect he could pay one he had heard so much of, but never expected to meet with. This is the very nectar of life, and I hope, I trust, it is not vanity to which the cordial owes all its sweetness. No; it gives me a feeling towards all mankind, which I am convinced is not unamiable; the impulse which begins with self, spreads a circle instantaneously round it, which includes all the sociabilities and benevolences of the heart."

As to the circumstances under which the Boat Song was written, these can best be learned from his own pen. In a note appended to the full edition of his writings, we find the following account :

"I wrote these words to an air which our boatmen sung to us frequently. The wind was so unfavorable that they were obliged to row all the way, and we were five days in descending the river from Kingston to Montreal, exposed to an intense sun during the day, and at night forced to take shelter from the dews in any miserable huts upon the banks that would receive us. But the magnificent scenery of the St. Lawrence repays all these difficulties. Our voyageurs had good voices, and sang perfectly in tune together. The original words of the air, to which I adapted these stanzas, appeared to be a long, incoherent story, of which I could understand but little from the barbarous pronunciation of the Canadians.

"The stanzas are supposed to be sung by those voyageurs who go to the Grand Portage by the Utawas river."

ET REGIMEN CANTUS HORTATUR. — QUINTILLIAN.

Faintly, as tolls the evening chime,
Our voices keep tune, and our oars keep time;
Soon as the woods on shore look dim
We'll sing at St. Ann's our parting hymn.
   Row, brothers, row, the stream runs fast,
   The rapids are near, and the daylight's past.

Why should we yet our sail unfurl?
There is not a breath the blue wave to curl!
But when the wind blows off the shore,
Oh! sweetly we'll rest on our weary oar.
   Blow, breezes, blow, the stream runs fast,
   The rapids are near, and the daylight's past.

Utawa's tide! this trembling moon
Shall see us float over the surges soon.
Saint of this green isle! hear our prayer,
Oh! grant us cool heavens and favoring air.
   Blow, breezes, blow, the stream runs fast,
   The rapids are near, and the daylight's past.

We have met with two translations of Moore's Boat Song into French, but neither of them are of much merit.

Besides these Boat Songs, the islands present many poetic associations that give to them peculiar interest. The late Caleb Lyon, of Lyonsdale, many years since, published a poem somewhat after the style of Byron's "Isles of Greece," that has been so often reproduced that we deem it proper not to include it in this volume.

The religious meetings that have been held upon Wellesley Island have given rise to some poetic reminiscences of peculiar interest, especially those relating to Mr. Philip B. Bliss, whose participation in the Sunday-School Parliament, in 1876, was brought sadly to mind by the railroad casualty that, before the next year, ended his life at Ashtabula, Ohio. This event has been made the subject of memorial verses by Miss Winslow, of Brooklyn. The following are the opening stanzas of this poem:

   Last year he stood amongst us all,
     Acknowledged King of Song,
   Last year we heard his deep tones fall
     The river side along;
   We saw his reverend mien, we knew
     His spirit true and bold,
   But of our singer's inner life
     The half was never told.

   We heard the story, as it flew
     On the western wires along,
   With bated breath we heard it true,
     God took our King of Song ;
   We read of fiery chariot wheels,
     Of wintry waters cold,
   But angels saw the agony—
     The half was never told.

THE "MILLE ILES" OF CRÉMIZIE, THE CANADIAN POET.*

This poem extends through more than fifty stanzas, in which the author lets his fancy

---

* Joseph Octave Crémazie, a native of Lower Canada, was gifted with a fine poetic talent, and produced several pieces that have been greatly admired for the elegance of their style, and the highly poetic sentiments which they express.

M. Crémazie was a merchant at Quebec, but proving unsuccessful in business, he went from Canada dwell upon what he would do, were he a swallow. He would fly to where the snowflocks fall, and make the wildest places echo to his song. He would visit Spain, where the almond blooms; the gilded dome of Alcazar, and the Royal Palace where the Caliph Omar reigned; Cordova, and Old Castile; Leon, with its brazen gates, and Sevillé; the Escurial and the Alhambra, and river banks fragrant with opening flowers. He would view the city of Venice, and the Lions of St. Mark; listen to the serenades of an Italian summer evening, and, in short, explore on light and rapid wing whatever region or place the wild world offers — in Europe, in India, or in the land of the Nile, that awakens poetic sentiments, displays pictures of beauty, or recalls the memory of great events.

Having thus touched, as it were, a thousand islands of interest throughout the world, he says:

"But when with floods of light, the balmy springtime comes, with its melodies, its mantle of green and its perfumes — its vernal songs with the morning sun, and all the freshness of awakening life, I would return to my native skies.

"When Eve plucked death from the Tree of Life, and brought tears and sorrow upon earth, Adam was driven out into the world to mourn with her, and taste from the bitter spring that we drink to-day.

"Then angels on their wings, bore the silent eden to the eternal spheres on high, and placed it in the heavens — but in passing through space, they dropped along the way, to mark their course, some flowers from the Garden Divine. These flowers of

to Brazil, and from thence to France, and died at Havre, January 17, 1879.

Mr. Lareau, in his Histoire de la Litterature Canadienne, in speaking of the style of this poet, says:

"There is something in Crémazie's talent that is found only in those of native genius — it is inspiration. By sudden and passionate flights, he carries you into the highest spheres of poetry and thought. He adorns his style with coloring the most brilliant, and in his hand everything is transformed and animated. He invests the most common of events with features that elevate and magnify, yet in this exuberance of coloring, and this wealth of words and ideas, he in no degree impairs the simplicity of his subject. The poetic thought of his writings is clear and refined, and his verse is natural, and flows from an abundant source."

changing hues, falling into the great river, became the Thousand Isles — the paradise of the St. Lawrence.

"The Thousand Isles; magnificent necklace of diamond and sapphire that those of the ancient world would have preferred to the bright gold of Ophir! Sublime and beautiful crown that rests upon the ample brow of the St. Lawrence, on her throne of the vast lakes that display the tinted rainbow, and return the echoes of thundering Niagara! The Thousand Isles — charming wonder — oasis on the sleeping waves — that which might be thought a flower-basket borne by a lover's hand! In thy picturesque retreats I find naught but peace and happiness, and spend the tranquil days in singing the lays of a heart content!

"Not proud Andalusia — nor the banks of Cadiz — nor the kingdom of the Moors sparkling like rubies — nor the poetic scenes of Florence and Milan — nor Rome with its ancient splendors — nor Naples with its volcano — nor that charmed sea where Stamhoul lifts its towers — nor the vales of sorrow where the fierce Giaours dwell — nor India in its native wealth, where Para-Brahma shines, or the seas of verdure that Kalidasa celebrate — nor the land of the pyramids — nor all the treasures of Memphis — nor the rapids of the Nile, where we seek and admire Osiris — shall ever thy echoes repeat from the notes of this lyre which is tuned amid these charming scenes."

GEOLOGY OF THE THOUSAND ISLANDS.

There is much geological interest in the rock formations of this part of the St. Lawrence, and in the evidences that they present as to the changes that the earth's surface has undergone since the beginning. For the most part, the islands consist of gneiss rock, belonging to the Laurentian period, which here form a connecting link between the vast Primary Region, so called, of Upper Canada, and an extensive district of the same in Northern New York. This gneiss is generally obscurely stratified, but with much confusion in the lines of original deposit, as if they had been softened by heat and disturbed by pressure, and the stratification, such as it is, is often highly inclined. The rock is composed largely of a reddish feldspar, with variable proportions of quartz and hornblende, and occasional particles of magnetic iron ore. In some places on the New York side it is found to contain dykes of trap and greenstone, that ramify into thin veins, as if injected under great pressure, and in a perfectly liquid form. It also contains, in Jefferson and St. Lawrence counties, most interesting crystalline mineral forms, in great variety and in Rossie, lead was formerly mined in this rock to a large amount.

Upon one of the Thousand Islands opposite Gananoque, the gneiss rock is quarried for cemetery monuments, which are sent to Montreal for polishing, and are thought by many to be as beautiful as the red Scotch granite for this use. The rock is there also quarried for paving blocks, and other uses.

At Gananoque, and at various places among the islands, the Potsdam sandstone occurs in thick masses, rising into cliffs fifty feet or more above the river, and affording a fine material for building, being easily worked when freshly quarried, and hardening upon exposure to the air. A little back from that town, gneiss forms the principal rock, rising in naked ridges, with intervening plains that indicate the presence of level strata of limestone or sandstone beneath. In this region, white crystalline limestone, steatite and various other minerals occur.

Before reaching Brockville, and for a long distance below, calciferous sandstone and the older limestones constitute the only rock in situ, and afford excellent quarries of building stone. These strata are for the most part level, and the very flat region in Jefferson county, lying a little back from the river, and extending several miles inland, is underlaid by this rock. It contains, in many places, the organic remains of lower forms of animal and vegetable life, that sometimes stand out in fine relief upon weathered surfaces of the rock.

At Kingston, and at various points upon both shores, and upon Carlton, Wolfe, Howe, Grindstone and other islands, the Birds'-eye and Black River limestones occur in nearly horizontal strata, and in some places are seen resting directly upon the gneiss, which comes to the surface, here and there, and often rises to a greater elevation than the adjacent limestone. It would appear that at these places an island existed at the time when the sandstones, elsewhere so abundant, were being deposited, and that the limestones were formed directly over the gneiss. This limestone is largely used for building purposes, at Kingston and elsewhere, and it makes excellent lime. From the lower and impure strata of this rock, water-lime, or hydraulic cement, was formerly made in Jefferson county. These limestones at various places contain fossil corals, sponges, shells, and other organic remains peculiar to the older Silurian period. The Black River limestone, in Watertown, Brownville, and other places, has extensive caves, worn by currents of water in former times. These have been explored to considerable distances, and appear to have been formed by the widening of natural fissures in the rock. Their section is more or less oval in form, sometimes wider than high, and nearly uniting along the line of the fissure, above and below.

The broken region, of which the Thousand Islands are a part, affords on either side of the river, in various places, a number of picturesque lakes, and within a distance of twenty miles in Jefferson county, there are extensive mines of red hematite, that have been wrought for more than fifty years, supplying several iron furnaces in their vicinity, and a large amount of ore for exportation to other points. Geologically, these iron ores occur in thick beds along the junction of the gneiss and the older fossiliferous formations, and they seem to extend downward to an unlimited extent.

In speaking of the Thousand Islands as a field for geological study, a writer, who has taken a great interest in this subject, says:

"One of the finest River Archipelagoes on the globe, is this of the St. Lawrence. Indeed, it is almost the only one that has such a vast number of islets, all of rocky formation; high, healthy, wooded, without muddy or marshy shores; small enough for inexhaustible variety, deep, navigable channels everywhere, and above all, the very crown and glory of the picturesque. * * * The location is one of the very best for geological study. The Laurentian system is reckoned the oldest exposure, or among the oldest, on the globe. The granite is largely composed of feldspar, and so differs widely from the famous granites of New England, in which hornblende forms so large an element, and which are nearly a true syenite. The Potsdam sandstone here lies directly upon the granite. Both show wonderfully the erosion of waves by which the great inland sea, of ancient geological ages, wore down this partial outlet to the sea. Both show, also, the grinding and planing action of the glacial drift, which here wrought with enormous power. There are drift striæ or grooves here, cut into this hard granite, some of them showing for several rods in length, straight as a line, and as wide and deep as half a hogshead divided lengthwise of the staves.

"A block of granite, as large as a small house, held fast in the under surface of a moving sheet of ice, as a glazier's diamond in its steel handle; another sheet of ice, hundreds of feet thick and thousands of miles wide, and creeping onward with a slow but irresistible movement — what a glass-cutter that! And when that whole sheet of ice is thickly studded on its under side with such blocks, great and small, we can get a conception of what an enormous rasp the hand of Omnipotence wielded in planing and polishing all the upper surfaces, especially the northern, western, and north-western exposures of these mighty rocks. The tooth-marks of this rasp are the glacial striæ of geologists, and this is an excellent place to study them.

"For half a mile, fronting on Eel bay, there is an almost continuous frontage of the glacier-planed rocks. At its western end, this rocky ridge breaks down abruptly in lofty precipices called the 'Palisades,' with a deep, navigable strait of the river, called the 'Narrows.' Here is an admirable place to study the cleavage and fracture of these rocks, and the whole is one of the finest scenic views of the Great River."

An anonymous writer, in a book of Travels "dedicated to the Wanderer by one of his class,"— but known to be John F. Campbell, of Islay, had his attention much attracted by geological phenomena, and in noticing glacial agencies, remarks as follows concerning this part of the St. Lawrence :

"At the foot of Lake Ontario, at Brockville, a rock of gray quartz in the town is so finely polished that lines on it were invisible, and almost imperceptible, till a heel-ball rubbing brought them out. Their main direction is N. 45° East (magnetic), and large polished grooves, in which sand-lines occur, are ten feet wide. At other spots on the same rock, lines point north and have other bearings, but the whole shape of the country bears N. E. and S. W.

"Beyond Brockville, the Thousand Islands of Lake Ontario closely resemble groups of low rocks off Gottenburgh. The solid rock foundation of Canada, up to the level of Lake Ontario, is glaciated. It is striated in various directions, but the main lines observed aimed from Belleisle towards Niagara. Upon or near the rock are beds of sand, shells, gravel, and clay, with large and well-scratched bowlders of foreign origin. Higher than these beds of drift are more beds of sand, shells, gravel, clay and bowlders as high up as the top of Montreal Mountain, and the top of Niagara Falls."

In noticing these phenomena of glacial action, it may be remarked that the whole surface of the country north and south, and to a great distance, is found strewn here and there with bowlders, some of them of immense size, and in other places are moraines or ridges in great abundance. Drift-hills composed of sand, gravel and bowlders, sometimes cemented by clay into "hard-pan," are a common occurrence.

LAKE RIDGES.

We may in this connection notice the "Lake Ridges," so-called, that occur on both sides of the lake, and various elevations above its present level. These particularly engaged the attention of Prof. Charles Lyell, the English geologist, who, in his journey in 1842, stopped at Toronto to examine them as they occur northward from that city. The first of the ridges was a mile inland — and 108 feet above the present level of the lake. It arose from thirty to forty feet above the level land at its base, and could be traced by the eye running a long distance east and west, being marked by a narrow belt of fir-wood, while above and below, the soil was clayey, and bore other kinds of timber.

The second ridge, a mile and a half further inland, was 208 feet above the lake at its base, as determined by canal and railroad surveys, and arose fifty to seventy feet high, the ground being flat both above and below, and at the foot lay a great number of bowlders, which, from their composition, showed that they came from the north. Some of these bowlders lay on the top of the ridge, but there were but few erratic rocks on the soil between these ridges.

Another ride of two miles and a half, in a northerly direction, brought him to a third ridge, five miles from the lake — less conspicuous than either of the former, being little more than a steep slope of ten feet by which the higher terrace was reached, only eighty feet above the base of the second ridge. Thus he went on, passing one ridge after another, sometimes deviating several miles from the direct course, to fix the continuity of level, and observing their general character. He saw no less than eleven of these ridges in all, some of which might be called cliffs, or the abrupt terminations of terraces of clay, which cover the silurian rocks of that region to a great depth, and belonging to the drift or bowlder formation.

The highest ridge was about 680 feet above the lake, the water-shed between Lakes Ontario and Simcoe being 762 feet. From the summit the slope toward Lake Simcoe descends 282 feet, and along down this, several ridges were found, showing that water had formerly flowed to a higher level than the present.

Mr. Lyell remarks that he had never before observed so striking an example of banks, terraces, and accumulations of stratified gravel, sand and clay, maintaining over wide areas so perfect a horizontality as in this district north of Toronto. He remarks that the hypothesis of the successive breaking down of barriers of an ancient lake or fresh-water ocean has now been generally abandoned, from the impossibility of conceiving here, as in the west of Scotland, as to where lands capable of damming up the waters to such height could have been situated, or how, if they have existed, they could have disappeared, while the levels of the ancient beaches remained undisturbed. He, therefore, inclines to the belief that they were the margin of the ancient sea, which has changed level from the upheavals of the continent. This must have been intermittent; so that pauses occurred, during which the coast-line remained stationary for centuries, and in which the waves would have time to cut cliffs, or throw up beaches, or throw down littoral deposits and sand-banks near the shore.

In support of this theory, he cites the example of Scandinavia, which has been slowly, yet perceptibly rising from the sea within the historic period, at the rate of two or three feet a century. We know too little of the laws that govern these subterranean movements, to deny the possibility of such intermittent changes in the level of the sea.

While the cliff margins might have been the abrupt shore in an extremely ancient period, the bars of sand on the highest levels may have been formed on the inland margin of shallow waters, at some distance from deep waters, as may be seen in course of formation in some places at the present time.

DEPTH OF THE ST. LAWRENCE.—TIDES IN THE LAKES.

The soundings in the river, among the islands, indicate a great irregularity of depth, the bottom being generally rocky, and quite as diversified as the parts that rise above the surface. The greatest depth is 120 feet, but the usual soundings are from thirty to sixty feet. As a general rule, the navigation among the islands is entirely safe to vessels of the size usually employed upon these waters, and all the dangerous rocks and reefs have their positions marked.

The level of the river differs one year with another, the extreme range being about seven feet. These changes are not the immediate effects of the excessive rains, such as cause floods in other rivers, but appear to be occasioned by the different quantities of rain falling, in some years more than in others, and which finds its way down months afterward. A series of several years of high water, and others of low water, are known to occur. The level of the river is also affected by strong prevailing winds, blowing up or down the lake, and several instances of rapid fall, followed by a returning wave of extraordinary height, have been reported. Some have supposed these sudden changes of level to be caused by earthquake-shocks, but a more probable theory appears to be that they are occasioned by the passage of a water-spout, or a tornado at a distant point. There is also found to be a slight, but well-marked tide in the lakes, depending upon lunar changes, like those upon the ocean, capable of the same prediction, and governed by the same laws. This fact has been proved by long-continued, self-recording observations. It may often be disguised by oscillation in the level occasioned by the winds. It was observed by Charlevoix, in 1721, that the level of the lake changed several times in a day, as may be seen anywhere along the shore, especially upon a gently-sloping beach. This is probably due chiefly to the action of the winds.

Boundary Lines Between the Two Governments.

In French colonial times, there was no boundary acknowledged by both governments, as existing between the French and English settlements. Each party claimed far beyond the point allowed by the other, and the encroachments of the former upon Lake Champlain and in the west are well known to have led to the war that ended in 1760, in the establishment of English authority over the whole.

The province of Quebec, as created by royal proclamation, was bounded on the south, from the Connecticut to the St. Lawrence rivers, by the line of 45° north latitude, and south-westward by a line running from the point where this line intersected the St. Lawrence to the south end of Lake Nipessing. A survey of the line of 45° was begun in 1772 by John Collins, on the part of Quebec, and Thomas Vallentine, on the part of New York, but the latter having died, Claude Joseph Sauthier was appointed in his place, and the work was completed October 20, 1774.

In the treaty of 1783, the line of the river and lakes was adopted as the boundary westward from St. Regis, but no surveys of this part were undertaken until about thirty-five years afterwards. The military posts on the American side of the boundary were held by the British for the purpose of protecting the claims of British subjects until definitely relinquished under the Jay treaty, signed November 19, 1794, under which it was agreed that they should be given up on or before June 1, 1796. In the meantime, the discussion as to boundaries continued, and Lieutenant-Governor J. G. Simcoe, of Upper Canada, was particularly strenuous in insisting upon an aggressive advance of the frontier, that should secure to British interests in the interior the magnificent empire which the French had endeavored to establish. He would have had Niagara the seat of government of this English America, and had his first concessions been allowed, the western boundary of the United States would have been the Genesee river, and a line extending from its headwaters to the sources of the Ohio, and thence southward, along the Alleghenies to the Gulf coast.

When this could not be secured, he proposed a line from Presque Isle [Erie, Pa.] to Pittsburgh; then the Cuyahoga, and, as a last extremity, the Miami river. Early in 1792, in a long letter to the home government, he pointed out the great advantages that would result to Canada from the adoption of a line that should run from Lake Ontario across the country to the southern end of Lake Champlain, including the disputed boundaries upon that lake. Until the last moment, he had clung to the hope of attaching Vermont to Canada, and the correspondence of that period shows that an expectation of this result had been encouraged by the turbulent leaders in that State as an alternative preferred to submission to the authority of either of the claiming States. He adds:

"I should think Oswego, and I question whether Niagara would not be a cheap sacrifice for such a limit, which would be strictly defensive on our part, and calculated to prevent future disagreements. I have heard that Carlton Island, the most important post on Lake Ontario, is on the British side of the line as the better channel is between that and the southern shore."

Again, in writing to the Rt. Hon. Henry Dundas, November 4, 1792, he says: "I beg to send a map of the river St. Lawrence, that in case of a treaty being entered into with the United States, it may plainly appear of what consequence it is to render it effectual and permanent, that the British boundary should enclose the islands of the St. Lawrence."

Under the treaty of Ghent, which ended the war of 1812-15, Peter B. Porter was appointed on the part of the United States, and Andrew Barclay on the part of Great Britain, as commissioners to run and mark the line. The survey was begun in 1817, and their report was signed June 18, 1822, subject to ratification by their respective governments. Their operations were conducted with much precision, and the details were reduced to maps that have never been published. Copies of these are preserved in the offices of record of the countries concerned.

While the boundary survey was in progress, Col. Samuel Hawkins, the agent of the American commission, gave a fête champetré upon one of the lower islands, to which the members of the commission on both sides were invited. The incident is described by Mr. Darby, who says:

"The day was even on the St. Lawrence uncommonly fine, and amid the groves of aspen, wild-cherry, and linden trees, the scene seemed more than earthly. Mrs. Hawkins presided, and in the bowers of the St. Lawrence recalled the most polished manners of civilized society in the crowded city. At the close of evening Major Joseph Delafield and myself walked over the island, and in full view of the objects which excited our feelings, concluded that no spot on the globe could unite in so small a space more to please, to amuse, and gratify the fancy."

The earlier surveys between the St. Lawrence and Connecticut rivers being made without precision, were found in 1818 to be almost everywhere upon a line too far north. At St. Regis the departure from the true latitude of 45° was found to be 1,375 feet; at the French Mills [Fort Covington] it was 154 feet; at Chateauguy river, 975 feet, and at Rouse's Point, 4,576 feet.

The government of the United States had begun to erect a fort on Lake Champlain, near what was the supposed boundary, soon after the war of 1812-15, and this was wholly carried over into Canada, by the survey of 1818. It had been christened "Fort Montgomery," but now in common parlance was called "Fort Blunder." The Americans being unable, and the Canadians unwilling to protect the property, it became the prey of whoever chose to plunder it of materials, as needed for building purposes. Finally by the surveys of 1842, the old line of 1774 was taken as a compromise, and the site being thus restored to the possession of the United States, work was resumed and carried, we believe, to completion under the original name.

In the surveys made under the Webster-Ashburton treaty of 1842, J. B. Bucknall Estcourt, lieutenant-colonel, was appointed by the government of Great Britain, and Albert Smith by that of the United States. They confirmed the line in the river, as it had been located under the treaty of Ghent, and the old line marked by Vallentine and Collins between the St. Lawrence and Lake Champlain. They were able to follow this line by the marks on the trees, still visible, or found by cutting into them; but where these could not be found, or where clearings had been made, straight lines were run between these old landmarks, and iron monuments were set at every angle of deflection, and at the crossing of rivers, lakes and roads. The boundary line is, therefore, not on the true parallel of 45°, nor in the middle of the channel, but it is a conventional line, agreed upon by both governments, and accurately defined by monuments and records.

The larger islands in the St. Lawrence, below Ogdensburg, had long been settled under St. Regis Indian titles, and were occupied at the time of the survey by settlers, who, up to that time, had been regarded as British subjects.

Some forty years afterwards, the persons who had sustained losses by this transfer applied to the State of New York for compensation, and their claims became the subject of investigation and of legislative action for their relief.

HYDROGRAPHICAL AND TOPOGRAPHICAL SURVEYS.

BRITISH SURVEYS.

The first surveys of Lakes Ontario and Erie were made in the summer of 1789, under the direction of Mr. Niff, an engineer. They only embraced the south shore of Ontario, from Carleton Island to Niagara, and the south shore of Lake Erie, from its eastern end to Detroit.

The engineer's instructions required him, in addition to the soundings, to note the locations proper for ship-building, the quality of land for settlement, and the kind of timber along the shores. It will be remembered that the whole of this region, now within the States, was then still held by the British military authorities, and it may be inferred from the above instructions that they were looking forward to a time when it should be permanently under their control.

Soon after the war of 1812–15, a survey of the eastern end of Lake Ontario and of the river St. Lawrence, as far down as the Gallop Rapids, was made by Capt. W. F. W. Owen, of the Royal Navy, with soundings, a definite delineation of the shores and islands, and some topographical details concerning the adjacent parts. This survey was completed in 1818, and published by the Hydrographical Office of the Admiralty in 1828, forming a series of five charts. These were re-engraved, with corrections, in 1861, and are found in the collections known as the "Bayfield Charts," which in all embrace an extensive series of lake surveys.

An elaborate survey of the region around Kingston, including the adjacent islands, upon a large scale, and showing the contour of surface and details of topography, with special reference to its military defences, was prepared a few years since, and a limited edition printed.

UNITED STATES LAKE SURVEYS.

For many years, the survey of the northern and northwestern lakes has been in course of execution by the corps of engineers of the war department. These trigometrical and hydrographical surveys were begun upon Lake Ontario and the river St. Lawrence about ten years since, and during the years 1871 to 1875, were extended along the river from St. Regis to the lake, under the direction of Brig.-Gen. C. B. Comstock. In 1876, the results were published in six charts, which represent the part of the river from St. Regis to the foot of Wolfe Island, upon a scale of 1 to 30,000 or a little more than two miles to an inch. They embrace the whole of the river, and the topography of both shores, but do not indicate the boundary line. A map of the eastern end of Lake Ontario, being No. 1 of a separate series, on a scale of 1 to 80,000, or about four-fifths of an inch to a mile, has also been published under the same direction. These charts all have a great number of soundings, with indications of the nature of the bottom, the contour and cultivation of the land on the islands and adjacent shores, the place of buildings, the lines of roads, and of streets in villages, and the character and extent of woodlands, with an accuracy of detail that proves the excellence of the work.

LIGHT-HOUSES.

A few facts concerning the light-houses along the St. Lawrence, may not be without interest:

The AMERICAN LIGHT-HOUSES are under the care of a "light-house board," in the Treasury Department, and the coasts and rivers of the country are divided into fifteen districts. Of these, the tenth district extends from St. Regis to Detroit, with the headquarters of the inspector and engineer at Buffalo. Within this district, there are sixty-seven light-houses, and about 150 buoys (spars and cans), anchored so as to show the course of the channel, or the position of dangerous places. These spars, etc., are taken up at the close of navigation, and replaced after the ice has disappeared in the spring. By their color and numbers, they give information that all navigators must understand. There are six American lights from Ogdensburg to Tibbett's Point, inclusive. They have all fixed white lights, with lens apparatus of the fourth or sixth order. Their names and position are as follows:

Ogdensburgh, on a rocky islet, 190 yards from south shore; built in 1834; refitted in 1870; a square tower, 42 feet high, with keeper's dwelling.

Cross-over Island, 20 miles above Ogdensburg; a tower 37 feet high, on keeper's brick dwelling; lantern black; built in 1837; refitted in 1870.

Sister Island, 6¼ miles further up; a tower on keeper's stone dwelling; lantern black, with red dome; built in 1870; height, 43 feet.

Sunken Rock, 6 miles further up, on Bush Island, about a quarter of a mile north of Alexandria Bay; an octagonal brick tower, sheathed with boards; white; height, 31 feet; built in 1847; refitted in 1855.

Rock Island, 7 miles further up; keeper's dwelling of brick, white, with a low tower on top; dome black; height, 39 feet; built in 1847; refitted in 1855. [Shown hereafter.]

Tibbett's Point, 23 miles above, at the outlet of the lake; a stone building connected by covered way with a round brick tower 67 feet high; white; built in 1827; refitted in 1854.

The oldest light-house on the lake is that near Fort Niagara, built in 1813; the next oldest is the one on Gallo Island, built in 1820. All the lights on the St. Lawrence and the Great Lakes are discontinued from January 1st until the opening of navigation, unless otherwise specially directed.

The DOMINION LIGHT-HOUSE SYSTEM is under the charge of the Minister of Marine and Fisheries, and at the beginning of 1880 embraced 482 lights, of which Labrador had 4; Newfoundland 3; Gulf and River of St. Lawrence 140 to Montreal—19 from thence to Windmill Point near Prescott, and 10 from thence to the lake; Saguenay River 6; Richlieu River 5; Lake Memphramagog 6; Ottawa River 16; Lake Ontario 29; Lake Simcoe 1; Lake Erie 15; Detroit River 2; Lake St. Clair 1; Lake Huron 32; Lake Superior 9; Prince Edward Island 29; Cape Breton Island 23; Nova Scotia (Atlantic Coast) 63; Bay of Fundy 48; St. John's River 13; Winnipeg 1, and British Columbia 7.

The Canadian lights from Prescott to Lake Ontario are as follows:

Cole Shoal, on a pier five miles west of Brockville.

Grenadier Island (S. W. point), two miles below Rockport.

Lindoe Island, five miles west of Rockport.

Gananoque Narrows, five miles below Gananoque, on Little Stave Island.

Jack Straw Shoal, on a pier, north side of channel, three miles below Gananoque.

Spectacle Shoal, on a pier, north side, one and a quarter miles west of Gananoque.

Red Horse Rock, on pier, S. E. side of channel, one mile above Spectacle Shoals.

Burnt Island, at S. E. point of island, north side of channel, half mile from Red Horse Rock.

Wolfe Island, on Quebec, or east point of island—and Brown's or Knapp's Point, on Wolfe Island.

These are all fixed single lights, with metallic reflectors, on white square wooden towers, and were all built in 1856, except Wolfe Island Light in 1861, and that on Brown's Point in 1874

STEAM NAVIGATION UPON LAKE ONTARIO AND THE ST. LAWRENCE.

The first steamboat that appeared upon this lake was the Oneida, in 1817. The boat was 110 feet long, twenty-four wide, and eight deep, and measured 237 tons, and had a low-pressure cross-head engine, and a thirty-four-inch cylinder with four-feet stroke. She had two masts, and used sails when the wind favored. It was indeed a new era in navigation, and from this time Durham boats, bateaux, and all the pleasant associations which boat songs recall were doomed to disappear. The new steamboat was indeed a wonder in this part of the world, and at every landing crowds assembled from far and wide, to catch a view of the first wreath of smoke from her stack, and to watch and wonder as she slowly and majestically came up, and as she independently departed on her appointed course. Every village that could muster a cannon, and every steeple that had a bell, announced the event, and joined in the welcome. Bonfires and illuminations, the congratulations of friends and interchange of hospitalities, signalized the event along the whole of the route, and the occasion was jotted down as one to be long remembered. The round trip from Ogdensburgh to Lewiston required ten days. Fare, $16 in the cabin, and $8 on deck. Master, Captain Mallaby. The Oneida ran till 1832, seldom making more than five miles an hour. The Frontenac came out from Kingston not long after. From this time down, the number has been legion; but since the completion of the Grand Trunk Railway, the importance of steam navigation has greatly declined, and several fine steamers were taken down the rapids never to return.*

But whatever the future may determine, as regards the lines of business travel, the St. Lawrence will always, in its islands and its rapids, present an attractive route for tourists in the summer season. We may never again witness a fleet of steamers as magnificent as those of the "Ontario and St. Lawrence Steamboat Co.," which in its best days had eleven such in daily use,—while the Canadians at the same time had numerous elegant steamers fully employed; but under the law universally true in business, that the supply will be regulated by the demand, we may confidently look for abundant comfort and elegance in these steamers upon the St. Lawrence. The history of steam navigation scarcely presents a more remarkable freedom from accidents than does that upon this lake and river — a circumstance due as well to the intelligence of those entrusted with their navigation, as to the sagacity of owners, who saw their true interest to consist in the certainty of their engagements, rather than in a reputation for extraordinary achievements in amount of business, or high rate of speed.

The fine boats of the Folger Brothers, as well as of the Richelieu and Ontario Navigation Company, have certainly reduced precision to perfection, and accidents to a minimum.

Life-saving stations were first established by the Government of the United States upon Lake Ontario, in the summer of 1854, consisting originally of Francis's Metallic Life-Boats, with fixtures, but without buildings to shelter, or crews to manage them. The system has since been perfected as the wants of the service required.

The present lines through the Thousand Islands are quite numerous, by far the larger part being owned and run by the Folger Bros., of Kingston. Their boats are in every way superior, and really leave nothing to be desired.

LUMBERING UPON THE RIVER ST. LAWRENCE.

In several of the descriptions given in the preceding pages, allusion is made to woodland scenes and woodmen's labor. One of the earliest and most extensive operators in this line was William Wells, eldest son of Thos. Wells, from Sandown, N. H., who came to Canada in 1787, and began lumbering operations about 1790, on the island to which his name is now often applied. He would establish a shanty at a convenient point, and with the aid of hired men, work up into staves all the timber suitable to his use within convenient reach, and when this was exhausted he would remove to another place. He thus went over the whole of this island and other islands in the river, until the business became no longer profitable. His market was England, by way of Quebec, to which place his stock was sent upon rafts. At a later period, Carlton Island for a short time became an important lumber station, and later still, Clayton, where for many years immense quantities of timber, brought down from the upper lakes in vessels, were made up into rafts in French Creek, and sent down to Quebec. It was there again loaded into vessels, for the European markets. In recent years, the foot of Wolfe Island, and Garden Island, opposite to Kingston, have been the principal lumbering

---

* A large amount of information concerning steamboats upon the lake will be found in Hough's History of St. Lawrence and Franklin Counties (1853), and in Haddock's History of Jefferson County (1895).

For many years Clayton was a noted place for steamboat building. Some of the finest steamers that ever appeared on these waters came from the shipyard of Mr. John Oades, of that place. Of these the New York and the Bay State,—truly magnificent in their appointments, were afterwards employed on government service in the South. Other lake steamers were used during our late war as blockade runners on the Southern coast.

stations on the river. The business has for a long time depended upon supplies brought down from distant points in the West, and is now greatly reduced from the exhaustion of supplies.

AUTUMNAL SCENERY OF THE NORTHERN STATES AND OF CANADA.

We have noticed in the descriptions of several travellers in the preceding pages an allusion to the coloring of the forests of this region towards the close of autumn, forming, indeed, one of the attractions most likely to fix itself in the memory in the declining season of the year. This was most fully given by the German traveller, Dr. Kohl, whose account of the islands will be found on preceding pages. We will commence the description with his arrival at Kingston, late on a warm, bright, richly-colored autumnal afternoon, when the setting sun presented a most imposing appearance. There was still enough of daylight left to get a fine view of the city and its suburbs, and he departed by steamer for Toronto the same evening. He describes the passage as one of exquisite beauty, the last glow of twilight shedding a glory over the apparently boundless water, which seemed, like the sea, without limit. As it grew dark, the waters presented the novel spectacle of moving lights near the shore, where the fishermen were following their business by torchlight ; and, later in the night, the heavens were lit up by the aurora borealis with unusual splendor.

It may almost be questioned as to whether, amid these shifting scenes of novelty, our worthy traveller got time for a moment's repose, for his description of the midnight aurora, with its gleaming pencils of light, its corona, and its dazzling arch, passes directly into the picture of a morning on the lake, that follows :

" But its splendors were far exceeded in beauty by the tender tints of the aurora orientalis that afterwards showed themselves on the eastern horizon, and then filled the whole atmosphere with their light. A delicate mist had risen toward sunrise, and the sun had made use of this gauzy veil to paint it with the loveliest pale tints. I do not wonder that the taste for coloring should develop itself in such a land of mist, where the palette of nature is provided with such a variety of finely graduated hues. The eye is sharpened to their differences, while in tropical regions, where the chief colors appear most strikingly, the senses are dazzled. As the sun rose, I remarked to my surprise that the redness of the morning dawn had not passed from the horizon, as it commonly does, but remained hanging as a very decided red segment of a circle, and the higher the sun rose, the further it stretched, till towards eleven o'clock it occupied one-half of the horizon, while the opposite side, which was of a light grayish tint, lost ground more and more, and at length the sun appeared as a radiant focus in the center of an atmosphere of light, which, with few variations, passed into red all round the horizon. I saw this remarkable phenomenon here for the first time, but afterwards frequently, and learned that it especially belonged to the ' Indian Summer,' and was known under the name of ' the pink mist.' "

A short time after, our traveller, in passing northward from Toronto, on the route to Lake Simcoe, had occasion to again revert to the glories of the autumnal forest, which he had already noticed in passing amid the Thousand Islands. His description has no local application, but will faithfully represent the impressions of an intelligent observer in the deciduous forests of any part of the Northern States, and of Canada, in the fading season of the year:

" The trees here still gloried in the rich coloring of their leafage, although in Quebec, a fortnight before, the vegetation had assumed a bare and wintry aspect. The elegant and much-prized maple was conspicuous among them, as it mostly is in Canada, and its leaves exhibited more shades and gradations of golden-yellow and crimson than can be found in the best furnished color-box. Even when you walk on dark cloudy days in the forest, the trees shed around you such gorgeous colors that you might imagine it was bright sunlight. You seem to be walking in the midst of some magic sunset of the declining year. The leaves of the maple are, too, as elegantly cut as they are richly adorned with color, and the Canadians pay them the same homage as the Irish do their green immortal shamrock. They are collected, pressed and preserved ; ladies select the most beautiful to form natural garlands for their ball-dresses. You see in Canada tables and other furniture inlaid with bouquets and wreaths of varnished maple leaves, and you see an elegant steamer with the name Maple Leaf painted in large letters on the side. Sometimes the Canadians would ask me, in their glorious woods, whether I had ever seen anything like them in Europe; and if I answered that, though their woods were especially beautiful, I had elsewhere observed red and yellow autumn leaves, they would smile and shake their heads, as if they meant to say that a stranger could never appreciate the beauties of a Canadian forest thus dying in golden flame. I have seen a Swiss, born and bred among the Alps, smile just as pityingly at the enthusiasm of strangers for their mountains, evidently regarding it as a mere momentary flare, and that they only could know how to value the charms of a land of mountains.

"The magnificent coloring of these trees strikes you most, I think, when the gilding has only just begun, and the green, yellow and scarlet tints are mingled with the most delicate transitions. Sometimes it seems as if Nature were amusing herself with these graceful playthings, for you see green trees twisted about with garlands of rich red leaves, like wreaths of roses, and then again red trees, where the wreaths are green. I followed with delight, too, the series of changes, from the most brilliant crimson to the darkest claret color, then to a rich brown, which passed into the cold pale grey of the winter. It seems to me evident that the sun of this climate has some quite peculiar power in its beams, and that the faintest tint of the autumn foliage has a pure intensity of color that you do not see in Europe. Possibly you see the climate and character of Canada mirrored in these autumn leaves, and it is the rapid and violent transitions of heat and cold that produce these vivid contrasts.

"The frost that sometimes sets in suddenly after a very hot day, is said to be one of the chief painters of these American woods. When he does but touch the trees they immediately blush rosy red. I was warned, therefore, not to regard what I saw this year as the ne plus ultra of his artistic efforts, since the frost had come this time very gradually. The summer heat had lasted unusually long, and the drouth had been extraordinary, so that the leaves had become gradually dry and withered, instead of being suddenly struck by the frost while their sap was still abundant, a necessary condition, it appears, for this brilliant coloring."

As if quite unable to tear himself from a subject that had so thoroughly awakened his attention, our keenly observant traveller, after describing many other scenes of Indian and Pioneer life, presented in his northern journey, again recurs to his favorite impressions. He had been so often interrupted by impertinent inquiries, as to who he was, where he was going, on what business, where he intended to buy land, and where he meant to settle, that he had devised a ready means of getting rid of these annoyances — for when he saw one of these inquisitors approaching, he at once began a short biographical recitation, stating where born, his origin, what he had come for and what not, and so forth, ending with the declaration that he did not intend to settle in the country, nor to buy land. As soon as everybody knew who and what he was, they cared little more about him, and having thus cheaply purchased a truce from further inquiry, he could settle down to the calm enjoyment of the scenery before him. He says:

"I would gladly give some idea of its beauty, but it is often difficult to convey impressions of this kind, without falling into repetitions, which, though often far from unwelcome in nature, where there are always shades of difference, are very apt to be so in books. To me, there was a never-ending enjoyment in gazing on the coloring of a Canadian forest in its autumnal glory, and observing the modifications of their colors produced by a greater or less distance. From the immediate foreground to the remotest point there was a scale of a hundred degrees. The trees near at hand were of a full rose or orange hue, and every leaf a piece of glittering gold, and yet every tree had something that distinguished it from all the rest, and although there were only leaves, the colors equalled those of a tropical forest in spring, when it is covered with blossoms. Farther on, the colors were melted together into one general tint of bright pink, then a little blue mingled with it, and there arose several softest tones of lilac; sometimes according to the conditions of the atmosphere, the distant woods appeared of a deep indigo, and then, perhaps, would interpose a little island of glowing red-gold upon an azure ground, but if your eye followed the line of forest to the east, the colors as well as the trees shrank together, and a great wood of leafy oak, elm and maple would look like a low patch of reddish heath."

The poet Whittier, in describing an autumnal scene, strikingly applicable to this region, although intended for another, says:

> Beneath the westward-turning eye
> A thousand wooded islands lie —
> Gems of the waters! — with each hue
> Of brightness set in ocean's blue.
> Each bears aloft its tuft of trees
> Touched by the pencil of the frost,
> And undulating with the breeze.

MISS CLARA BARTON,
President of the American Red Cross, now distributing relief to the sufferers in Armenia.

TO sufferers from war, famine and catastrophe the name of Miss Clara Barton is a familiar one. She was born in Massachusetts in 1830, and in her earlier years was a school teacher, afterwards obtaining a situation in the Patent office at Washington, which place she held when the war broke out.

Just before the first battle of Bull Run, Miss Barton advertised in Massachusetts papers that she would receive stores and money for wounded soldiers at the front, which she would personally distribute. The appeal was so liberally answered that she filled a building with goods. She went with the army and worked night and day nursing, relieving suffering and distributing supplies throughout the war. Through her efforts, thousands of graves of the unknown soldier dead were discovered and marked. Congress recognized her efforts in this direction by awarding her $15,000.

After the war, Miss Barton lectured 300 nights, for which she received $30,000, and drew crowded houses wherever she spoke. In 1869 she went abroad for rest and recuperation. The next year the Franco-Prussian war broke out and she did some effectual work among the wounded, especially at Strasburg. From Strasburg she went to relieve the suffering after the fall of the Commune at Paris. Her services won for her the Prussian order of merit, gave her acquaintance with the working of the Red Cross agencies in Switzerland and Germany, and brought her to the notice of the Empress Augusta.

In 1881, after many disappointments and delays, which seem incredible at this day, the American National Red Cross Association was formally recognized by Congress, and Miss Barton was elected its president.

The first real relief work of the association was done in 1882 when the Mississippi overflowed its banks. Having less than $1,000 in the Red Cross treasury, Miss Barton started for the scene of the disaster. Before she left Washington the wires flashed appeals for aid to be sent at once to Clara Barton at Cincinnati. Aid poured in from every direction. So generous was the response, that more came than was needed. Always frugal, Miss Barton put by the surplus for the next great disaster, which soon followed in the overflow of the Ohio in 1883, and the Louisiana cyclone of the same year. In the following year, the Red Cross

REMARKABLE POT HOLES NEAR THE PALISADES, IN EEL-BAY.

again found work in the overflow of both the Ohio and Mississippi.

In 1884, the government having appropriated $3,000 for the purpose, Miss Barton went to Europe, accompanied by Mr. A. S. Solomons and Hon. Joseph Sheldon, to represent the American Red Cross at the international conference at Geneva.

In 1886, the drouth in Texas necessitated more work by her agents. When the Charleston earthquake occurred the same year, Miss Barton was in California endeavoring to regain her health, but she visited the scene and gave her aid.

The terrible Johnstown disaster occurred May 30, 1889. After Miss Barton arrived on the field, the distribution of clothing was under the personal supervision and direction of the "National Red Cross Headquarters." The entire sum expended by the society, at Johnstown, was $40,000.

The Sea Islands hurricane, which occurred in 1893, and caused widespread destruction of life and property, are still fresh in the recollection of the public. The population of the islands directly affected was about 9,000. The fringe of coast which felt the storm was inhabited by about 35,000 people, the large majority of whom were colored.

Miss Barton had some experience with the negroes of this region in the first months of the war, and so knew how to deal with them. A rigorous system of economy was adopted from the first — a system far more efficacious in the end than any lavish system of charity could have been. [See article upon The Red Cross, page 51.]

FISHING OFF THE HEAD OF "LITTLE GRENADIER," CANADIAN CHANNEL.

EARLY RECOLLECTIONS OF ALEXANDRIA BAY.

BY WILLIAM FAYEL, ESQ., OF ST. LOUIS, MO.

ALEXANDRIA BAY, when I first knew it, just before the existence of railroads in the United States, was a place of small importance. It was a dépôt for the back-country merchants and new settlers who sent lumber, staves and potash, principally for shipment to the Quebec market, and returned with dry goods, salt, etc., for the village stores. Except river transportation, the place was side-tracked on the landward side by the most abominable roads, almost impassable in the spring and fall, so that for years butter and cheese and other country produce were under the control of contractors, forwarded to Watertown and Sackets Harbor, it is true, over better roads, but a much longer route. Owing to its isolated situation, the Bay, which within a few years has attained a magical growth and become the central attraction of the most popular summer resort in America, was, at the time mentioned, unfrequented by the tide of pleasure seekers, except perhaps a few local fishermen. The mode of transportation was then by stage-coach and canal. The world of fashion resorted to Saratoga Springs, the Catskill Mountain House, Niagara Falls, and some favorite sea-side resorts now seldom heard of. The most famous resorts and watering places were brought into journalistic notoriety by letter writers, some wielding graceful pens, as N. P. Willis in the New York Mirror, and Willis Gaylord Clark, the "Ollapod" of the Knickerbocker Magazine. Some of these descriptions were extensively copied, and showed the advantages, as one mode of judicious advertising, in turning the tide of travel and posting the public on the charms and striking beauties of the places described.

I first saw Alexandria Bay in 1832, the cholera of that year having struck Quebec, the earliest outbreak of the dread pestilence on the continent, and then following up the St. Lawrence, it visited Kingston and the large cities, leaving the Bay entirely untouched. The village contained about a dozen frame dwellings and shops, scattered promiscuously among the granite knolls and level grounds, wherever a favorable site offered. The only store, a red frame structure, owned by John W. Fuller, was at the steamboat landing on the lower point jutting into the Bay. The only tavern, a weather-worn frame structure, at the end of the main street, leading to the right on entering the village, was kept by Smith. The front was marked by a flight of wooden stairs that led to the bar-room. This important feature, like all country bar-rooms, had the upper portion of the bar shielded from outside intrusion by a grating of round wooden rods, through which could be seen a row of flint-glass decanters, surmounted by heavy stoppers of the same material. The upper shelf had round glass jars, containing sticks of ribbon-colored candy and Jackson balls.

The edibles consisted of small crackers (two for a cent), then in universal use, and "cookies," a second cousin of the popular ginger-cake. A box of dried herrings was also temptingly displayed to satiate the pangs of appetite, especially when irrigated by draughts of strong liquor. On wooden pegs in the proper place were hung yellow slippers for the retiring guests at bed-time. Tavern customs and the empire of fashion have very materially changed since those pristine days. The open tavern shed, with a loft for hay and oats over head, was located on the Bay at the extreme end of the street. Between the tavern and the store on the water front, was a large wooden warehouse in which the goods, shipped to country merchants were stored until called for. In the open spaces near the warehouse immense piles of staves and lumber were corded up, awaiting shipment, and constituted quite a feature in the river commerce of the place.

In my early recollections of the scenery I recall with curious interest the intensely sea-green color of the waters of the Bay, and the beautiful displays of graphic granite sometimes seen in the rounded granite knobs.

The arrival of a steamer at the wharf in rear of Fuller's store was always an event that enlivened the drowsy quietude of the village. A few passengers would usually step on shore to ease their sea-legs, but the most important personage was the faultlessly-dressed clerk of the steamer who stood on the wharf, with a lot of invoices in his hand noting down or checking the discharge and shipment of freight. To the boyish fancy he was an envied individual, a stupendous official character, through whose deft fingers all business transactions between the shore and steamer had to be transmitted before the boat could leave the wharf. Sometimes a glimpse was obtained of singular people and outré characters, emigrants from foreign lands, making their way towards the illimitable West. At a period somewhat later I saw twenty or thirty young French Canadians land from an up-bound steamer. They were a lusty looking set of youths in robust health, hardy visage, well developed, athletes in strength and physical symmetry of form. They were dressed in fine new suits, rather flashy, and wore their boot-legs outside up to the knees, bound on top with red morocco, with fluttering tassels dangling therefrom. These adventurous young men had left their homes at Chambly, St. Johns and Montreal, and were bound for Green Bay, thence to the fur-trading town of St. Louis. Some thirty years afterwards, while accompanying the Indian Peace Commissioner among the Sioux of the Upper Missouri, I encountered an Indian interpreter, who, as near as time and place could be indentified, was one of the party seen at Alexandria Bay at the period mentioned. This man, like all the French Canadian traders and interpreters, had an Indian wife and a numerous progeny. Our interpreter abandoned his Indian wife and married a respectable white girl at North Platte — General Sherman and the other commissioners being invited to attend the wedding. The relatives of the old squaw came to kill the interpreter's horses in revenge for his desertion of the once attractive and dusky maiden of his youthful days.

Alexandria Bay was slow in coming to the front as a fishing resort, owing to the adverse causes mentioned. In this respect, for several years, Theresa, in the same township, rather took the lead. The stream at that then remote village abounded in the spring with mullet, and throughout the season that king of the piscatory tribe, the muscalonge, came up the Indian River, to the falls at Theresa, and was taken with the spear or trolling spoon. The Sixberries had long beaten up the ground, and the Indian River with its tributary lakes, became the paradise of the hunter, trapper and fisherman. Theresa, as the headquarters for the outfit of boats and fishing tackle, came into note, and was made popular by the annual excursions down the river from that point, of Mr. Norris M. Woodruff, of Watertown, and his friends, who brought with them Loren Soper, an old fisherman acquainted with the ground, and then the keeper of the United States Arsenal at Watertown. There was a fascination amid the scene and haunts of nature, in the wild scenery and freedom from the public gaze in a jaunt of this kind, that a large river, open to all the world, did not possess. No man enjoys reading his newspaper in the thronged thoroughfares.

In spite of these little rivalries of neighboring fishing resorts, Alexandria Bay, in no spirit of jealousy, abided its time. The fame of its waters in yielding abundance of pickerel and muscalonge to the sportive fishermen, became extended far and wide. Of the last named fish it was reported that a big one, the real sockdoger, had been captured by an amateur sportsman from Syracuse, and that in his vain glory he had a full-length picture of himself taken by an artist, with the big fish, held up by the gills, painted by his side.

In due time the Bay became the resort of some famous men, and it is but repeating a twice-told tale to state that among these noted characters were Silas Wright and Martin Van Buren. Of these two distinguished men, I may, in passing, be permitted to mention a phase of their personal traits. Old fishermen tell of the generosity of Silas Wright, in quietly slipping into their hands, on returning from a trip, a liberal "tip," while Mr. Van Buren, less thoughtful, to put it mildly, never exceeded the exact sum stipulated in the contract by dispensing the expected douceur to his boatmen.

It is probable that political friendship, as well as the genial hospitality of the host, rather than the fish, drew these great men to the Bay. The Waltons stood high in social distinction throughout that section. I am speaking from boyhood impressions. They were the first in a small town, and in the neighboring villages were regarded as superior beings. Their arrival at Theresa on a transient visit produced a sensation, among the younger people especially. The head of this family, Mr. Azariah Walton, I regarded as a grand old man, by whom I was always treated with kindness and courtesy. At his store, I frequently saw his massive figure seated behind the counter employed in thumping some refractory substance into use for trolling spoons.

The shelves in the rear were garnished with lines, hooks, bright brass spoons and other fishing tackle. In one corner was seen a forest of fishing poles, some of these being suspended by wooden supports overhead, like the old-time rifle on hooks, in the hunter's cabin. In the winter section, skates were suspended, showing that a demand for these articles could be supplied at all seasons.

Mr. Walton was collector of customs for the port. He never disparaged the duties of the office, and spoke with pride of his success in checking and finally putting an end to smuggling, that formerly prevailed to the detriment of the goverment. He once told me that the revenue collected from customs in the Cape Vincent district, to which he was attached, exceeded in amount that collected in any other port of the United States, as the official figures would verify. He was withal a warm political partisan, the leading Democrat in that section, and though his mercantile partner, John W. Fuller, was a pronounced Whig, no disputes on that score seeming to disturb their business relations. But to his outside political opponents he was not sparing in his jibes and sarcastic hits at their expense. With what unction would the words "Whig" and "Whiggery" roll from his tongue, in contemptuous tones and in utter depreciation of the claims of that young and growing party.

In those anti-Masonic and early Whig days, the election was held on three successive days in separate precincts. Theresa was then attached to the town of Alexandria, and when the election was held in that precinct, Mr. Walton always came up in full force, a dreaded opponent, in his withering gibes, to the leading Whigs, Squire Nathan M. Flower, Anson Ranney and Benjamin Still. The division of the town at length gave these good men a rest. Amid his multifarous business and official duties, Squire Walton found leisure to court the poetical muse. He composed campaign songs, which were never written out or read; one of these he recited to me, the burden of which extolled in the popular rhymes of that day, "The Favorite Son of Kinderhook."

In closing this imperfect sketch of a notable man, I desire to add, that although a violent partisan, he was a patriotic lover of his country. When the Mexican war broke out, he everywhere, in and out of season, denounced the opposition to President Polk and the war, declaring that it was unpatriotic in private individuals and bar-room ranters, to question the right or wrong of the war, when the honor of the country was at stake.

His eldest son, George Walton, followed in the footsteps of his father, as a politician, and as his active life, too early cut off by the fell destroyer, comes within the period under consideration, a word may be added. Much might be said in praise of this gentleman who bore "the mould of beauty and of form," but one incident only will be given, illustrative of the times, in his connection with "general training day," that great event of mustering battalions and parody on grim war, always looked forward to by wondering youths and gingerbread-vendors as a gala day, now gone into desuetude, and is only a memory of the past. George Walton was the colonel of a militia regiment; and his brother-in-law, General Archibald Fisher, commander of the brigade, transferred the general muster, from Antwerp, where it assembled from time immemorial, to Theresa. Col. Walton, as the ranking officer, superintended the customary evolutions, and towards evening he headed the perspiring troops in their march from the Cooper farm, where the muster was held, to the village. The militia companies were halted, and on being massed in regulation order for dismissal, the gallant colonel in a grandiose speech, not unmixed with a quiet undercurrent of humor, wished the men a safe return to their homes, their waiting wives and children, and capped the climax of dismissal by designating the brigade as "soldiers of the great American Army."

As if to add to the ludicrous character of the scene, an auctioneer from the Quaker settlement, named Kirkbright, who had been vending gingerbread during the day, brought forward for sale a menagerie of wild and tame sugar animals. Having disposed of the elephants at a fair valuation, he then held up between his thumb and finger a two-cent rooster, with red comb and gills, about the size of a small ball of yarn. The bids started at one cent, with no raise for some time, when the auctioneer shouted forth indignantly, "Soldiers of the American Army! How can you stand idly by, with arms in your hands, and see property thus sacrificed in the market place?"

Recurring to matters at the Bay, I once, on a visit there, met with an enjoyable incident, characteristic of the chronic characters that one frequently meets with. I was attracted by two gentlemen in front of the hotel, who appeared hotly engaged in a religious discussion,—the one a skeptic; the other, whom I took to be a religious enthusiast by the warmth with which he supported his side of the argument. Gifted in speech, he overwhelmed his antagonist with a torrent of excellent advice, as well as sound argument.

The reverend gentleman proved to be the Rev. P. C. Headley, the author of a popular "Life of the Empress Josephine." He was then quite a young-looking man. He informed me that he was settled in the ministry at Adams, Jefferson county, and was on the way to join his brother, Rev. J. T. Headley, also a widely-known author on war heroes, for a trip through the great Northern woods, then, as may be remembered, unvexed by the Rev. Adirondack Murray and his fellow tourists. Mr. Headley turned out to be a most genial companion, full of animal spirits, and ready to indulge in boat excursions and other pastimes, except playing billiards, then a favorite amusement among the frequenters of the place.

A boat party was made up to sail among the islands, with Mr. Ed. Tanner, collector of the port, in charge. We trolled up the streams, and encountering a squall, landed on a nameless island. While there, a large sail boat, it might be called a yacht, also landed on the island, driven in by stress of weather. An elderly, sturdy-looking man came on shore and looked anxiously around. The newcomer proved to be the famous Bill Johnston, whose name became linked with the Thousand Islands.

He wore a blouse, a plain-looking old gentleman, with strong features and an expression of determination about the mouth. Otherwise he would be taken for a very ordinary farmer, in general appearance. He was rather reticent and conversed in a low tone of voice, as is usual in men supposed to have some great secrets locked up in the breast. He was a man just to Mr. Headley's hand, who pumped the old gentleman as to the history of the islands and his connection with them during the late troubles. Johnston, meantime, had a far-away look, his mind reverting to his boat and the condition of the weather. After the detention of a couple of hours we parted, on a lull in the gale.

Before the extension of telegraph lines, and with limited postal connections inland, the people of the Bay were behind their neighbors in getting the news. But this was not always the case, very important news reaching there by river in advance of the neighboring villages. An instance may be given. About the 12th of July, 1850, going with a party to the Bay, when arrived within three miles of the place, we met old Ezra Cornwall, father of George W. Cornwall of Theresa, coming up the road on foot, who imparted the intelligence that General Taylor, President of the United States, was dead. The news was received at the Bay by steamer from Oswego, and was unknown at Theresa until obtained from this source.

My last visit to Alexandria Bay was in 1867, when, after the absence of some years, great changes in the aspect of the town were visible. Two hotels, the renowned Crossmon House, widely known, and the St. Lawrence Hotel, kept by Edward Fayel, assisted by his sister, Mrs. Sophia Spalsbury, were in operation. Since then a greater change, amounting to a perfect "transformation scene," has supervened, supplementing the wonders of natural beauty with the improvements suggested by unsparing wealth, art and taste. But despite all these enchanting improvements, effected by man, the great natural features of rocky islands and glorious river will stand unaltered till the end of time.

JONATHAN THOMPSON.

Among the earliest to forsee and urge the advantages of the Thousand Islands as a resort for pleasure seekers, and the establishment of a hotel to entertain them, was doubtless Jonathan Thompson, of Theresa. Thompson was a genial character, quaint in speech, or rather of cute sayings, a harmless romancer with a brain fertile in projects. He was a man past middle age, buoyant in hope as a grown-up boy, had seen something of the world, and, in fact, among his early experiences, had "gone out" with the Green Mountain Boys in September, 1814. In working up his scheme he had visited the islands, selected one of the group to erect a fishermen's resort upon. But the time had not come for the realization of such an enterprise. Other more favorable and fortuitous circumstances had to arise before the scheme could become practicable. Thompson would have made a good second to a man of financial ability; a good chief of a restaurant, and a capital entertainer of guests.

A few years before this time, Thompson had pitched upon one of the most romantic little lakes, situated between the Indian and St. Lawrence rivers, much nearer the first named stream, as a home, which he intended to improve. It was an expanse of clear, limpid water, nestled among wood-crowned shores, six miles from any settlement. It had lost its Indian name, the lake being on the main water route followed by the Canadian Indians during the French and Indian War, and up to the War of the Revolution, in their predatory incursions to the Dutch settlements on the Mohawk. In recent times the hulks of their abandoned boats could be seen lying deep through the clear water on the lake bottom. It was known as Lake of the Woods, latterly as Thompson's Lake, from the new proprietor, and was three miles in length north and south, and from one mile and a half to half a mile in breadth.

In a spirit of enterprise and unbounded hopes that inspired visionary schemes, Thompson pre-empted a few acres, near the western cove, which a squatter had cleared up and abandoned, leaving his deserted log cabin among the assets of the place. On obtaining possession, his original design was to stock the ranch with geese, as his flocks would have the unlimited privilege, like himself, of the lake. But, owing to a change in domestic economy (except among the blanket Indians, who still adhered to skins for bed clothing), feather beds began to be discarded, and a demand for feathers consequently ceased. He, therefore, was compelled "to feather his nest" in some other more profitable product. Whereupon, like Thoreau, the hermit of Waldon Pond, he determined to cultivated a bean patch, finally adding to his agricultural operations crops of potatoes, cabbage and cucumbers. On an adjoining little islet, that rose like a wart above the bosom of the lake, the only excrescence of the kind that fretted the ripples into complaining murmurs, he erected a house of primitive accommodation. In its construction, he was ably assisted by a Watertown journalist (JOHN FAYEL), who, seeking recuperation for broken health, found pleasant recreation in the exercise of his constructive talents upon very scant materials. Poles were ferried across from the opposite beach, and the deserted log-cabin of the squatter was dismantled of its boards, shingles, nails and window sash, to supply the needed material. That house was a "daisy," and ranked with the common shanty in architectural adornment, having a door swung on hinges, and a window to admit the light. It was a large single barrack-like room, and for years became also the sleeping apartment of tired pleasure-seekers, who, rolled up in their blankets on the board floor, were lulled to sleep by the monotonous chafing of the ripples on the beach.

Meantime, chance visitors to the lake returned with enchanting descriptions of its varied beauties. Mr. Thompson, on his return to the village, exhausted the vocabulary of adjectives in extolling its wonders. It was "the land of promise" spoken of in the Scriptures, the original "Fountain of Youth," sought after by De Soto, "the loveliest spot under the canopy," to use his favorite expression. In truth, his representations could not well exaggerate the admitted beauties of the lake and wild surroundings.

Curiosity was worked up to a high pitch, and to gratify it by actual realization, an expedition was fitted out, composed of some twenty or thirty citizens, who descended the river in boats. Mr. Thompson took the lead alone in his little canoe, ballasted with a few sacks of provisions. As commodore of the fleet, he issued instructions, and paddled ahead, a happy man, not unmindful of his glory. From long experience he became a marvel in handling a paddle, which he did as deftly as an Indian. He protested against a useless waste of power and misapplied movements of the arm in paddling. "Never," said he, "dip the paddle too far ahead, as the force would then be expended in lifting up the keel of the boat, but when the paddle falls in a perpendicular line with the rower's body, then the back-push against the resisting medium gave the only impulse forward to the boat." In his progress, to show off his dexterity and knowledge of the river, he sometimes cut across a bend, through rushes and over lilly-pads, thereby avoiding a long detour in keeping to the currents. About seven miles down the river a landing was made for a march of three miles over the carrying place to the foot of the lake. The landing place was designated by a beacon seen from a long distance above, consisting of the stub of a big tree on the bluff, which had been splintered by a thunderbolt. From the landing place to the lake, the labors of the traverse commenced, sometimes through thickets and underbrush, over fallen logs, and across swails and quagmires; but a portion of the route was unobstructed. The men started cheerily forward, lugging paddles, fishing poles, and sacks of flour, salt pork and other supplies of the commissary department. Thompson took the lead as generalissimo of the expedition overland, limping briskly forward, shouting words of encouragement, and ready to diverge from the route to show up some remarkable scenery; in one of these, for instance, from the brink of a precipice, was seen, spread out beneath, a vast marsh, carpeted with moss, extending for miles towards the river.

Arriving at the foot of the lake, a halt was called, when the generalissimo expatiated on the wonders of the scene soon to open on the astonished gaze. To many minds, striking images, thus presented to the imagination, through the ear, even when conveyed through the medium of gushing, bloviating rhetoric, leave a stronger impression than when conveyed to the eye by careless observation.

At the place of embarkation on the lake there was but one canoe and two leaky skiffs to take the party to the Island House, the terminus of their toils. When tired and hungry, curiosity lags, and the most romantic scenery loses its charm. The party divided, some passing up one side and others on the opposite side, to the nearest point, until Mr. Thompson, having landed the first installment from the boats, could cross over and take them to the island. The shouts of the men in their slow progress along the heavily wooded shores, the Sabbath day, hundreds of visitors flocked to the lake, some to fish, but mostly others to gather huckle (whortle) berries, blue-berries and raspberries, which abounded in their proper season on the bluffs and in the swamps; but Mr. Thompson received little or no revenue from these people, who accepted his hospitality rather as friends than as paying guests.

The lake abounded in black bass, a most edible fish. He had a favorite spot, a headland, for catching them, and having captured a lot of small frogs for bait in the damp grass

AN ICE-BOAT, WINTER OF 1895-96.

and the responsive shouts from the opposite side, kept up continuously for several hours, startled the three loons seen sailing on the lake, causing the bewildered birds to tack from one point to the other, for no such yells had stirred up the wild varmints in that region since the ancient war-whoop was sounded by the Indian warriors that passed through on their scalping expeditions.

In the course of time boating facilities were increased, and some days, more particularly on the evening before, at dawn would paddle out in his canoe, that could be seen courtseying in the distance like a dark bubble, and returning with "the beauties," as he called them, had them served up for breakfast. On rainy days he rowed to the east side of the lake, where the deep water was filled with the branches of dead cedar trees that had fallen in, and rowing slowly along, in perhaps two hours' time, he would return with the bottom of his boat covered by the flopping beauties.

He had an intimate knowledge of the habits of fish — those shrinking creatures best studied when out of their native element. Of birds and beasts, he also possessed an intimate knowledge of their habits and instincts. Regarding the loons, to which reference has been made, he believed with old hunters that they could not be killed by a rifle while on the water, though he would not permit the experiment to be tried upon the loons that frequented his lake. The tradition concerning these wary birds is that they can dodge a bullet after seeing the flash, for instantly diving down, they remain for some time under water, and emerge to the surface a long distance from the spot where they went under. Thompson said he could predict a change of weather from the movements of his loons. It was observed that owing to their heavy conformation they could not rise in a calm much above the surface of the lake, and when inclined to change their present habitat, they flew against the wind, which lifted them above the woods, thus affording an exit beyond their old prison limits.

He declared that his loons, before a storm, would sail to the head of the lake, and when the south wind blew they would rise, and, flapping their wings, seem to walk on the water, but rising gradually, the wind buoying them upward higher and higher, until they reached the lower end of the lake, three miles distant from the place of starting, they would attain such an elevation as to clear the highest trees, and, thus regaining their freedom, seek "fresh fields and pastures new." He remarked the curious fact that though they could dodge a bullet on the wave, they could not dodge a tree in a calm.

Talking about the instincts of animals, he once remarked on a curious habit of the bears. On a heavily wooded ridge along the west side of the lake, there was a certain tree that on one side was deeply gashed, as if made by some huge gnawing animal. It would heal over for a time, like the scar made on a maple tree by the sugar-tapper's axe, and then it would exhibit a freshened appearance, like the re-opening of an old wound.

This peculiar phenomenon, old hunters declare, was the work of bears. It was a guidepost to them in their journeys, the same as blazed trees were to any backwoodsman. The bears, in traversing the woods from Canada to the great northern wilderness, thus left their mark as a guide to the other bears which followed them on the same path. Each bear in passing would stand on his plantigrade feet, gnaw out a fresh chunk, to be freshened up by his successors, and thus the great bear-route, a genuine international line, was kept open.

I once asked Prof. Ebenezer Emmons, the geologist of our district, his opinion as to the truth of the statement. The eminent naturalist rather doubted the explanation, and attributed gnawing of the tree to the rutting season of those animals.

As the novelty of Mr. Thompson's kind of life wore away he turned his eye to the Thousand Islands with the outcome as before stated.

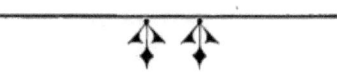

THE GULF OF ST. LAWRENCE.

IT may happen that this book will fall into the hands of some one who is more than a mere pleasure-seeker among the Thousand Islands, who shall desire to know more of the ocean end of the great St. Lawrence river, which flows down through the finest scenery in the world, from grand Lakes Superior and Michigan, through Huron, St. Clair, Erie and Ontario —

"Vast lakes, which float the grain and ore
Of mighty States from shore to shore,
A thousand billowy miles and more."

If the reader be such an one, he will be glad when told that the author of this Souvenir is one of the few whom he may meet who has traversed the whole Gulf, even from Labrador, Belle Isle and Newfoundland, up to Quebec.

Passing by the many interesting towns below Quebec, and reserving for another article the journey up the grand Saguenay, as well as a description of some of the delightful summer resorts where the fashion and beauty of Lower Canada disport themselves during the short but warm Northern summer months, we will pass down the great river straight to Anticosti island (some 400 miles below Quebec) where the Canadian authorities maintain a light-house. It is almost a barren island, but the time will come in the not distant future when its size and location will make it an important spot, perhaps a summer resort. It lies in the Gulf, longest from west to east, but is so much nearer the north shore of the Gulf as to be readily passed unobserved by vessels traversing the center of that wide roadstead. By bearing north by east from Anticosti you would reach Labrador at the straits of Belle Isle, after sailing about 450 miles. But it is not in that direction we will now conduct the reader, though one who has a summer to spend and don't care much where he spends it, two months on Labrador would be wholly unique and perhaps interesting. It is a land without a local government, being so far away and so essentially uninviting as not to be worth the cost to Canada of maintaining courts, or those other formulas by which civilization is supposed to be advanced. But Canada maintains light-houses there. The writer made some good friends on Labrador in his youthful days, and recalls that region by many pleasant memories.

But we will bear south by east from Anticosti, traversing the wide Gulf of which every one has doubtless heard, but few are aware of the attractions it offers to the tourist and artist. Even to those who have given it much thought it is generally regarded as a region of mists and storms, and more or less enveloped in hyperborean gloom. But recently sportsmen and yacht sailors have begun to visit the southwestern shores of the Gulf, and the summer rambler finds that this part of the world has been more or less maligned, and that during July and August it offers a variety of attractions hitherto almost unknown. To make clear our idea we will take the reader into one town, upon one of the main islands of the great Gulf.

If the traveller were to desire to cruise around a part of the Gulf of St. Lawrence, and should make Charlottetown, Prince Edward's Island, his starting point, he would be in a situation to get a vast amount of real pleasure from his journeyings.

Tuesdays and Fridays are the days when Charlottetown shows the most evidence of activity and commercial prosperity. In the square where the government buildings are located may be found the market-house. On these days it is crowded by both the town and country folk, and among the latter will be found now and then an Indian. An active barter for provisions is kept up for a greater part of the day. But this delightful town is not what it once was. The Dominion government has made such drastic laws that nearly all the American fishermen have been driven away from these waters, where their enterprise and industry once made business lively. Thus the goose has been nearly killed that laid the golden eggs, and places like Charlottetown suffer from unwise legislation.

In Summer, Prince Edward Island enjoys a delightful temperature, the mercury ranging for about three months from 60 to 76°. The air is dry and almost entirely free from fogs, and as the winds inevitably come off the sea, the island is very healthful, nearly all the old people being obliged to move away to die. The island has peculiar advantages for summer visitors from the liberal supply and the comparative cheapness of all kinds of country produce. Personal pleasure is enhanced by the lovely drives in every direction over a country that is gently undulating and always in sight of the sea. The rivers, notably the Dunk, the Hunter and the Morell, abound with fine salmon and trout, and the long reaches of land along the easterly shore are frequented by snipe, plover and duck resting there on their journeys northward or southward. At Rustico and Arcadie the summer landlord is much in evidence, and there the best accommodations can be found. And it is in the flitting thitherward of the migratory summer visitor, with pockets full of gold, that the islanders may look for the return of that prosperity driven away by the laws which shut out American fishermen from neighboring waters.

The facilities for observing the unique scenery of Prince Edward Island are much enhanced by the narrow-gauge railroad, kept up by the Dominion government, but which does not yet repay expenses. Lobster canning has also assumed considerable dimensions upon the island, but it can hardly be classed as a stable or certain industry, for these homely crustaceans cannot be altogether depended upon. Singular as it may appear, they take no interest whatever in the philanthropic designs of capitalists and fishermen to ship them to market in elegantly labeled tin cases, and declining to co-operate in these schemes, they have a disagreeable way of remaining away at seasons when anxiously expected.

Gazing over the pleasant landscapes and breathing the ozone-laden air at Prince Edward Island, one hardly comprehends that for many months the island is covered with snow to an enormous depth, but is also shut out from the rest of the world by a tremendous barrier of ice. From January to May, Northumberland Strait is frozen over. The mails are carried across at the narrowest part, near Cape Tormentine or Jourimain, a distance of nine miles. The carriers drag a boat over the hummocks of ice, the boat being provided with runners like a sleigh. When they come to open water they launch the boat. It is an arduous and perhaps dangerous journey, and the mail carriers have few passengers. Were it not for this prolonged hybernation and being shut out from the rest of the world amidst immense bodies of snow, Prince Edward Island would be a veritable paradise.

Money goes a great way upon this island, for it is scarce. The people are mostly of Scotch descent, but there is still a remnant of the Mic-mac tribe of Indians occupying a reservation on Indian island in Richmond Bay. There are some descendants of the original Acadian French yet upon the island, about Rustico and Ingowich. These are farmers. They have a convent at the latter place. But the Highland Scotch are far the most numerous people upon Prince Edward Island. They came originally from the Hebrides, driven away by the religious oppression of the lairds. They have increased and multiplied. Nearly half of the inhabitants are Roman Catholics, though there are many Protestant Scotch. They are more than usually tolerant towards each others' religious views.

A region so remote as Prince Edward Island and shut in for seven months of the year from the "wide, wide world," must of necessity produce many unique characters. One of the most prominent families upon the island is that of James Yeo, who accumulated a large fortune in shipbuilding. His sons were in the Dominion parliament. He came out from England as a cabin boy, and the rough school in which he was bred marked his character and his speech. He once lost a brig, and three of the crew perished. Alluding to the misfortune he lamented: "Poor things—two souls gone and one Irishman."

We ought to mention, historically, that Prince Edward Island was discovered by Cabot, who called it St. John's Island, which name it retained until 1800. Verrazzino took possession of it for France as early as 1523—473 years ago. The island became British by the treaty of Fontainbleau.

We have thus very briefly sketched one town upon the Gulf of St. Lawrence and enumerated one island. There are many islands of more or less repute and population, and there are other towns. Had we space we would take the reader further east—to New Brunswick, Paspebiac, the Bay of Gaspe, Nova Scotia, the Bay of Chaleurs, the Magdalen Islands, the Gut of Cansu and far-away Newfoundland. What we have said may open the eyes of some traveller to the fact that the regions upon the southeast side of the Gulf of St. Lawrence are not uninviting, nor inhabited by savages. There are delightful places of sojourn in summer, with the best fishing in the world, and the least expensive living if we take quality and quantity into account. We know of no place where the people are more healthy, hospitable and independent. Individual and unique characters are plentiful, as is usually the case in a region where man is cast mainly upon his own resources. While not learned, they are peculiarly practical, possessing that kind of ability which makes the most of every surrounding, and forces nature itself to yield to the industrious persistence of man. We can but express again our regret that our limited space precludes further reference this year to this most interesting section of British North America.

A SUMMER INSTITUTE ESTABLISHED AT THOUSAND ISLAND PARK.

AMONG the bills signed by Governor Morton is one providing for three summer institutes to be held under the direction of the State Superintendent of Public Instruction.

Superintendent Skinner has located one of these schools at Thousand Island Park, St. Lawrence river, to be held from July 15th to August 7th, 1896, inclusive. It is the intention that this institute shall rank with that which has been held for several years at Chautauqua and at Glens Falls, each of which has had a very large attendance of teachers. The superior facilities of Thousand Island Park and upon the adjoining islands, the beauty of the river, its matchless scenery and bracing air, should make it one of the most attractive places in the State for an institute, and the teachers of the northern portion of the State who have been remote from these facilities so long will, without doubt, attend in large numbers. Arrangements are made for cottages for those teachers who may desire to organize a club and provide their own home, thus combining a pleasant vacation at one of the healthiest summer resorts on the continent with the advantages of instruction by many of the most prominent school men in the United States.

It is confidently expected that this institute will become a permanent matter at Thousand Island Park or at Murray Hill Park, the new resort which has come into prominence in 1896, and gives promise of a great future.

A FEW "DON'TS" FOR EXCURSIONISTS.

DON'T be in too great a hurry, you will get along easier.

DON'T rush to get on board the steamer until the passengers are off, and then you can get on board without rushing.

DON'T push, and jam, and crowd, either in going ashore or aboard; you only hinder and delay.

DON'T stop to gossip on the gang-plank, it blocks the passage and delays others.

A PARTIAL VIEW OF MURRAY HILL HOTEL.

MURRAY HILL HOTEL AND PARK.

DURING the whole season of 1895 visitors to the Thousand Islands were surprised to see the vast piles of lumber, timber and building material being collected on the head of Hemlock Island, just at the entrance to Eel Bay, and at a point where a bold back ground had given away to a breadth of shore that seemed to invite a stately building. All summer long a great array of work-people were kept there, and at last the object of all this labor and material was manifest in a great hotel, four stories high, over 300 feet long, and containing rooms for 500 guests. When snow began to fall this noble building was turned over by the contractor to the proprietors, and it has been fitted up with every appliance that taste and comfort can require, and there has sprung into existence, without any great amount of advertising or newpaper mention one of the largest and most complete hotels upon the St. Lawrence river.

The public owe this grand improvement to the organizing mind of Mr. A. Corbin, Jr., of Gouverneur, and to the indefatigable industry and activity of Capt. " Jack " Taylor, the original proprietor of Hemlock Island, for which he once recklessly paid $100 in cash and a second-hand shot-gun. The island could not now be bought for $100,000. But no matter who bought the island or built the hotel, there they stand "in evidence," with surroundings the most enduring and beautiful on the river. These are the points the visitor is interested in, and they form the attractive influences which will draw to this spot those who seek for rest and enjoyment and yet wish to be " right in the swim." The railroad docks at Clayton are in plain sight from Murray Hill Hotel, no boat can pass up or down that is not visible from its windows, for every room has an out-of-door out look. It is readily reached, is the second landing below Clayton, in the very centre of the best fishing on the river, and yet enough secluded to prove a veritable resting-place for those who wish to avoid noise or hurly-burly. We predict for this great improvement a decided success, and that the foresight of its proprietors will meet with a just reward for their labors and their investment.

FOREST G. WEEKS.

FOREST G. WEEKS.

FOREST G. WEEKS, of Skaneateles, was born in Draycott, Somersetshire, England, August 2, 1832. His parents were Stephen and Ruth Weeks. Forest G. Weeks, the subject of this sketch, was one of a family of eight children, seven of whom came to this country. Forest G. was only seventeen years of age when he left his native country to seek his fortune in the new world. The success he has achieved is evidence that he possessed the metal and ability to make his way against the many obstacles that beset the road even of the native born American. He came to Skaneateles in 1849 and at once apprenticed himself to learn the blacksmith's trade. His time and talents were devoted to this occupation for the succeeding five years. Then not being satisfied with the education so far acquired, he wisely concluded to attend school for a time. This was carried out by taking a course at the Falley Seminary in Fulton, Oswego county, N. Y. The winters in the meantime were spent in teaching school, and thus accumulating sufficient money to defray the expenses of his course in the seminary.

After having completed his course of study at the seminary, Mr. Weeks returned in 1857 to Skaneateles and entered upon a business career that has now continued with remarkable success for nearly forty years. He did not return to the occupation of blacksmith, but at once engaged in the teasel business, which was then an important industry in Onondaga county. Mr. Weeks not only raised this product, but carried on a large business as a dealer in teasels. The enterprise proved eminently successful, and so Mr. Weeks remained in that line till 1867. In the meanwhile energy and good management had enabled him to accumulate money to extend his business interests in other directions. That year (1867) he purchased a one-half interest in the paper manufactory, which is now known as the Brick Mill. This mill is situated on the Skaneateles outlet about three and one-half miles from the village. The firm name then was Bannister & Weeks, and so continued four years, when Mr. Weeks by purchasing the interest of Mr. Bannister, became sole proprietor. He still conducts this mill, turning out a large product. It was destroyed by fire in 1872, but was at once rebuilt and enlarged with more modern design and equipment. Its output is now from six to seven tons of paper per day.

The Draycott Mill was established a little later, the daily product of which now averages five to six tons per day. The third mill, which is now owned by Mr. Weeks, was formerly owned and run by the Skaneateles Paper Co. Mr. Weeks first purchased a minority interest in this company but at the same time bought the entire product of the mill. This business continued several years when Mr. Weeks also purchased the total capital stock of the company, thus becoming sole owner of the property. This mill too has an output of eight tons of paper per day. In 1882 another extension of the business was made by the purchase of the Earll, Tallman & Co. distillery, which was remodeled and converted into another paper mill. It is run as a stock company and is known as the Lakeside Paper Co. In this mill are manufactured mill wrappers, building paper, carpet paper, felts, etc., turning out about six tons per day. These comprise four of the largest mills on the stream. Besides these, Mr. Weeks in company with Mr. Edwin R. Redhead, established what is now known as the Victoria Mills Paper Co., at Fulton, Oswego county, N. Y. The company a little later bought the upper power on the Fulton side of the falls and erected thereon a large wood pulp mill, now producing thirty-five tons of pulp per day. In 1890 Mr. Weeks and Mr. Redhead separated, Mr. Redhead taking the Victoria Mills and the former the Upper Falls Pulp Mill, which he still owns. Thus it will be seen that Mr. Weeks is one of the largest manufacturers of the paper product in the United States.

Associated with Mr. Weeks in his many business enterprises are his three sons, Charles G., Forest G., Jr., and Julius S. Besides these there is Mr. H. L. Paddock, formerly of Wolcott, Wayne county, N. Y., who married Mary L., eldest daughter of Mr. and Mrs. Weeks. She is a graduate of Cazenovia Seminary. They also have another daughter, Sara L., who graduated at the Syracuse University. Mr. Weeks married in September, 1859, Sarah A. Monell, of Mexico, Oswego county, N. Y.

Mr. Weeks is also a stockholder and director in the Thousand Island Park Association, at which place he, together with his family, spend the summer. He is a member of the Methodist Episcopal Church and represented the same in the General Conference of 1880. He is, besides this, one of the trustees of Syracuse University and Cazenovia Seminary. The deep interest he has always taken in educational institutions, and especially those named, has been backed by his upbuilding influence and a generous contribution of money. Mr. Weeks has always been an active, earnest Republican in politics, and had he been so inclined, would have been honored by an election to almost any office within the gift of the citizens of Onondaga county. In this as in all other matters he has the confidence and esteem of all who know him.

YACHTING.

BY GEORGE A. STEWART.

In "OUT-DOORS," published by the Pope M'f'g Co., the Original Bicycle Manufacturers.

IT is a well known fact that lovers of the sea consider yachting to be the highest of all sports. The fundamental principle which underlies all the best sports we have—that of a life out-of-doors, where fine air and sunshine do their glorious part in building up the physique—applies to yachting, in common with foot-ball, base ball, rowing, bicycling, tennis, cricket, and other sports a-field.

One grand feature of sports in the open air is that they simulate uncounscious exercise, and herein lies half of their beneficial effect. It is idle for the physician to prescribe a gymnasium-course for the average young man of sedentary occupation, for he looks upon such exercise as so much work, and soon tires of it. But put the same young fellow into a game of ball, or on a bicycle, or aboard a yacht for a cruise—whichever may be his particular hobby—and he will go to bed with a delicious sense of physical weariness without having appreciated that he was doing any work at all.

Sports are the salvation of our youth, and it is remarkable that they should have been frowned upon, or at best tolerated, for so long a time. The most natural tendency of a growing boy, or girl for that matter, is to play at some game all day long. Nature is wiser than man in this, as in all other things, and the present age has learned to follow nature, and to encourage the young to healthful exercise.

Which is the best form of sport is not for anyone to decide. They all have their virtues, and the taste and circumstances of individuals may be best left to select the most useful. While yachting has not so many devotees as some other sports, its admirers make up in enthusiasm what they lack in numbers. It can be pursued to advantage only on the open sea or on some tolerably large lake. That was the reason for the Chippewa Yacht Club locating in that wide arm of the river. (See p. 79.)

The number who sail the seas for pleasure is astonishingly large, and rapidly increasing, for the water rarely loses its fascination for those who have once tasted its allurements.

There is more or less of an opinion prevalent that yachting is an expensive sport, one to be indulged in only by the rich. Such an idea is as far as possible from the truth. It is true that the millionaire finds plenty of opportunity of gratifying expensive tastes in that connection, and palatial Alvas and Atalantas attest the royal scale upon which yachting may be enjoyed. Yet it is doubtful if a Vanderbilt or a Gould gets any more real pleasure out of a half-a-million dollar steam yacht than the owner of a snug little single-hander, who lives more cheaply on his yacht than he could possibly live ashore.

I remember a striking instance of this. A well-known millionaire yachtman was standing idly on the bridge of his 200-foot steam yacht one day, when a friend of his sailed by in his 30-footer. The millionaire's eyes kindled as he saw the fun his friend was having, and with a touch of sadness in his tone, he called out: "I wish I could get as much fun out of my big boat as you do out of your little one." The two men were intimate friends, so there was nothing of snobbishness about this remark, nor of impertinence in the reply of the owner of the 30-footer, which was: "The trouble with you is that you own so many things you don't know how to enjoy any of them. I've only got one plaything, and so I make the most of it."

Take a party of four young fellows off for a cruise on the wide St. Lawrence, or on Long Island Sound, or along the Maine coast, and they realize nearly the acme of human pleasure. Their yacht may be small and inexpensive, they may have to put up with cramped accommodations, and a doubtful diet prepared by their own hands, each officiating as *chef* in turn, yet the two weeks or more which they will spend on the cruise, will be weeks of solid fun.

The supposed perils of the water have kept many from this most fascinating of sports. The truth of the matter is that yachting is one of the safest of sports. There is just enough danger to add that spice of adventure which attracts the Anglo Saxon race. Quick judgment, skill, pluck and endurance are continually called into play by an association with the sea.

Quite distinct from cruising, and becoming more so every year, is the sport of yacht racing. The idea of combining the cruiser and racer in one hull is a very attractive one. Not many years ago, indeed at the present time, in nearly all classes, the clever yachtsman could cross the finish line of a hard-fought race in the smoke of the winning gun, hastily dump a few stores and extra gear aboard his craft, and set sail for the eastward for a cruise in as staunch and comfortable a craft as one could wish to own.

Keen racing competition, however, is driving the sport into craft built especially for racing, with no thought of cruising comfort. As the family horse is no longer harnessed to the sulky, nor the trotter tied up to the carryall for the family driving, so the tendency is to divide the racing and cruising yachts more sharply.

Take the little fleet of this year, how fine and thorough-bred they all look to the racing man, and how ugly to the cruiser. The latter protests they are not yachts at all, but "machines." Presently he ranges along side with his sturdy cutter, and is first amazed and then lost in admiration of the wonderful speed of the tiny craft. As he tacks ship, and runs in for the anchorage, he murmurs grudgingly to himself: "I guess the darned little things have come to stay," and the chances are that he will order a "fin" or a "sand-bagger," or something even worse, with which to "do up" the fleet the coming year.

It is the great advantage of yacht racing that it is, and must remain, a "clean" sport, unhurt by the evils of professionalism. It costs so much to build and run a racing yacht, and the prizes are so small that there is no money in racing for the prizes as a business. The racing man must race for the love of the sport and the ambition of winning. The gambling spirit finds little to feed upon in yachting contests.

For the skillful amateur there is nothing more full of interest than a yacht race. From the time that the preparatory signal is given, he is all alert, counting the seconds so as to have his ship just on the line when the starting gun is fired. Once away, and every sense is at its keenest pitch, to catch the slightest advantage of varying wind or tide, or to keep one's competitor from getting the best of it. The elements of the water are stable enough in nearly every race to let the fastest boat win, yet there is just enough uncertainty and possibility of "fluke" to make every sailor in the fleet work his hardest and not give up till the winning gun is fired.

For those who object to the extreme competition of the racing classes, with its consequent "out-building" and a new boat every year or two, handicap racing offers a good deal of sport. In the handicap class the cruisers and out-built racers meet and each receives an allowance of time which is supposed to put all on an equal basis. The slower the boat the more time allowance she receives. Such races as these invariably attract large entries, and the tail-ender who lags in half an hour behind the first boat and wins by the aid of his 35-minute handicap, feels as proud as the owner of the Volunteer. Hot arguments on the injustice of the handicap ensue, and it behooves the regatta committee to "lie low" and not appear at the club house till the storm has abated.

It is the varied nature of yachting, and the different conditions under which it can be enjoyed which make the sport so universally popular. Who does not remember the intense interest over the American-cup races of 1885–87 which spread from Maine to California, and which caused thousands who did not know a spinnaker from a marlin-spike to scan the bulletins eagerly during the progress of the races? Then the wonderful 46-footers of 1891, and the still more remarkable 21-footers of 1892, have won the admiration of the yachting public and stimulated interest in the sport. Steam yachting attracts the busy man, who must know to an hour when he can get back to Wall or State street, and the steam fleet multiplies even more rapidly than the sailing craft.

As in any sport, the beginner should be started aright in yachting. Give him a handy little non-capsizable cutter with a snug rig, and you have amply provided for his safety. Make what blunders he may, he cannot tip her over, and he will have hard work to come to any grief at all. To make assurance doubly sure, send him out for a time in the care of a good boatman, or make him serve an apprenticeship under some of his skillful yachting friends. If he has the right stuff in him, it will not be long before he is sailing his own boat nearly as well as the crack sailors of the fleet, and he will soon acquire a readiness to meet emergencies, a coolness under possible danger, which will make him safer on the sea than he is on shore, and which will stand him in good stead in facing the difficulties which he will meet in his other walks of life.

THE FIRST PRINTERS UPON THE ST. LAWRENCE.

IN the admirable article by General Neilson, on page 195, the beginning of newspapers and other printing on the St. Lawrence, is ably discussed. Singular as it may appear, and it illustrates the manner in which the migratory spirit in man carries forward great movements in art and science, these early efforts at establishing printing presses in Canada had their inception in the city of Philadelphia. On page 200 General Neilson mentions "S. Miles" as the founder of the Kingston Gazette, in 1810. A son of this Stephen Miles (Rev. Harvey Miles) is now a minister of the Congregational Church at Canton, N. Y., and from him we have been able to procure a short biographical sketch of his father. Rev. Mr. Miles is about the same age as the author of this volume (in his 73d year), but his handwriting is as clear and bright as if written by a young man. He has sent us a copy of his father's newspaper, the Kingston Gazette, dated September 5, 1815. It is a folio, 17x24 inches in size, and fully up to the newspapers of that era, filled with advertising—a sure sign of the progressive spirit of the business men of Kingston. Of his father, Mr. Miles says:

"Stephen Miles was born in Royalton, Vermont, October 19, 1789. His father, Ephraim Miles, was a soldier in the Revolutionary war, and fought in the battles of Saratoga, under General Gates, and was present at the surrender of General Burgoyne and his army to the American forces. He was also at West Point, under General Benedict Arnold, when that officer betrayed his country and fled to the British in New York, in 1780. While quite a lad, Stephen was apprenticed to learn the art of printing in the town where he was born. Before his time of service expired, his master sold his office in Royalton, and went to Montreal, Canada, to establish an office there, taking young Miles with him. After completing his apprenticeship, a favorable opportunity presenting itself, he went to Kingston, to continue in the printing business. A paper called the 'Kingston Gazette,' had been started there by a young man of the name of Kendall, but he, coming from the 'States,' and being dissatisfied and discontented with his surroundings, disposed of his printing office to interested parties in Kingston, who were anxious to have a paper printed in that town. By correspondence with Mr. Moore, of Montreal, Mr. Miles was engaged to go to Kingston, take charge of the office, and finally, purchasing it, the 'Kingston Gazette' became a permanent and promising investment. This, I believe, was the third paper printed at that time in Upper Canada. In subsequent years, Mr. Miles became a Methodist minister, and a member of the annual conference of that body. and after spending many years of active service, age and infirmities compelled him to retire from active work. He died at Ernesttown, some 18 miles north of Kingston, December 13, 1870, in his eighty-second year."

POINT VIVIAN.

THIS is the name given to a peninsula containing about eight acres of land, pleasantly situated on the great St. Lawrence River, about two miles above Alexandria Bay. It was purchased of Captain W. H. Houghton, in the year 1877, by a number of Evans Mills residents, who had it surveyed by H. L. Scott into forty building lots, leaving a large public square in front and a neat little park. They also have a good road leading to the regular town highway; a well has been drilled, and pure cold water obtained in abundance; it has a large ice-house which is filled each season affording plenty of ice for all. About thirty-five cottages have been erected. It has two stores, a boarding-house and a post-office, where the mails are received every day during the pleasure season. The place is easy of access by all the largest boats, as it has one of the best docks on the river, and is nearly 200 feet long. The association is governed by a president and three trustees. The names of the present officers are E. O. Hungerford, president, Evans Mills; Wm. M. Comstock, secretary and treasurer, Evans Mills; Richard Rodenhurst, Theresa; O. W. Van Wormer, Watertown, and Mr. Harrigan, Gouverneur, trustees.

The following is a list of the present property owners at Point Vivian: Allen Cook, Theresa; Geo. W. Adsit, Watertown; Geo. Taylor, Watertown; Charles Austin, Watertown; Mrs. G W. Davenport, Evans Mills; Rezot Tozer, Evans Mills, W. S. Cooper, Felts Mills; Mrs. Chadwick, Theresa; Mrs. A. M. Cook, Evans Mills; A. B. Cutting, Gouverneur; Ed. Grieb, Alexandria Bay; Theodore Gegoux, Watertown; M. Horton (present postmaster), Watertown; Miss Jennie Hungerford, Evans Mills; E. O. Hungerford, Evans Mills; Mrs. Mary Sharon, Evans Mills; Lorenzo Smith, Gouverneur; Mrs. Albert Utman, Syracuse; O. Van Wormer, Watertown; Mrs. Van Epps and Klock, Watertown; Alexander Whitney, Gouverneur; M. Wainwright, Gouverneur; Mrs. Wm. Youngs, Watertown; Mrs. Hannah Jane Saxe, Watertown; John Ball, Watertown; O. W. Barnes, Watertown; Miss Mary Hungerford, Syracuse; Miss Agnes Hungerford, Syracuse; J. D. Harrigan, Gouverneur; Henry Goodrich, Theresa; Miss Ida M. Isdell, Albany; L. E. Jones, M. D., Buffalo; Mrs. J. J. Kinney, Evans Mills; Mrs. T. C. Kellar Est., Watertown; Mrs. Charles Ehrlicher, Watertown; Andrew Kinney, Gouverneur; Henry Lewis, Watertown; Nathan Lennon, Watertown; Geo. W. Mowe, Watertown; H. H. Marsh, Gouverneur; B. G. Parker, Gouverneur; Richard Rodenhurst, Theresa. A Mr. Henry has established a large boarding-house, and also keeps a store [1896].

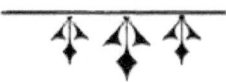

The Murray Hill.

"As we journey through life, let us live by the way," never forgetting that there is a distinction between "living" and merely "existing."

THIS newest of all the "new" hotels on the St. Lawrence, will be opened June 25th, 1896.

It will be patronized by the sort of people one likes to meet. As Murray Hill Park is largely owned and represented by the younger class of business men from New York, Philadelphia, Trenton, Pittsburg, Chicago, Cleveland, Buffalo, Rochester and Syracuse, an atmosphere of good fellowship will surely be found under the hospitable shelter of Murray Hill.

Weekly Concerts will be inaugurated, and held under the oaks, for which the best of music will be provided, and to which all cottagers among the Thousand Islands will be invited.

In short, it will be our aim to make the Murray Hill famous for its hospitality and good cheer. The Murray Hill is situated on Murray Hill Park, the latest popular resort established among the Thousand Islands. It has the largest Dining Room, largest Office, largest Ladies' Parlor, largest Ladies' Billiard Room and the widest Piazza of any hotel on the St. Lawrence, and will be supplied with Elevator, Electric Lights, Fire-places, Electric calls, etc. There is a post-office and telegraph office in the hotel.

It is surrounded by broad waters for yachting, and Eel Bay, the best fishing grounds on the St. Lawrence, washes the shores of Murray Hill Park.

Terms, from $2.50 to $4.00 per day.

MURRAY HILL PARK CO.,
Murray Hill, Jefferson County, N. Y.

HADDOCK'S
Centennial History of Jefferson County
REDUCED IN PRICE.
Original Price $5.50. Now offered at $4.00.

IT is a singular fact that no book offered for sale in Jefferson County has elicited so much praise as this HISTORY. Originally intended for 480 pages, the author was constrained to increase its size to over 950 pages, weighing eight pounds, on fine paper, and this without any increase in the price. The book is a complete historical synopsis of the last hundred years in the social, religious, agricultural, mechanical and financial growth of Jefferson County, beginning with the earliest frontier settlements, and following the country's progress up to 1895. The book has many new features; there is not a dull page in it, and not one person who has bought it would part with it for what it cost. It stands unchallenged as *the* HISTORY of the County.

Excellent as are its articles and beautiful as are the illustrations, the book has been handicapped by the hard times, which have affected all classes; to this should be added the increased expense of every household on account of the hard winter of 1895-6. To bring the HISTORY within the reach of every family the subscriber has determined to put the price **down to cost.** The price has been $5.50; it is now $4.00, at which it is expected that the balance of the edition will be speedily exhausted. It is safe to say that in ten years a person desiring to sell his HADDOCK'S HISTORY can obtain $10.00 for it.

We can fill a newspaper with the commendatory articles relating to this work. Even a casual examination will convince a person of its superior excellence. It takes the place of Hough and the two other alleged histories that have been produced since 1854, when Hough's was published. HADDOCK'S HISTORY is the only one written by a native of the County, one who for over fifty years has been more or less intimately in touch with all its personalities, who knew the leading men of the County from 1840 to 1895 as no one else has known them — and many biographical sketches of many such are presented in a way that is instructive yet truthful. From Perley G. Keyes and Orville Hungerford, followed by Charles B. Hoard and Roswell P. Flower, the political record comes down to and includes the later crop of equally able partisans. This is a new departure, and the Political Chapter is alone worth the price of the book.

Its record of the War for the Union is the most complete yet published, and graphically describes many incidents in which the writer participated, as well as philosophically discusses the causes which led up to the war. It is a soldier's book, written by a soldier, one who "marched with the troops." The portraits of the soldiers who went to the front form a galaxy of rare pictures, growing more and more valuable each year, and transmitting to posterity the very lineaments of some of the men who fought to save the government from destruction.

This work should be in every household. The opportunity for its purchase will soon pass away.

Secure it now, and transmit it to your children.

☞ A Post Office Order or Cash to the amount of $4.00 secures you the book by express.

JNO. A. HADDOCK,
Watertown, N. Y.

Haddock's Popular St. Lawrence River Books for 1896 contain many new pictures and articles, and are worthy of a place in any library. The volume in your hand is one of these books, and speaks for itself.

INDEX OF WHOLE-PAGE ILLUSTRATIONS.

[Many pictures are not included in this index. They are scattered all through the book, and are worthy of the reader's notice. In looking for illustrations, please remember that pages A to P follow page 64, and that Q to Ff follow page 80.]

A   Calumet Island, Summer Home of C. G. Emery, of New York.
B   The Summer Residence of C. G. Emery, of New York (Calumet Island).
C   The Veranda, Looking Eastward, Summer Home of C. G. Emery, Calumet Island.
D   Calumet Island, the Summer Home of C. G. Emery, of New York.
E   The fine Steam-Yacht "Sophia," Capt. H. W. Visger, of Alexandria Bay.
F   Mr. J. P. Billings' Beautiful Cottages at Thousand Island Park, on Garden Avenue.
G   Composite Plate of Steamboat Captains.
H   The Fiddler's Elbow, Canadian Channel.
I   Composite Plate of Steamboat Captains.
J   The Old Seth Green House, on Manhattan Island, now owned by Hon. J. C. Spencer.
K   In the Rift — Canada and the United States.
L   Big 45-pounder Mascolunge.
M   The "St. Lawrence" on her Search-light Excursion.
N   Yachting on the St. Lawrence.
O   Composite Plate of Steamboat Captains.
P   Steamer "Empire State."
Q   The Beautiful Steam-Yacht "Captain Visger."
R   Island Kate, the property of G. W. Lascell, of Lynn, Mass.
S   Judge Spencer's Residence, Manhattan Island.
T   Prof. Blandner's Naptha Launch.
U   The Pullman Hotel, Grinnel Island.
V   West Side of the Square at Thousand Island Park.
W   Residence of W. E. Dewey, Esq., on Friendly Island.
X   The Frontenac, Round Island — Steamer "St. Lawrence" making a landing.
Y   A Scene on LaRue Island.
Z   The Water-front of Alexandria Bay.
Aa The Thousand Island House, Alexandria Bay.
Bb River-front of the city of Brockville, Ont.
Cc View in Gananoque, Ont., showing Water Power.
Dd One Day's Catch of Bass. (Not much of a day either.)
Ee The Sentinel.
Ff Residence of W. C. Browning, Esq., opposite Alexandria Bay.

[253]

INDEX.

A.

	PAGE.
Abbey, Dorephus	147
Alexandria Bay, Recollections of	233
Algerian, The, in Long Sault Rapids	74
Algonquins, Huron and Iroquois	10
Alvord, Hon. Thos. G. (Portrait)	44, 86
Amherst, Expedition of Lord	39
Angel, Gen. William H. (Portrait)	88, 134
Anticosti Island	76
Adirondacks or Algonquins	32
Arsenal at Watertown robbed	143
Art of the Angler	177
Arthur, President C. A.	87
Articles, Leading, in this Volume	5

B.

Backus, Rachel	164
Henry, Awakening of	160
Baker, Col. Lafayette	116
Balloon Voyage of La Mountain and Haddock	150
Barton, Miss Clara (Portrait)	53, 54, 230
Barry St. Leger, Colonel	43
Beauharnais Canal	72
Bell, Robert, of Ottawa	159
Benton, Col. Z. H. (Portrait)	131
Bethune, Rev. Doctor	45, 86
Billings, J. P., and his Hotel on Garden Ave., 1000 Island Park (Illustrated on page F)	50
Blanchard, Joseph	100
Boatmen of the St. Lawrence	46
Bonaparte in Northern New York	96
Bond Head, Sir Francis	148
Bon Voyage, Steamer entering Alexandria Bay	139
Booth, John Wilkes, the Assassin	108, 111
Boundary Line between Canada and the United States	223
Britton, Freeman, of Gananoque	188
Brockville, Ontario, the Gate city	70, 189
Burgoyne, Gen. John	43
Butterfield, Theodore (Portrait)	129

C.

Canadian Boat Songs	215
Camp, Col. Elisha	13
Cameron, Angus	156
Canada's West Point	28
Carlisle, Mrs., Cottage at Grinnell Island	81

	PAGE.
Carlton Island, with Diagram	41
Sir Guy, Governor of Canada	43
Will, The Poet	4
Cartier, Jacques, the Explorer	9, 10
Castorland Colony, The	169
Champlain, Samuel, the Explorer	10, 32
Chapman, Captain	78
Chippewa Yacht Club	79
Members of	79, 80
Clayton, Village of	81
Description of	81
Business People of	82
Old Bridge at (Illust.)	82
Coburg, City of	70
Comstock, Alf., and Tom	45
Conkling, Hon. Roscoe	87
Cooper's Pathfinder and Station Island	80
Cornwall & Walton	13
Hon. Andrew	13
Canal	72
Corbin, A., Jr., of Gouverneur, N. Y.	244
Corsican Running Lachine Rapids (Illust.)	74
Count de Survilliers (Joseph Bonaparte)	96
Curtis, Gen. N. M.	93

D.

Dayan, Rev. J. F	47
De la Barre, Governor of Canada	36
De Nouville, Expedition of	37
Description, General, of the Islands	31
Devil's Oven (Illustrated)	63
Dickinson, Mr. E. D., of the "Frontenac"	79
Dutton, the Music-teacher, of Utica	44

E.

Emery, Mr. C. G	44, 83
Cottages of (Picture pages A, B, C, D).	

F.

Fairbanks, Jason	136
Fayel, William, author and editor	233
Fishing, the Technique of	182
Flower, Hon. Roswell P. (Portrait)	19
Mrs. Sarah M.	21
Emma Gertrude (Mrs. J. B. Taylor)	21
Anson R.	21

[254]

	PAGE.
Flower, John D.	21
Fred S	21
Folger, Howard S. (Portrait)	59
Forrester, Capt. E. F.	64
Forty-fifth parallel	72
Fowler, John N.	17
Miss Jane C. (Mrs. E. G. Merick)	17
Melzar	17, 204
French Missionaries	35
Frontenac Hotel	78
The Count (Portrait)	211, 212
The Fort	35
Expedition of Count	37
Destruction of Fort	39

G.

Gananoque, past and present	184
Geology of the Thousand Islands	219
George, Daniel	147
Gilmour & Co., of Ottawa, Ont	157
Glen Cove Cottage, Hemlock Island	207
Good place for Bass	71
Green, Seth, the fish culturist	45, 87
Grennell, Saml. B.	58, 94

H.

Haddock, John A. (Portrait)	Frontispiece.
His Balloon Voyage	150
Centennial History of (Advt.)	252
Haldimand, the Fort	42, 43
General	43
Hamilton, City of	70
Hancock, Mabel	161
Happy Islands, The (Mr. Bragdon's Poem)	4
Health, the Value of	14
Henry Keep Home	24
Hennepin, Louis	35
Hiawatha, The Legend of	32
Hinckley, Captain C.	61
Hinds, Prof. F. A.	178
Historic Ground	86
Hudson, Captain H. C.	61
Hugo, Frank	61

I.

Indian Mission at Oswegatchie	37
Indians, How They Learned the Rapids	76
Indian Traces on the St. Lawrence	34
Race, Creation of	34
Ingalls, Hon. L.	100
International Park	51
Book	30
Introductory and Descriptive	7
Iroquois Inroad upon the French	37

J.

	PAGE.
Johnston, Capt. S. G.	54, 76
Mrs. Emmeline H.	55
Capt. Henry T	62
"Kate"	63
William	143, 144

K.

Kendall, Capt. Aldridge	56
Capt. Eli	57
Capt. Chas. H	57
Capt. Frank	65
Miss Nellie M. (with portrait)	84
Keep, Henry	21
Henry Keep Home	24
Kinney, Rev. M. D.	48
Kingston, City of	70
Kennedy, George N.	90
Charles L. Hon	90
Knights of the Blue Gauntlet	108
of the Golden Circle	110
Keyes, Perley G	138
King, Hon. Preston	146

L.

LaFarge, John	101
Lake of a Thousand Islands	12
LaMountain, John, æronaut	150
LaSalle, the explorer	208
Portrait of	209
LeRay, James Donatien	96
Lost Channel, The, an Allusion to	165, 166
History of the	177

M.

Maple Island	102
McCormick, Mrs. C. H	17
C. H., reaper manufacturer	17
McKenzie, William Lyon	142
McLennan, Hon. P. B	90
McLeod, Capt. Alexander	143
McNab, Sir Allan	144
Miller, Captain Andrew H	84
Miles, S., founder of Kingston Gazette	200, 249
Montreal, the city of	73
Mudd, Dr., surgeon for J. Wilkes Booth	115
Murat, Joachim	101
Murray Hill Park	244
Mystery of Maple Island	102

N.

Navigation by Steam on the St. Lawrence	226
Neilson, Gen. J. L. H., Biog. Sketch of	201
Portrait of	202
New Island Wanderer, view of	124
Nightingale, Florence	52

INDEX.

O.
	PAGE.
Oswegatchie under the English	40
Oswego, Capture of	38
City of	69
Old "Just About," pop-corn vendor (Ill.)	155

P.
Pahud, Hon. Joseph	132
Parsons, Chesterfield	13
Patriot War, The	18, 142
Patterson, Commodore Ned	45
Payne the Ruffian	112
Peel, Sir Robert, Burning of Steamer	133
Pic-Nic on La Rue Island (Ill.)	77
Pot-Holes in Eel Bay (Ill.)	231
Point Vivian	250
Lot owners at	250
Prescott, City of	70
Printing, origin of, on the St. Lawrence	195

Q.
Quebec, City of	74

R.
Rainy Day at the Islands	13
Rapids of the St. Lawrence Enumerated	71
How the Indians Learned to Run the	76
Reuse, Captain Chester W	62
Red Cross, The	51
Rest, The Value of	14
Richelieu and Ontario Navigation Co.	70
Roberval, the Huguenot	76
Rochester, City of	69
Roque, Francis de la	10
Round Island	78
Cottage owners of	79
Trustees of	79
The "Frontenac" at	78

S.
Safe Day for the Fish (Ill.)	69
Sailing Vessels, Disappearance of	73
Savage, Miss Annette	132
Scenery, Autumnal, on the St. Lawrence	228
"Sir Robert Peel," the Steamer	12
Spencer, Hon. J. C	25
Skinner, G. M., of Clayton	183
Spicer Family, The	206
Sportsman's Song	195
Staples, Col. Orin G	13
Steamboat Captains, some old ones	58
Steam Yachts for Hire	83
St. Lawrence, Song of the (Carlton)	4
River and Inland Navigation	68
Why the River Runs Where it Does	178
Light Houses of the	225
Navigation of, by Steam	226
Lumbering on the	227
Gulf of	241
Summer Institute on the	243
Stone, Colonel, of Gananoque (Portrait)	185
Sturgeon, Picture of a	6
Surratt, Mrs., the Conspirator	112
Summer Institute on the St. Lawrence	243
Sweet, Captain George	67
Captain Vernon	68
Mrs. Catherine	67

T.
Taylor, Capt. Jas. A	66
Frank H. (Portrait)	168
Toronto, city of	70
Thompson, Jonathan	237
Thousand Islands, Geology of	219
Surveys of	224
Light houses of	225
Park	47
Original trustees of	48
Present trustees of	48

V.
Van Rensselaer, General (Patriot War)	142
Visger, Capt. Elisha W	64
Capt. Walter L	65
Capt. H. W	84
Von Shoultz, Niles Sobelitcki	145

W.
Walton, Azariah	13
War of 1755, The	165
Webb, H. Walter	124
Weeks, Forest G	245
Webster, Timothy, the Detective	105
Williams, Hon. Pardon C	90
Windmill, Battle of the	12
Whittlesey Affair, The	136
Mrs., her Will or Statement	140
Woodruff, Martin	147
Wright, The Story Teller	88

Y.
Yacht Club, The Chippewa	79
Yachting, by George A. Stewart	247

www.ingramcontent.com/pod-product-compliance
Lightning Source LLC
Chambersburg PA
CBHW032054220426
43664CB00008B/993